D1736605

Andalusian Ceramics
in Spain and New Spain

Andalusian Ceramics in Spain and New Spain

A Cultural Register
from the Third
Century B.C. to 1700

Florence C. Lister
and
Robert H. Lister

The University of Arizona Press, Tucson

THE UNIVERSITY OF ARIZONA PRESS
Copyright © 1987
The Arizona Board of Regents
All Rights Reserved

Published with the assistance of the
J. Paul Getty Trust.

Library of Congress Cataloging-in-Publication Data

Lister, Florence Cline.
  Andalusian ceramics in Spain and New Spain.

  Bibliography: p.
  Includes index.
  1. Andalusia (Spain)—Antiquities. 2. Mexico—
Antiquities. 3. Pottery—Spain—Andalusia.
4. Pottery, Andalusian. 5. Pottery, Andalusian—
Mexico. 6. Pottery industry—Spain—Andalusia—
History. 7. Spain—Antiquities. I. Lister, Robert
Hill, 1915—   . II. Title.
DP302.A465L57 1987   936.6   87-23781
ISBN 0-8165-0974-3 (alk. paper)

This book was set in 10/12 Linotron 202 Palatino
Manufactured in the U.S.A.

British Library Cataloguing in Publication data are available.

A CRAFT OF TWO PEOPLES

Muslim:
"O potter, before opening the kiln you should
perform ablutions, O good mannered one, and
after that recite this verse, and the kiln will
be blessed: 'Come, sweet patience. Allah's
succor is there in your misfortune'."
>   From the Potter's Book, *Kulal-nama*, Pakistan
>   Rye and Evans 1976: 192

Christian:
"I am like a broken vessel."
>   *Psalms* 31:12

Contents

Figures

Tables

Preface

The ceramic research upon which this book is based had its origins in the late 1930s during our undergraduate studies at the University of New Mexico. There we became aware of a few fragments of tin-glazed earthenware, or maiolica, being recovered at both Spanish and Pueblo Indian archaeological sites along the Rio Grande Valley that dated to the seventeenth and eighteenth centuries. They were believed to represent the colonial Mexican phase of a continuum of Spanish pottery-making extending back many centuries. In those days, however, regional archaeologists were concerned almost exclusively with Native American materials, and so the European fragments were stored for some future day.

A schoolmate, John M. Goggin, returned to his native state of Florida to pursue his career, and there he found similar kinds of pottery in sixteenth- through eighteenth-century settlements. That prompted him to spend a decade studying the problems raised by these European ceramics in the New World through excavations in the former Spanish Caribbean islands, a surface reconnaissance in central Mexico, and a survey of resources in Europe. Goggin died in 1962 before his monograph *Spanish Majolica in the New World* was put in final form. His mentor at Yale University, Irving Rouse, posthumously prepared the study for publication, even though provenience data for some specimens were not available. It remains a basic field manual for type identification but is now outdated, partially incorrect, and the taxonomic system based upon Southwestern practice has proved less successful when applied to pottery types with an international distribution.

Six years after Goggin's death and thirty years after our first exposure to maiolica, we decided to continue this ceramic research. Because a spate of work was being done or being planned in Spanish colonial sites in the Southwest, Florida, the Caribbean, and central Mexico, we anticipated that the pioneer endeavors of our colleague could be augmented, verified, or perhaps revised. Armed with galley proofs of the Goggin monograph, we went to Iberia in 1968 for the first of a number of background trips throughout the Spanish world. Although the study was narrowed principally to Andalusia and Mexico, tracing the ancestry of the borderland fragments we had known proved a far more challenging task than originally supposed. Much of our leisure time for the ensuing seventeen years was devoted to field, laboratory, museum, gallery, classroom, and library efforts on five continents.

At the outset our goals were those of traditional archaeology: to determine places of origin of the Western Hemisphere maiolica and its associated utilitarian wares and to reconstruct a stylistic evolutionary sequence that could be dated relatively, if not absolutely. As our knowledge broadened and deepened and the focus of American archaeology in general shifted from tangible artifacts to intangible patterns of human behavior indicated by those artifacts, we were increasingly drawn into considerations of the complex cultural milieu from which the Andalusian potting craft had grown and of the voiceless, anonymous body of artisans who practiced it. In the belief that there had been a high degree of continuity through the centuries in Spanish ceramic technology, vessel forms, and their functions, we spent a great deal of time observing modern potters at work under a variety of circumstances and in our own studio tried to duplicate their products. That gave us a necessary depth of understanding not only of techniques and chemical knowledge, but also of the more subtle sensual pleasures found in the yield of moist clay between the fingers. It also created a very personal bond, a *simpatía*, between us and the potters, dead or alive. Social anthropologists customarily live among those they study in order to gather firsthand data and impressions, but archaeologists seldom have the opportunity to bring the past into the present. Southern Spain affords an oustanding laboratory for doing so; for example, one can visit a Roman kiln in the morning and in the afternoon see an identical kiln being fired in a functioning workshop.

While we were deep in such self-education, scientific research in Spanish colonial matters on the American side of the transatlantic problem steadily produced the stuff of analysis. At first, much of the effort was put into straightforward archaeological substantiation of former use of particular places. Often this was done so that structures could be restored for public visitation. On occasion it resulted from municipal improvements. Associated with these programs were studies of ceramic technology, distribution of products, and descriptions of their varieties. We personally analyzed and published upon two major collections excavated by government workers from beneath Mexico City, but there were other assortments

coming to light wherever digging in colonial horizons was
carried out.

On the borderlands some tentative dating of maiolicas
in the late fifteenth through early nineteenth centuries was
indicated, which was used to cross-date materials from
areas where similar archaeological efforts had not been
made. Once a corpus of these data accrued, it became
possible for scientists to probe related anthropological
questions, such as status and ethnicity of probable users of
the pottery. Patterns of colonial adaptation were postulated based upon presence or absence of Iberian ceramics
or percentage of those to other available pottery. Physical
scientists aided social scientists in analyzing clays to determine places at which the pottery likely had been produced. It was obvious that in addition to imported Spanish
earthenwares, derivative colonial types were present.

In Europe the problem was one of distinguishing Spanish trade pottery from ceramics made in the various countries with which Hispanic commercial ties had been
maintained from as early as the thirteenth century.
Research in Great Britain, southern France, the Low Countries, and Italy added information about shapes of vessels,
modes of decoration, and, most important, probable time
of manufacture of a variety of Spanish pottery that
included known Andalusian products. At the same time,
studies were devoted to the local wares of those countries
that were important to Spanish work because of these
same reciprocal trade exchanges. Before the enthusiasm
for Italian medieval research that characterized the 1970s,
for example, it would not have been possible to identify
some of the Italian wares that were sold in Andalusia
and the American colonies.

Work on the north coast of Morocco likewise provided
evidence about shared and imported Muslim and Christian Andalusian ceramic technology, vessels, and their
probable places in the scheme of things, both internally
and externally. The value of these data was enhanced by a
set of reliable dates derived from documents and coinage
to place the materials in their proper temporal slot, the
latter part of which fortunately spanned the period of
Spanish penetration into the Americas.

Interest in Spain prior to World War II in post-Roman
pottery of Andalusia typically focused on its exotic
expressions, particularly the famous lusters of the thir-
teenth- and fourteenth-century Granadine emirate and the
sixteenth-century polychromatic Sevillian tiles. Lack of
ready access to a great body of both Muslim and Christian
documentation and the known extraordinary continuity
of certain types, each in its own way hampering temporal

placements, discouraged further research. A series of
stratigraphic studies that might have offered opportunity
for cross-checking of data did not exist. In Sevilla, which
played a pivotal role in the overseas transmission of
regional pottery and its technology, attempted archaeology
had been thwarted by disturbed cultural deposits attributable to long intensive occupation and by an exceedingly
high water table that quickly drowned out excavations.
Moreover, numerous known floods and an ancient custom
of using ceramics in construction were thought to have
devoured the pottery record.

Happily, during the last three decades there has been a
turnaround. A new generation of archaeologists is analyzing old collections in accord with modern methods and
perspectives, and sites of a more domestic nature than the
palaces that drew earliest attention are being explored.
This eventually will lead to a fuller understanding of the
lifeways of the common people. Until recently, archaeological interest in the period of contact with the Americas
has lagged. But several Sevillian municipal projects,
undertaken in a time of prolonged drought that reduced
subsurface moisture, have spawned an awakening concern
with the archaeology of this era. Precise dates for various
local ceramics are not yet forth-coming, nor have there
been the kinds of analyses that can offer insight into past
human behavior. Still, corroborative specimens at last
are coming from the ground.

Primary historical documentation is spotty, but what
is available adds a human dimension to the inanimate
artifact record. Two potters, separated by two and a half
centuries, wrote treatises that are now an invaluable
resource for clarifying the old maiolica technology. One
was Abū'l Qāsim of thirteenth-century Persia, whose
Persian text was translated into English only within the
last decade. The other was Cipriano Piccolpasso of
sixteenth-century Italy. On two occasions his work has
been critiqued by modern English ceramists, which ampli-
fies a text that at times is obscure. Archives in Sevilla
and Mexico have yielded information about potters and
their personal affairs to vivify history. Compilations of
these data have been published in convenient form. Data
retrieved from cargo registers housed at the Archives
of the Indies at Sevilla, a search commissioned by Goggin,
are included in Appendix 2 with the permission of the
late Charles Fairbanks. They substantiate a pattern of
transatlantic trade in Andalusian ceramics that is critical to
economic assessments.

The following pages, then, are a synthesis as it is presently perceived of the narrative of Andalusian pottery,

its makers, and their contributions to the offshoot colonial
ceramic industries. It is set against a historical backdrop
in order to provide a necessary structuring through time
and a controlling baseline for interpretation. An arbitrary
cut-off date of 1700 was selected because Sevillian pottery
technology had been implanted overseas and was by
then in a state of decline at home; Mexican maiolica was at
a summit, but within fifty years it also would decline.

Anthropological jargon is avoided as much as possible
in order to make the text more readable for the layman.
Spanish rather than Arabic names for vessel forms are
introduced because of their current usage, but it should be
borne in mind that form terminology as used by the Spaniards is very loose and inconsistent. Because of the
acknowledged unbroken ceramic continuum, the drawings
of vessel forms for various periods should not be taken
as mutually exclusive. Pottery type names used by American scholars are, in the main, replaced by descriptive
phrases. Nor is the work intended as a definitive archaeological report, owing to remaining lacunae in the documentary and excavation records. Nonetheless, we hope
this review will serve as a substantial foundation upon
which to build. Continuing studies in the Americas and in
Europe surely will contribute new facts and ideas and
refine or correct old ones. Such glacially slow amalgama-
tion of detail is the way of most cultural evolution in
the first place, and that of those who choose to study it in
the second.

Heartfelt thanks for many kinds of help given during
this long project go to countless museum workers, priests,
small boys, Peace Corps Volunteers, Cultural Affairs
Officers in various United States embassies, and potters at
work. To all these folks, who never will read these lines,
we are forever grateful. As for our colleagues, we have
learned that their generosity, helpfulness, and sincere concern with the pursuit of knowledge is boundless. They
have greeted us warmly, allowed us access to collections
and library stacks, given us study materials, taken us
to visit regional sites, shared ideas and good times. We
cannot name them all, but we surely must formally recognize some. Their professional affiliation at the time we
met is indicated.

In Spain, Jesus Bermúdez Pareja, Museo Nacional de
Arte Hispano-Musulman, Granada; Luis Diego Coscoy,
Museo Arqueológico, Santa Cruz de Tenerife, Islas Canar-
ias; the late Concepción Fernández Chicarro and Fernando
Fernández Gómez, Museo Arqueológico Provincial, Se-
villa; Balbina Martínez Caviró, Museo Valencia de Don

Juan, Madrid; Salvador de Sancha Fernández, Museo de
Artes y Costumbres Populares, Sevilla; Juan Zozaya
Stabel-Hansen, Museo Arqueológico Nacional, Madrid.

In Morocco, El Merini Abelfattah and Mohamed Alaoui,
Service Ceramique a la Direction de l'Artisanat, Rabat;
Ahmed Aqallal, Ministry for Cultural Affairs, Rabat; Driss
Mosaddak, Inspecteur Regional de l'Artisanat, Meknes;
Ahmed Sefrioui, Direction des Arts Plastiques des Musees
et des Expositions, Rabat; Mohamed Maji, Musee Batha,
Fez.

In Italy, Guido Farris and Tiziano Mannoni, University
of Genoa, Genoa.

In England, John Hurst, Department of the Environment, and Rosemary Weinstein, Museum of London.

In the Caribbean and Central America, Elpidio José
Ortega and Mario Veloz Maggiolo, Museo del Hombre
Dominicano, Santo Domingo, República Dominicana; José
María Cruxent, Instituto Venezolano de Investigaciones
Científicas, Caracas, Venezuela; Luis Glaize, Dirección de
Turismo, Historico y Social, Panamá; Edwin C. Webster,
Balboa, Canal Zone, Panamá; Richard Cooke, Museo
Nacional, Panamá; Dr. William Hodges, Limbé, Haiti;
Luis Luján Muñoz, Instituto de Antropología e Historia,
Guatemala City; Edwin and Virginia Shook, Antigua,
Guatemala.

In Mexico, Ignacio Bernal, Museo de Antropología,
Mexico City; José L. Lorenzo, Gonzalo Lopez Cervantes,
and Florencia Müller, Instituto Nacional de Antropología e
Historia, Mexico City; Vicente Medel Martínez, Jaime
Ortiz Lajous, and Jorge Olvera, Dirección de Restauración
de Inmuebles Federales, Mexico City; Hugo Nutini, Uni-
versity of Pittsburgh and Fortín de las Flores; Carmen
Pérez de Salazar de Ovando and Carlos de Ovando, Mex-
ico City; the late Isabel Kelly, Tepepan, D.F.; Alicia de
Araujo, Museo Bello, Puebla.

In the United States, Kathleen Deagan and the late
Charles L. Fairbanks, University of Florida; the late Hale
Smith, Florida State University; Robert Harper III, Historic
St. Augustine Preservation Board; Dee Ann Story, Bal-
cones Laboratory, University of Texas; Kathleen Gilmore,
North Texas State University; Mardith Schuetz, San Anto-
nio Archeological Laboratory; Curtis Tunnel and Dan
Scurlock, Texas State Historical Survey; Yvonne Lange
and Christine Mather, Museum of International Folk Art,
Sante Fe; Florence Hawley Ellis, University of New Mexico; Helene Warren and Alden Hayes, National Park Service; Richard Ahlborn, Jacqueline Olin, Emlen Myers,
Marino Maggetti, Albert Jornet, the late Clifford Evans,
and Betty Meggers, Smithsonian Institution; Rex Gerald,

El Paso Centennial Museum, University of Texas at El Paso; the late Charles DiPeso, Amerind Foundation, Dragoon, Arizona; Bernard Fontana, Mark Barnes, and James Ayres, University of Arizona; Ronald May, San Diego State University; Mike Hardwick, Mission La Purísima Concepción, Lompoc, California; Arnold Pilling, Wayne State University; A.B. Elsasser, Lowie Museum, University of California, and Charles Redman, State University of New York at Binghamton.

Funding for various aspects of the general research has been provided by the American Philosophical Society, University of Colorado, University of Arizona, Museum of International Folk Art, and the Smithsonian Institution.

Finally, we wish to thank our son, Gary, for his many unstinting efforts in the dark room.

Chronology

Andalusia

Roman occupation of Guadalquivir valley	218 B.C.–A.D. 414
Visigothic occupation	A.D. 414–711
Muslim invasions	711–912
Cordoban Caliphate	929–1009
Taifas, Almoravids, Almohads	1009–1266
Sevilla recaptured by Christians	1248
Nasrid Emirate of Granada	1238–1492
Reign of Isabela and Fernando	1469–1516
Reigns of Hapsburgs	1516–1700

Canary Islands

Isabela of Castile takes possession of Gran Canaria and Gomera	1477
Portugal renounces its claims in Treaty of Alcacovas	1479
Tenerife and La Palma captured by Spanish	1496

America

Discovery of San Salvador	1492
First colony on Hispaniola	1493
Santo Domingo named first capital	1502
Spanish Main exploited, losing importance	1519
Panamá Viejo establishes Spanish on American west coast	1519
Aztecs conquered	1521

Andalusian Ceramics
in Spain and New Spain

Prologue

The day the Spaniards first set foot in the Caribbean they introduced products that were part of a ceramic complex having a convoluted linkage back to the hearthstone of Western civilization. The last fifteen hundred years of that evolutionary process had occurred in the southern part of Spain known as Andalusia. Within a half-century the methods for making Andalusian pottery took root in central Mexico, and kilns, potter's wheels, workshops, and a glaze formulary evolved over millenia made their first appearance in the New World. From that time in the sixteenth century to the present the homeland craft and that passed on to her American colony have persisted with remarkable vigor. None of the ceramics of other European colonials in the Western Hemisphere can claim such a venerable unbroken lineage.

Thus, culture historians working with the ceramics and technology brought as freight attendant on the Spanish conquests in America meet the craft in its maturity. The problem is to understand the full range of implications of these ceramics prior to, as well as after, that Columbian moment in history.

We organized a two-front attack on the problem, theorizing that a review of the growth environment of the Andalusian ceramic craft from historical and archaeological points of view would prove the two approaches complementary. Political, social, and economic history were to be gleaned for a necessary chronological framework and relevant data to explain the world in which the craft functioned. Iberian historians have paid scant attention to the masses of the citizenry at any period, but we hoped to gain some insight into a group of artisans heretofore ignored. The pottery itself would speak more clearly of the common denominators of human activity and attitudes that would help knit disparate historical events into an understandable, everyday cycle. Each vessel and each fragmentary reminder of a once whole and functioning object was viewed as a complicated entity incorporating many subordinate but informative factors. The plasticity of prepared clay, which permitted it to be turned into items both useful to their maker and expressive of his aesthetic urges, external contacts, or societal needs, and the subsequent fires that preserved them had created a uniquely sensitive register of technical and cultural development. Our goal was to read that register from as many perspectives as the physical and documentary perimeters would allow, augmented by observation of current practices. We postulated that not only would the evolutionary patterns of the craft be demonstrated, but also that more light would be thrown into the shadowed recesses of Hispanic social history.

PART I

History of the Craft

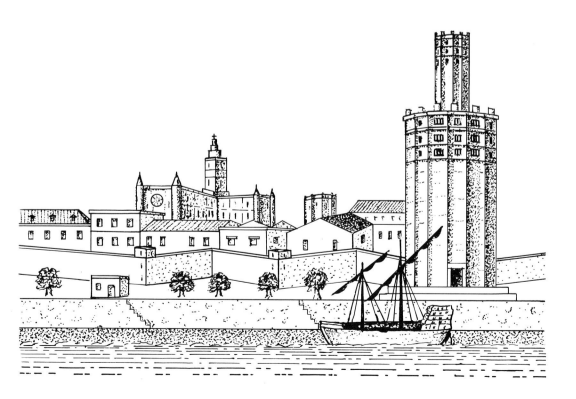

THE BEGINNINGS

Andalusia is that southwestern bastion of Spain that fronts both upon the Atlantic and the Mediterranean as it straddles the Straits of Gibraltar and brings Europe upwind of the continent of Africa (Fig. 1). Today its focal point is the province of Sevilla, flanked on the south and west by the provinces of Cádiz and Huelva, on the northeast by Córdoba and Jaén provinces, and farther east by Granada and Almería provinces. With this strategic position and the blessings of temperate climate, varied topography, fertile soil, a major river system, and mineral deposits, Andalusia has from its earliest human history attracted invaders, influences, and ideas from beyond its borders. Depending upon the tenor of the times, many of these have been accepted, absorbed, and then transformed to provide much of the unique underpinning of regional life. On occasion, as with its pottery, the resulting physical and cultural mutations have diffused outward again in the never ending ebb and flow of civilization building.

The first potters of Andalusia were Neolithic folk of about 4000 B.C., who formed simple containers by pinching or coiling moist unwashed clay into a restricted number of bulbous, wide-mouthed forms. These resembled gourds or leather bags, from which they may have been copied. Some were covered with a red ochre slip, which was polished after firing with a scrap of leather. The vessels were decorated with incised zigzags, double triangles,

Figure 1. Modern Andalusia.

circular eyes, or anthropomorphic figures, and were fired
in open hearths. Presumably, the idea of pottery slowly
had diffused to the Andalusians over the course of many
centuries from an original source somewhere in the
eastern Mediterranean, and their pots differed little from
others then in use by their neighbors.

Gradually, from about 1700 B.C. to 1200 B.C., a more
elaborate Bell Beaker mode of handmade earthenware
evolved. It generally was black, owing to smoky firing,
and bore crudely incised reticulated patterns in bands
around rims or central body zones, the patterns filled with
a white chalky substance.[1]

From the eighth century B.C. those successive, inveter-
ate voyagers of the ancient world—the Phoenicians, the
Carthaginians, and the Greeks—planted isolated trading
colonies on Andalusian shores. Most of the pottery they
left behind had been made in their home bases. Some,
however, appears to have been produced in the west to
replenish stocks diminished through breakage. These, in
turn, exerted influences upon the cruder local wares. By
the fifth and fourth centuries B.C., Iberian tribes of Baja
Andalusia, most notably the African-Celtic Tartessians
who dwelt in the area known as Turdetania along the
lower Río Guadalquivir basin, were turning out thin
pottery with decided Ionian overtones (Fig. 2). The clay in
their pottery fired to a light creamy color, which would
remain characteristic of the area to the present. Typical
forms were those of a sophisticated people having use for

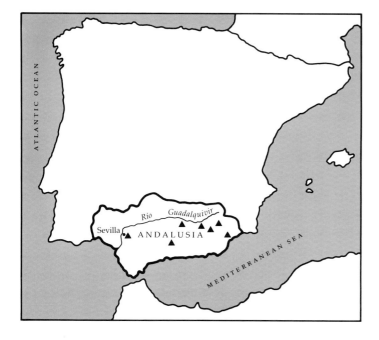

Figure 2. Distribution of sites in
Andalusia yielding Iberian
ceramics (after Arribas 1964).

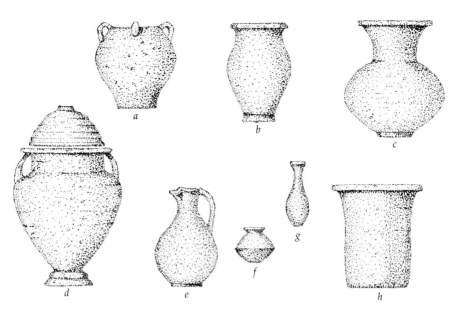

Figure 3. Some typical Iberian ceramic vessel forms: *a*, four-handled jar; *b*, wide-mouthed jar; *c*, large flared-neck jar; *d*, large lidded urn; *e*, spouted pitcher; *f*, small carinated jar; *g*, small bottle; *h*, wide-mouthed beaker.

goblets, tiny perfume bottles, lidded handled jars with flat rims and platform bases, small jars, pitchers, plates, wide-mouthed bowls, straight-sided cylinders, footed jars with flared necks, enormous bulbous jars for storage, and funerary urns, amphorae, and masks (Figs. 3, 8b–c). Geometric decorations arranged in bands were painted in red, chocolate, and black over white slips.[2] Thus, at the dawn of Andalusian pottery history in the beginning of the Christian Era there appeared the first traces of orientalizing concepts that would reappear often in the centuries to follow.

Although examples have yet to be found, it is believed that the Iberian pottery was fashioned on a primitive so-called slow wheel, or *torno lento*.[3] In a strict sense, such a device may have been a mere pivoted turntable incapable of producing sufficient centrifugal force for throwing; in most cases, it probably could not be prevented from oscillating. Nevertheless, it represented a notable technical advancement over more time-consuming, cumbersome hand modeling methods. While the turntable spun around, the potter shaped the rotating clay with both hands. When the tension of work slowed the wheel, the artisan paused to set the machine in motion once again. A true compound potter's wheel consists of a fly wheel connected to a wheel head by means of a vertical axle. It is capable of continuous rapid rotation through foot propulsion and may have been in use in the area shortly thereafter. Although local evidence for the slow wheel remains inconclusive,[4] such an implement very likely did spread westward from the Aegean as part of a group of ceramic

traits that also included horizontal tunnel kilns made
of stone and clay.[5] Unquestionably some preconditioning
for later ceramic methods existed in Andalusia at places
like Galera and Toya. There, wheel thrown pots have been
recovered. They were made in Graeco shapes, with the
diagnostic thickened flat rims, straight vertical handles,
and platform bases, and were decorated in encircling bands
separated by silhouette figurative motifs in the Greek
Geometric Period style. A matter of some three centuries
separated the Greek models from the Andalusian copies,
which continued up to the time of Roman occupation.[6]

ROMANS: THE FIRST CULTURAL TRANSPLANT

Historicultural Background

The attractive physical features of Andalusia prompted
the Romans to stay for six centuries after they had fought
a major battle there in 206 B.C. during the Second Punic
War (Fig. 4). Known to them as the province of Baetica,
it was transformed through retail and export commerce,
small industry, agriculture, fishing, and mining into a very
important arm of the Roman Empire. The city of Itálica
just west of the lower Betis River, later the Guadalquivir,
was an outstanding example of a flourishing provincial
center.[7] Elsewhere, farming and mining activities were so
intensely pursued for Rome's benefit that peninsular
lands were left sterile, in the absence of rejuvenation prac-

Figure 4. Roman province of
Baetica (after O'Callaghan 1975).

tices, or were stripped of their nonrenewable mineral
resources. For example, the tin deposits of the northern
provinces of Lusitania and Gallaecia (modern Portugal and
Galicia) were depleted by the year A.D. 250 as a result of
massive hydraulic operations.[8] Even with these long-
term detrimental effects, much of Roman material culture
remained to enrich local life. Among these were constructions such as harbors and docks, roads and bridges, canals
and river locks, houses oriented inward around atria,
sewer systems of lead and terra cotta piping, public baths,
aqueducts, and amphitheaters. Introduced assemblages
of tools and simple machines included levers, augers,
winches, cranes, pulleys, mill wheels, and windlasses.
Urbanization brought a gamut of crafts dependent upon
the intermediary Roman technology but ultimately derived
from Middle Eastern antiquity. Some of them were not
strong enough to survive the later Visigothic eras.[9]

Pottery History

One of the handicrafts introduced to Andalusia was the
making of pottery in typical Roman styles by customary
Roman methods. Two distinct groupings of this pottery
were used for different purposes and were formed by
different techniques.

Foremost was a large-scale rural industry geared to the
exportation of foodstuffs. On the gently rolling Andalusian hills and in the broad, flat, warm Betis valley extensive dry farming of wheat, grapes, and olives led to
establishment of scores of workshops to fashion earthenware containers to carry these products or their derivatives
back to Italy. Comparable workshops dotted the coast to
make containers for various fish sauces. Bonsor, an
English archaeologist who early in this century explored
Andalusian Roman remains, found evidence of numerous
such potteries along the banks of the great Betis River
and its tributaries. Many of them had been exposed or
partially eroded away as the river bed had repeatedly
changed. Millstones for the preparation of clay, concentrations of kilns, and heaps of wasters and broken pots were
scattered about these places. Nearby warehouses and
quays had been constructed with coursed potsherds, tile
fragments, or orifices of jars set in mortar.[10]

A trade pattern is obvious. Thrashed wheat, wine made
from grapes, or oil extracted from olives had been transported in bulk to the river's edge from processing stations
scattered through the countryside. Córdoba, Astigi (now
Ecija), and Hispalis (now Sevilla) were the largest clear-
inghouses; there, various products were put first into

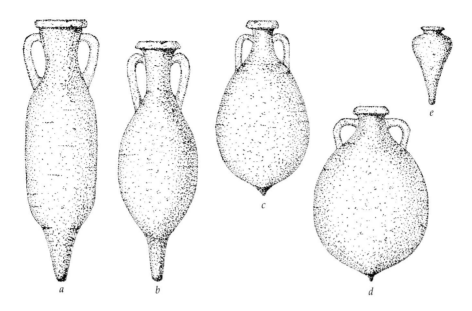

stationary ceramic vats. After fermentation, wine was
racked off into prepared amphorae, which were placed in
the sun for up to four years to mature the contents. Then
the containers began a long journey downriver to the
Atlantic and east through the Mediterranean. Those not
destined for Italy were transferred to river craft near
Marseille. From there they were moved up the Rhone and
down the Rhine to the English Channel. Other ships
carried the jars on to Britain.

In the vicinity of Roman Gades, or Cádiz, ships tied up
along the shores near fish-processing stations to take jars
of seafoods on board. An aromatic condiment known as
garum, made of small salted fish, was especially notable.

With a history extending back into Near Eastern antiquity, the Roman shipping and storage container was the
amphora form. Several variations were used in Spain.
Most typical and unique to the area was a globular jar with
a short neck, a pair of bowed stout handles, and a small
nub at the base (Fig. 5c–d). Also present were long,
torpedo-shaped jars with tall necks, a pair of heavy strap
handles from neck to vessel shoulder, and a tapered base
ending in a solid knob (Fig. 5a–b). These are judged to
have been standardized at 26-liter capacity. The heavy
body walls and seemingly awkward shape must have
made them difficult to handle. However, the basal knob
facilitated lifting them and pouring out the contents, and it
could be secured for shipment into a rack or bed of sand
or straw. Although no positive association has been established, some researchers believe the long amphorae were

Figure 5. Roman amphorae
forms characteristic of Baetica:
a–b, possibly used for storage and
shipment of wine; *c–d*, possibly
used for storage and shipment of
olive oil and fish sauces; *e*, possibly used as base for torches in
river traffic.

Figure 6. Sample of stamped
factory marks on Roman
amphorae from Baetica (after Días
et al 1939).

for the storage and transport of wine, while containers
for oil and the salted fish or fish sauces of the coastal areas
were the round-bodied amphorae.[11] All the vessels were
sealed with plugs of unfired clay, wood, or cork, held
in place with pitch, resin, or gypsum. Because the pots
were unglazed, they sometimes were rubbed with oil to
keep out air.[12] While still warm from the kiln, the presumed wine jars were coated with pitch on their interiors
to prevent seepage, a treatment which likely caused the
wine to taste much like modern Greek retsina. On their
handles most of the jars carried a stamped impression of
the names of makers or factories (Fig. 6). Painted inscriptions, unfortunately now often weathered away, contained such vital information as weight, contents, estate
and its locality, taxes, and merchants dealing in their
commodities.[13]

So many earthenware containers were used in the
Roman Andalusian seaborne trade that they reached from
the western empire in Britain to Italy. They have been
identified as Baetican through factory marks.[14] Outside of
Rome at the port of Ostia there used to be a prominent
hillock formed primarily of spheroid Andalusian amphorae
sherds. One estimate places the number of individual
pieces dumped there at forty million.[15] It has been argued
that such a mass of sherds accumulated at Ostia because
cargo, once it reached warehouses, was transferred to
storage cisterns or huge stationary ceramic *dolia*. Bonsor
felt that the emptied jars that had contained oil were
no longer usable, as they had become unintentionally
impregnated with their contents, and so were discarded.[16]
Regardless of whether absorption of oil by porous body
walls was accidental, it is obvious that the manufacture of
amphorae in Andalusia was a flourishing, specialized,
rural industry devoted to rapid, cheap production of a

single, standardized, efficient but expendable item. Farm
and sea market needs underlay its manufacture. In apparent relationship, the volume of exportation of olive oil
and wine declined after A.D. 250, the locks and quays on
the river fell into ruin, and the number of common potteries decreased.

With large volume output came some secondary usage
of discarded amphorae for purposes other than random
construction fill. After the second century, for example,
Roman architects adopted a practice of placing such jars in
the haunches of vaulted public buildings to reduce the
weight of the superstructure.[17] This usage unquestionably
expanded to Iberia, but to what degree is only speculation
at present because roofs have collapsed. Amphorae also
commonly have been found in Andalusia serving as ready
made sarcophagi for humble citizens. For infant bodies,
the jar necks were broken off to allow the remains to
be inserted, and then were replaced (Fig. 7). For a large
corpse, the amphora was laid on one side. A section was
removed from the upper side to permit a tightly flexed

Figure 7. Amphora infant burial
being excavated at Roman site
of Orippo, near Sevilla. Such jars
often were used for inhumation of
commoners (courtesy Museo
Arqueológico Provincial, Sevilla).

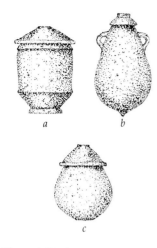

Figure 8. Earthenware cinerary ceramics from Andalusia: *a*, Roman; *b–c*, Iberian. Cremation was replaced by inhumation in the second century. Rectangular earthenware slabs then were used to mark graves of Andalusia's various ethnic groups. Inscriptions in Spanish, Hebrew, Arabic, or a Romance language predecessor to Castilian Spanish were either etched or painted on the slabs, depending upon whether the deceased were Christians, Jews, Muslims, or mozarabs.

body to be crowded into the vessel, and the makeshift lid was replaced. The amphora and contents were buried in designated areas near towns, without markers.

The same riverine Roman workshops also turned out architectural materials, such as terra cotta floor tile and ceramic tubes for water and sewer lines, which would continue to be characteristic of the region for centuries. Well jars, cook pots, canteens, and receptacles for storage served many domestic purposes, and virtually all had passed into Roman culture as a heritage from older civilizations bordering the eastern Mediterranean. Some were of a variety now called African Red Slipped Ware. Commodious plain gray or cream-colored funerary urns were fashioned to be used when cremation was practiced (Fig. 8a). These, found in considerable numbers in the great neocropolis at Carmona, disappeared from the ceramic repertory with the Romans.

Although at the beginning of Roman occupation some fine-grade tablewares may have been traded into Andalusia from other parts of the empire, it is believed that in time a second major potting industry was begun to produce the red domestic and display wares characteristic of Roman potters elsewhere. This branch of the craft likely was located in urban areas, since its output was designed for city dwellers. One of the main southern production centers seems to have been in the vicinity of Andújar, still a leading regional pottery-making town now known for its unglazed white water jars.[18] Representative of the better grade of ceramics was a red gloss ware called *terra sigillata* or *sigillata hispánica*,[19] bearing small-scale molded embellishments. These generally were less lavish than their counterparts from Gaul or Italy. Barbotine, employing raised slip patterns, and roulette modes, which repeated impressed designs, were present. Additionally, a few lead-glazed vessels may have been made by the Spanish Roman provincials.[20] Small, thin-walled, ring- or pedestal-footed bowls with carinated rims; two-handled

Figure 9. Some typical *terra sigillata* and African Red Slipped Ware ceramic vessel forms in Roman Baetica: *a*, cup; *b*, vase; *c*, lidded tripod bowl; *d*, plate; *e*, oil lamp; *f*, hemispherical bowl; *g*, canteen.

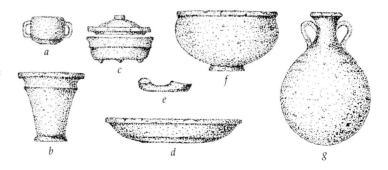

cups; platters; wide-mouthed jars; long-necked bottles, and tiny, flat-topped oil lamps were typical forms (Figs. 9, 10).

Figure 10. Late Roman handled jugs and canteen (courtesy Museo Arqueológico Nacional, Madrid).

Pottery Technology

A compound potter's wheel obviously was used in the manufacture of the container amphorae, but no examples of this machine have been identified in Roman Spain. Presumably, the wheel was made of wood, which has disintegrated.[21] The amphorae, fashioned from the light-colored Guadalquivir marly clay,[22] were thrown in sections. The basal portion was shaped upside down over a mold attached to a wheel head. Spiraling marks of finger impressions extending to the basal projection confirm this technique. The upper portion with neck was thrown erect, and was welded to the lower body at the leather hard stage, at which time handles were attached.

The *terra sigillata* was made by means of molds. These may have been fastened to the wheel heads or they may have been separate. From this time on, the use of molds would remain popular for certain kinds of rapidly produced or elaborated wares.

The usual Roman kiln in Spain was a two-chambered, vertical, updraft type, the exterior outline being elliptical to circular and domed in form. The lower chamber serving as a fire box often is all that now remains, although one kiln with upper chamber intact has been reported near Cádiz.[23] Being partially subterranean, the walls of the fire chamber

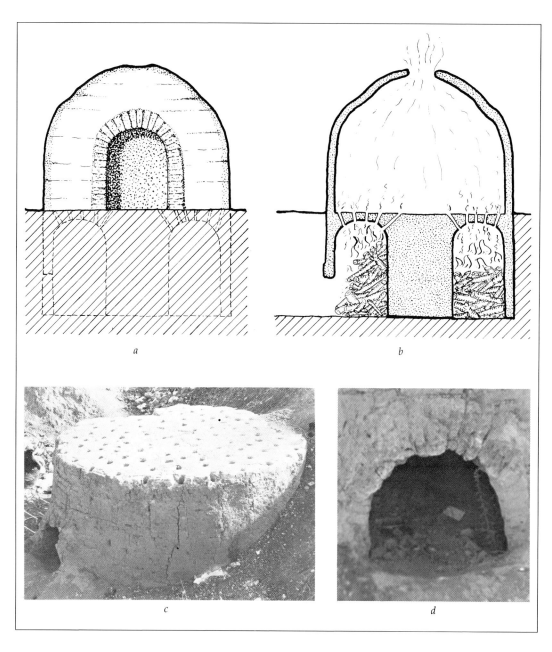

a

b

c

d

Figure 11. Reconstruction of a Roman two-chambered, updraft kiln (*a, b,*). A central pier supports a perforated floor between combustion and baking units. The combustion unit is entirely subterranean. Combustion chamber of a partially preserved extant structure (*c, d*) at Orippo, near Sevilla.

were not so easily destroyed by heat during use or by vandals later on. Occasionally an adjacent hearth or baking box was located to one side of the lower unit, converting the structure into a three-part affair usually typical of Greek practice.[24] Modification of the fuel chamber into a horizontal tunnel was not uncommon. The walls of most kilns were constructed of rubble incorporating amphorae sherds, bricks, or stone, and were covered with roughly dabbed-on clay. Some were made of tiles laid in courses. The typical units were separated by a floor perforated with many randomly spaced holes, a grill now called a *parrilla*, which allowed the heat to flow upward and out through ceiling port holes. If of large circumference, the kiln's upper central area was supported by a pillar of clay from beneath. A variant kiln form was supplied with a large central column, upon which horizontal clay rods, or fire bars, were laid radially to separate combustion area from baking area.[25] Entrance to the lower kiln chamber was an arched opening often faced with brick.[26] Many kilns were of a relatively small size, measuring 1m to 2m in greatest dimensions, although some estimates are that as many as thirty thousand small objects might have been fired in them at one time.[27] Amphora kilns were larger, as shown by one still extant in Orippo, just south of Sevilla; that kiln measures approximately 3m across (Fig. 11). Given the enormous numbers of sherds to be seen around Roman sites, common kilns must have been in use almost constantly. Fuel to fire them undoubtedly was a problem in an area where trees were not abundant. The lack of carbon deposits around the kilns and the degree of calcination still evident may indicate that the Romans found a solution in the oily residue left from olive pressing operations. Estimates are that the vertical kiln type used by the Romans could achieve temperatures in the 1050°C. to 1150°C. range, which would have been adequate for their *terra sigillata* or for the more ordinary earthenwares,[28] the latter surely requiring a considerably lower temperature.

Socioeconomics of the Craft

Roman pottery-making was a commercial activity practiced by male specialists working exclusively in either of the two branches of the craft. The commercialism arose from population growth and the needs of empire. There is no evidence the potting industry was state-controlled; it more likely was a reflection of a nascent capitalism based on a money economy. It involved large numbers of independent businessmen and artisans, although some of the workers likely were slaves.[29] Like those in other trades, potters may have been loosely organized into cooperative societies and may, to a limited extent, have shared in the prosperity of Baetica. Indicative of the focus of the craft, both the potter's wheel and molds allowed accelerated production and easy duplication of sizes, shapes, and designs.[30] Hence, huge quantities of ceramics could be made for sale either as containers for other products or as objects with their own intrinsic value. Organizations of middlemen are known to have been active distributors of such manufactured goods. In the case of the earthenware containers, several disposal outlets may have func-

Figure 12. Spanish potter patron saints Justa and Rufina. Painting by Bartolomé Murillo, 1682, contains the iconographic symbols of palm fronds for martyrdom and a model of the Giralda tower for Sevilla. The associated pottery is that of the artist's own time, rather than that of the Roman era when the sisters lived (courtesy Museo de Bellas Artes, Sevilla.).

tioned simultaneously. Producers of substantial amounts of wine and olive oil are thought to have operated their own amphora-making workshops, but there also may have been wholesalers who acquired such ceramic goods for resale to those persons who ran lesser enterprises. Surprisingly few duplications among the enormous number of known factory marks on such jars points to a veritable army of people engaged in some aspect of the trade.

Roman control provided later Iberian ceramists with one more thing, a pair of patron saints (Fig. 12). These were Justa and Rufina, potter sisters living in Hispalis who became Christian martyrs during the reign of Diocletian (A.D. 284-305).[31] In the thirteenth century, when the city was recaptured from the Muslims, a common grave thought to be that of the sisters was found. No datable reliquaries were associated with the fragmentary bones.[32] Nonetheless, Justa and Rufina became household figures, guardians of Spanish potters, and emblematic of a legendary city.

Retrospective

The result of Roman pursuit of the potting craft in
Andalusia firmly implanted there a basic appreciation for
the usefulness of pottery for a great many purposes and a
generally maintained high standard of craftsmanship in
formation. The region was opened to a flood of eastern
Mediterranean influences that would continue. An elaborated technology involving human-powered mechanized
equipment was introduced. Vertical, two-chambered,
updraft kilns, in some cases outfitted with fire rods and
fueled on olive residue, became standard. Specialized
categories of wares and makers and a range of vessel
shapes that for centuries would constitute the substratum
of Spanish ceramics were routine. Moreover, the Romans
were responsible for the use of disposable earthenware
containers of set sizes for various products, a concept that
would be of utmost importance in the future of regional
ceramics. Also, as would happen repeatedly as the winds
of fortune shifted, the finer grade of pottery ceased to
be made with the military and political defeat of the clientele for which it was created. The common objects of
use in daily life continued, just as did the common people
who used them.

THEN, THE VISIGOTHS

Following the decline of the Romans in the early fifth
century, Baetica was swept by Byzantines and Germanic
Siling Vandals (Fig. 13). The former held Córdoba for
a long time, and the latter razed Hispalis. The Siling Vandals were replaced by other German speakers, the Asding
Visigoths. They came out of the northeast having already
assimilated some aspects of Latin culture. In Spain they
established a court at Toledo to the north of the Guadalquivir Valley, adopted Roman law, made Latin the official
language, and in debased form preserved some classical
traditions in the arts, although they themselves may not
have been the actual craftsmen. Lacking in technical skills,
they let Roman roads, aqueducts, and towns decline into
ruin as a deep sense of localism emerged.

Because the Visigothic invaders were pastoralists, pottery traditionally was of little consequence to them. They
used it sparingly, relying more heavily on metal vessels.
Their cultural level remained relatively low,[33] so the forms
of such earthenwares as were used were few in number
and uncomplicated in contour. These probably were

Figure 13. Visigothic and Byzantine penetration of Roman Baetica (after O'Callaghan 1975).

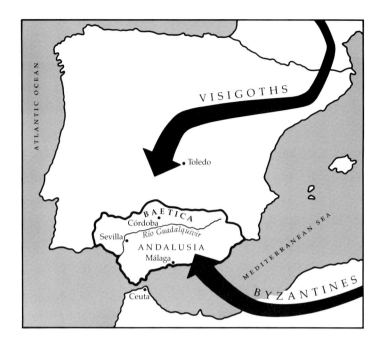

turned out by potters from the old Hispano-Roman population, which comprised the majority. As time passed there remained only a dim memory among the conquerors and the conquered of former classic styles and standards, although the basic methods for making pottery on the wheel and firing it in a two-chambered, updraft kiln were retained. Some lingering classicism may be seen in weak imitations of late Roman forms and red *sigillata*, either plain or bearing stamped decorations of doves, human figures, or geometric elements.[34] More usual were pieces made of highly micaceous clays that fired gray to black.

Some forms in this category were chunky baglike receptacles with crudely incised decorations that suggest a reversion to old Iberian prototypes. Typical vessels included spouted pitchers; jugs with single handles and straight necks; two-handled, round-bodied, necked ollas; small cups, and pilgrim bottles or canteens. New contributions to the inventory of Andalusian pottery shapes were a tall, necked bottle with a rib at the point of handle attachment, a pear-shaped pitcher made with a small pouring spout pressed down at the rim, and a single-handled jar thought by some to have been a beer jug with a broad, erect spout attached to the body bulge (Fig. 14b–d). The former Roman-style oil lamp now had a neck to control draft, a more adequate handle, and a pronounced lateral spout for a longer wick, the latter two features being added by hand at the leather hard stage. Once this lamp variation was adopted into the regional assemblage of

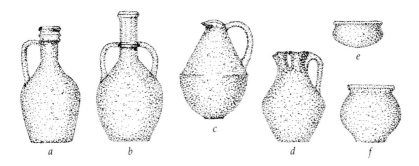

Figure 14. Some typical Visigothic ceramic vessel forms: *a*, one-handled bottle; *b*, two-handled bottle; *c*, spouted pitcher; *d*, spouted jug; *e*, hemispherical bowl; *f*, wide-mouthed jar.

ceramic forms, it continued to be made for the ensuing thousand years. Large rectangular earthenware slabs used as grave markers were derived from Roman marble proto-types. After Christianity became the official religion in the late sixth century, many of the slabs were decorated with moldmade relief or stamped designs taken from Catholic iconography.[35] Some long, pointed or rectangular terra cotta tiles and bricks with molded designs forming sepulchers completed the list of Visigothic ceramics.

Meanwhile, Byzantine potters in Andalusia had intro-duced white wares with stamped or painted decoration. These had limited distribution and are not well known. Spanish archaeologist Juan Zozaya dates them between A.D. 621 and 711.[36]

During Visigothic times the narrow strip of water at Gibraltar had become a cultural moat, although the Visi-goths held control of Ceuta on the southern shore until they were routed by the Byzantines.[37] This barrier was breached at the beginning of the eighth century as Mus-lims, originally from many distinct backgrounds but becoming united by language, religion, and a broad spec-trum of cultural compatibilities, poured into Andalusia. Hispalis, situated on an important Roman road to the interior, fell to them in A.D. 712.

ARABS AND SYRIANS: THE SECOND CULTURAL TRANSPLANT

Historicultural Background

The old Roman city that became Sevilla, surrounded on two sides by the Río Guadalquivir and on the third by the smaller tributary called Tagarete, was at the low-lying hub of an expansive plain radiating away from the water-courses. It sat only twenty-five feet above sea level, but deep clayey soils beyond its perimeters, rejuvenated by periodic flooding, offered promise for sustained exploita-tion. Flowing southward past the city walls, the river then twisted some sixty miles through a great, flat, salty marshland to empty into the Atlantic northwest of the sandy spit of land on which the port of Cádiz sat. It was navigable by seagoing craft as far inland as Sevilla. From there smaller vessels could proceed another hundred miles upriver, as the great waterway turned eastward into a loamy basin near Córdoba. Recalling much of the environment of the Fertile Crescent, this Andalusian setting appealed especially to groups of uprooted Syrians, who arrived in about the mid eighth century as the Umayyad dynasty in their homeland began to collapse in a pool of blood. According to Dozy, in about A.D. 742 Syrians routed the earlier Arab invaders in some parts of the new holdings, such as the Syrian division of Emesa that was settled in Niebla and Sevilla on public lands turned over to it.[38]

The Spanish peninsula already may have been familiar to some Syrians. During the preceding century a number of them, who together with Egyptians were known collectively as *Syri*, had dominated a maritime trade that connected Asia Minor with the western Mediterranean. Their ships carried cargoes of wine, spices, and manufactured goods to North Africa and Spain and then proceeded to England to secure return loads of tin.[39]

One of the displaced Syrians in Spain was Prince 'Abd al Rahman I, a royal Umayyad survivor, who quickly rallied followers (Table 1). In A.D. 756 he set himself up as rightful leader and encouraged other Syrians to head west. The result was that by the end of the eighth century

Table 1. Muslim Masters of al Andalus.

Umayyad Emirs:	
'Abd al Rahman I	A.D. 756–788
Hisham I	788–796
al Hakam I	796–822
'Abd al Rahman II	822–852
Muhammad I	852–886
al Mundhir	886–888
Abdallah	888–912
Umayyad Caliphate:	
'Abd al Rahman III	912–961
al Hakam II	961–976
Hisham II	976–1009
Taifa kings	1009–1090
Almoravids	1090–1147
Almohads	1147–1248 (Sevilla)

Figure 15. Al Andalus, eighth to mid-eleventh centuries.

the lower Guadalquivir Valley was experiencing a phenomenon which a modern historiographer has termed a
Syrianization of the landscape.[40] In the countryside
numerous plants native to the eastern Mediterranean were
introduced, became rapidly acclimatized, and flourished
through the widespread instigation of irrigation. The
rural settlement pattern was one of small villages surrounded by farm lands, rather than dispersal of individual
families as in northern Europe. This practice afforded
greater security, but also encouraged seasonal cottage
industries and weekly markets for regional exchange.

In the territory of al Andalus (Fig. 15), as the Muslims
called their Spanish holdings that extended over two-
thirds of the Iberian peninsula, canals and large, wooden,
vertical hydraulic wheels brought water to the fields.
There were such constructions along the Guadalquivir and
its tributaries Genil and Guadajoz. They were turned by
the water currents and consequently were known as *norias
de vuelo* (Fig. 16). In the heartlands of the Guadalquivir
drainage neither the Roman practice of dry farming nor
irrigation by gravity flow from the river was practical
for the kinds of intensive plantings the new arrivals from
the Near East preferred. Moreover, at the time of the
Muslim invasions the area seems to have been experiencing hotter and drier climatic conditions.[41] Under Muslim
hands scores of deep wells were sunk, their waters
brought to the surface by means of geared wooden

Figure 16. Vertical water wheel, *noria de vuelo*, ringed with attached earthenware jars and paddles turned by water currents. Introduced to Andalusia by the invading Muslims, it derived from Syrian prototypes. Many of these vertical-lifts were erected along the great Río Guadalquivir and its major tributaries.

wheels. A horizontal wheel just above ground level was turned by animal power to rotate a lower vertical wheel, to which a long chain of pots was attached by means of a pulley. The pots filled with water when submerged and then, as the wheel brought them up, dumped the contents into a trough. These were *norias de sangre*, or *saquiyahs*, their repetitive screeching as wood ground against wood adding grace notes to the hum of farm life (Fig. 17). Their prototype was to be found commonly in Syria, where they had been developed in the Hellenistic period.[42]

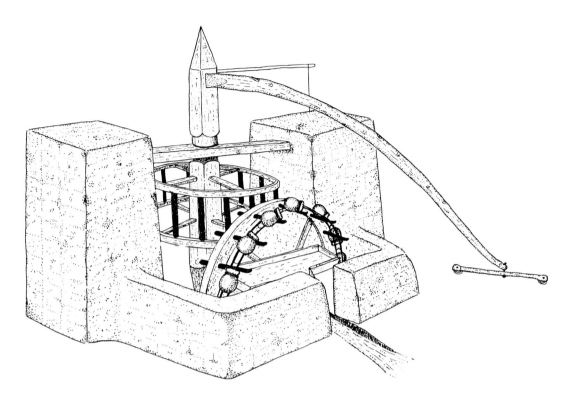

The bountiful yield from three or four crops a year formed the basis of a thriving export trade, which in turn subsidized increasing urbanization. There were two principal urban centers built over Roman remains in the Guadalquivir Valley. These were Sevilla and Córdoba, where Syrian building techniques and decorative tastes created for homesick Levantines the image of a remembered Damascus. Trade was geared to exchange values within the Mediterranean Islamic world. Profit based on calculated outlays and anticipated returns and loans with interest were aspects of commercial life, even though there were religious sanctions against them.[43] A ninth-century document written in Damascus listed three kinds of merchants, which likely also typified the trade in al Andalus. The three were he who travels, he who stocks, and he who exports.[44] Various familiar mechanical arts supported by wealth from agriculture flourished in an expanding, specialized economy, but in this formative period in the western Islamic province there is no indication that manufactured goods were shipped abroad.

Politically, the first two centuries of Muslim presence in Spain were chaotic. A succession of emirs ruled as tribal chiefs over clans who maintained their own range of

Figure 17. Horizontal water wheel, *noria de sangre*, turned by means of a draft animal attached to a lever. Geared wooden wheels lowered and raised a chain of ceramic jars into a deep well. Thousands of these introduced constructions were in use throughout Andalusia where gravity flow irrigation waters were not available.

authority. This promoted a feudal structure in which ordinary citizens had little power. Particularism, a system
in which each regional grouping felt free to pursue its own
ends and which the multi-strained invasion encouraged,
grew.[45]

During the eighth and ninth centuries there were three
other polities within the western world with whom the
Spanish Muslims had contact. Most important was the
ʿAbbasid dynasty, with its capital at Baghdad. Even
though nearly three thousand miles away, its cultural and
commercial effect on western Islam was dominant until
the eleventh century. Also in the eastern Mediterranean
was the Byzantine empire. At this period its influence
came to Spain through Syrian intermediaries as absorbed
aesthetic viewpoints, rather than by direct intercourse,
owing to the presence of strong Muslim fleets that increasingly controlled central and western Mediterranean sea
routes. To the north of al Andalus was the Carolingian
empire. After having been stopped at Poitiers in A.D. 732
by Charlemagne's grandfather, Charles Martel, the invading Muslims withdrew south of the Pyrenees and had
little further communication with the Franks.[46] Charlemagne reinforced the barriers between his empire and that
of the infidels by securing a buffer zone, the so-called
Spanish March, from Barcelona on the east to Basque territory on the west. The agrarian Carolingian empire, with
its barter system of exchange, had little to offer in international commerce, but its strong hierarchial social organization of king, clergy, and peasants and its deep piety found
favor among the Christian kingdoms of northern Spain
after the establishment of the pilgrim routes from southern
France to the shrine of Saint James at Compostela.

Pottery History

Lacking information from documents or archaeology, it
can only be speculated that among the transferred Syrian
handicrafts surely was that dedicated to earthenwares.
If so, it was merely an areal expansion of a cluster of craft-
related traits and not a cross-societal diffusion. It is further
suggested that rural and urban industries functioned as
in Roman times, but that more or less the same range
of vessel forms was turned out in each. This idea is substantiated by a broadly shared lifestyle among the populace, with little status differentiation in material goods
yet being apparent in the evolving culture.

Scattered smaller villages across al Andalus likely could
provide a living for no more than a man and his sons
engaged in making earthenware objects needed for the

routines of country life and for carrying local produce to
market. Because the forms devised for mundane purposes
were rudimentary and undecorated, except perhaps for
some bands of encircling grooving, their fashioning could
have been achieved with almost mechanical rapidity.
Zozaya believes a network of such potteries spaced about
20 km apart spread through the Muslim province, but
this idea still has to be treated cautiously until further digging is undertaken.[47] So many workshops making the
same objects may have been necessary because of the difficulties of getting unwieldly breakable goods to potential
purchasers. Trains of pack animals, rather than wheeled
vehicles, were the norm in the Muslim world, and few
roads built during the Roman occupation were still in ser-
viceable condition.

It was potters working on this lowest level who were
responsible for the great constant body of Andalusian
earthenwares that endured through the ages, because they
were most resistant to change. Once successfully designed
for specific functions, modification of form purely for
the sake of fashion was impractical. There may have been
some regional specialization in particular types of vessels
that were traded at some distance, but these, too, experienced little alteration through time. Because Andalusia
continues to be basically agrarian, poor, and conservative,
it is this aspect of the ceramic tradition that has most
completely survived.

Among typical rural forms were amphorae of the same
general tapered-based contours made during Roman
times. These were used to store the olive oil that was universally used for cooking, and for cereals, water, and
wine.[48] They surely served as containers for the export
trade, too, but unfortunately neither local factories nor foreign deposits of discarded Spanish Muslim amphorae
are known, as they are in the Roman horizon. Of related
interest is the fact that the contemporary Byzantine maritime trade was flourishing in the Aegean Sea and Black
Sea, partly as a result of what economic historian Archibald Lewis terms a container revolution, in which the
classical amphorae were replaced by lighter weight, stack-
able wooden casks.[49] The lack of timber resources, as
well as an entrenched custom of former desert dwellers,
precluded such an innovation in al Andalus. Lamps,
urinals, basins, jugs, and bowls rounded out the complement of country household pottery and did not differ
appreciably from that made and used by townsfolk,
regardless of their individual social or political status (see
Figs. 18–22).

Figure 18. Some typical Spanish
Muslim commonware vessel
forms, unglazed or lead-glazed;
household furnishings: *a–b*,
chamber pots; *c–d*, oil lamps.

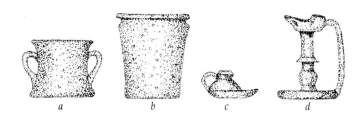

Fig. 19. Some typical Spanish
Muslim commonware vessel
forms, unglazed or lead-glazed;
storage and shipping receptacles:
a, ánfora; b, lidded *tinaja, c,* winged
tinaja; d, small carinated jar; *e,*
cantimplora.

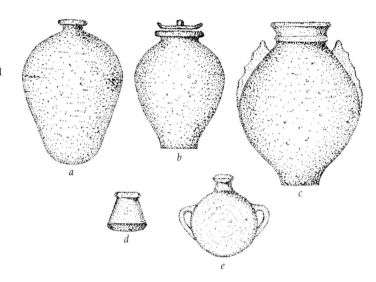

Figure 20. Some typical Spanish
Muslim commonware vessel
forms, unglazed or lead-glazed;
food preparation receptacles:
a, basin, *lebrillo; b, c, e, ollas;*
d, *cazuela; f,* bowl.

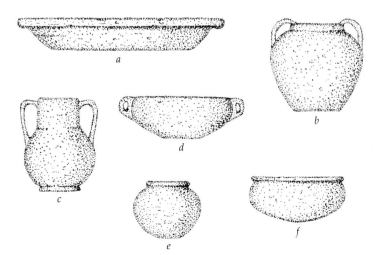

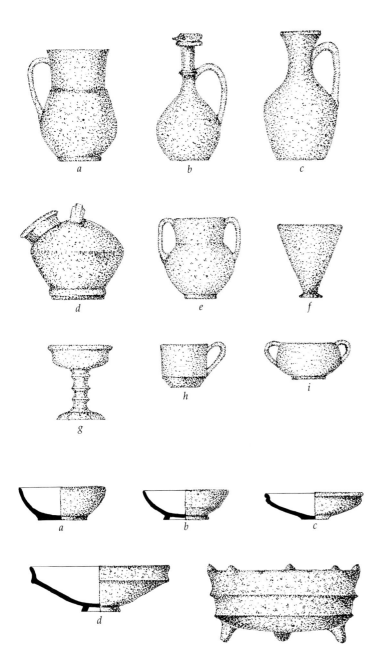

Figure 21. Some typical Spanish Muslim commonware vessel forms, unglazed or lead-glazed; serving vessels: *a, c,* pitchers; *b,* handled bottle; *d, botijo; e,* two-handled jar; *f–i,* cups.

Figure 22. Some typical Spanish Muslim commonware vessel forms, unglazed or lead-glazed; serving bowls: *a,* unfooted hemispherical bowl; *b,* ring-footed hemispherical bowl; *c,* unfooted conical bowl; *d,* ring-footed conical bowl, *cuenco; e,* nubbed tripod bowl.

As in the Roman era, agricultural pursuits underlay a major potting activity. For Andalusian Muslims, the mainstay of rural workshops was the ubiquitous bag-shaped jars attached to the rims of vertical water wheels or mounted in series and suspended on the vertical element of the horizontal wheel.[50] This basic *arcaduz* form took several wide-mouthed modifications, but each had a central groove to ease its fastening to the wheels (Fig. 23a).

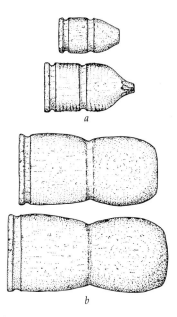

Figure 23. Earthenware water wheel jars, *arcaduces* or *cangilones*: *a*, Muslim style; *b*, Christian style.

Some were equipped with a basal knob for additional security. Walls were left with throwing ribs to add strength. Those jars most characteristic of Andalusia held approximately 5 liters.[51]

The number of such earthenware receptacles made in Andalusia over a span of more than half a millennium must have been enormous, since the wheels not only raised water but supplied hydro-power for grist and other mills. Glick suggests sixty pots per wheel at any given time, with the total number of functioning wheels likely well into the many thousands. The replacement of jars must have been a continual process as they hit against the wells, burst from water pressure, or fell because of rotted lashing. One variation of the well jar had a hole in the bottom. Glick considers this to have been a clepsydra, or hanging irrigation water clock, the contents flowing out in a determinable time.[52] One can imagine that many artisans grew up in potteries producing the well jars and spent their entire working lives making just this one vessel form.

One type of ware believed to have been brought to southern Spain by the country-dwelling Berbers, rather than by their Near Eastern contemporaries, fired to a whitish color and was decorated in red-to-brown vertical stripes. Its most common shape was a simple unfooted dish. Owing to low iron content, some clays still used in Andalusia turn a similar light color when fired, but modern tribes of northern Morocco are credited with more nearly continuing this particular stylistic tradition associated with the Muslim conquest horizon. Descriptions do not indicate how it may have been formed. As with present Berber wares, chances are that it was hand-built. It could have been a parallel, but unrelated, development in the story of Andalusian commercial earthenwares. Fruitful lines of future inquiry might determine Berber occupation of locations marginal to the main Guadalquivir basin through evidence afforded by their customary hand-made pottery, which they probably continued to use even after moving from their ancestral territory. There has been no archaeological investigation to substantiate that suggestion, but recent examination of a scattering of contemporary sites in northern Morocco suggests that non-urbanized communities there, likely composed of more Berbers than of the invading Muslims, clung to the indigenous technology in direct ratio to demographic and, quite surely, ethnic factors.[53]

It was in the urban communities that potters were most innovative and quickest to adopt methods and styling diffused from elsewhere, in order to please the tastes of a more cultivated clientele. Therefore, as political and social circumstances evolved at various times, it was the modes pursued in Córdoba, Granada, and Sevilla that represent the apexes of Andalusian ceramic history. The number of active shops in such places can be assumed to have increased in proportion to the needs of the expanding population.

Although few actual specimens of the early Muslim period in Andalusia can be positively identified, it is thought that the usual household repertory for all urban economic classes was composed primarily of ring-footed, hemispherical bowls of several sizes, perhaps some tapering directly down to a narrow base; one- or two-handled jugs, some with vertical, wide spouts; globular, wide-mouthed *ollas* without handles; broad, squat, cylindrical urinals; small jar-shaped oil lamps with a troughed, lateral wick spout; round canteens that could be suspended by two small handles from a saddle or carried over a user's shoulder; tall-necked pitchers, typically with a neck ridge over which a cap of linen or leather could be secured; porous water jars with flat, knobbed lids; deep, broad, straight-sided basins; amphorae; and wide-mouthed storage receptacles (Figs. 18–22). Cooking pots and casseroles would have had convex bases formed by careful compression outward with the hand after the vessel had been removed from the wheel. This process made it conform to the shape of the firing unit over which it was to be used. Had the base been pushed inward, it would have compacted the clay and reduced the risks of breakage from heating and cooling.[54]

Cooking was universally done on portable braziers, either of earthenware or metal. The ceramic examples were composed of a cylindrical base, open at one side for air circulation and ash removal, topped by a bowl with a perforated base in which charcoal was placed (Fig. 24). The cook pot was set above this, resting on prongs or nubs fastened around the bowl rim. Use of such a device meant that most cooked foods were simmered in water or oil, although some grilling over direct flame was possible. It likely also imposed a cuisine of one-dish hot meals upon its users. Large open hearths, typical of colder northern Spain, were not characteristic of Andalusia. The number of individual braziers used in the south for a millennium (until the introduction of metal stoves in the eighteenth century) must have reached into the millions, yet archaeological reports are strangely silent about them. The limited research in domestic structures, the commonness of the objects, and their likely end as fire-blackened, warped fragments account for their usual absence from ceramic discussions.

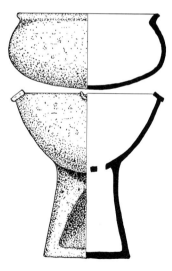

Figure 24. Earthenware brazier, *anafe*, consisted of a pedestal base open on one side for draft and an upper bowl with perforated bottom for charcoal. Cook pots were held above the fire by nubs or prongs attached to the fire bowl.

Figure 25. Spanish pharmaceutical earthenwares: *a*, small two-
handled jar (Muslim, *mudéjar*,
and Nasrid); *b–c*, albarelos (Muslim and Christian); *d*, *cántaro*
(Muslim and Christian); *e*, *orza*
(Christian); *f*, *bote* (Christian); *g*,
mortar (Muslim and Christian).

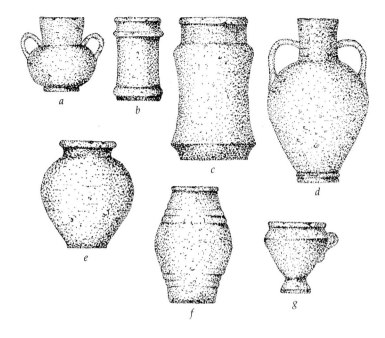

Figure 26. Thirteenth-century
miniature painting of a pharmacy
scene in an Arabic edition of
the De Materia Medica of Dioscor-
ides, believed to have been
made by copyist Abdallah ibn al
Fadl in Baghdad about 1224.
The classical two-handled *cántaros*
on the upper tier likely contained
medicinal preparations such as
that being brewed in the lower
scene. Apothecaries, similarly outfitted, are speculated to have
been common in Muslim Spain
(courtesy the Metropolitan
Museum of Art. The Cora Timken
Burnett collection of Persian
miniatures and other Persian art
objects. Bequest of Cora Timken
Burnett, 1957).

Another complex of earthenware forms as yet unrecognized among early Spanish Muslim remains includes those related to the processing and dispensing of medicinal concoctions (Fig. 25). Having been heirs to the classical *materia medica* and in direct trade contact with India and its exotic plant life, eastern Islam early in its history pushed to the forefront in the new sciences of pharmacology and toxicology. Such necessary equipment as mortars, distillation apparatus, and storage receptacles likely had earthenware as well as glass and metal components. One can surmise that in the cities of al Andalus small drug shops lined with shelves of pottery containers opened to the market streets (Fig. 26).

A clue to further use of pottery as containers for other products is provided by an early Arab historian, who wrote of his contemporaries in Cairo:

Every day they throw a thousand dinars' worth of waste production on refuse heaps and in the rubbish pits. This is the debris of the red terracotta pots in which the milk suppliers sell their milk, the cheese merchants place their cheeses, and the poor consume their meager meals on the premises of the cooks' shops.[55]

Architectural earthenwares assumed a special importance in southern al Andalus because, first, neither stone nor wood were plentiful locally, and, second, they had not been commonly used in the lands from which the bulk of the western Muslims had come. Moreover, earthenwares were well suited to a hot dry climate. Included among these terra cotta materials were thin rectangular bricks, flat paving tiles, curved roof tiles, and tubular water ducts (Fig. 27). Most were strictly functional, but one example of more elaborated earthenwares can be seen in a mosque begun in 785 over an older Cordoban Visigothic church. Borrowed from Damascus examples, which

Figure 27. Tapered earthenware tubes were connected to serve as water ducts, sewer pipes, and downspouts. The illustrated elbow, based upon specimens at the Museo Arqueológico Provincial, Sevilla, is essentially a wide-mouthed jar with lateral arm. Introduced to Andalusia by the Romans, comparable architectural earthenwares continued in use until modern times.

in turn were taken from Roman models, they are the
large white and red bricks forming the famous striped
horseshoe arches supported on marble columns that carry
the weight of the mosque roof. Not notable as ceramics,
they do signal an important future in Andalusian architecture for decorative earthenware.[56]

In general terms, this hypothesized repertory is based
upon knowledge of earlier and related ceramic complexes.
If correct, it represents a continuation of some Hispano-
Roman and Visigothic forms, supplemented by others in
contemporary use in the eastern Mediterranean. Although
their variety likely was limited, they would have revealed
a significant dependence upon earthenwares for widely
divergent purposes. One suspects their substitution for
bags and boxes that might have been fashioned of other
materials had they been abundant, or perhaps it was
partially a consequence of an early ingrained commitment
to the use of ceramics. Whatever the reasons, it is known
that ceramics from this time forward continued to play
a far more important role in Andalusian lifeways than they
did in those of any of the European societies to the north.

Pottery Technology

Behind an appraisal of the eighth- and ninth-century
technology of pottery-making followed by western Muslim
artisans must be recognition of the fact that these men
were inheritors of the oldest known complex of ceramic
traits in the world. Present evidence is that it was in the
Syrian uplands of the Near East that the pottery process
itself—that is, chemical alteration of clays through application of heat to achieve impermeability—was first discovered. Some examples of pottery and enclosed kilns there
date back seven to eight thousand years before Christ.
In the same broad geographical zone simple potter's
wheels are found from about 3500 B.C. They may have
been preceded by more primitive machines of perishable
materials that have not survived.[57] Copper-lead glazes
and the beginnings of an involved chemical formulary followed by 2000 B.C.[58]

Once the discovery of pottery was made and for some
seven millennia prior to the unifying force of Islam, the
expanded domain of which Syria was the lodestone witnessed a bewildering succession of unadorned utilitarian
earthenwares made to serve a host of everyday needs.
For special functions there were elaborately painted or polished objects in literally hundreds of shapes formed of
the earth from which Neolithic civilizations sprang.
Regional variations existed. Nevertheless, there was a
remarkable sameness imposed by limitations of the

medium, the environment, and the human factor. Of the
many ceramic developments that evolved, those coming in
the several centuries before Christ were particularly outstanding. At that time Hellenistic and Roman technical
and stylistic refinements in the craft were grafted on to the
older root of ceramic knowledge. Both these extensive
pottery heritages, that from antiquity and that from the
classical world, inevitably were thoroughly integrated into
the new cultural expression being developed and consolidated in the same region during the early Islamic period.
This was particularly true in the Syrian area, where little or
no destruction had taken place during the Arab conquests,
leaving Hellenistic remains intact.[59] These various patterns
of pottery making then spread with the westward drift
of Orientalia to its toehold in Iberia. There, a receptive
body of craftsmen, indigenous and migrant, already was
conversant with many of their attributes.

The pottery workshops of southern Spain, both those
left over from the Hispano-Visigothic era that were
brought back into operation and new ones created by
incoming Muslims, resembled scores of others scattered
from Samarra to Kairouan. Kiln form, wheel style, grinding pits and settling tanks, workyards, and a basic set
of primitive hand tools and larger stationary equipment
were part of the complex of associated traits generally
shared by all the potters of the Mediterranean basin.
Available raw materials and personal aptitudes in execut-
ing communally sanctioned principals of design varied
from one locality to another, but free trade and the
extreme mobility of Islamic artisans tended to even out
these distinctions. Therefore, from this moment on the
Andalusian craft was one of widely shared styles that persisted for centuries. It was overlaid with regionalisms
that had briefer temporal significance.

A SUDDEN BLOOMING

Historicultural Background

At a time when the rest of western Europe was still
feudalistic and floundering in a subsistence level money-
less economy, the second, or consolidation, phase of
Muslim occupation occurred in Spain. This period saw the
flowering during the tenth century (912–1009) of a capitalistic, independent, although intensely Arabized, Umayyad
caliphate, which maintained its capital in Córdoba rather
than in Sevilla. The agricultural wealth upon which much
of the economy was based was centered in the Guadalquivir Valley where both were situated. A half dozen other

cities, eighty large towns, three hundred smaller communities, and a host of villages dotted southern and eastern
Spain,[60] but it was in the capital that artistic, commercial,
and intellectual resources were concentrated. In the effort
to demonstrate its supreme success as an imperial power
in its own right, the western caliphate sought to outshine
the eastern Islamic centers, but it actually ended up
emulating them. Córdoba, a city of an estimated 100,000
persons, was adorned with Oriental splendors beyond
anything previously seen in Europe, but which would
have been at home in any comparable nucleus of contemporary eastern Islam.[61] Its uniqueness was its distance
from the main centers of power in western Asia, from
which it drew inspiration, and its total rejection of any
European flavor.

Geographically separated though Córdoba was, local
leaders likened their city to Damascus or Baghdad. There
was sound reason for such comparison: a marked interna-
tionality began to prevade the arts and crafts of Islam
wherever they were to be found. This frontier-to-frontier
unity of culture eventually spread over portions of three
continents.[62] Thus, beginning with the Umayyad caliphate
in Córdoba, complex influence from both sides of Asia
became embedded in Spanish Muslim life.

There were three main contributors to the easternization
of the caliphate. There existed an astounding network of
land and sea trade channels by which the goods and
ideas of the east flowed to the far Atlantic shores and back
again. This was because the Muslims successfully opened
up the Mediterranean, with Almería at the eastern edge
of modern Andalusia as the major western port. Round
ships capable of hauling bulk cargoes sailed in seasonal
convoys from east to west via Sicily and the Maghreb and
returned with supplies of foodstuffs.[63] Traders and merchants were extremely mobile, unknowingly serving as
informal but prime agents in cultural diffusion. Secondly,
artisans traditionally moved from capital to capital as
dominance and patronage shifted. This may have caused
some conflict, but it also served as a stimulant. Themes,
preferences, and worldviews from old and new sources
became amalgamated and sought expression. And there
was outright importation here and there of foreign, even
non-Muslim, craftsmen to carry out projects too advanced
for lesser local skills. Moreover, throughout Islam the
westward diffusion of both tangible and intangible riches
from the Far East was greatly enhanced. Earlier important
contact had been made between the Roman and Han
empires, but the intercourse truly blossomed beginning
with Islamic 'Abbasid and Chinese T'ang rules of the ninth

century. The flow of technical information was consistently from east to west.[64] Persia often served as intermediary on the northern land route across central Asia, and Mesopotamia functioned similarly at the terminus of the sea lanes that crisscrossed the Indian Ocean.[65]

Surviving documents tend to dwell upon the upper ranks of the society of the Cordoban caliphate, on their acquisitiveness and appreciation of luxurious trappings, on their support of the decorative arts, education, and commerce, and on their emphasis on religion, while at the same time wholeheartedly seeking theoretically immoral personal aggrandizement. They also describe Córdoba's many elaborate homes, public buildings, gardens, and the Great Mosque upon which fortunes were lavished to make it a jewel of early Spanish Muslim art. Less dramatic information was that the city was divided into twenty-one districts, each with a square, mosque, and bath.[66]

The production of most handicrafts was concentrated near the principal square by the leading mosque, each activity occupying a separate street or grouping of buildings which served as workshops or salesrooms. It is said that Córdoba and its sister cities of al Andalus had more active artisans than were present in any other part of tenth-century Europe. They contributed to the expanded economic base through silk-weaving, leatherwork, armaments, and fine metalworking.[67] That entailed the introduction of an assemblage of tools and mechanical devices ranging from precision looms, to smelting furnaces, to wheel-turned lathes. These were accompanied by an extensive understanding of raw materials and their behaviors under certain conditions. Tools and technology as applied to earthenware production likewise were part of this new vitality.

Pottery History

Pottery production is believed to have continued in both rural and urban workshops; especially at the latter, several grades of wares were made for a society grown more complex. Unfortunately, information is not as detailed as might be wished. The key center of caliphate Córdoba, for example, was nearly destroyed in the eleventh century. Relatively little archaeological research has been undertaken there because over the centuries the earlier remains were dismantled, and the city was rebuilt in less spectacular style. Presently it is so densely occupied that excavations generally are unfeasible unless undertaken in conjunction with public works.

It is especially regrettable that exploration of the potters' districts is not possible in Córdoba, since for the first

Figure 28. Extramural locations
of potteries in caliphate Córdoba.
Note their juxtaposition to cemeteries. A dam with water wheels
and grinding mills is indicated
on the Río Guadalquivir (after
Lévi-Provencal 1957).

time in the Muslim period their approximate locations are
identified. Unlike those crafts at the heart of town, the
two principal concentrations of Cordoban caliphate potteries are thought to have been outside the northern city
walls adjacent to outlying cemeteries and near related
brick and cement works (Fig. 28).[68] All of these inherently

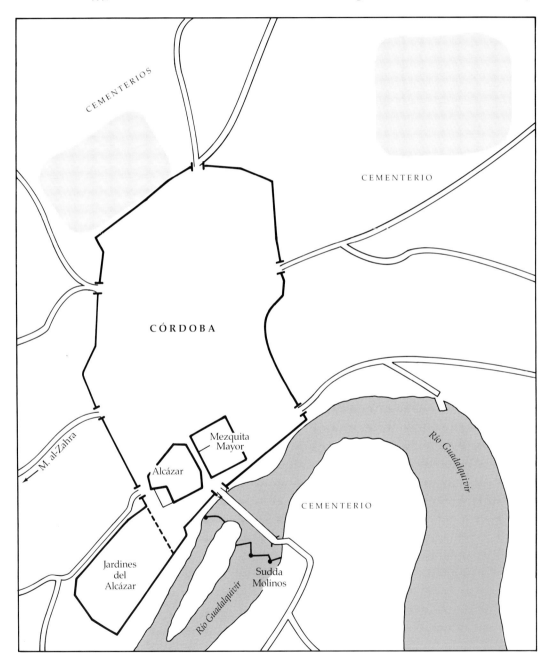

dirty enterprises produced objectionable clutter and smoke, were potential fire hazards, and required constant replenishment of bulky raw materials brought to the city by mule trains. Hence, their placement immediately inside or outside of walls became customary wherever such enclosures existed. Otherwise, they were clustered in the farthest suburbs. If excavated, the area of the Cordoban potteries, once called *kutah rasho*[69] and now covered over by businesses and residences, doubtless would provide a vivid picture of an entire craft having been lifted as a culturally determined entity from the eastern Mediterranean and set down thousands of miles away on another continent.

In addition to random ceramic finds beneath Cordoban streets and buildings, caliphate age pottery has been retrieved at sites such as Medina Elvira near Granada, Mesas de Asta in the vicinity of Jérez de la Frontera, Alcalá la Vega, Almería, Toledo, Ibiza and other places in the Balaeric Islands, Bobastro Castle near Málaga, Medinaceli in the vicinity of Soria, Alcalá de Henares, and some additional locales in a line up to the northern border of Muslim territory along the Río Duero. These ordinary vessels were of the same rough-textured, heavy-walled, low caliber as had been known earlier. Used by all citizens, these primarily were a half dozen basic shapes that can be separated into jar, bowl, urinal, and portable charcoal brazier categories. If alterations in or additions to that established complex of utilitarian shapes occurred they were not significant. When a vessel broke it was replaced by an identical item. This continuity reflects the fundamental conservatism of the mainstream of Spanish Muslim ceramics perpetuated by a core of native workers long conversant with local biases. If the artisan force was augmented by migrant potters from outside al Andalus, they must have come from comparable workshops and quickly have fallen into step with their Spanish colleagues. Users moving into Spain from the eastern Mediterranean basin likewise would have been immediately comfortable with local pottery because of the universality of common earthenwares throughout the Islamic world. The constancy of ordinary vessel form may also be a sign that the impoverished, harsh life of most of those who used this pottery remained about as it had been, despite great wealth in high places.

Most vulgar hollow wares were undecorated, but some bore simple, crudely applied, geometric, matte designs in white over a red-burning base clay or red or black patterns on a tan paste (Fig. 29).[70]

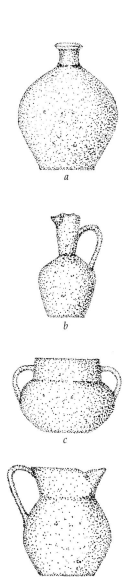

Figure 29. Some typical Spanish Muslim fineware vessel forms, low grade: *a*, black–on–tan; *b, d* white–on–red; *c*, red–on–tan.

The low-level pottery industry obviously had economic importance. Troops of journeymen and supporting laborers must have been engaged in mass producing simple domestic earthenwares used in all homes and farms, because during caliphate times the province became the most populous sector of Europe. These workers were to be found in settled localities throughout the domain; if Zozaya's theory proves correct, they were concentrated at approximately every twenty kilometers. Add typical friability and hard usage of such pottery to enormous demand and one can appreciate a thriving, ceaseless activity catering primarily to nearby internal markets. Although it is not likely that empty common vessels were a commodity in the active export trade, containers for Andalusian foodstuffs shipped abroad unquestionably were a significant part of the basic pottery output. Whether these containers were made in rural localities close to the source of the agricultural products is not known. Nor has the role of the river system in commercial transport of them and other goods been studied. An interdependence between those who prepared *esparto* coverings for some ceramics and the actual potters is notable.

Some records of the time further emphasize the function of common ceramics in the heightened caliphate commerce. A few vessels became standard measuring units in the selling of produce. Their sizes supposedly were graded by the overseers of the markets, although regional variations were common. Smallest was a jar called a *thumn* or *azumbre*. It accommodated 4 pints of liquid or one-eighth of an *arroba* of dry foods. A medium vessel was the *qulla* of 12 *azumbres* capacity, and the largest measuring jars were *jabujas*, which held 20 *arrobas*. There were jars of special sizes for honey and vinegar. The milk *azumbre* held 6 pints of liquid.[71] The exact contour of these receptacles is unknown, but they likely were short-necked, round-bodied vessels with one or more handles to facilitate pouring. It will be recalled that standardization of vessel size was an important aspect of Roman amphora production.

On a higher level of pottery making, an innovation in the Spanish sequence was the use of lead glaze. Because such glaze served both functional and decorative purposes, it was widely used and has persisted in Spanish ceramics to the present day. In the Near East its origins extended backward to about the second millennium B.C., but it had not gained common acceptance because its flushing action tended to blur favored painted patterning. Later Romans residing in Asia Minor did make use of lead glaze on vessels decorated by various surface modifications, some examples reaching as far westward as Great Britain and Spain. Byzantine potters continued the common use of such glazes.[72]

Responsive to the dry, bright sunlight and bleached coloration of much of their desert homelands, Arab artisans early displayed a fondness for the jewel-like qualities of lead glazes. Their flash and the brilliant colors possible with mineral additives were appealing. They found that surface manipulations achieved through incising, gouging, appliquéing, stamping, or fretting, which they had been leaving uncoated, allowed pooling of liquid glaze. This created highlights and shadows on what otherwise were flat grounds. Again, such treatments were not original with the Muslims. Roman and Byzantine potters before them had decorated some of their ceramics by the same means. Still, the combination of plastic design and lead glaze was diffused to Andalusia during the tenth century. There, relief under lead glaze generally was created by molds, with a spiraling or diagonal orientation of pattern being characteristic.

Other means of vessel enrichment illustrate the complexity of cultural crosscurrents at work. Painted designs of simple intersecting lines or a brief inscription were executed on one surface in brown or black pigments and were covered with either colorless or honey-colored clear glaze. The opposite surface frequently was decorated solely by a green or amber glaze. The fluxing action of the glaze often caused painted lines to bleed. Comparable underglaze painting was present in ninth- or tenth-century Syria, which is suspected of being the immediate donor of this particular trait.[73] A rare variant was a turquoise glaze that resulted from use of copper oxide in an alkaline glaze, a Mesopotamian innovation copied in the west. A few examples of a yellow, rather than amber, glaze is a possible clue to Byzantine influence. Stevenson reports that a canary yellow coating had been perfected at Byzantium by the late ninth century.[74]

The most dramatic impact of eastern Islam on the ceramics of tenth-century Andalusia occurred in the finer wares meant for use by the affluent. For the first time in Muslim Iberia some earthenwares assumed shapes of certain metal pieces commonly found in wealthy establishments. Among these were porringers with sharply angled sides, shallow straight-sided bowls on stubby tripod feet (Fig. 22e), and tiny jar-shaped oil lamps (Fig. 18c). The classical background of the ancient Mediterranean is hinted at in tall-necked jars with tapered curved spouts and high arching handles (Fig. 21b), small round-bodied bottles, cups with walls sharply flared from a very constricted base (Fig. 21f), and other delicate forms. It was in the caliphate era, too, that painted decorations became of sufficient importance to constitute a second distinct branch of the pottery-making industry. Their differences from anything previously known locally, the variety of techniques they demonstrated, and the kind and quality of design execution clearly indicate the arrival of a group of artisans versed in the ceramic maturity and vogues of the eastern Mediterranean. A small number of artisans was involved in making fewer objects in this branch of the industry. Their ceramics were traded throughout the extent of al Andalus, but there is no evidence thus far that they were an integral part of the external commerce.

Stylistic and technological evidence supports the argument that one contingent of potters moving into al Andalus in response to the richness of upper levels of caliphate society and their patronage of the arts originated in Baghdad. There they had worked under similar conditions generated by the 'Abbasid dynasty, but which by the tenth century had begun to dissipate, scattering artisans like dandelions on the wind. 'Abbasid art had evolved out of the dominant stimulus of Sassanian Persia to the northeast and the lesser influence of the pervading classicism of the Near East to the northwest. Both these aesthetic orientations as interpreted by Mesopotamian Muslims can be observed in the new style of earthenwares that seem to have suddenly appeared in the west.

Prior to the fall of the eastern Umayyads in 750, the Byzantine world had been a leading contributor to the new Islamic culture evolving at the capital of Damascus. According to Grabar, what was taken was not Byzantine art but some methods and motifs.[75] That complex of traits passed to the 'Abbasids in Baghdad. Isolated elements from Byzantine sources cannot be positively attributed to artisans from Byzantium having been active in the royal workshops at Córdoba, although such men have been documented in caliphate crafts such as stone carving, tiling, ivory carving, and woodworking.[76] In an earlier time Córdoba had experienced a long Byzantine occupation. At the caliphate period, however, either there was imitation of introduced models present at Córdoba, or, more likely, the potters had absorbed classicism expressed in a variety of media through long confrontation in the Near East.[77]

The distinctive new caliphate style that most vividly reveals the complex cultural forces to which Andalusia was subject once was regarded as court ware, which probably would have been unknown to rank-and-file tenth-century Andalusians. Information about it came primarily from two sites. One was the Romanized villa-palace compound of Madinat al-Zahra (also Medina az-Zahra) tumbled over

a rocky hillside west of Córdoba, which was begun in
936 and occupied for less than a century. An analysis of
the pottery recovered there was included with a 1912 excavation report, which has been reviewed recently in the
light of modern research.[78] The other source was a similar
noble establishment near Granada known as Medina
Elvira, which was occupied and destroyed at almost the
same time as Madinat al-Zahra. It was excavated from
1870 to 1875. These two archaeological zones provide a
documented chronology unique in the studies of Muslim
Spain, in that recovered artifacts can be securely dated. As
research has progressed, however, the range of this type
of pottery has been greatly expanded. It now has been
recovered from diverse sites elsewhere in former al Andalus, most of which cannot be pinpointed so precisely in
time. The comparative abundance of this type makes
its designation as a restricted palatial ware improbable.[79]
Not unexpectedly, it disappeared from the regional
ceramic record as soon as foci of exotic Arabized Muslim
life faded. As was to recur many times, its makers packed
up and moved on to an ascending capital. But with the
tenacity of Spanish ceramic traditions, traces of the methods of production of the type's specialized design and
palette submerged into the Andalusian aesthetic background to resurface from time to time.

Made of a clear red-firing clay quite distinctive from the
lighter materials of the lower Guadalquivir, this most
unique caliphate pottery came in a number of shapes (Fig.
30). The three that were most frequent afforded the best

Figure 30. Some typical Spanish
Muslim fineware vessel forms, top
grade, white-slipped with green
and brown decoration under clear
lead glaze, Córdoba caliphate
age: *a, cántaro; b,* spouted bottle or
jug; *c, e,* bottles; *d, alcuza; f,*
handled jar; *g,* plate or bowl; *h,*
handled cup; *i,* inkwell;
j, large jar or *jarrón.*

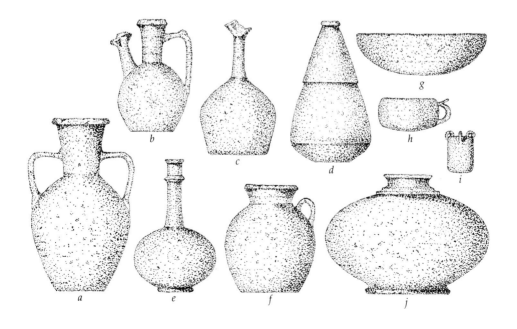

fields for design. They were a broad, footless plate that gently sloped up to a direct rim, a tall-necked jar with a pair of sharply angled handles, and a bottle with a very slender neck that sometimes widened into a flower-shaped, spouted top (Fig. 30a,c,e,g). A ridge below the orifice on the tall throat of some bottles may have inspired a similar feature on Far Eastern vessels of a much later date, which in the latter case is termed a string rim.[80] Also present in the style were small handleless jars, inkwells, other jars with four handles, a conical water container, and lamps. All the shape variations, reflecting a refined level of use beyond that of simple peasantry, had eastern or late classical affiliation. So did the decorative process, in which pattern was laid on a white engobe, a treatment dating to at least 5000 B.C. in the eastern Mediterranean.[81] This was a decorative method widely used in Fatimid Egypt, contemporaneous with the caliphate, whereas ʿAbbasid decorators in Mesopotamia already had more commonly adopted a different technique. In Spain the bisqued and slipped caliphate ware was fired after being painted, dipped in a lead glaze solution, and refired for a third time.

As was usual in Islamic art, a stock of motifs was shared by artisans engaged in diverse crafts. Therefore, pottery decoration as applied to this special ware restated the ʿAbbasid preference for relatively sparse patterns used as bands, isolated large-scale single elements, and all-over arrangements (Fig. 31) seen in stone, textiles, ivory, and woodwork. Rim patterns were suspended lunates or running palmettes of ʿAbbasid derivation or lanceolate leaves more typically Byzantine. Also characteristic were radial compositions or the quartering or dividing of fields of design into thirds.

The most frequently seen motif was the calligraphic rendering of the phrase *almulk*, the empire. If the phrase had been complete, it would have read *almulk lillah*, the empire belongs to God. This epigram was executed in large Cufic, foliated Cufic, or pseudo-Cufic as a solitary ornament on plate obverses or, when drawn in small size, was laid in an encircling band on plates or cylindrical jars. The style of foliated Cufic was an early form and appeared on no other western Islamic pottery. The concentration on a single calligraphic inscription differs from the usual ʿAbbasid practice of using the potter's name, isolated words, or propitious phrases as elements of design.[82] Among other motifs taken from Hellenistic Persia and assorted pre-Islamic decorators were doughnut circles, guilloche, arcades, palmettes, or *atauriques*. Lanceolate leaves, or what can be regarded as ʿAbbasid florals

a   b   c

d   e   f

having Sassanian ties, often appeared on Cordoban ceramics as a central medallion arranged so that the leaves pointed outward around a central square and were separated by smaller units. These combined to form a starred pattern that further evolved into a six-lobed flower.[83] Other star devices were framed by squares overlapping larger diamonds. Parallel designs can be seen on earlier plaster work at Samarra in Mesopotamia, in marble at Byzantium, or on contemporary luster tiles at Kairouan in Tunisia. The latter was a trade and religious center midway on the route from Cairo to Sevilla. The designs also occur in stone sculpturing or wood ceiling patterns from Madinat al-Zahra and the mosque in Córdoba. The so-called peacock's feather motif on some al-Zahra vessels comes from the Byzantine background, although it also is present at Samarra.[84] Rims of plates frequently were enlivened on interiors with pendant lunettes and bands of curling leaves derived directly from 'Abbasid grammar.

Of special interest were numerous stylizations of animal figures borrowed from 'Abbasid roots (Fig. 32). All are now believed to have had iconographic or zodiacal significance to makers and users alike, and were executed in the figural style of decorators at Baghdad. They reaffirm

Figure 31. Typical compositions used on Cordoban caliphate green–and–brown–on–white fineware: *a*, balanced isolated floral; *b*, center, Cufic inscription, with lunate rim border; *c*, stylized encircling band with lunate rim border; *d*, center, Cufic inscription, stylized geometric encircling band, lunate rim border; *e*, three-part field with stylized florals and lunate rim border; *f*, off-center four-part field of geometrics and stylized florals (after Pavón Maldonado 1967).

Figure 32. Some animal motifs appearing on Cordoban caliphate green–and–brown–on–white fineware (note that all have abstracted foliage in their mouths): *a*, deer with ears and horns indicated identically; *b*, horse with bird riding a saddle; *c*, hare; *d*, peacock; *e*, duck; *f*, addorsed peacocks (after Pavón Maldonado 1967).

that strictures against representations of these elements had not yet been adopted by some sects, especially if they appeared on secular objects and were not rendered realistically. Animal depictions have remained a part of Spanish design to the present. Furthermore, the spritely portrayed ducks, doves, peacocks, rabbits, cranes, gazelles, wolves, and stags, often carrying foliage in their mouths, have many eastern Mediterranean counterparts.[85] Addorsed peacocks facing a central column on a *cuenco*, or large bowl, could have come right off Sassanian textiles. Large horses appear to trot across several plates, one bridled and with a bird on its back holding the reins in its beak.[86] Their large size filling the field of design vividly recalls Nishapur decorations. The dots or circles that speckle animal bodies may have been suggested by niello elements on contemporary bronze work.[87]

Around the fat body of a specialized long-necked bottle form typically are designs of human figures drawn in a simple sketchy way, with a few lines indicating facial features, hair, and clothing (Fig. 33). There is no mistaking them, but the treatment is not realistic. One such bottle displays five men apparently playing musical instruments

Figure 33. Some human motifs appearing on Cordoban caliphate green–and–brown–on–white fineware (after Gómez Moreno 1951a; Pavón Maldonado 1967; Torres Balbás 1957).

and a sixth waving a baton. The meaning of the scene is puzzling now, but there is little doubt that it represented a ceremony familiar to tenth-century Spanish Muslims. What appear to be representations of warriors carrying shields and lances, women, and a falconer decorate several other fragments. These closely resemble some contemporary examples found along the North African Mediterranean coast.[88]

Most of the borrowed eastern motifs originally had appeared on lusterware, but in the west they adorned fine polychromes. The caliphate renditions of many of these figures displayed a spontaneity of execution and imaginative detail that made them less rigid or stereotyped than the models. In these variances from the 'Abbasid norm can be detected a timid emergence of Spanish Muslim artistic independence. Still, in general, the figurative art of the Cordoban potters conforms to many of Grube's hallmarks of the eastern style. These include its extreme simplicity, monumentality of individual figures, perfect balance, powerful expression with limited means, large size of animals in relation to the vessel's surfaces, and animals depicted in motion.[89]

Usual decorative colors of this elaborate Cordoban type were a green obtained from copper and a brown from iron or manganese that verged on purplish tones. The green was the filler of elements, the brown the outline. Zozaya, who considers the style to have been principally of Byzantine origin, cites regional variations that include the use of yellow for ground or minor accents.[90] This color, as well as red and black, probably came from iron solutions. Contemporary sherds recovered from Algerian kilns are similarly decorated and are thought to have represented a slow drift westward along the North African littoral of decorative ideas from Egypt.

The process of applying white engobe to a surface and then laying on colored pattern covered by a lead glaze was used for curved bricks in the cupola of the mosque at Córdoba, dated 965 to 968. These marked the closest thing to glazed tile to have developed there at that early date.[91]

When black or red slip was placed on pottery, it was painted in light-colored pigments and left unglazed. Rarely, it was lightly scratched with fine-lined elements. Stylized floral designs, simple bird or animal figures, and geometrics were most usual. The motifs and color schemes are said to be comparable to coeval materials from Algeria.[92]

A further surface treatment came through mixing mineral pigments with lead glaze and using such a compound to paint a patterned band around a pot, leaving the remainder of the body uncoated with glaze. Vessels also were molded with all-over relief patterns, which sometimes were subsequently glazed. Among these were heavy, large, octagonal well mouths, or *brocales*, also present in marble.[93]

To keep molten mineral oxides within the boundaries of a given pattern, caliphate potters toward the end of the tenth century sometimes drew primary outlines in a mixture of a greasy substance and impure manganese, which burned out during firing to leave a dark matte line. The elements, usually boldly drawn circles, leaves, letters, and dots, were painted with various pigments that vitrified. These produced yellow, green, and purplish-brown colors, with associated white passages being a chalky slip. Occasionally the entire vessel was then coated with clear lead glaze. Perhaps in these uncommon ceramics were the real luxury types of the period, originating in the shops of Madinat al-Zahra but copied in a few other places.[94]

Figure 34. Some typical Spanish Muslim fineware vessel forms, top grade, *cuerda seca*: *a*, chamber pot; *b*, large jar; *c–d*, small two-handled jar; *e*, lidded bowl; *f*, handled bottle.

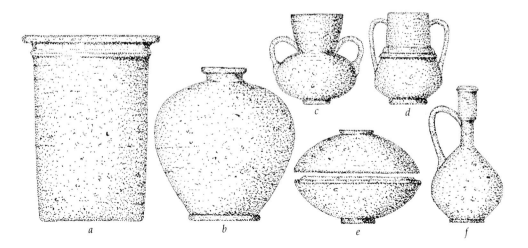

a   *b*   *c*   *d*   *e*   *f*

In Spain this approach to decoration, another of those which may have diffused west from Egypt by way of the Tunisian coast,[95] became known as the *cuerda seca*, or dry cord, style. Caliphate potters used it primarily on small jars or plates (Fig. 34). However, one of the most intriguing of the series was a heavy-walled cylindrical chamber pot of a large diameter suitable for use in one of the communal lavoratories found in the palace at Madinat al-Zahra.[96] It carried bold alternating palmette and divided circle motifs in three encircling registers and was lead-glazed on both interior and exterior surfaces.

The most impressive trade pottery was called *reflejo metálico*, or lusterware. Its significance was due to its nature and not to its number, because it was rare in tenth-century Spain. It was accomplished by painting oxides of silver or copper over fired tin-glazed pottery and then refiring the articles a third time in a muffle kiln held to low temperature. The present consensus of opinion among art historians and archaeologists is that these few known fragments were remnants of trade pieces or royal gifts from Mesopotamia. It was there that the technique was invented and kept a closely guarded secret until craftsmen moved on to other work places. Both obverse patterns of a large solid animal surrounded by a contour line and a background filled with dots or stylized florals and exteriors treated with large circles separated by carelessly placed dashes are common ninth- and tenth-century Mesopotamian devices (Fig. 35).[97] Susa has been suggested as another possible supplier of these particular vessels.

A westward traffic in comparable ceramics from the ʿAbbasid area is substantiated by the occurrence of luster tiles at the mosque of Sidi ʿAkba in Kairouan, completed in

Figure 35. Tenth-century Mesopotamian *reflejo metálico*: *a*, specimen at Detroit Art Institute, with central figure considered to be a camel bearing an *'otfeh*; *b*, specimen at Fitzwilliam Museum, Cambridge, showing comparable treatment of background with contour outlining of main single element; *c*, fragment recovered from Madinat az-Zahra that appears to have been decorated in the same style with a camel and *'otfeh* (after Pope, A.U. 1964 and Torres Balbás 1957).

836.[98] Although these commonly are ascribed to Baghdad, one researcher believes a few of them with some similarities to sherds reclaimed at Madinat al-Zahra actually may have been made at Susa by itinerant potters from the 'Abbasid capital.[99] Regardless of which locality may have been responsible for the Andalusian and Ifriqiyan specimens, there was an unquestionable appreciation in the western Islam settlements for the lusters of the east. It was not until a century later that similar pottery may have been made in Spain, although there is disagreement on this point. Then Toledo, taken back into Christian hands by that time, seems to have been the place where it was manufactured.[100]

Architectural ceramics had not yet become important in Spain, other than at the palace of Madinat al-Zahra. There some plain floor tiles were laid with stone in contrasting patterns. Similar use of floor terra cottas occurred in contemporary Tunisia. At Toledo, tenth-century insets of honey-colored tiles have been found on columns of a mosque.[101]

With so much of the 'Abbasid ceramic complex being diffused to the western caliphate, it is hard to explain the absence of what already had become a standard item in Mesopotamia. That was a kind of pottery to become known later in Spain as maiolica, which bore lead glaze made opaque and white by the addition to the liquid solution of a small percentage of tin oxide. Such glaze usually was the base for the imported *reflejo metálico*.

The process of opacifying common transparent lead glaze had been developed in the ancient Near East, but over the centuries it had been forgotten.[102] In one of the cyclic reconstitutions of lost ideas that has characterized the slow advance of man's engineering prowess, ninth-century Mesopotamian craftsmen rediscovered it. To them, it was a means of making their wares vaguely comparable to the first Chinese wares to reach the west. These were T'ang porcelaneous products coming to them through the efforts of a large Muslim colony living at Canton.[103] If such a motivation had not been present, the tin glaze that is used by most contemporary folk potters throughout the world might well have remained deep in the bank of rejected technology that comprises the rind of human civilization. Tin-opacified glaze had the advantage of concealing the base material of which pottery was formed, thus eliminating the need for engobe. Also, because tin additives reduced the fluxing action of lead, designs painted on top of unfired coatings could be counted upon to remain sharp and permanently fixed through firing.

Had the maiolica technique been introduced to caliphate
potters, the court ware would have had a richer quality,
because designs would have been within the semi-lustrous
glaze rather than beneath a clear coat. Although lead
glaze was a base on some occasions, it is probable that the
potters also needed knowledge of the maiolica process
in order to produce *reflejo metálico*. That may explain why
that kind of ware was not made.

The reasons for uneven diffusion of Mesopotamian
ceramic knowledge to Spain are unclear. Necessary raw
materials were available. The chalky clays of the Guadalquivir Valley, with their high lime content and light firing
color, were desirable for maiolica manufacture. Tin was
already being used for engobe solutions.[104] If a greater
supply of tin were needed, it was certainly available from
Christian traders in the northern Iberian peninsula or
from the more usual Cornwall sources. The kilns in use
were capable of heats sufficiently high to mature the glaze.
One possible answer to the lack of caliphate maiolica
may be the total absence of known examples in Spain of
Mesopotamian maiolica, other than the *reflejo metálico*.[105]
Lane is of the opinion that tin-glazed pottery made in
ninth- or tenth-century Mesopotamia, decorated in blue,
green, purple, and occasionally yellow, customarily was
exported to Persia, but not to Syria or Egypt.[106] That would
have put it out of reach of western decorators.

Pottery Technology

Of more lasting consequence than introduced pottery
styles was introduced technology. As for machines and
hand tools, these represented a set of objects suggested by
a generalized Middle Eastern Bronze Age heritage, which
in Spain was substantially reinforced by previous Roman
practices there. However, certain aspects distinguished
this complex of traits from what had been known earlier.
The wheel brought to Spanish shops by the Muslims
doubtless was of the compound type (Fig. 36). That is, it
was a large, heavy, wooden basal disk, probably about
3½ ft in diameter, turned by a forward thrust of the craftsman's right foot. This initiated movement of a vertical
axle of either wood or metal, seated in a pivot stone or
heavy wooden block beneath the fly wheel, which spun an
upper disk a foot in diameter, on which the raw clay
rested. The throwing head probably was formed of two
rather thick wooden disks of the same circumference
pegged together, which was pivoted into the center axle.[107]
The wheels resembled those already known to the native
artisans. Indications are that its positioning differed from
former custom. Admittedly, no wheels or intact factories

Figure 36. Muslim-style potter's wheel introduced to Spain: ABOVE, view from above: *A–B*, center axis, wheel to left side of potter's seated position; *a*, throwing wheel head; *b*, lower wooden fly wheel; *c*, axle connecting two wheels; *e*, foot rest; *f*, plank across pit opening to support potter, other planks across pit opening forming work table. BELOW, cross section of potter's wheel recessed into a pit: *A–B*, center axis; *a*, wheel head; *b*, fly wheel; *c*, axle; *d*, pivot stone in which axle is seated; *e*, foot rest; *f*, seat.

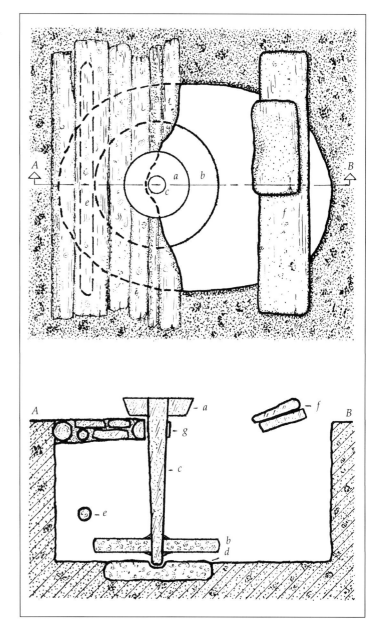

of the caliphate age are thought to have survived, but rare accounts of pottery processes observed in Spain in following centuries report that wheels customarily were set in trenches dug in workroom floors, so that the throwing head was at ground level.[108] The potter sat directly on the ground, his legs extending down into the trench so that his right foot could comfortably reach the fly wheel. At some unknown period a slanted wooden seat or brace was set into the pit edge for the potter, and this in due time sometimes was attached to the base of the wheel framing. The ground surrounding the wheel or planks stretched across the pit opening became a work table of sorts, where tools, bowls of lubricating slip, and freshly thrown pots could be placed.

Substantiation for the physical arrangement of Muslim potter's wheels comes from excavation of a ninth-century workshop at Sirāf on the modern Iranian coast of the Persian Gulf. There, bearings for the vertical shafts of potter's wheels and pits to secure the legs of a surrounding work table were exposed. If the publication descriptions are interpreted correctly, the wheel position was as suggested here.[109]

Survival of traditional methods is an explanation for continued use of the pit wheel in some modern Spanish potteries, in towns such as Granada, Cuellar de Baza, Ugijar, and Guadix in the province that was the last Muslim stronghold in Spain and where Moorish flavor persists.[110] It is universally employed throughout Morocco in maiolica factories and in potteries making common grade wares.[111] The pit wheel still is used in many folk potteries in the Near East, Pakistan, and Iran.[112]

If one may speculate further from observation of modern practice, the throwing wheel was placed slightly to the potter's left rather than directly in front of him. Such relationship of worker to wheel presently is typical in Spain, Morocco, Spanish America, and parts of the Middle East, and probably has been so for a very long time.[113]

General kiln configuration copied Roman models, likewise derived from a basic Near Eastern example. Eastern Islamic examples of that sort are those encountered at ninth-century Sirāh in Persia and at Egyptian Fostat.[114] The Spanish Muslim kiln, the *horno arabe*, was a beehive, or domed cylindrical structure, although rectangular models also are known (Fig. 37). The kiln consisted of a partially subterranean tunnel and large chamber for the burning of irregularly shaped fuel, and another unit placed vertically over part of it to contain pottery to be baked. The walls of the lower unit were buttressed by the earth. From above, the outline would have been of a keyhole or rectangular shape. An opening in one side of the upper chamber permitted easy stacking, the opening being sealed at each firing with bricks, potsherds, and copious amounts of mud that hardened with heat. The two compartments were separated by a clay or stone floor punctured with holes to allow free circulation of hot air. This floor was supported from below by arches or a central pillar, but was subject to collapse because of excessive heat or weight. Walls were of broken bricks, stones, and pottery fragments

Figure 37. Andalusian two-chambered, updraft kiln styles: *a*, subterranean combustion unit, firing chamber open at top; *b*, subterranean combustion unit, standard enclosed firing chamber, usually elliptical or round; *c*, rectangular construction with combustion unit partially subterranean or completely above ground, firing chamber outfitted with saggars.

mudded together with clay. Overall size ranged from 2 to 5 m in greatest dimensions, the height being about 3 m. Examples of such kilns have been unearthed at Manises in Valencia province and on the grounds of the Alhambra palace at Granada.[115] In both cases these post-dated the caliphate, but once were operated by *morisco* or *mudéjar* potters thought to have followed traditional ways.[116] Whether single-chambered kilns existed in Muslim Spain, as they did in ancient Persia, is not known.[117] Although not of an efficient design—owing to great heat loss, inability to achieve and maintain temperatures higher than those necessary for earthenwares, cold spots, and the need for considerable fuel reserves—the two-chambered updraft kiln remained typical of the Mediterranean until modern times.[118] Kilns in use around the lands overrun by Islam seem never to have incorporated chimneys, although they would have promoted better draft. The one exception is those designed to be used for the creation of lusterware. In common Spanish Muslim kilns, one or more ports in the roof served to pull hot air upward and maintain an oxidizing atmosphere within the kiln.[119] Some reduction would have resulted from use of oil rich substances for fuel, but prolonged reduction would have volatilized the lead in glazes. There may have been no roof whatsoever on kilns used to fire the lowest quality of earthenwares, large potsherds being placed as a temporary covering over greenware mounded within. This has not been confirmed and does not represent present practice in usual Muslim or Spanish shops, although it is occasionally reported in some rural Moroccan potteries. Most likely, brick kilns were completely open at the top.

As in earlier times, fuel for many Andalusian kilns may have been either *ramón*, the branches and leaves of olive trees, or *borujo*, the by-products of olive oil processing. In all instances, this was loose bulky fuel necessitating a commodious firing chamber. These materials were added to the fires by means of a typical two-pronged Muslim pitchfork to other more readily ignited materials, such as grape vines or *chamiza*. The olive residue of pits and skins still is burned in some regional Andalusian potteries and in the active tin and lead glaze industries in Fez, Morocco.[120] Later records from the Valencian area, where olives did not thrive with such abundance as in Andalusia, show that brush, furze, *chamiza*, and various other plants were burned.[121] Furze is used today in Granada. Depending on kiln load and kind of pottery, most firings lasted about a day. The outer openings of the kiln then were sealed with rubble or broken pots, and the kiln was left to cool overnight, or even for several days.

Dehydration, the point at which soluble earth converts irretrievably into insoluble pottery, occurs at temperatures near 600°C. For greater durability, fusible earthenwares need to be further heated to at least 900° to 950°C. Fully matured glazes containing tin usually require a slightly higher temperature of approximately 1050° to 1060°C, at the uppermost limits of the usual *horno arabe*. In Muslim and later Spanish view, therefore, unglazed pottery meant for routine house or farm functions was considered finished after only one firing. Probably low grade unfired wares occasionally were sprinkled with granular galena, or

sulphide of lead, which melted and flowed during baking
to form a thin glassy surface in a single firing. Vessels
to see table or special use most commonly were bisqued in
one firing, dipped in glaze, and fired a second time.

Whether in caliphate workyards there were separate
kilns for bisque and glaze firings or for domestic and finer
grade wares presently is unknown. These may have been
later refinements. A reverberatory kiln for the calcination
of metals used in glaze preparation likely was an integral
component of the customary workshop.[122]

Knowledge of kiln furniture used during caliphate times
is limited. Although saggars were mentioned by Abū'l
Qāsim, a Persian ceramist of the early fourteenth century
whose brief treatise is the oldest remaining discussion
of the Muslim maiolica process,[123] it appears that they
never became part of usual kiln setting practice in pre-
sixteenth-century Spain. Large bowls might well have
been put to use for the same purpose of protecting individual objects from damage by undesirable fumes, fly-ash,
or contact. That method is known to have been employed
by Roman potters.[124] Several sizes of three-pronged cockspurs of fired clay separated stacks of lead-glazed pieces.
Most vessels retain obvious scars where the supports
fused at point of contact to body parts. Such stilts had a
very long usage in the eastern Mediterranean, going back
to the earliest discoveries of glaze. In Spain there is no
record of balls of clay being used to separate vessels during
firing, as seems to have been done in Egypt. Particularly
intriguing are fired ceramic rods, or *birlos*, about 40 cm in
length and 8 cm in diameter, recovered from thirteenth- to
fifteenth-century debris and walkways around *mudéjar*-
operated kilns in Manises[125] and from recent excavations
beneath Sevilla. Series of these fired earthenware bars
formed support shelves within a kiln load. This was an
improvement over contemporary European methods,
which until the nineteenth century utilized no shelving of
any kind. In traditional shops in Granada today the *birlos*
are supplemented by stacked hollow cylinders, originally
made to serve as water conduits, or by saggars. Roman
kilns also used fire rods, but their ultimate origin possibly
was in the wellspring of most of the other aspects of pottery-making methods, ancient Eurasia.[126]

In lead glazing, vessels first were fired to a temperature
sufficient to drive out chemical and physical moisture
and to harden the walls. The bisqued pots then were
dipped into a solution formed of a compound of pulverized quartz sand, a bit of clay, and crushed lead oxide.
Finally, the pots were fired a second time, but to a higher

temperature. When matured, the coating emerged as a vitrified, glossy, transparent, and colorless surface, rendering a vessel impervious to liquids and attractive in appearance. The glaze often was altered by the addition of ground mineral oxides, such as copper, iron, or manganese, to achieve green, amber, or brown hues; these could be lightened or darkened, depending upon the strength of the admixture. Less expert potters may have merely sprinkled their greenware with powdered galena, the action of heat and fumes during baking forming a thin glassy surface.[127] Heraclius, author of a book about tenth-century craftsmen, described a process of lead glazing by making a solution of powdered red potter's earth (clay?), glue, and oil, which was spread over a pot, covered with flour and water paste, and then sprinkled with lead oxide.[128] Such a procedure is not known to have been used by Muslim potters.

Retrospective

The Andalusian pottery craft introduced by the Muslims was a wheel industry operated by free men. There was little place in the Islamic sphere for women making kitchen vessels by hand and then firing them in a depression in the yard. To the present, such procedures remain rare in southern Spain. Since the principal markets for earthenwares naturally were the places of greatest concentrations of people, it was in them that major commercial potteries were set up.

In the relatively short span of one hundred years, the tenth century, the first key period in Andalusian urban ceramics had been experienced. It had firmly established ways and modes that were to endure. The underlying stimulus for advancement was the influx of talent and inspiration from elsewhere in Islam, which was encouraged by and thrived under royal patronage. The effects of that support trickled down through lesser ranks of the society. The path of much of this diffused knowledge originating in the Near East passed along to al Andalus by way of the Muslim settlements on the North African Mediterranean coast. The Andalusians soon made the new methods and styles their own, modifying them to suit local skills and taste. The pottery decorations achieved by many means indicate a worldly people still open to aesthetic suggestion. Although some of these exotic expressions were to vanish with the caliphate and others temporarily went underground, there remained a pool of creative talent trained in some of the most advanced ceramic technology of the day.

BERBERS: THE THIRD CULTURAL TRANSPLANT

Historicultural Background

After the Umayyad rule ended, numerous political factions divided al Andalus into twenty-six principalities called *taifas* (Fig. 38). They were under control of provincial Muslims or Berbers. The one centered at Sevilla, which reached across Iberia to the Atlantic, quickly assumed a dominant role in the Guadalquivir region. The city was elevated to an important status it never lost. Of critical importance was its position as a fluvial port, although it opened to the Atlantic rather than to the Mediterranean. Because travel was unencumbered with legalities and because cosmopolitan scholarship and mercantilism were eagerly sought ways of life, through her river harbor sailed a colorful, restless parade of characters drawn from all ranks of life. Sailing ships, oared galleys, and small coastal craft tied up at the quays to unload spices from Ceylon, textiles from Persia, metals from Ifriqiya, or copper pots from India. For their return voyages they took on cargoes of local foods, raw minerals, and artisan wares. Within the city a bimetal economy existed, with one gold *dinar* coin equal to ten silver *dirhem* coins. It fueled active hand industries that gave rise to a prominent middle class notable for its secularity and hedonism. The rich farm lands around the city continued to produce abundantly. One geographer of the time wrote of Sevilla:

She is great and populous, her walls and bazaars are massive. About her lies the Aljarafe, a fine country always green with a fertile soil. So many olive branches are enlaced over it that the earth is barely exposed to the sun.

Al Idrisi, a contemporary geographer born in Ceuta on the Moroccan shore but raised in Córdoba, provided more details:

This last city [Sevilla] is large and densely populated. The walls are solid, the markets numerous, making it a great commercial center, the populace is rich. The principal article of commerce of this city is olive oil, that is sent east and west by land and sea; this olive oil comes from the territory of Aljarafe, forty miles distant and covered with olive and fig trees; it extends from Sevilla to Niebla, a width of more than twelve miles. There exist in this area eight flourishing villages with a great number of baths and beautiful buildings.[129]

A Romance language was spoken in *taifa* Sevilla, though Arabic remained the language of diplomacy and science. Besides a mixture of Arabs, Berbers, Syrians, and Yemenites in the Muslim population, there were Jews and a dwindling number of Old Christians, or mozarabs; both

Figure 38. Three eleventh-century *taifa* kingdoms within the area of modern Andalusia. That of which Sevilla was capital extended across Iberia to the Portuguese Atlantic coast (after O'Callaghan 1975).

were allowed to participate in many aspects of life. Some of the citizens adopted eastern dress, although most Andalusians no longer considered themselves Orientals. The Christians who remained are said to have been primarily artisans being assimilated into a *muwalladun*, or convert, class.[130]

After about eighty years an abrupt Africanization began that dramatically changed the flavor of life. This was because in 1090 the Almoravid Berber dynasty from southern Morocco gained control of Andalusia to end the *taifa* reigns. Their rule lasted merely fifty-seven years, but it made Sevilla the European capital of an African kingdom. Puritanical in belief, the Almoravids set about exterminating vestiges of materialistic Arabism and suppressing the local mozarabs. They imposed a strict orthodoxy on a society that had become lax. More than a thousand of the Christians were expelled to North Africa, where many were rescued by Portuguese sailors. Jews went scurrying north into France, Germany, and Italy, taking with them some of the cultural baggage they had shared with the Muslims.[131]

While these changes were taking place in eleventh-century al Andalus, the Christian Europeans to the north and east were beginning to stir from their long feudalistic dormancy. A rise in rural and urban population was made possible by more efficient farming techniques, which enabled them to work additional lands. An increase in the number and size of towns, especially in Flanders and

northern Italy, resulted from an extensive trade on both
local and international levels. Two principal spheres of
maritime commerce emerged whose effects stimulated
growth on the coasts and in the interior. On Europe's
southern flanks Muslim control of the central Mediterranean was threatened by the emergence of Venice, Genoa,
and Pisa as new sea powers in competition with Byzantine
merchantmen. In the north Scandinavians steadily were
becoming more active throughout the Baltic and North
Sea.[132]

Religious interests soared, drawing hundreds of monks
and nuns to the introspective mysticism of monasteries.
In these closed worlds the almost forgotten work ethic was
reinstituted, education was encouraged, classical works
were preserved through tedious copying of manuscripts,
and the venalities and decadence that had nearly
destroyed the fiber of the Catholic church were combated.
The Cluniac Order of south central France was to play a
prominent part in bringing French mores and Gothic art to
Spain as the reconquest gathered momentum. Great
barrel-vaulted Romanesque cathedrals, whose sculptured
facades provided visual moral lessons of sin and redemp-
tion, towered over more than fifteen hundred villages,
such as Vézelay (1120–32) and Autun (1130–35). Throngs
of tireless pilgrims trudged to Christendom's shrines,
while the more adventuresome undertook crusades to the
Holy Land. In northern Spain knights in armor rode off
to do battle with the Moors, and by the end of the eleventh
century had driven the hated Muslims from the central
tablelands of Castile and its prize city of Toledo.

The next act of the Andalusian drama opened with the
defeat in 1147 of the fanatical Almoravids by another
camel-herding Berber dynasty. This was that of the Almohads from the Atlas Mountains (Fig. 39). Their effect on
the capital city of Sevilla during a century of control was
more substantial, thanks in part to their supplies of
Sudanese gold and a pronounced focus southward. At the
same time, Hilali incursions into the Tunisian domain,
Mongol and Turkish conquests farther east, and the
strength of Italian sea traffic in the Mediterranean
deflected communication with eastern Islam. For the first
time, western Islam was essentially isolated into a Maghreb sphere.[133]

The Morocco men set about embellishing Sevilla with
structures similar to those their architects were erecting in
Marrakesh and Rabat. Extensive repairs were made to
old features, some of which dated from Roman foundations. These were outward changes visible in the city to
the present. Their styles were in keeping with the Almohads' sobering interpretations of the Islamic faith,

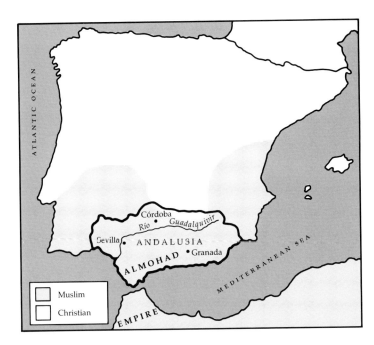

Córdoba
Río • Guadalquivir
Sevilla • ANDALUSIA
ALMOHAD • Granada
MEDITERRANEAN SEA
EMPIRE

☐ Muslim
☐ Christian

ATLANTIC OCEAN

Figure 39. Thirteenth-century Almohad empire extended into southern Spain from North Africa.

although a softening tendency under the enervating influence of luxurious living at Sevilla can be detected. Absent is the flood of inspiration from elsewhere in Islam. On the other hand, important in the history of decorative arts was the Almohads' sanctioning of the return of the banished mozarabs, many of whom had become as manually adept as their Muslim colleagues. Although most of the former exiles preferred to move on north to Christian-held Toledo, the strong contacts between Castilian and Andalusian artisan communities led to a mutual aesthetic point of view.[134]

Meanwhile, Christian adversaries of the Almohads and other followers of the teachings of Mohammed were enjoying unanticipated fruits of conquest. The continuing wave of crusades of the twelfth and thirteenth centuries led to contradictory epic heroism and self-indulgence. As a result, central and western Europe was opened up to the material and intellectual advancements of the Middle East, of which westerners formerly had been ignorant. Luxury trade with the enemy prospered; scientific, medical, and creative interests were stimulated; and standards of living were raised because of the Islamic example. Under such renewal of zest for living and acquisition of the mechanical skills to make the impossible seem obtainable, the solid Romanesque architecture rooted to the soil gave way to the ethereal Gothic. Built almost contemporaneously with the Almohad minaret tower in Sevilla, now known as the Giralda, was the cathedral of Chartres (1194–1220).

Pottery History

Progress in ceramic evolution never has been at a uniform rate. Characteristically, as in civilization itself, there have been periods when social climate has spawned rapid developments such as those that arose during the Cordoban caliphate. These have been followed either by retrogression and loss of expertise or by breathing spells when potters have seemed content to continue to perfect, rather than to invent, techniques. The *taifa* and Berber periods represent both a time of continuity and of change.

In the mid-eleventh century, regional distinctions in pottery reflected political fragmentation. Although the great body of ceramic knowledge, like the great Guadalquivir, flowed on, everywhere there was evident a subtle lowering of the quality of wares. Pastes and glazes were poorly prepared; throwing was haphazard, with carelessly executed forms, indifferent ring feet, and central humps or bosses becoming common. Styles and individual motifs most explicitly associated with the then despised Arab culture disappeared. Draftsmanship decayed.[135] But, so far as is presently known, Berber hand-building processes in pottery making were not adopted.

Under Almohad control there occurred a gradual solidifying of Spanish Muslim design grammar, fashions already known being stated with an increasing technical command of the craft and minor alteration of details. The number of forms made was reduced from the extravagant days of the caliphate to comply with the Almohad worldview. For example, potters were forbidden to create vessels for the serving of wine.[136] There was also a democratic sharing of all ceramic modes by the general populace, with no kinds, other than possibly some *cuerda seca* elaborations, being ostensibly of a luxury grade. The closed nature of the dynasty precluded foreign trade ceramics.

Many Almohad forms were so like earlier vessels extending back to Visigothic times that dating based upon stylistic characteristics is suspect. What had become the usual range of vessel shapes consisted of conical bowls (Fig. 22c,d), bowls whose rims turned inward, small straight-sided bowls or jars, cylindrical handled chamber pots (Fig. 18a), and convex-based cook pots (Fig. 20d,f). New forms primarily were associated with the use of water. One was a small, tall-necked, two- to four-handled jar with a perforated disk in the throat through which liquid was filtered (Fig. 20c).[137] Taken from the repertory common to Near Eastern desert dwellers, the Almohad filters were not elaborately pierced, although floral elements are apparent. Other jars of the same general contour, but lacking the filter, may have been the earliest kind of vessels made for storage of the medicines being created by a growing group of pharmacists (Fig. 25a).[138] The other water jar was the *botijo* (Fig. 21d). This was a flat-bottomed, bulbous, enclosed jar of moderate size with a wide pouring spout and a circle handle over the rounded top.[139] In later periods it would carry two spouts, one for filling and one for pouring.

It is fitting in this area where water and agriculture were fundamental to life that an important category of large pottery objects continued to be related to them. Most of them demonstrate a remarkable physical control of the medium and of the tools of the trade, as they are of tremendous volume and weight. Getting them successfully through the entire production process would have been no small feat. One such diagnostic earthenware form was a massive wellhead, or *brocal* (Fig. 40). Averaging about

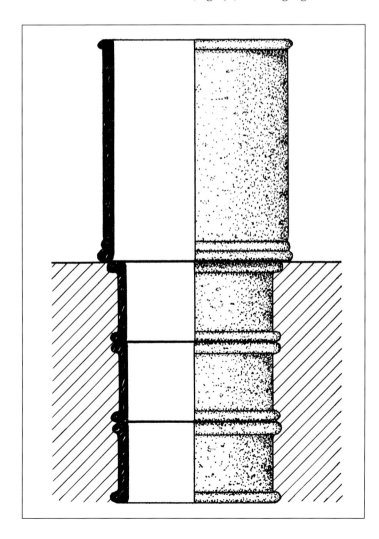

Figure 40. Earthenware wellhead, or *brocal*. A large, usually decorated cylinder, round or octagonal, sat above ground. Below it, plain ceramic tubing formed the well casing. These were common *taifa*, Almohad, and *mudéjar* ceramics, but identical specimens in marble came from the tenth–century caliphate ruins at Madinat az-Zahra.

a meter in diameter and height, it was essentially a thick-walled collar, usually circular but occasionally hexagonal or octagonal. It was open top and bottom, with heavily compacted rims for added strength. These wellheads were the richly decorated aboveground components of a plain, sectioned, tubular casing of nearly the same dimensions that extended below the ground surface; they were based upon Roman and caliphate marble and, in the latter case, earthenware examples.[140] Hundreds of them must have been in service in Sevilla, where the high water table allowed the sinking of shallow household wells. When one well became contaminated, another could be put down a few feet away. *Brocales* are among the most frequently seen *taifa*, Almohad, and later *mudéjar* remains in Andalusian urban sites. The earliest dated specimen so far recovered from Sevilla was made in 1039.[141]

A second specialized kind of earthenware devoted to storage of water was based upon the old amphora shape, but with modifications and of greatly increased size. Necks were reduced in height and bodies were fattened into a nearly globular profile, but the bodies tapered to a very narrow flat base (Fig. 19b,c). Its top-heavy instability required some kind of basal support. The amphora's paired handles became winglike appendages, which suggests some latent Sassanian iconography at work. Some wings were of prominent size rising from upper jar shoulders; others were mere vestigial arc-shaped stubs. Fired only to relatively low temperatures, the porous walls and tapered bases of these *tinajas* permitted evaporative cooling and filtering.

Other great, high-shouldered jars for the storage of various provisions were so commonly used in warehouses that structures were described as having the capacity of a prescribed number of *tinajas*. Whether those for water or those for other purposes, these vessels must have been thrown in several sections and joined when leather hard. Some may have been moldmade.

In the country, thousands of *arcaduces* continued to be made to equip the all-important irrigation water wheels. Their style remained unaltered (Fig. 23a).

The pastes of *taifa* and Almohad pottery unearthed at Sevilla are of two types. One was sandy in texture and white-to-cream in fired color. It is this clay that has attracted most attention because of its uncommonness outside the Mediterranean basin. The other was an iron-bearing clay that fired red and had frequent mica inclusions. Because both these clay bodies had been in use in the area from the earliest pottery known there,[142] they must be assumed to be of local origin.

For decoration of the cumbersome reddish brown *brocales* and *tinajas*, Almohads showed a preference for plastic treatment of ceramic surfaces echoing current architectural detailing. Patterns, achieved by use of molds or stamps, consisted of well spaced, small scale, carefully repeated stylized leaf or geometric motifs placed in encircling rows over entire exterior surfaces. Small individual vessels bore a poorly controlled partial *cuerda seca* pattern, were covered partially or totally with dark engobe through which simple motifs were scratched, were incised with band patterns of parallel lines of zigzags, or had colorless lead glaze either on all surfaces or as decorative bands. Unstructured linear underglaze painting continued (Fig. 41). Although colorless lead glaze was most common, a deep copper green lead glaze was especially popular over relief decoration and sometimes was used as a substitute for pitch lining of utility jars. Amber *melado* glaze was used on one or both surfaces of bowls. Patterns painted in copper green, manganese purplish brown, or both revealed not only survival of an older method, but also an increased concern for stylized vegetal elements added to traditional interlaced geometrics or Cufic inscriptions. The animal or human figures seen on Cordoban polychromes only partially disappeared from the grammar. Perhaps this reduction was due to the greater conservatism of the more orthodox Almohads, but it did not kill local interest in such elements. Black-to-brown decorations often were applied to unglazed surfaces, forecasting what was to be a more important vogue among Nasrids. Rare blue decorations occurred as irregular lines on flattened rims.

Notable at Sevilla was the appearance there under the Almohads of contrasting frets of brick and glazed tile in architecture. Later renovations under Christian rulers removed most examples, but some small sections of Almohad tiling have been found. The four twelfth-century towers of Santa Catalina, Homenaje, San Marcos, and the Torre del Oro, and the square minaret of the great mosque built between 1184 and 1196 once had such tiles on portions of their floors, facades, or domes. These were mosaic panels, or *alicatado*. One indication of a generally later impressed technique was in the Claustro del Lagarto.[143]

Exactly what kind of pottery a type called *mukhfiyat* might have been is unknown; it was identified by Goitein as a specialty of the west. It is reported that eight pieces of the ware were sent from Spain to Egypt in 1137.[144] Perhaps they originated in Sevilla and were taken east by Italian traders.[145]

Figure 41. Muslim lead-glazed
vessels with underglaze manganese decorations; *a, taifa* oil
lamp with lateral wick spout; *b,
taifa* flat-based bowl; *c,* Almohad
bowl with wide horizontal brim;
d, Almohad pedestal-based oil
lamp; *e–f,* Almohad conical bowls,
cuencos (courtesy Museo Arqueológico Nacional, Madrid).

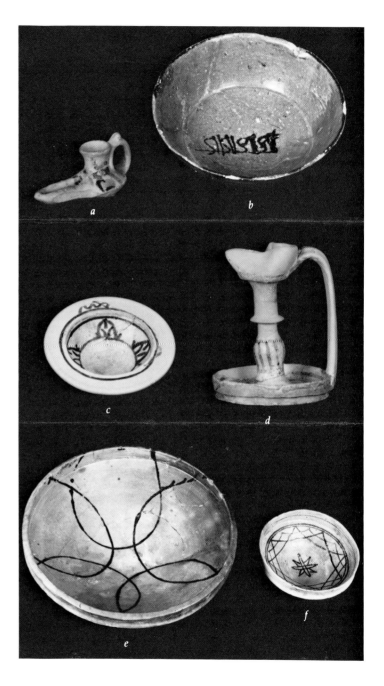

Retrospective

   At the end of the Muslim occupation of Sevilla in the
middle of the thirteenth century, basic procedures and
equipment, as well as many decorative principles and
individual motifs that would continue to be characteristic
of the ceramics of that part of Spain until the arrival of

the Renaissance in the sixteenth century, were in place. Even the language of the craft was to pass into Castilian Spanish.[146] Refinements of technique and modifications of style would follow, the latter often in tandem with *mudéjar* trends at Toledo. The foundations upon which the craft continued to develop would forever be essentially those of the Muslims, who were there longer, in greater numbers, and had a fuller dedication to pottery making than any of the preceding conquerors. However, from the symbiosis of Arab, Berber, and ancient Romano-Visigothic cultures climaxing under Almohad rule came the native florescence known as Moresque.[147] With rare exceptions, never again would there be "pure" Islamic interpretations in Andalusia.

The ceramic developments of eastern Islam that were to find little or no favor in Andalusian Spain were slip painting, frit ware, sgraffito splashed with green or amber under lead glaze, fine quality plain whites, polychrome overpainting, and carved pierced ware. Not only was there selective diffusion to the recipient culture in the west, but there was no reciprocity. Apparently there were no Andalusian technical innovations or styles that appealed to the more advanced Near Eastern potters.

MUDÉJARES AND NASRIDS: POTTING COMPETITORS IN A NEW ANDALUSIA

Historicultural Background of the Early Reconquest Period

Of the urban centers under Almohad control, Sevilla had assumed such particular prominence that it was coveted increasingly by the Christian kingdoms to the north. In the early thirteenth century the Castilians took the lead in eating away the lands of al Andalus, working southward toward Sevilla. Meanwhile, Aragonese armies under James I launched a similar offensive against Almohad positions in eastern Spain. In 1238 they retook Valencia, successfully completing their campaign to return to Christian political control all of the peninsula east of the pincher thrust along the wedge of mountainous country surrounding Granada and Málaga, where the Muslims were being cornered. On the western front, Castilians marched down through the passes leading into modern Andalusia, toppling Muslim defenses as they went; on November 2, 1248, Sevilla passed once more into the Christian camp. The heartlands of al Andalus were on the verge of becoming those of Andalusia (Fig. 42). A century later, Fernando III (Table 2) was made a saint for reconquering Sevilla for Christ.

Figure 42. Completion of the
Christian reconquest of Spain in
the thirteenth century left the
Emirate of Granada—(a large
chunk of modern Andalusia) isolated on the southern coast
(after O'Callaghan 1975).

Table 2. Castilian Rulers.
Thirteenth to Sixteenth Centuries

Fernando III	1217–1252
Alfonso X	1252–1284
Sancho IV	1284–1296
Fernando IV	1296–1312
Alfonso XI	1312–1350
Pedro I	1350–1369
Enrique II	1369–1379
Juan I	1379–1390
Enrique III	1390–1406
Juan II	1406–1454
Enrique IV	1454–1474
Isabela	1474–1504

Peace terms gave the Muslims three days to pack or sell
their possessions and to leave Sevilla and environs. The
king generously provided a fleet of fourteen ships to
transport evacuees across the Straits of Gibraltar to Ceuta;
safe conducts were given those who preferred to move
south toward Jérez (Fig. 43). It has been estimated that as
many as one hundred thousand persons made their way
directly to Morocco, a figure that surely is excessive. By
some accounts another three hundred thousand traveled
to Jérez, although O'Callaghan perhaps more correctly
places the latter figure at thirty thousand.[148] Others went

on to Tunis because a governor there earlier had been
a popular governor in Sevilla. This group was said to have
included potters.[149] An undetermined number of Muslims
fled one hundred thirty-five miles eastward to Granada,
where a new kingdom under domination of a dynasty of
the Nasrid lineage was to be permitted to exist for another
two and a half centuries. Records confirm that thirteenth-
century Muslim Sevilla was the largest metropolis in
Europe. It must also have been one of the most colorful,
constituting a teeming Oriental emporium jammed with a
stunning diversity of peoples and products drawn from
the entire Mediterranean world.

What the conquerors found at Sevilla was a city plan as
complexly knotted as a Muslim decorative scheme, but
far less orderly.[150] Because little had remained of the origi
nal Roman settlement pattern, the incoming eighth-
century Arabs and Syrians had been able to establish
themselves in their customary manner. That meant enclosure of town and homes for defense and privacy and
the development of focal points for business and worship.
In a limited public area around a central 'Adabbas mosque
were shops dealing in religious or academic articles.
Centrally located also was the *alcaicería*, a block of small
lockable salesrooms where luxury commodities were
dispensed. Unlike the medieval cities farther north, there
was no guildhall. Because no wheeled conveyances were
used, the dirt streets that twisted mazelike through living
and work areas at the town's core were pinched into
mere pathways. These wound tortuously among buildings
of several stories, often ending in dark cul de sacs. It
was here that the workshops of carpenters, weavers,
metalsmiths, or tailors and assorted food markets were to
be found. Engulfed among them were a few broken
Roman temple columns and sections of walls. Areas near
the city gates were allotted to the saddlemakers, the dealers in pack animals, the vendors of produce brought in
from the farms, and the seamen and shipbuilders. At the
very limits of town were the crafts, such as dyeing and
tanning, that were attended by undesirable disorder and
odors, that used fire in their work, or that required larger
space and plentiful water.[151]

Little now remains of the city's finer homes, but records
show that during *taifa* times many workers had been
especially occupied in making bricks and floor and roof
tiles for common construction. Such material remained
typical of the region because the scarcity of stone and
wood reserved those materials for rich edifices. The use of
terra cotta building materials spared Sevilla the conflagra-
tions that repeatedly swept through Europe's medieval

Figure 43. Jérez de la Frontera,
on the line of Muslim southward
retreat, as depicted in the thirteenth-century miniatures of *Las
Cántigas de Santa María* (after
López Serrano 1974).

settlements. Without apertures in exterior facades, most
homes opened their hearts to cramped arcades encircling
unroofed courtyards, or *corrales*, where private lives were
protected from public view.[152] Water was piped to all
palaces, and numerous public baths and a central tank for
drinking water served the lesser populace who lacked
house wells. Because Muslims generally came from arid
environments, in special places such as Sevilla they saw to
it that fountains splashed in gardens lush with imported
plants.

A surprising mixture of social groups had been tolerated
in the Almohad capital. This contributed to its deliverance
to Christian invaders. Jews, assorted Italians, Frenchmen,
Spaniards from other provinces, and even some Muslim
occupants served as a potential underground for Fernando. Many of these people remained after the city's fall
to impart an international flavor to a greatly shrunken
town.

Sevilla was segregated by the Christians into twenty-
four *collaciones*, each estimated to contain two hundred
vecinos, or tax-paying heads of households; each was
named after one of the saints, martyrs, prophets, or vir-
gins traditional to Catholicism. As had been customary in
the Muslim town, certain trades or craftsmen were located
together, such juxtaposition promoting group identification.[153] Hideworkers, for example, were in the *collación* of
San Lorenzo, *esparto* weavers in the *collación* of San Ilde-
fonso, makers of coifs in the *collación* of San Nicolás.[154] If
potters were recognized as a viable craft group, there is no
known documentation of their assigned sector (Fig. 44).

The new administration established districts for the varied ethnic entities concentrated in the city, each complete
with public baths, workshops, markets, granaries, and
bread ovens. Appropriate religious centers—synagogue,
mosque, or church—were permitted. In contrast to
reported estimates of the number of departing Muslims,
Christian repopulation probably did not amount to more
than twenty-four thousand persons at the most. Many
of the original invaders soon abandoned the properties
granted them on terms of five or twelve years' occupancy
and returned to the north.[155] Sevillian population dropped
to about fifteen-thousand during the fourteenth century,
owing to the famines and plagues that swept all of
Europe.[156]

Exactly how many Muslims chose to stay behind after
the reconquest is unknown, but the number was sufficient
to lead to the designation of a neighborhood, or *morería*,
to accommodate them. Located centrally so as to be well
away from the city walls, the *morería* (also known as the

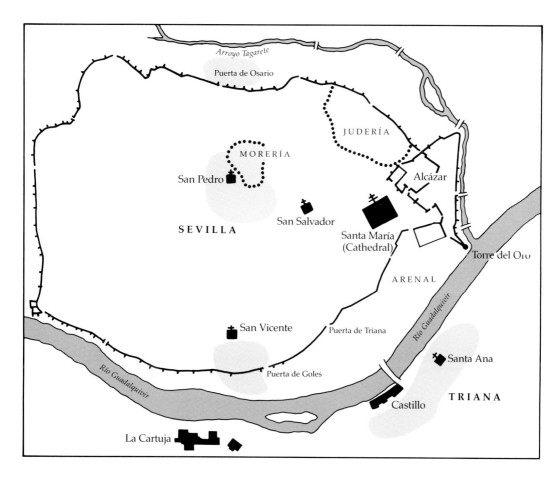

Figure 44. Shaded areas indicate probable location of potteries in Christian Sevilla.

Adarvejo de los Moros) disappeared during the fifteenth and sixteenth centuries with absorption of its residents into the populace, mass conversion, and, finally, exile of its residents. Prior to those events, the Sevilla *morería* expanded to take in refugees from towns of surrounding conquered territories, and it tenaciously clung to its own customs, religion, and justice. Within its walled compound, the markets dealing in vegetables, meats, tallow, wax, spices, and cosmetics continued as before.

The Muslims who chose to live under Christian political authority were termed *mudéjares*. Although it is unclear in the repopulation statistics, most appear to have been craftsmen or manual laborers.[157] Commonly mentioned by historians as remaining under Christian rule in the cities were innkeepers, shoemakers, horse dealers, blacksmiths, masons, and carpenters, the last two having skills needed to repair the Sevillian *alcázar*, or fort, and the dockyards. Even with this residual labor force, the emptying of the Andalusian urban centers, especially Sevilla, led to a catastrophic decline of the provincial economy because replacements did not follow. Unquestionably, any remaining pottery industry would have suffered from lack of workers and customers.

In outlying sections of reconquered Andalusia demographic changes were as profound as in the cities. Particularly in the Campina south of Córdoba, many of the farmers who continued to work the land were Muslims, although ownership passed to ennobled Christians, military orders, or the church.[158] For a time these peasants were tolerated because they had the farming and irrigation knowledge the Spaniards lacked. Due to concentration of both urban and rural physical labor with the Muslims and intensification of ethnic cleavages, highborn Castilians, then forming a disproportionate percentage of the population, soon rationalized themselves above such labor. They preferred to confine their own endeavors to warfare, governmental posts, or the clergy. That shortsighted attitude caused further impoverishment when eventually even country Muslims were driven away. With their departure, the emphasis shifted to stock raising. Irrigation water jars were threatened with obsolescence.

During the twelfth century, meadows lying southwest of the Guadalquivir opposite Sevilla had been farmed by a group of mozarabs, whose wine reportedly presented a temptation to abstemious Muslims. They may have had storage buildings by the river.[159] Some houses scattered about a nearby castle and along land paralleling the west bank of the river gradually became known as Triana, an incipient industrial district peopled with low types, such as artisans, sailors, fishermen, galley slaves, manual laborers, winemakers, and workers at a soap factory begun in the thirteenth century. During that and the following century the three dirt streets of Triana—Tejar, Santa Ana, and Castilla—never housed more than some sixty citizens.[160] Nevertheless, to commemorate the Christian victory Alfonso X (see Table 2) ordered the construction there between 1266 and 1280 of a church named for Santa Ana (Fig. 45).[161] To this day the part of Triana surrounding the old edifice remains a working man's part of town.

The sociopolitical condition in Andalusia in the early reconquest years was comparatively enlightened. Sevilla and other cities were granted near autonomy in controlling their civic affairs, a step that increased the sense of local patriotism and regionalism that hindered the political unification of Spain for centuries. Religious tolerance was encouraged by the Crown, especially under the rule of Alfonso X, who assumed the throne just five years after the Almohad capitulation. He proclaimed his kingdom the

Figure 45. Modern view of Santa Ana parish church in Triana. Built between 1266 and 1280, it served the main body of Sevillian Christian potters. Formerly, as now, it was crowded in among working class homes and artisan shops.

land of three religions. Jews were prominent in education, medicine, some crafts, and business. Many served as money changers and tax collectors. The former occupation was critical in the trading activities of a port like Sevilla, owing to the multiplicity of coinage characteristic of the Middle Ages. The changer charged a small fee for his services, accepted and kept deposits safe, and extended loans for interest. In short, he was on the way to becoming a true banker. Usury was condemned by the Jewish religious leaders, but as in the case of the earlier Muslims and later Christians, it was practiced nonetheless.[162] Farming the taxes, while profitable for the Jews, brought the ire of their contemporaries down upon their heads. *Mudé-jares*, more frequently comprising the lower social ranks, were permitted to continue their crafts by payment of a crown tax.

An interdependence grew between the peasantry of the surrounding countryside, who provided foodstuffs, and city dwellers, who contributed a great variety of durable commodities and services. Village markets were weekly; city markets were permanent. There was an additional market held in Sevilla on Thursdays, as it had been in Muslim times and continues today. Sevilla and Córdoba also had two annual trading fairs modeled after those in France and Flanders. As had been true in Muslim towns, the markets were placed under an inspector who checked weights, prices, and quality of articles for sale. Direct selling from maker to consumer was encouraged, in order to eliminate middlemen. The weight of the non-productive, tax-exempt military aristocracy and church was burdensome for all citizens.

Slowly the depression that followed the reconquest eased, and for fifty years after about 1280 the lower Guadalquivir experienced a period of growth. But neither urbanization nor industrialization matched that taking place elsewhere in Europe.[163]

Pottery History of the Early Fourteenth Century

There is oblique documentary evidence that some Muslim potters remained in Andalusia after the reconquest. Alfonso X, an admirer of Islamic decorative arts, ordered that no potteries be built in Córdoba unless they were in Muslim style.[164] In actuality, that edict probably was unnecessary. If Christian potters had moved down from the north to replace departed Muslims, they would have been mozarabs from Toledo with exactly the same technical knowledge. Elsewhere in northern Spain the art of pottery making had progressed little beyond the most rudimentary handmade vessels being turned out by women working in their yards. There had been no stimulus for Castilian development of this craft because the economic borders between Spanish Muslims and Christians had remained so porous that the better made wares of the south surely were available.

It is the extant transition period pottery in Andalusia that confirms an unbroken craft continuity, despite the political upheaval. Such strength of technical craft knowledge continued because the composition of the work force remained unchanged. In terms of style other than vogues that came with later evolution, it is impossible to distinguish the work of a Muslim father working before

1248 from that of his *mudéjar* sons working later in the century. Only in the range of forms is there a clue to underlying cultural redirection, and that was not due to a new body of workers. A comparison of Figures 18–23, 29, 30, and 34 with Figures 55–58 reveals the great diversity of Muslim vessel shapes and design groups as compared to those of the Christian period up to the middle of the sixteenth century. This must be attributed to a more vigorous, complex Muslim society exposed to greater foreign trade and contact.

Beds of potting clays on the west bank of the Guadalquivir opposite Sevilla probably had attracted craftsmen to that locality from the earliest times. During Roman occupation, shops may have been situated nearby to make the necessary amphorae in which to ship wines and olive oil produced in the Aljarafe back to Rome. Some are now known at the site of Orippo, just to the south. Perhaps invading Visigoths and then Muslims took over various of these work areas.[165] Kilns have been found along the river front at Sevilla. So far as can be determined, no description exists of their type or of the debris associated with them.[166] Chance recovery of ceramics inside Sevilla itself suggests that Muslim potteries may have been operating in the *morería* and later *collaciones* of San Vicente, San Pedro, and San Salvador, or were located near the north wall close to a gate called Bab-Alfar, the potter's gate (see Fig. 44).[167] The entrance later was renamed Puerta de Osario because it opened to the Muslim cemetery,[168] indicating a relationship between potteries and graveyards comparable to that which had existed at Córdoba and which can be observed today at Fez. Any potting installations that may have been near the Triana castle doubtless would have been wrecked during the unmitigated fighting of the reconquest. The unpredictable river, which on many occasions has left its banks or changed its course, and limited archaeological exploration have combined to leave unresolved this matter of Muslim use of the west bank as a center for making earthenwares. It also is not known whether there was any spatial relationship between potteries and the glass factory, such as existed in contemporary Fostat.[169]

The establishment of potteries followed the spread of small craft industries to Triana. Although attached to an urban area, pottery production in Triana remained essentially a peasant industry, with small-scale producers employing nonindustrial technology.[170] The artisans, a large class of free men, were encouraged to settle by the availability of clays in the nearby meadow, on islands in the river, and at the village of Castilleja de la Cuesta on the cart road toward Huelva.[171] Fuel for kilns and certain minerals needed in large quantities for glazes were transported by boat from more remote sources to be stockpiled along the river's edge until needed. Sevillian gates facing the river acquired the names of Puerta del Alcohol (Gate of Galena) and Puerta del Carbón (Gate of Charcoal) because minerals for simple glazes and woods for kilns and baking ovens were dumped there. The earliest reference to such a Triana workshop is a notation dated 1314, which records a *corral de ollería con sus hornos* on Calle Santa Ana, next to an orchard and a mill.[172] Other potteries probably were there or soon followed.

From these beginnings in the fourteenth century, or perhaps earlier, to the present time Triana has been known as the potting quarter of Sevilla, although *morisco* and later Italian potteries are documented within several parts of the city proper. A pottery market, *alcaicería de la loza*, flourished in San Salvador *collación* near the market for foodstuffs. Artisans from all districts, whose role did not end with production of pots, took some of their work to this central point for sale.[173] The proximity of shops selling domestic pottery and the foods to be cooked or served in it has remained common Spanish practice.

A number of things came together during the thirteenth century to give Andalusian ceramics a lasting character. So long as the Almohads firmly controlled both shores of the western Mediterranean, they also dominated the waters. As their power started to dissipate, the Italian city states of Genoa, Pisa, and Venice, which had steadily been building up merchant fleets, gradually expanded their orbit of trade out into the Atlantic to reach England and northwestern Europe. Putting in at Spanish and Maghreb harbors was routine. Included with the spices, glass, alum, woad, and Oriental specialties in the westbound cargoes was surely Persian cobalt.[174] Another theory has cobalt being brought by Persian artisans to the Emirate of Granada, from which it soon reached Sevilla.[175] Regardless of how it was transported, this mineral was the basis for blue pigment used in pottery decoration. Slabs of tin from Cornwall were carried back to the Mediterranean on the Italian ships.[176] A small percentage of tin oxide added to the customary lead glaze solutions made the fired covering on earthenware opaque and white. Although minor deposits of low grade tin were known in parts of Spain and cobalt from Morocco likely had been used infrequently at an earlier date, this more purposeful distribution of raw materials at about the middle of the thirteenth century resulted in white-glazed earthenwares decorated with a few blue elements appearing at the two main urban potteries of southern Spain.[177] This change cannot be directly attributed to the new Christian element. Although the *mudéjares* of Sevilla made their versions, so did the *moros* of Málaga. A style with a combination of blue and manganese purple designs apparently was widespread in Andalusia at about the same time, but its exact source and date are yet to be determined.[178]

Potters in the Spanish Levant, Aragón, and Catalonia, who contemporaneously took up the production of maiolica glaze, did not begin to use blue until the second half of the next century.[179] This was because of the entrenched vogue of a green and brown palette. Farther to the east in the Mediterranean, tin-glazed ware bearing polychromatic ornamentation with the addition of green, yellow, and brown to blue elements appeared in the early to middle thirteenth century, prior to the blue–on–whites of Andalusia. Such pottery was made in southern Italy, from where it was taken to Greece, Syria, and Egypt by Crusaders on the move.[180] Thus, some four centuries had passed between the first appearance of maiolica in Mesopotamia and its earliest adoption in the Mediterranean communities. It would take another three centuries for its technology to be transmitted to Europe north of the Alps.

Fashioned primarily from the highly characteristic calcareous clay of the Guadalquivir drainage, with perhaps a small admixture of red-burning clay, the early Sevillian maiolicas essentially duplicated the variety of moderate sized domestic utensils that continued to be lead glazed. Parallel output of pitchers, jars, and bowls bearing one or the other kind of glaze may be a clue to an evolving price structure, with greater value being given the new color format. That, in turn, would lead to user differentiation. Noteworthy more often in maiolica were shallow, flared-rim plates and small, straight-sided drinking bowls. The plate form may be regarded as original, without a direct predecessor in the Muslim past. Cups, however, had been used by the Muslims, although apparently not in significant numbers. As objects for individual use, the plate innovation must have come from market demand attributable to changing social habits. The many conical *cuenco* serving bowls basic to collections of medieval Muslim ceramics were used for communal eating from a centrally placed vessel. These continued in the thirteenth to fifteenth centuries just across the Mediterranean in Merinid Qsar es-Seghir.[181] Although in late thirteenth-century Sevilla the dishes were made by *mudéjares*, the main customers were Christians who may no longer have wished to share common pots. The presence of personal crockery may hint not only at changed ethnic circumstances, but also at the broader trend during the European Middle Ages toward the rising importance of the individual.

Some idea of other kinds of pottery made for home consumption in *mudéjar* Sevilla is indirectly provided by the miniature paintings meant to accompany *Las Cántigas de Santa María*.[182] These were four hundred poems in the Gallegan vernacular compiled by Alfonso X and set to music. The verses extol the powers and glory of the Virgin Mary, whose cult was at peak popularity in all the Christian West between the twelfth and fourteenth centuries. The miniatures, which are anecdotal scenes executed by a corps of laymen artists, afford an exuberant, but stylized, cross section of thirteenth-century Castilian secular and sacred life in all its varied faces. Of the four copies made of these miniatures, one set was kept at Sevilla, where the king frequently held court. Many of the backgrounds glowingly rendered in the paintings obviously are of that area. We see that even then there were whitewashed facades, crenellated city walls, balconies, horseshoe arches, *mirador* towers, monastery cloisters, and tiers of red-tiled roofs.

Among the persons shown against these backdrops are all ranks of medieval Spanish society at their best and at their worst. There are tonsured monks decorously singing in choirs or conducting mass, but also lounging in bed with lovers, while nuns carry on their daily tasks even though very pregnant. Kings and nobles strut through the courts. Slaves grovel at their feet and modest householders, who have prayed for intervention of the Virgin in order to please their betters, hover nearby. Peasants tediously work the fields, armored cavalry soldiers charge off to do battle with the Moorish army, artisans laboriously erect buildings, and midwives deliver babies. The darker side of life is revealed by pitiful cripples beseeching help, beggars biding their time, misguided citizens applying their own brand of justice, and common highway robbers plying their trade. How disappointing that there are no potters, hands brown with mud, making household crocks.

So detailed are the drawings that an astounding assortment of cultural elements of the sorts not usually retrievable from the impersonal archaeological record are exposed. Information can be gained of such diversities as regional architectural idiosyncracies; costumes typical of male and female Christian, Arab, and Jewish segments of the society; massively carved or canopied furniture; sailing craft with rigging, sails, and cargo; horse trappings, armor, military banners; ornamental tents in a gaudy style popular with the Muslims; tapestry-draped altars; and, for the purpose of this study, mundane pottery.

Minor features in the drawings, the earthenware form shown on tables or in room backgrounds most usually

is the flat-based, high-shouldered *cántaro* type (Fig. 46e). The frequency of its appearance in the drawings substantiates its universal use as a multi-purpose household accessory. A touch of humor appears in some scenes, wherein the jars are used to thoroughly drench devout persons being baptised (Fig. 47). Some of the *cántaros* have paired appendages, others a single handle. A variation of the latter is a spouted pitcher with a knobbed lid. Depicted in brown, the *cántaros* are known to have been unglazed.

Also in brown, however, are collared, footed bowls seen on dining tables (Fig. 46a). That color was chosen by the artists either to contrast with white tablecloths or to represent *melado* glaze.

Figure 46. Some ceramic vessel forms suggested in thirteenth-century miniature paintings in *Las Cántigas de Santa María*. Although indistinct, the drawings suggest a range of domestic wares in use in Andalusian settings: *a*, bowls and cups; *b*, *albarelo* drug jars; *c–d*, jars; *e*, *cántaros* (after Guerrero Lovello 1949 and López Serrano 1974).

Figure 47. Typical rendition in the thirteenth-century *Las Cántigas de Santa María* of a ceramic baptismal font, *pila bautismal*, in use. If these drawings can be taken literally, immersion in the tublike bowl seems to have been practiced for individual baptism, however physically awkward it would have been. Production of such large, sturdy ceramics, appropriately decorated to become special objects, would have made exacting demands on potters.

An item being popularized in most urban potteries in southern Spain was the drug jar meant to hold hundreds of different herbs, aromatic waters, elixirs, ointments, pills, and medicinal preparations. Thought to have been inspired by the sections of bamboo in which medicines often were shipped from the Orient, the drug jars shown in the *cántigas* lined up on apothecary shelves were of several profiles. One was a small, lidded, high-shouldered jar. Another was the wide-mouthed, cylindrical *albarelo* that would become a hallmark of Spanish-tradition ceramics in both undecorated and elaborately finished versions (Figs. 25c, 46b). For what were considered sanitary reasons, these vessels always were either lead- or tin-glazed, although the chemical reactions between jar and contents occasionally may have been deleterious.

The baptismal font, or *pila bautismal*, was an expectable addition to the *mudéjar* repertory in the wake of the Catholic religious fervor stirred by the reconquest. It consisted of a pedestal base several feet in height, on top of which was mounted a large, heavy bowl approximately a meter in diameter (Figs. 72a, 73a). If ever there was a ceramic hybrid, this was it. First, it was based on a Visigothic and on a later Muslim fountain conception as seen at Madinat al-Zahra in marble; the latter may or may not have been associated with the ablutions prerequisite to Muslim prayers.[183] Its association with water eased its transfer to a Christian ritual in which the use of water was necessary. Under *mudéjar* transformation, this old stone object became an elaborated ceramic construction created by a skilled combination of throwing and molding techniques. Secondly, composition of field and raised motifs inspired by Muslim aesthetic dictates enhanced exterior surfaces, which most characteristically were covered with a Muslim-introduced green lead glaze. The font essentially was an Oriental product meant to be used by the Christian majority, although it was purchased specifically by the religious practitioners of the community. The *cántigas* show persons to be baptised sitting in the font bowl (see Fig. 47). Possibly this was artistic license. It is ironic that the time came when the *mudéjares* themselves were forced to renounce their own religion by being annointed with the holy waters in this vessel to seal their conversion.

The frontals of the altar on which the Santa María and Child were placed in at least one scene of every six-part story pose some questions. The panels on either side of a central double-rowed pattern taken to represent tapestry appear to be flat-surfaced, square tile. These are not known to have come into use as early as the second half of the thirteenth century; present evidence is that only glazed relief tiles with castle, cross, or escutcheon elements in black, *melado*, and green were made in Sevilla and Córdoba during this period.[184] The small-scale, alternating white and amber patterned motifs in an all-over arrangement may have been intended as references to *alicatado* mosaics introduced in Sevilla a century earlier by the Almohads.

For years after the reconquest of Sevilla there was skirmishing with stragglers to the southeast,[185] who were aided by an informal blockade at the Straits of Gibraltar by the new Merinid rulers of Morocco. Finding it difficult to sail into the Mediterranean, the trading naos out of Sevilla headed for Great Britain and the Low Countries, and for the first time reoriented Andalusian commerce northwestward. Such sea going ventures of Spanish bottoms had become safer with the new requirements decreed in the Siete Partidas of Alfonso X for all ships to be equipped with rudders. It is also a possibility that Italian ships carried Sevillian products on to England. The earliest record of Genoese ships being in dock at Southampton is dated 1278, with the Flanders Galleys of Venice following shortly thereafter.[186] It is not surprising, therefore, that finds of a complex of Andalusian pottery have been made at Southampton, London, Bristol, and Dublin (Fig. 48). At present, they are the only such fragments whose dates reasonably can be fixed as early as the late thirteenth century.[187]

The earliest Sevillian maiolicas reclaimed in excavations in Southampton and London are pieces of tall-necked pitchers with beaked spouts, small ring-footed bowls, drug jars, vertical-walled cups, and shallow plates with flared rims. Most are glazed in plain white, but several also carry

Figure 48. Some late thirteenth- and early fourteenth-century Andalusian vessel forms recovered in Great Britain: *a, ánfora; b, cantimplora; c, cántaro; d, pitcher or handled jar; e, jar; f, plate; g, basin, lebrillo.*

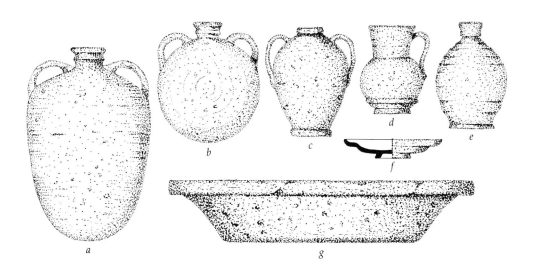

a sketchy blue or blue and purple linear design. The possibility must be considered that this white pottery found a ready market in England or on the opposite continental shores, as the local tablewares there still were a dismal dark brown or gray. It is likely that then as now, many persons considered food more palatable when served on light-colored dishes. However, the number of finds of such intrusive pottery is not great. It may be that the thirteenth-century Sevillian maiolicas scattered about the British ports were not trade goods at all, but were discarded possessions of Spanish seamen. Furthermore, had shipments of Sevillian low-caliber maiolica been dispatched along the northern shores of the Mediterranean, there probably would have been little demand for it because the same kind of pottery was being made nearly everywhere.

Attribution of the two other categories of Spanish earthenwares recovered from thirteenth- and fourteenth-century English sites is not so obvious, primarily because there have not been a sufficient number of verified specimens for study. There could well have been several sources for this pottery, since all formerly Roman and Muslim held sectors of southern Portugal and Spain shared a basic form vocabulary. It is the clay of the archaeological fragments that has prompted several suggestions of derivation outside of Andalusia. Until detailed comparative geological analyses are undertaken of both archaeological ceramics and clay deposits from which their raw substance might have been drawn, the arguments cannot be definitely settled. Nevertheless, historical and archaeological deductions support a premise of Andalusian origin for at least a substantial number of the exported vessels, if not in Sevilla itself, perhaps in its satellite countryside potteries.

The pots in question were coarse earthenware containers for various footstuffs, not items of trade in themselves (Fig. 48a–c, e). All the unglazed shapes were those meant to hold liquids, in this instance probably olive oil, inasmuch as wine from the Rhineland and France was more available to British customers. Based upon known practice, the containers must be assumed to have been made at or near the place where that oil was prepared. It is possible that, as in Roman times, rural shops around Andalusia supplied the entire commodity—pot and contents—and brought it to the city by river craft or the wheeled carts that to a large degree had replaced Muslim pack trains. Or the urban workshops may have provided shipping containers for agricultural goods sent in bulk

to the port. In any case, by the thirteenth century Sevilla
had for a millennium commanded the western Mediterranean outlets with such exports in such packaging. As
to the paste, a red-firing clay with mica and metamorphic
rock inclusions similar to that observed in the fragments
reclaimed in England is widespread in southern Spain,
and was in fact used in Sevilla to make many heavy duty
objects and tiles. Its generally dark color, as compared
to the English fragments, may be due in part to incomplete
oxidation in firing the thick walls of the usual variety of
forms. Recent finds in Sevilla and in the American colonies
of specimens comparable to the debatable sherds at least
leave open the likelihood of their derivation in Andalusia.

There are reasons to question the possible origin of
these particular earthenwares in either the Estremadura
area of west central Spain or in the adjoining Alentejo
province of Portugal, as has been proposed.[188] The former
is an infertile region lacking exportable agricultural
resources. It is in the center of the peninsula distant from
any seaport, and its antique Roman road system had
decayed by the thirteenth century. Even if wine or olive oil
had been produced there, hauling them any distance in
heavy, breakable jars would have been a formidable,
not to mention pointless, task. The Alentejo is a better
candidate: although it was similarly isolated in the interior,
farming was more productive. In those instances when
it was possible to get crops and containers to the Atlantic
coast, commercial exchanges between Portugal and England had existed since the previous century.[189]

There are three shapes of the exported unglazed jars
meant for liquids. One was the round-bodied canteen
known in Spain as a *cantimplora* (Fig. 48b). Its lineage in
Spain goes back to the Romans, who had assimilated it
from the ancient Near East. It has continued in use in
Andalusia until the present, with very few modifications
from what it was at the beginning of the Christian Era.
During the early transatlantic trade with the American colonies it saw service as a kind of container that has come
to be called an "olive jar" by American archaeologists.[190]
Actually, other forms would have been better suited for
the shipment of olives.

A second kind of storage jar was the amphora, or *ánfora*
(Fig. 48a). It continued the short-necked globularity of
Roman and Byzantine versions believed to have carried
Andalusian olive oil.[191] Its pedigree in Spain is just as long
as that of the *cantimplora*, but changes in it have been more
marked. For example, during the seventeenth and eighteenth centuries it lost its handles and neck to metamor-

phose into the customary jar in which millions of gallons of wine and olive oil went to the colonies. This form also is known in the Americas as an "olive jar."

A third coarse ware vessel shape that reached England in the late thirteenth or early fourteenth century is the *cántaro* (Fig. 48c). This is a high-shouldered jar, usually with prominent paired handles and a flat base. However, sometimes the handles are absent, the base is indented, and the neck height is slightly increased.[192] Ultimately modeled on classical prototypes, the *cántaro* has remained the main support of many potteries all over Spain.[193]

One glazed vessel form that might occasionally have functioned as a container for some items with which seepage was a problem was a flat-bottomed, vertical-walled, thick-rimmed, wide-mouthed basin, or *lebrillo* (Fig. 48g).[194] Typically covered on one or both surfaces with a bright green glaze, it, too, was used for centuries in Andalusia and remains a routinely produced type in modern shops in Triana. The green lead glaze had been used on a variety of utilitarian forms since the tenth-century caliphate period, although it had been known in the Near East for two centuries previously. In the case of this ware, physical tests of the clay have confirmed its Andalusian source.[195]

The directions indicated in this thirteenth- and fourteenth-century evidence of the foreign trade or unintentional distribution of Sevillian ceramics were to continue through the four future centuries dealt with in this book. Whether through sale, use, or accident, low quality tin-glazed domestic utensils turned out in the cramped dirty shops by the Guadalquivir would find their way into scattered human debris on both shores of the Atlantic. In terms of numbers, hastily made unglazed or lead-glazed receptacles of a half-dozen form and size variations, designed as expendable merchandising necessities, would continue to account for the greatest percentage of Sevillian ceramic exports. Once their contents were removed, they were discarded around the world.

Historicultural Background of
Late Fourteenth Century Andalusia

The second half of the fourteenth century was a dark period in European history. Slack population growth, stagnant economies, and social unrest were worsened by the devastating Black Death that wiped out entire communities. In Andalusia the European phenomenon was matched by successive floods, earthquakes, and famines. Population dropped dramatically.[196] Social friction increased. Anti-Jewish sentiments came to a climax in 1391, when Sevillian synagogues were razed and some

four thousand Jews were murdered. That tragedy was followed by mass conversions among Jews whose religious
convictions already were wavering.[197] A *converso* class
was thereby created that in the next century would be the
target of the Inquisition initiated in Sevilla. Incessant
infighting between landed Christian families and running
battles with Muslim forces still controlling the Mediterranean coast and Straits of Gibraltar disrupted any lingering
peace.[198] These unhappy events caused widespread misery
and placed a damper on significant cultural achievements.
The queen city of the Guadalquivir, which had promised
Castile a doorway to wealth and power, was sinking
into murky provincial backwaters. Royal families continued to maintain seasonal homes there, basking in winter
sunshine and fleeing sizzling summers. But while French
High Gothic monuments were changing skylines in northern and eastern Spain and cities there were growing rich
with new enterprises, the south lived on amid its crum-
bled ruins and its memories. Much of the motivation
or ability for artistic and other growth was seeping away.
The ranks of laboring men had become so depleted that
Sevilla appeared to be a city of females.[199]

Pottery History of
the Late Fourteenth Century

Such a troubled state of affairs had obvious consequences in a male occupation like pottery making, which
was inexorably linked to prevailing economic conditions
and at the same time hampered by a growing Castilian
antipathy toward handwork. The small number of known
examples of pottery correlated with late fourteenth-
century Sevilla may substantiate a ceramic decline as much
as it does a lack of archaeology. Fewer vessel forms and
decorative modes, as compared with the Muslim repertory, reflect a cultural impoverishment.

There was one significant exception to the seeming
stagnation in local pottery making. That related to refur-
bishment and new construction at the *alcázar*, begun in
1360, which quite openly was based upon the contemporary Granadine palace of the Alhambra. Christian Pedro I
(see Table 2) seems not to have cared, or realized, that
the architectural artistic enrichments achieved by Muslim
craftsmen were in their eyes an expression of their religious convictions. Although it is believed that the carved
plaster decoration may have been accomplished by
imported Nasrid workers, the tile panels that enliven the
walls below it were, in all probability, the work of local
mudéjar talent. Competence in this kind of ceramic work
was apparent in several projects completed in Sevilla prior

to the ouster of the Moroccans.[200] However, the design
style was so different from anything seen earlier that some
kind of cultural interplay within the Muslim sphere as a
whole is implicit. Based upon the underlying aesthetics—
not only in terms of design expression, but also considering the fascination with architectural beautification of
this sort—the most logical conclusion is that there was a
diffusionary trajectory from Seljuk Turk or Persian backgrounds to Tunisia, across the Mediterranean to the Emirate of Granada, and on west to Sevilla.[201]

The manufacture of the basic tile blanks was an uncomplicated process. Small, uniform balls of prepared red-
firing clay were rolled flat to an even thickness over a surface lightly sprinkled with sand to prevent sticking. Using
a template, the desired form was trimmed with a sharp
implement and set aside to dry. A weight of some kind
may have been placed on rows of these blanks to prevent
warping. Following bisquing, each tile was dipped into
a vat of one of several colored glaze solutions made
opaque with tin oxide, thus a maiolica coating. The most
common colors were green, yellow, black, and white;
blue glaze appeared for the first time. During the glost firing the tiles may have been fired vertically, held in position by pins or wads of clay so as to avoid the use of
cockspurs. Today, however, tiles generally are fired flat in
special racks. This step in the making of the primary
resource for *alicatado* was simple enough to have been
done by anyone in the workshop.

The installation was the aspect of the mode calling for
sensitive designing and technical finesse. Patterns had
to be conceived in accord with prevailing canons of taste
to properly fill the prescribed space—a field of design
framed by borders—and colors played off against one
another to achieve positive or negative values as desired.
Further, designs had to be considered in relation to the
room as a whole in order to provide a bold basal balance
in harmony with adjoining spaces. *Alicatado* in Nasridian
and Sevillian application most commonly formed a wainscoting, above which was a fanciful stucco confection
that, although intricately detailed, imparted a feeling of
lightness. One must assume a master plan, even if observation of current projects in progress seems to deny this.

Patterns consisted of a number of complexly intertwined geometric, calligraphic, or six- to twelve-pointed
stellar motifs, all angular and easier to cut than the curvilinear designs favored in Persia (Fig. 49c–d). They were
set so as to be seen as continuous bands rather than as
small contiguous units. This placed additional demands on
designers and executors. Many panels were bordered at

the top by solid stepped triangles. These were suggested
by freestanding roof line embellishments at Córdoba. They
probably had ultimately derived from Near Eastern examples dating back at least to Ninevah, and possibly gave
rise later to ceramic *remates*, or finials, that became thoroughly identified with Sevillian architecture.[202]

The next step of *alicatado* preparation was its installation. On the job, working in front of a particular panel,
workmen broke fragments, or tesserae, from the larger tile
blanks to suit the patterns. Some were left rather large,
but most were small. These were known as *aliceres*. The
single tool used was a double-headed hammerlike object
with a chisel edge called a *pico*. It was struck decisively
against the blank in certain ways to produce proper frac-
ture. Suitable results were obtainable only through practice. The waste of tile material must have been
considerable. Fragment after fragment was carefully placed
over a previously prepared cartoon. The composition
then was covered with grout. When set, the panel was

Figure 49. Polychromatic tile
wainscoting in Sevilla: *a–b, cuenca,*
Casa de Pilatos, early sixteenth
century (Raised borders of elements prevented flow of molten
glaze, and designs continued
the complex intertwined compositions favored by the Spanish
Muslims.); *c, alicatado, alcázar,* second half of the fourteenth century;
d, close-up of star element, showing irregularities of mosaic fragments due to fracturing of larger
base blanks.

backed with stabilizing timbers to allow the section to be raised and secured in place. The final step was removal of the cartoon and excess mortar. Finished units were somewhat flawed, since handwork never attains machine precision (see Fig. 49d). This drawback was redeemed by strong color and dynamic pattern.

Alicatado ranks as one of the highest expressions of Spanish ceramic art of the period. It grew out of a twelfth-century ceramic background in Persia, which passed through a stage of combining brick with interspersed glazed pieces to an all-over glazed mosaic. The technique came to full maturity in thirteenth-century Anatolia, then under control of the Seljuk Turks.[203] Possibly through the stimulus of Nasrid contemporaries, it seems to have revived Sevillian interest in architectural ceramics, which, after undergoing many variations, continues unabated. Until the sixteenth century, however, tiles were used only by rich individuals. The Sevillians could as well have adopted a method of creating figural panoramas similar to Roman tesserae floors still to be seen in the fourteenth century in some of Sevilla's baths and in the ruins of Itálica,[204] but they did not. Fourteenth-century panels that the Sevillians are believed to have laid in such local monuments as the Casa de Olea, Omnium Sanctorum, San Gil, Santa Marina, San Estéban, and the *alcázar*, in Córdoba and Santiponce, as well as far away in Zaragoza and Salamanca, are still *in situ*.[205] From this time on there was a rigid division in the Sevillian ceramic craft between those who made and laid tile and those whose activities were devoted to fashioning *vasija*, or hollow ware.

A century later, after the Nasrids were driven from the hilltop Alhambra, it was tilers from Sevilla who made repairs to damaged dados there and who subsequently were called upon for tile projects of *alicatado* and other styles at their own *alcázar*.[206] The name of Juan Pulido stands out as one of the best known of these artisans.

Nasrid Ceramics

Before that happened, the major pottery industry in closest geographical proximity to that of Sevilla was that in the Emirate of Granada, also in the part of Spain now classed as Andalusia. Málaga on the Mediterranean coast was the site of the most active Nasrid potteries, but others probably operated in the cities of Granada, Murcia, and Almería, and small towns such as Andarax, Arjon, Guadix, Antequera, and Berja. The largest part of the artisan work force came into those urban centers under the military pressures of the first half of the thirteenth century, where it quickly found an environment favorable to the pursuit of the decorative arts. An infusion of talent, a modicum of political stability, an intensification of cultural identity, support of the elite, public awareness and appreciation, arrival of foreign methods and possibly of artisans, and a commercial success that opened widening opportunities all combined to produce a series of ceramics still regarded as masterpieces. One of the ironies of the westerly Andalusian reconquest was that all of these same elements were at that time absent from the Sevillian scene.

Seeking ways to bolster revenues in its reduced territorial circumstances, the Nasrid leadership had the foresight to especially encourage its pottery industry. Quite coincidentally, that craft apparently was refreshed at inception by an infiltration of expert Persian craftsmen fleeing invasions of their homeland. In an assemblage of introduced eastern pottery traits, which incorporated certain vessel shapes, design preferences, *alicatado* tiling, and perhaps cobalt, was the technology of lusterware. This was to prove of utmost importance to the financial health of the emirate and put Granadine ceramic exports on a totally different level than those of neighboring Sevilla.

Actually, a small lusterware industry may have been begun in Málaga by Egyptian refugees adrift after the fall of the Fatimids in Cairo in 1171, but concrete archaeological evidence is lacking. Most of the Egyptian potters are thought to have moved on to Rakka in northern Syria or to Rayy or Kashan in Persia, but some conceivably could have gone west.[207]

From such a murky beginning, there evolved a wholesale Nasrid concentration on the manufacture of lusterware, or *reflejo metálico*, which lasted from about 1250 to 1450. Its high point came near 1350, when the wandering Muslim geographer Ibn Battuta wrote of "gilded pottery" in Málaga.[208]

The manufacture of *reflejo metálico* was expensive. This was not so much because of the silver and copper metals required, which actually would have been relatively small amounts, but because under the usual uncontrolled primitive firing methods the loss of or damage to pottery incurred during this crucial stage was excessive. Some estimates of rejects range as high as ninety percent. That, combined with the need to employ topflight artisans, the imported raw materials needed, and three necessary firings—which meant added consumption of time, labor, and fuel—resulted in costly objects.[209] Capital was required to support such an industry. As the frequent appearance of the dynastic emblem in the decoration confirms, the treasury of the Nasrid court underwrote its manufacture.[210] In return, and without competition, this luxury grade pottery dominated a market stretching around the entire Mediterranean world and into northern Europe.[211] Much of the actual shipping was in the hands of the Genoese, who converted the port of Málaga into their own stronghold.[212] Characteristically, the artisans responsible for elevating lusterware into the rarified atmosphere of fine art remained anonymous, even though they were instrumental in what has been termed one of the six major flowerings in the history of all Islamic ceramics.[213] It is lamentable that the metallic pigments have not stood up well through time. Few examples recovered archaeologically retain their original brilliance.

Some of the vessel forms adopted for the display of *reflejo metálico* decoration, such as the pedestal-based pitcher with a sharp beaklike spout at rim line or the sling-supported, tubular-spouted ewer, enjoyed popularity only so long as that kind of ware was an important commodity; their shapes were borrowed from eastern metal vessels for what began as an alien mode attempting to resemble metal. They vanished with that mode. Others were put to new use. For example, a lidded tureen for ceremonial occasions became a baptismal font in Christian hands (Fig. 72c). The cylindrical drug jar was an unusual survivor (Fig. 50g). It paralleled numerous Syrian and Persian examples that were exported during the thirteenth and fourteenth centuries for use in European pharmacies.[214] More common were the flaring, narrow-footed, conical *cuencos* with jutting rims (Fig. 50d), hemispherical footed bowls (Fig. 50c), unfooted basins, and wide plates typical of the non-lustered categories of contemporary wares.

Figure 50. Some typical Nasrid ceramic forms (With the exception of *b* and *e*, all occurred with varied decorative modes, primary among them being simple lead glazing, manganese patterns under lead glazing, etched patterns through colored slip, blue–on–white maiolica, and the same maiolica with the addition of luster overglaze pigments.): *a*, winged *tinaja*, the Alhambra Jar; *b*, ribbed storage jar; *c*, hemispherical bowl; *d*, conical bowl; *e*, *cantimplora*; *f*, pitcher; *g*, drug jar; *h–i*, two-handled jars apparently inspired by mosque lamps; *j*, torch holders.

Most interesting of all was the winged *tinaja*, whose mixed genealogy was both eastern and western Mediterranean (Fig. 50a). As their consummate display of virtuosity, Nasrid potters took what up to then had been a common Andalusian service form, enlarged it to extraordinary size (approximately four feet in height), reduced its globular profile to an elongated pear shape, pulled its ribbed neck to great heights, expanded its wings into arcing prominences with modeled upper elements leaning inward toward the neck, glazed it with solutions made special by the presence of opacifying tin, and graced it with their finest brush work in expensive silver and, occasionally, cobalt.[215] A single white maiolica *tinaja* of this type but lacking luster or blue overlay is known.[216]

This was the Alhambra Jar, so named because several were found in the rubble of that palace. Unfortunately, they were not filled with gold dust, as some romantics like to say, but when in use more likely were filled with water, just as were the coeval Sevillian *tinajas*. Their glazed surfaces would not have permitted seepage or consequent cooling through evaporation. Some scholars have suggested their use as display objects set in specially enhanced structural niches (Fig. 51).[217]

Also remarkable in their intricate patterning and huge size were a few large door jamb slabs in blue and luster pigments over white maiolica glaze. They resemble carpets hung on the wall. Producing them without warpage or cracks was a spectacular accomplishment. A famous example at the Instituto Don Juan de Valencia in Madrid was made in the second decade of the fifteenth century, at which time it may have been one of the final superior Malagan examples of the technique.[218]

Nasrid decorative art—elegant, elaborate, and expressed through *reflejo metálico*—was typified by dense all-over imbricated patterning that incorporated an array of traditional elements in accord with Islamic point of view. Some of these had metaphysical implications but were reinterpreted to Moresque taste. Networks of sinuous or angular lines carried a pattern out into infinity. Motifs bent arbitrarily or twisted to fill prescribed spaces and thereby passed from realism to abstraction. Cufic and Nashki calligraphy with poetic, religious, or felicitous messages was so elaborately presented as to be nearly illegible. These treatments and repetitious arabesques were part of the style. The use of figural elements, which sporadically appeared in the Spanish Muslim arts of all periods, persisted. They may have had some symbolic meaning not now understood. Exteriors of bowls carried hastily executed circles, ovoids, or splashes reminiscent of tenth-

Figure 51. Late fourteenth-century Nasrid winged *tinaja*, the so-called Alhambra Jar, carried for three centuries around central Europe as spoils-of-war, finally in 1648 becoming part of the Swedish royal collection. The bronze adornments and dark marble stand are eighteenth-century additions (courtesy Nationalmuseum, Stockholm).

Figure 52. Typical patterns on reverses of Islamic bowls: *a–b*, Nasrid *reflejo metálico*; *c* and *e*, tenth-century Nishapur; *d*, eleventh-century Fatimid Egyptian *reflejo metálico* (after Grabar 1976, Lane 1958, Llubiá 1967).

century Nishapur or eleventh-century Fatimid work (Fig. 52).[219] Also hidden in the intricacies of pattern were compositions and minor motifs that had filtered into Muslim shops everywhere as a result of the influence of Chinese Ming blue and white porcelains.

Chinese ceramics were traded across the Asian steppes during the time of the Mongols. As early as the late Sung dynasty (960–1279), a twelfth-century list compiled by an Inspector of Foreign Trade in Fukien (Fujian) Province showed knowledge of trade routes extending as far west as Morocco.[220] Under the western Muslim decorators who copied the imported Chinese wares in underglaze painted patterns, the penchant for flat, non-realistic, decorative effect greatly altered the final results. Still, they point up an interesting reciprocal diffusionary sequence. Ming dynasty (1368–1644) artisans, eager for change after the long Sung emphasis on undecorated surfaces, adopted the use of figurative patterning against a white ground, as well as the cobalt mineral itself, from the Persians. Persian artisans, in turn, copied some of the styling of the Chinese. Over years, elements of this Sino-Persian package of designs worked their way westward. Perhaps they invaded the cultural gear of migrating Persian decorators, eventually to appear in Muslim Spain after having crossed two major continents in their journey.

After the mid-fourteenth century, an increasing number of figural and heraldic motifs taken from Christian Gothic sources and characteristic of Spanish Levantine potteries to the east of the emirate appeared on vessels coming from Nasridian kilns.[221] Among them were fish, griffins, and ships. They and the color blue had symbolic meaning in Christian art, although it is doubtful that Muslim decorators were aware of that.[222]

In Granada, small potteries operated on the hill east of the Alhambra palace.[223] Presumably for members of the court and for other highly placed Nasrid customers, there were additional decorated wares, including the typical two-handled, small jar (Fig. 53); conical or small ring-based bowl; necked bottle; tall pedestaled lamp on a saucer base, and other forms. One was decorated in black on an unglazed straw-colored ground, another was a white with relief decorations glazed in green or purple, a third was a dark blue-on-white maiolica, and a more ordinary ware was glazed in green with black underpainting.[224] The types with most decoration echoed the painters' bent for involved repetitive patterning through use of such means as bands of small calligraphic figures, the tree of life, khams or hands of Fatma,[225] and dotted and arabesque fillers. The assortment of accompanying country pottery, or that used by lesser city dwellers, included the same sort of unglazed or lead-glazed mortars, water wheel jars, pedestal-based handled candleholders, urinals, basins, and cooking pots that were known in the Guadalquivir Valley. Eared ceramic slab grave markers recall Roman and Visigothic specimens.

Figure 53. Nasrid small jars with typical black decoration over an unglazed straw-colored ground (courtesy Museo Arqueológico Nacional, Madrid).

Figure 54. Nasrid jar of brick red paste and a decoration using inlaid white feldspar chips. In Andalusia this kind of pottery is identified with Guadix, from which it was dispersed into the environs of Sevilla and, subsequently, overseas to the Indies and central Mexico. This specimen is thought to date to the sixteenth century, as are most of the examples recovered archaeologically in the Americas (courtesy the Hermitage of Nuestra Señora de la Defensión, La Cartuja, Jérez de la Frontera).

One unusual and infrequently fashioned type came from the mountain village of Guadix. It may have been a mode borrowed from fellow Muslims elsewhere, but in Andalusia its manufacture appears to have been centered in this locality. Of a distinctive dark red color and principally formed into small jars, the type was decorated with some burnishing, a few incised lines, and tiny white chips of feldspar set into patterns while the clay was leather hard (Fig. 54). Firing temperatures obviously were insufficient to vitrify the rock. Emphasizing the great continuity in Spanish ceramics, a similar kind of pottery is made today in the same town,[226] which remains a refuge for Muslim-influenced life. In pottery-making endeavors, pit wheels and *hornos arabes* indicate survivals there from the past.

Mindful that the commercial success of *reflejo metálico* production was dependent upon a tight monopoly, the Nasrids managed to keep its technological details from neighboring eyes for more than one hundred years. But trade secrets are no better kept than any other kind. In the late fourteenth century a Valencian entrepreneur named Peter Boil (or Buyl) was able to take advantage of his diplomatic appointment to the Granadine court to ferret out the process by which the overpainted metallic patterns were achieved. He learned that they resulted from a complicated procedure of calcinating the proper metallic oxides with sulphur, then mixing them with red ochre and vinegar, and finally applying them over fired tin glaze. The third firing, wherein a reducing atmosphere was essential, had to be held to a low temperature sufficient only to melt and fix the minerals.[227]

Back in the Levantine village of Manises, where Boil and his successors served as patrons for a colony of *mudéjar* potters in return for ten percent of the pots they made,[228] he went about creating his own lusterware empire.[228] It is rare on this earthenware level of pottery production for one person to have affected so great a change, but one must bear in mind that other factors, such as extensive pirating on the seas, duties extracted, and cultural exhaustion, also were involved. As a result of Boil's espionage and of the innovations and backing he brought to the Manises endeavor, within a few years the Granadine industry floundered, although it continued to turn out lower quality, and presumably less costly, *reflejo metálico* until almost the very end of the emirate. The fifteenth- and sixteenth-century *reflejo metálico* fame belonged to eastern, not southern, Spain.

The Nasrids did not send abroad cargoes of container jars filled with regional delicacies as did the Sevillians, because such resources were urgently needed to sustain their hemmed-in dense population. Nor did they export coarse tin-glazed tableware. What they had for several centuries sent out into the most sophisticated and richest markets of the time were the best ceramics then being made in Europe.

Retrospective

The one hundred fifty years following reconquest of Andalusia, except in the case of the Emirate of Granada, were characterized primarily by the continuation of the basic technology and styles introduced by the Spanish Muslims over the course of the preceding half-millenium. This continuum is attributable to the craft's having remained largely in Muslim hands and serving a clientele following the same general modes of life as earlier Andalusians, regardless of religious affiliations. Most utilitarian vessel shapes, with origins in the ancient Near East, already had been in use in Iberia for centuries. In some instances their production can be better documented than formerly, owing to the circumstances of foreign trade.

Innovations that did appear were comparable to those of the contemporary Mediterranean basin. Most notable was the adoption of tin-opacified glaze and of cobalt decorative pigment, which would continue to dominate Spanish earthenwares to the present. Several changes in vessel forms derived from new social forces, such as small plates and bowls for personal use and a baptismal font for Christian churches that was based upon a Romano-Visigothic stone fountain style, but which at this period was treated with *mudéjar* motifs and glaze. The introduction of *alicatado* tiling confirmed a sharing of ceramic information with neighboring Nasridians and forecast an important future in Andalusia for decorative architectural ceramics.

THE CRITICAL FIFTEENTH CENTURY

Historicultural Background

A quickening rhythm of life in fifteenth-century Andalusia ushered in the beginning or culmination of a number of events that directly or indirectly had bearing upon local pottery. To the south of Sevilla a string of fortified castles and settlements was left behind as the Muslims steadily receded from that frontier. Christians followed in the wake of their retreat to reoccupy the land. Agriculture gradually assumed its old importance, and a new breed of *latifundistas* engaged in cattle and horse raising.

Meanwhile, even though the provincial economy

remained committed to working the soil and the animals
that grazed upon it, Sevilla's population, estimated at
fifty thousand at the beginning of the century, [229] steadily
swelled through the attractions of the pleasure and profit
to be had there. After one hundred and fifty years of
Christian reoccupation, the city was just approaching what
had been its estimated size at the end of Muslim rule.[230]
Watching the shipping of the Mediterranean tie up at their
docks once the Genoese finally broke the Gibraltar blockade, Sevillians increasingly sensed a future linked to trade
and exploration westward into the Atlantic and southward
into the Berbería. The *barrio de mar* lined along the street
from the main church to the river grew proportionately.
In San Salvador *collación* small markets sold a great variety
of produce and meats brought into the city from surrounding farms and handwrought articles for daily life made
in town. It was there that the *alcaicería de la loza* offered
domestic ceramics to householders. A list of fifteenth-
century artisans of Sevilla includes more than eighty-nine
categories of workers who manufactured such varied
items as fans, embroidered textiles, helmets, cabinets,
chests, crossbows, muskets, shields, purses, quilts, sad-
dles, belts, knives, locks, mirrors, and combs.[231]

This body of workers mirrored the dramatic change that
had taken place since the thirteenth-century reconquest,
when the usual settlers more often were displaced peasants or former soldiers whose style of living had no need
for some of the luxuries now created. Life spilled outside
the city in all directions. The sandy beach between the
walls and the Guadalquivir became a rowdy zone associated with fishing and freighting and of shacks occupied by
innkeepers, gamblers, prostitutes, hawkers of second-
hand clothes, or *cacharreros* peddling cheap earthenware
crockery. Beyond the Río Tagarete, where the wastes
of the city accumulated and fouled the air, was a cluster of
slaughterhouses and the hovels of butchers. Along the
river numerous flour mills were turned by oxen and ovens
yielded the city's bread. In the district of Triana the making of soap, a royal monopoly until the fifteenth century,
made use of two local resources, oil from olives and
potash from the *barrilla* plant, to make a hard white soap
that became a Sevillian specialty. It proved so successful
that a second factory for dark soap opened in San Salvador
collación. Also in Triana, *casas de ollería* housed a pottery
industry utilizing the same resources, which expanded to
rank third in the city in number of men employed. The
clouds of black smoke from their kilns hung over the city
each morning.

Royal officials, clergy, and members of large, important,

noble families formed the upper layer of Sevillian society. They and a clique of traders, most of whom were Italians or Jewish converts, controlled whatever wealth was available and had their spacious homes decorated with a panoply of *mudéjar* arts expressed in tiles, textiles, and inlaid furniture. It was a totally different situation among the fuller lower ranks of petty officials, shopkeepers, construction workers, craftsmen, laborers, seamen, vendors, and a sizable throng of picaresque elements who lived in one way or another off the labors of others. Impoverished, most of the people existed from day to day, never able to accumulate adequate funds or goods to give them hope of a better future. There were eleven specific years notable for plagues and fourteen years when famine was devastating.[232] Under a thin veneer of progress festered sores of racial and religious intolerance that pitted Jews, Muslims, Italians, Frenchmen, and Castilian Old Christians against one another, class feuds rooted in the stranglehold on or contests for power among noble families, and widening chasms between economic layers that bred injustice and anger.

Catholic religious orders were expanding in size and number all over Spain during the fifteenth century. Sevilla, with a racial mix given to passionate extremes, seems to have offered many of them a particularly attractive home. One of the groups drawn to Sevilla, and one that would play an important role in the lives of many potters, was the Carthusians. Construction commenced in 1401 on a Carthusian *comunidad*, or residence, to be known as Santa María de las Cuevas. The *cuevas*, or caves, may have been associated with kilns reported in the area,[233] and perhaps were pits from which clay had been extracted. Santa María de las Cuevas on the west bank of the Río Guadalquivir grew to include quarters for seventy monks, seven chapels, a refectory containing marble-topped tables, a library, gardens of citrus and palm trees with jasmine and flowers planted in beds around fountains, orchards of fruit trees watered by mule train from the river, and a small graveyard where descendants of the Dukes of Alcalá wished to be buried.[234] There was a tower on the grounds where the monks could go for contemplation and to enjoy a view of Sevilla across the river and of the surrounding fertile plains of Baetica, which one traveler said seemed like an entrance to Paradise.[235] Life was further sweetened for the fifteenth–century residents of the *comunidad*, as attested by Jerónimo Munzer, a German who came through Sevilla in 1495. He wrote that in the spacious cellars of La Cartuja there he counted ninety-three enormous earthenware *tinajas* of fine wine. These are estimated to have held some twenty-three hundred gallons when full.[236] Drawing support from the local populace in the form of gifts, alms, foodstuffs, and taxes, this chapter additionally received forty thousand *ducats* of annual rents, some of which were for houses and kilns used by potters in Triana and Sevilla.[237]

Most notable among the non-Spaniards dwelling in fifteenth-century Andalusia were the Genoese. The cramped setting of their home city state, with its back to the mountains and its feet in the Ligurian Sea, had guided many of them into a way of life dependent upon trade, most of it seaborne. From the twelfth through the sixteenth century fleets of trading ships from landless Genoa vied with those from Pisa, Venice, and Barcelona for lucrative Mediterranean markets, thus curtailing the earlier Muslim monopoly of that inland sea. Growing commerce and Crusader traffic took them from the Black Sea to Flanders. By the fifteenth century there were Genoese trading colonies as far from Genoa as Lisbon, Bruges, and Antwerp.

A small number of Genoese traders had been in Andalusia from the time of the Almohads.[238] In recognition of their aid to Christian forces during the reconquest, Fernando III granted them a neighborhood in the Sevillian *collación* of Santa María and allowed them to enjoy a satellite Italian world with their private chapel, cemetery, consulate, baths, and bread ovens. At the same time, other of their countrymen who had gathered in the Andalusian towns of Córdoba, Jérez, and Cádiz also were given special privileges. Not confining themselves to dealing with fellow Christians, the transplanted Genoese soon deeply penetrated Muslim markets on both shores of the western Mediterranean. Their participation in all sectors of Andalusian life and their aggressive commercialism quickly propelled them into positions of power as moneylenders, shipowners, merchants, and entrepreneurs.[239]

The Catholic Kings ascended their respective thrones in the last quarter of the fifteenth century, Isabela to that of the Kingdom of Castile in 1474 (see Table 2) and Fernando to that of Aragón in 1479. Even though their dynasties remained independent in many ways, they achieved a unification of Spain that theretofore had been only an idle dream. Through shrewdness and diplomacy, these monarchs gradually brought about administrative, religious, military, and economic reforms that affected all levels of society and laid the groundwork for Spain's future as a world power.

Among measures to aid artisans were those attempting to organize the chaotic urban economy. Standardization of weights and measures, laws to foster shipbuilding and international trade, tightening up of tax collection procedures together with the abolition of many internal duties, encouragement of regional trade fairs, and monarchial sponsorship of some manufacturing activities produced a period of relative gain from which monarchs and subjects all benefited financially. Unfortunately, the search for order and justice led to overregulation. The institution of trade guilds, which were being abandoned in neighboring countries, was one aspect of this tendency.

At the same time, there was prosperity throughout Europe which, according to some economic historians, lasted from about 1450 to 1550.[240] Seaborne commerce had been redirected from the eastern Mediterranean because the strategic port of Constantinople had fallen to the Turks at mid-century. The Hundred Years War had come to an end. The Portuguese were getting toeholds on both of Morocco's shores.

The concentration of power in the Spanish Crown gradually produced a period of internal peace, security, and hope unlike any Christian Spain had known, and Andalusia seemed on the threshold of a cultural flowering. Catholic artisans from Italy and Flanders, thought to be more versed in the mechanical arts than Hispanic craftsmen, were invited to emigrate to the country under an incentive program. Some of them chose to come to the Guadalquivir valley because of the attraction of possible markets in an inviting temperate environment. The northern Italians already had family ties there. Shopworn Muslim and Gothic conventions were about to be confronted by those of the Renaissance. Then, like a clap of thunder, came the frightful racial and religious travail that would spawn the infamous Black Legend of Spanish paranoia. Two of Spain's three racial/ethnic/religious components were on the block.[241]

Sephardic Jews had been in Spain since the time of the Romans. For more than a thousand years they had been alternately persecuted and tolerated by more powerful groups sweeping across the peninsula, but through it all they had survived and increased their numbers. The invading Muslims of the eighth century had allowed them some measure of participation in economic and social life, which greatly expanded during the Cordoban caliphate. Then, experiencing a growing resentment, many of them moved northward into the Christian kingdoms. There, Jews were settled along the pilgrimage routes to Santiago de Compostela to protect the peace. From this proximity to France, they dispatched luxury goods, spices, and goldwork to their coreligionists north of the Pyre-

nees.[242] Ancient *fueros*, or local laws and customs, guarded
their rights, which were considered equal to those of
the Christians. Over the next several centuries, as Castilians, throbbing with a crusading mentality, pushed back
south to oust the Muslims of al Andalus, Jews were in the
vanguard. For this service they received grants of land
and other rewards, including a distinctive internal jurisdic-
tion over their own affairs. Toledo became an important
home for many of them. They contributed heavily to
its glowing reputation as a center of learning. The thirteenth-century *Las Cántigas de Santa María* depicted Jews as
merchants and pharmacists, but others were translators,
fiscal agents, doctors, mathematicians, and cartographers.
But by the fourteenth century attitudes toward them
steadily deteriorated, until horrible pogroms precipitated
by the despair of the Black Death destroyed hope of peaceful integration.

The *conversos*, Jews who had nominally accepted Roman
Catholicism but whom many Old Christians felt acted
out of convenience and to ensure their survival rather than
out of conviction, by the fifteenth century were considered
subversive to what was becoming the state religion and
a primary obstacle to national unity. In common eyes
these converts were Judaizing heretics in sympathy with
the large body of unconverted Jews still in Spain, who
impeded their assimilation. Barriers had been placed
between the two groups because the Jews not only practiced an unacceptable religion but by then were considered
a culturally and racially alien people. Unconverted Jews
were forced back into the old ghettos they had left behind
in more relaxed times. One of these Jewries was the *barrio*
of Santa Cruz in Sevilla (see Judería, Fig. 44). To further
isolate them, Jews were forbidden to practice medicine or
handicrafts or to trade with Christians.[243] These measures
were ineffective. Moreover, penetration of the *conversos*
into the highest ranks of government and society and their
financial success inevitably caused resentment among
those who lacked the skill and drive to emulate them. Still,
their wealth and high positions shielded them from official
wrath until the Catholic Kings declared a cornerstone of
their governing policy to be unity and purity of faith.

The Spanish Inquisition, charged with rooting out heresy among the *conversos* and known for its autos-da-fé,
was formed in 1480 and was housed in the Triana castle.
Varying estimates state that seven hundred to two thousand Jewish converts died in Sevilla at the hands of that
tribunal in an eight-year period, five thousand were sen-
tenced to imprisonment or penance, and so many others
fled that the city gates were ordered closed. Forced con-

formity became an accepted tenet of Spanish life. Since properties confiscated from *conversos* went into the royal treasury, it has been suggested that the Inquisition was a tragic means of defraying the expenses of driving the Muslims from Spain.[244] Finally, in 1492, just three months after the defeat of the Nasrids, the royal spotlight turned on the unconverted Jews. After a millenium of life in Iberia, they were abruptly expelled to begin yet another diaspora. Eight thousand Jewish refugees sailed from Cádiz on ships piloted by Genoese, but thousands of others fled overland to Portugal, Italy, and the Ottoman Empire.[245]

The economic effects resulting from driving out the Spanish Jews were severe and rippled through the entire community. Equally disastrous were the narrowed social and intellectual values reinforced by the Inquisition. However, although Jews generally are believed to have constituted a large block of the artisan group active in textile, glass, and metal crafts, their role in local pottery making is thought to have been minimal. This cannot be proved as yet because vulgarization of surnames has concealed their identity in surviving documents, just as a commonality of aesthetics makes identification of individual works impossible. Nevertheless, the prejudice against them that ended in their exodus was a significant factor in the invitation extended to foreign Catholic craftsmen, among whom were Italian potters.

The *mudéjares* of Andalusia through two and a half centuries under Christian political domination had retained a strong cultural identity. They continued to wear distinctive garb, adhere to a religiously prescribed diet, follow social mores different from those of the Christians among whom they lived, speak privately in Arabic, and heed their own religion. Earlier, some Andalusian Christians had affected *mudéjar* trappings, but by the fifteenth century there was a growing tide of resentment against this stubborn refusal to conform to the Castilian norm. This was furthered by the official Isabelline policy of strict orthodoxy in all aspects of life for the entire realm. Yet there also was widespread appreciation for *mudéjar* craftsmanship and a wry recognition that without *mudéjar* willing hands and backs much of the toil of everyday life would come to an abrupt halt. Therefore, passing over this immediate problem of unassimilated elements in their own domains, the Catholic Kings felt compelled to tackle the unfinished business of the reconquest and to drive the Nasrids of Granada into the sea.

It took eleven years and all the royal resources. With ultimate victory in 1492, which owed as much to demorali-

zation of the enemy as to the dogged determination of
the attackers, the Castilian people were triumphant in
religious righteousness and a perception of their own
racial and cultural superiority. A military class had been
heroized in the name of God and Spain. Then, in a chival-
rous magnanimity, the defeated were allowed a choice
of leaving or staying in dignity, with their culture and religion intact. Those promises were soon to be forgotten,
but the long struggle had forged a national character typified by toughness, dedication, and self assurance that
was to be put to the test in the unfolding Age of Discovery. The price of the victory was yet to be fully understood.

Pottery History and Technology

To meet increased needs arising from a repopulation of
the countryside, country potteries, possibly operated seasonally, sprang up in areas with suitable clay deposits,
such as at Jaén, Andújar, La Rambla, and Bailén to the
north and on the plains of Tablada south of Sevilla, where
they continue to the present day.[246] Their wares, destined
primarily for local consumption, came from that fundamental stratum of Spanish ceramics based upon a simple,
unchanging, agrarian way of life.

Because nothing was made without there first being a
need, valid conclusions can be drawn from these earthenwares about the lifeways of the peasantry. For the creak-
ing wheels that brought life-sustaining water to fields
and garden plots, there were the ever present *arcaduces*
(see Fig. 23b). They continued to be made of clay because
wood, metal, or leather all were beyond the farmers'

Figure 55. Some typical Christian
ceramic vessel forms, unglazed, or
lead-glazed. Storage and shipping
receptacles: *a*, large jar, *jarrón*; *b*,
cántaro with lid, *tapadera*; *c*, *cántaro*;
d, *cantimplora*; *e*, *ánfora*; *f*, *tinaja*.

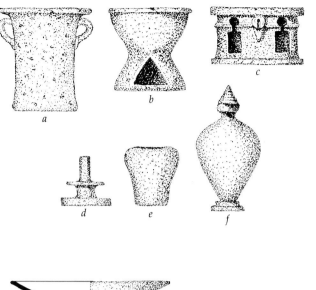

Figure 56. Some typical Christian ceramic vessel forms, unglazed, lead-glazed, or tin-glazed. Household furnishings: *a*, chamber pot, *bacín*; *b*, brazier, *anafe*; *c*, pot rest; *d*, suggested reconstruction of candleholder, *candil*; *e*, mortar, *mortero*; *f*, finial, *remate*.

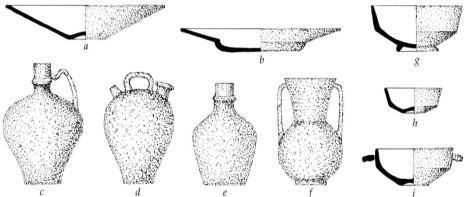

means. Another major concern were large storage and shipping receptacles for agricultural products. These were the ancestral earthenware *tinajas*, *ánforas*, and *cántaros* in use as long as anyone then could remember (Fig. 55). Out in the yards somewhere were rabbit hutches, pigeon lofts, and chicken feeders, all made of clay. Domestic furnishings of earthenware included cylindrical, two-handled chamber pots; candleholders consisting of a vertical shaft cupped at the upper end to receive a tallow taper and set on a saucer base to catch melting wax; and flat-bottomed tubs in which clothes could be washed (Fig. 56).

Earthenwares to hold water and beverages were a special consideration in the hot, dry Andalusian climate. For the horseman or foot traveler, there was the canteen, or *cantimplora* (Fig. 55d). For more stationary users, double-spouted *botijos* were fashioned with closed tops to keep out dust and insects and often with a looped handle for lifting (Fig. 57d). From time to time an orange likely

Figure 57. Some typical Christian ceramic vessel forms, lead- or tin-glazed. Serving receptacles: *a*, principal plate form until mid sixteenth century; *b*, plate form after mid sixteenth century; *c, e*, jugs or cruets; *d, botijo*; *f*, two-handled jar; *g*, drinking bowl, *taza*; *h–i*, porringers, *escudillas*.

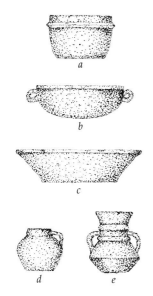

Figure 58. Some typical Christian ceramic forms, unglazed or lead-glazed. Cook pots: *a,* straight-sided bowl; *b, cazuela; c,* basin, *lebrillo; d–e, ollas.*

was jammed down on the pointed spout to keep the water sweet-tasting. Pitchers of many variations held the wine that over the centuries had become a staple for all classes of Spanish society.

Although Muslim-introduced vegetables, fruits, spices, and sweets made the Andalusian diet more varied than was usual in medieval Europe, culinary methods were uncomplicated and required no specialized utensils (Fig. 58). The predominance of broad-mouthed, deep sauce pots is attributable to the typical fare of braised foods, usu-ally onions, carrots, or other vegetables, with meat, poul-try, or game being added on special occasions. Similar wide, heavy casseroles, some lidded, were designed for deep frying in olive oil such things as fish, potatoes, or, for holidays, certain pastries. Jar-shaped pots with uncon-stricted throats were preferred for slow simmering of *gara-banzos* or beans, the form being one that exposed a wide surface to heat and still helped conserve cooking liquids. Because they were commodious and stable, large flat-bottomed basins were very practical for mixing a variety of sausages or for making bread. Short cylindrical or globular shapes made easier the removal of cheeses, honey, or preserves. The many small bottles with a single handle at the rim were for the native olive oil and vinegar that were common seasonings. Grinding jars, which imitated in cheap clay the bronze mortars to be found in more lavish households, were essential for crushing hard lumps of sea salt gathered from coastal estuaries (see Fig. 56e). Small braziers, which continued to be standard, could be taken to the fields for the midday meal (see Fig. 56b).

Generally, this variety of commonware was fashioned in quantity with a casual dexterity resulting from long practice. Capable, experienced potters were able to throw hundreds of such items each day. Minor individual varia-tions were usual because no kind of sizing or contour control was used. Within each form, even so, there was remarkable homogeneity. The prevailing quality of potting was comparatively high. Hard, thin-walled vessels were left with throwing ribs and fingerprints from handle attachments unobliterated, imparting an appealing sense of spontaneity to the objects.

The commonly used light-firing clay of the Guadalquivir valley was calcareous, typically incorporating occasional spicules of sea urchins.[247] Such material normally produces a relatively porous, lightweight fired body that would not have been practical for vessels meant to hold liquids. However, recent physical experiments on clays containing calcium as large-particle grit have demonstrated that they actually have refractory properties similar to noncalcar-

eous clays.[248] In other words, greater vitrification obtainable with these clays would have made for denser, less
porous pottery. The fact that from pre-Roman times on the
Guadalquivir light-firing clay was used for amphorae and
other containers for liquids, such as pitchers, jars, and
bottles, and that these objects frequently received neither
pitch lining nor glaze would appear to substantiate this
conclusion. Moreover, the vessels emerged from the kilns
in a range of color from off-white to a warm pink. American archaeologists erroneously have identified the white
surfaces as being slipped, when in fact they were
scummed by an insoluble white stain. Such stain resulted
from the carbonates of calcium being dissolved by the
free water in the clay body and brought to the vessel surfaces where, if the atmosphere during firing happened
to contain sulphur contaminates, they were converted to
white scum.[249] Engobe was not customarily used on
unglazed objects. Local red-firing clay was preferred when
extra body strength was needed, as in the case of huge
storage casks. It also was desired for cook pots because
calcareous white clay expanded and cracked when put
over brazier fires. No decoration was added to vessels of
either paste, except for occasional lead glazing on one
or both surfaces. Interior glaze customarily dribbled down
unglazed exteriors. Regardless of glaze color, these vessels
usually were referred to as yellow or common wares (loza
basta or loza común). There was a noticeable preference
now for colored, rather than clear, glaze for these objects.

The fifteenth-century ceramic industry at Sevilla holds
most interest for American archaeologists because it has
been assumed that this was the most likely source for
the earthenwares diffused to the Americas with the initial
Spanish conquests. It has proved particularly frustrating,
therefore, that two principal features of the Andalusian
cultural and national landscape appear to have been
responsible for the near eradication of the ceramic record.

One was the grand cathedral that looms above the
skyline. Begun in 1401 and requiring one hundred twenty
years to complete (Fig. 59), it now stands as the world's
largest Gothic cathedral, although it was built at a time
when the French Gothic already was two hundred fifty
years old. During construction, local potters received some
contracts to supply architectural terra cottas and tiles.
Unfortunately for science, their greatest contribution was
in ceramics that would never be seen. In keeping with
an architectural practice introduced to Spain by the
Romans and later also pursued by the Byzantines there,
spaces above the vaulting were filled with large, hollow,
earthenware jars. These served to lighten the load of

Figure 59. Modern rear view
of Sevilla cathedral, built between
1401 and 1525. The lower two-
thirds of the Giralda bell tower
was the minaret of the principal
twelfth-century Almohad mosque.
The upper portion of the tower
and the rounded Capilla Real
were later sixteenth-century
additions.

the superstructure. Through time the Spainards must have
forgotten or misunderstood the purpose of these ceramics,
because at the cathedral they further added masses of
broken vessels and potsherds of all types to cram the voids
with weighty ballast (Fig. 60).[250] Archives record that in
1467, as masons began the task of closing the seventy
ogival vaults over the nave and four side aisles, local potters sold or gave unwanted ceramic materials to church
officers to be used as fillers. Similar transactions took place
in 1498, 1511, 1513, and 1515, when construction of various other units of the cathedral had reached the vaulting
stage.[251] Workyards and trash deposits must have been
cleared of untold amounts of the accumulated residue of
years of pottery production. Perhaps the river banks also

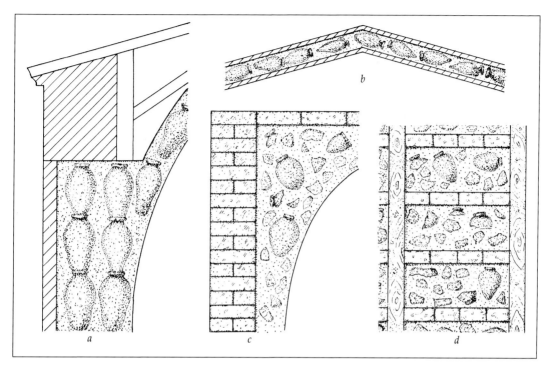

were mined of consolidated lenses of potsherds and discarded kiln furniture that had been dumped there. The
archaeological record of many fifteenth-century ceramics in
most common use in Sevilla was jeopardized, if not
erased.

Another blow to the study of Sevillian ceramics of all
periods was the repeated flooding of the Guadalquivir.
From Roman times to the early twentieth century, it
repeatedly left its banks, backed up into the city's streets,
destroyed boats, weakened houses, and drowned or
marooned residents. Sixteen major inundations occurred
in the span of sixty-three years between 1587 and 1650,
for example, because of torrential rains and increasing silt-
ing of the river's outlets.[252] Although circled by a drainage
through its meadow, the potters' district of Triana was
especially vulnerable. One account related how after three
weeks of flooding the holy image was taken from the
Santa Ana church there in a prayerful procession to the
Triana castle, where river waters reached high on the
walls. Only then did the torrent subside, or as the writer
noted, *se fué el río a su madre*.[253] Unquestionably, such flood
waters flushed riverside waster dumps and the piles of
general refuse that banked the city's walls down through
the marshes lying between Sevilla and the Atlantic.

Even with these losses to science, there are enough
extant specimens to permit a broadly sketched reconstruc-

Figure 60. Various ways in which
complete earthenware vessels
or fragments were used in Andalusian and Caribbean construction:
a, complete amphorae in walls
and haunches; *b*, complete
amphorae in vaulting; *c*, complete
vessels and potsherds as random
fill in walls and haunches; *d*,
complete vessels and potsherds as
random fill beneath floors.

tion of the ceramic industry as it was evolving during
the period leading up to the dramatic overseas expansion
of *hispanidad*. These have come from minor excavations
and random finds within the old city and outlying sectors
served by it, as well as from heirloom collections.

Of particular importance in yielding appropriate specimens thought to have originated in the workshops of
Sevilla has been the Carthusian monastery at Jérez de la
Frontera, sixty miles to the south. Jérez was recaptured
from the Muslims little more than a century after the
reconquest of Sevilla. In recognition of the defense
believed given by the Virgin to Christian forces in their
victorious battles there, in 1368 a hermitage called Nuestra
Señora de la Defensión was established on the Río
Guadalete outside of town, not far from where the original
Muslim occupation had begun some six and a half centuries earlier. The site passed to the Carthusian Order during
the next century. Work began on an important monastery
there in 1463.

During the sixteenth century the Jérez Carthusians
grew wealthy from their fertile lands and their breeding of
horses for the royal herd.[254] La Cartuja de Nuestra Señora
de la Defensión became known for its many art objects,
most of which disappeared following secularization in the
early nineteenth century. To protect the buildings from
further vandalism, they were declared a national monu-
ment in 1856. Subsequently, after one hundred thirteen
years of abandonment, the monastery was returned to the
Carthusians, who commenced restoration in 1948. During
the course of this work many pieces of pottery were
recovered that are believed to date from the second half of
the fifteenth century through the seventeenth century.
However, precise stratigraphic data are lacking. Fortunately, an important site on the Moroccan side of the
Straits of Gibraltar provides some temporal corroboration.

Five categories of earthenware articles routinely were
produced in the Triana and other local workshops by
a variety of methods. They were made for several levels of
urban society in Sevilla and in foreign markets. Some
classes of vessels also were widely distributed among village dwellers who did not have access to such pottery
in their own towns. Their relatively few stylistic variants
are indicators both of an economically poor consumer base
and of a fundamental conservatism among producers
and users. It can be presumed that there were three informal groupings of potters, but how much specialization
of skills there may have been is unknown. Some crossover
within the decorated wares is probable.

The group of potters needing the least chemical and
decorative expertise made the basic *loza basta* of kinds

identical to those from the rural Andalusian workshops, with the possible exception of water wheel jars. Some required partial or total lead glazing, but most did not. These were items useful in the daily routines of homes and businesses.

Necessitating physical strength and superb manual control were enormous storage jars, which were considered a specialty of Triana (see Fig. 55a). They probably owed their existence to a scarcity of wood for barrels and kegs. With capacities of from 25 to 75 gallons, these huge jars generally repeated the usual Andalusian profile of a high-shouldered body slimming down to a narrow flat base.[255] Because of their size, production involved carefully measured sections luted together when leather hard. The accurate fit of parts demanded a keen judgment learned only through experience. Users of such jars were those having need of ample storage facilities, such as convents or monasteries with many residents, taverns, or retail shops dispensing certain commodities. Distribution of these objects would have been restricted, owing to the difficulty of transporting them.

The container jars that carried regional agricultural surpluses abroad were the responsibility of this body of workers. There was no reason to alter their long-tested *tinaja*, *ánfora*, *cántaro*, or *cantimplora* shapes (see Fig. 55b–f). Interior coatings of clear or brown lead glazes were more frequent on the *cantimplora* shapes than formerly. Small flat lids with tiny knobs, *tapaderas*, were made to be used with some of the jars, but without the benefit of securing flanges. The lids would have been sealed in place with pitch for shipping. It is believed that these containers continued to reach many foreign markets, from England, France, Flanders, and Italy to some Greek islands and North Africa, despite increasing commercial competition from elsewhere.[256] Of the four form variants for liquids, only the *cantimplora* has been recovered at the strategically located Moroccan site of Qsar es-Seghir, which was occupied by Portuguese troops from 1458 to 1550.[257] The conclusion is that the others carried substances not needed by the garrison.

The large, flat-bottomed green basins that originated in the thirteenth century continued to be made (see Fig. 58c). These basins are viewed by some as possible containers, and perhaps were formed by this group of workers.

Another subgrouping within the category of ordinary earthenwares was one in demand during the fifteenth century for construction within the city, most notably at the *alcázar* and the new cathedral. Local potteries supplied standardized units of cylindrical tubing, slightly larger at one end than at the other, so that the individual parts

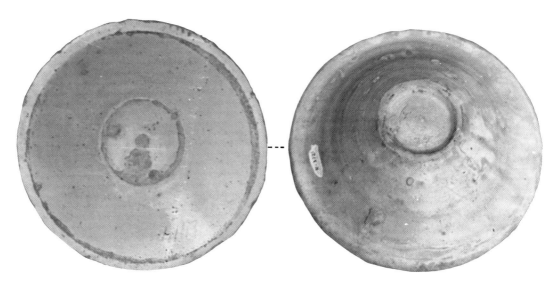

Figure 61. White maiolica plate typical of Sevillian commercialized jigger-and-jolly production from perhaps the fourteenth into seventeenth centuries. Lack of ring foot, thin glazing, trimming facets, and many surface defects were characteristic (courtesy Museo de Artes y Costumbres Populares, Sevilla).

could be fitted together into longer sections or angled with use of earthenware plumber's joints to form water conduits, downspouts, and sewer lines (see Fig. 27).[258] The *atanores* also served secondarily as supports for kiln stacking. As today in Granada, they may have been struck into masses of wet clay to help draw out the excess moisture. Perhaps moldmade in enormous numbers, the tubes were the efforts of a body of workers having fewer skills and lower economic expectations. On the same level were the masons responsible for bricks and terra cotta curved roof tiles, who in the craft hierarchy were not considered potters, even though they molded earth and fired it.

Three other assortments of Sevillian earthenwares may have been the work of the same body of workers, perhaps depending upon market requirements, but the differences in their finished quality would seem to deny this. Showing the least amount of care were the kitchen and tablewares, with essentially the same shapes being either lead or tin glazed. The most common articles were unelaborated thick plates with flaring sides and diameters standardized at about 15 to 20 cm (Figs. 57, 58, 61). Rims were direct and thick, in contrast to the collared rim characteristic of the usual Muslim work. Plate depths, suggesting modern soup dishes, made them suitable for the customary braised foods. Obverses always had a slightly raised central configuration, indicating upside down production over a mold or jigger attached to a wheel head (Fig. 62). This was a point of weakness because glaze tended to wear away from the low protuberance. Bases were slightly concave and compacted, the vessel resting on the outer vessel wall rather than on a ring. Exterior walls were cut away with a single pass of a template or jolly, which faceted rather than smoothed the surface. A jigger-and-

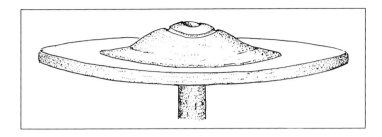

Figure 62. Suggested method for mass production of plates, upside down over jigger attached to wheel head, with reverse being roughly trimmed by a template. The jigger left a characteristic central ridge on obverses.

a

b

c

d

Figure 63. Carinated porringers, *escudillas*, typical of commercialized Sevillian ceramic production during the fifteenth and sixteenth centuries (exteriors trimmed by template and surface defects are characteristic): *a c*, covered with white tin-opacified glaze; *d*, covered with comparable glaze darkened to a gunmetal color through addition of iron oxide or manganese to glaze solution, leaving typical light paste evident; *b*, low ring foot on inverted view may suggest its comparatively late manufacture in the continuum. Specimens average 7.5 cm in diameter (courtesy Museo de Artes y Costumbres Populares, Sevilla [*a–c*], and Museo Arqueológico Provincial, Sevilla [*d*]).

jolly technique also has been detected in contemporary Granadine work, so it cannot be regarded as a method unique to Sevilla.[259]

Small handleless cups or drinking bowls called *tazas* and porringers known as *escudillas* were from 7 to 15 cm across and were easily formed through a throwing technique known to modern potters as "off the hump" (Figs. 57 g–i, 63, 64a). In this method one vessel after another was pulled up from a residual mass of clay revolving on the wheel head. It was a faster procedure than using a single ball of clay for each item. When leather hard, the pieces were recentered upside down on the wheel to be trimmed with an angled iron and one whirl of the wheel. A prominent low carination was formed as the body merged into a narrow, ringless or ringed foot. On the porringers, pairs of solid small lugs with scalloped edges occasionally were attached horizontally in a style common in medieval Europe. A variant appendage was a vertical raised ledge applied to the exterior body walls. The cups and porringers were more variable in size than were the plates, but were similar enough that they could be easily nested together for shipping. The smallest served as *saleros*, or salt cellars.

a

b

Figure 64. White maiolica bowls of commercialized Sevillian ceramic production during fifteenth and sixteenth centuries: *a*, carinated drinking bowl, *taza*, 15 cm in diameter (contour duplicates many contemporary *escudillas*); *b*, flat-based serving bowl with incurved rim (courtesy Museo de Artes y Costumbres Populares, Sevilla).

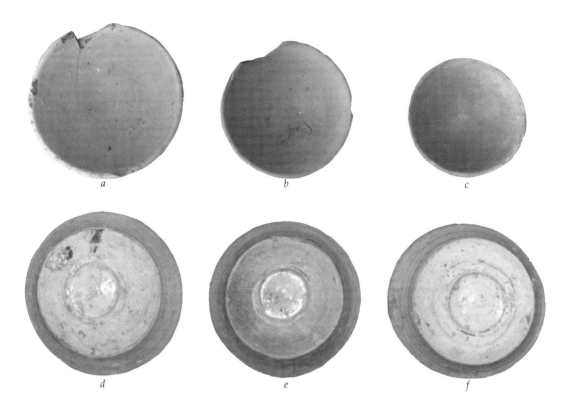

Figure 65. White maiolica bowls typical of fifteenth- to seventeenth-century commercialized Sevillian ceramic production: *a–c*, obverses; *d–f*, reverses (courtesy Museo de Artes y Costumbres Populares, Sevilla).

Less frequently seen forms were somewhat larger bowls of varying dimensions, with flat or convex bottoms and nearly vertical or flared walls (Fig. 65); hemispherical shallow bowls with concave bases; shallow, broad basins (see Fig. 58c); short, flat-based jars with a thickened rolled rim and one pulled handle attached from just below the rim to the lower body (see Fig. 57c); drug jars with a slightly indrawn waist (see Fig. 25b–c); and chamber pots that were straight-sided, broad-mouthed cylinders about 30 cm in height, with wide, thick, horizontal rims and paired looped handles (see Fig. 56a). The large specimens may have been thrown on individual bats secured to the wheel head by slurry. This would have assured their removal from the wheel undamaged. Candleholders had by then replaced the ancient inefficient oil lamps, and were cylindrical tubes springing from a wide saucer base (see Fig. 56d).

The great majority of these housewares were left untrimmed and undecorated, except for simple glazing. Among the lead-glazed vessels, *melado* or green were favored colors. If colorless lead glaze was used and added enhancement was desired, it was an unplanned swipe across the surface with a brush laden with manganese pigment that left a brown, linear, free-form pattern under a

Figure 66. Two blue–and–purple–on–white maiolica plates of a style that appears to have been widespread throughout al Andalus during the fourteenth and fifteenth centuries. The border patterns may represent the last vestiges of the use of Arabic calligraphy in Spanish decorative art (courtesy Instituto Valencia de Don Juan, Madrid).

clear, glossy glaze covering. Most shallow bowls so treated cannot be visually distinguished from bowls made five hundred years earlier.

In the maiolicas, plain whites were most numerous. Otherwise, three general kinds of painted design were used. That with most pronounced ties to the past were pseudo-calligraphic scrawlings between band lines, as though the decorator no longer could write his native tongue but remembered a tradition for using it decoratively (Fig. 66). A second style consisted of encircling lines around centers or rims of open forms laid on by holding a brush against the pot as the wheel revolved, or perhaps as a tow filled with cushioning grass was turned by hand (Figs. 67, 68a). A variation was paired rim lines (Fig. 68b). Occasional Spanish inscriptions across obverses suggest the makers were from the Christian rather than the Muslim component of the potter work force (Fig. 69). A third category of decoration was composed of crudely drafted geometrics spread in a band between encircling lines, with a centerpiece often consisting of a simple crest motif (Fig. 70).

Manganese purple, iron brown or black, copper green, and cobalt blue made up the palette of decorative pigments used against the white glaze. As the century wore on, blue became more common than the other colors, probably as a consequence of growing Italian commercial involvement with Andalusia. It was consistently grayed because of poor refining methods at the source of the cobalt. The green seldom appeared in linear pattern, being seen more often as a glaze solution into which a vessel being finished was partially dipped. Near the end of the century a dark blue ground glaze appeared on exteriors of small drug jars.

The paste used for table and associated domestic wares other than cooking pots was generally the sandy, light-firing Guadalquivir type. The potters were not consistent, however, because some red serving pieces are known, usually bearing lead glazes.

Figure 67. Two small white maiolica plates with decoration of paired blue encircling lines. This was one of the most characteristic modes of Sevillian potteries for much of the fifteenth to mid-seventeenth centuries. The vessel's irregular contours, the uneven lines, and many surface flaws were typical of mass-produced common tablewares used by all levels of Andalusian society, a ware that helped sustain the industry (courtesy Museo de Artes y Costumbres Populares, Sevilla [top], and the Hermitage of Nuestra Señora de la Defensión, La Cartuja, Jérez de la Frontera [bottom]).

2

22

Figure 68. Two small vessels of
the simplest blue–on–white
fifteenth- to seventeenth-century
Sevillian style: *a*, tiny bowl probably used as salt cellar; *b*, squat
chamber pot (courtesy the Hermitage of Nuestra Señora de la
Defensión, La Cartuja, Jérez de la
Frontera [*a*], and Mueso de
Artes y Costumbres Populares,
Sevilla [*b*]).

a   *b*

Figure 69. Two small white
maiolica plates of characteristic
Sevillian paste and mass-
production styling dating from the
second half of the fifteenth century. They were recovered from
an excavated well at the Carthusian monastery outside of Jérez de
la Frontera, and are believed to
have been ordered by the purchasing agent for the friars for use
by lay personnel at the *comunidad*.
The central inscription, painted
before firing in brown pigment,
translates "Servant of the prior."
A single blue line frames the
obverses (courtesy the Hermitage
of Nuestra Señora de la Defensión, La Cartuja, Jérez de la
Frontera).

The three leading tablewares—plates, drinking bowls,
and porringers—that are first known in volume for the
fifteenth century, but that very likely evolved during the
previous century, pose many questions. Why was their
potting so careless, when even the most ordinary of the
contemporary utilitarian vessels often were better made?
Why were their walls left heavy and chunky, their contours misshapen from uneven drying or improper stacking, their glazes blemished with extraneous matter and
cockspur scars? What had happened to the promise of the
white glaze, which on these vessels more often was cream
and shiny, and very thin, heavily crazed, and pitted at
that? When earlier plates and bowls had had ring feet, as
did contemporary Nasrid maiolica, why were they most
often eliminated on this pottery?

There are several explanations for this apparent back-
sliding in technique. One was an inherited attitude that
placed little value on technical perfection in pottery. A
wide latitude of flaws was acceptable, even in the luxurious Nasrid *reflejo metálico*. The almost mechanical precision
of contemporary Italian potting and design was totally
absent in Muslim Spain. The other was an obvious overriding commercialization of this grade of pottery, in which
rapid, volume output was essential because the wares
were sold in unit lots rather than by the piece. Although it
was necessary in order to speed the formation process,
the use of the jigger mounted on the wheel head made it
too time-consuming to thin and compact rims with a
chamois, as might have been done otherwise, or to determine wall thickness by finger pressure. The addition of
a ring foot was a step considered unnecessary for dishes,
which were just as functional without such a finishing
touch. To keep costs down, a semblance of white could be
gained with only a tiny fraction of the usual amounts of
tin oxide, owing to the light color of the base clay. That
allowed the paste to remain visible and the less durable
glaze to become shiny rather than semi-matte, as would
have been the case had more tin been used. It was a matter

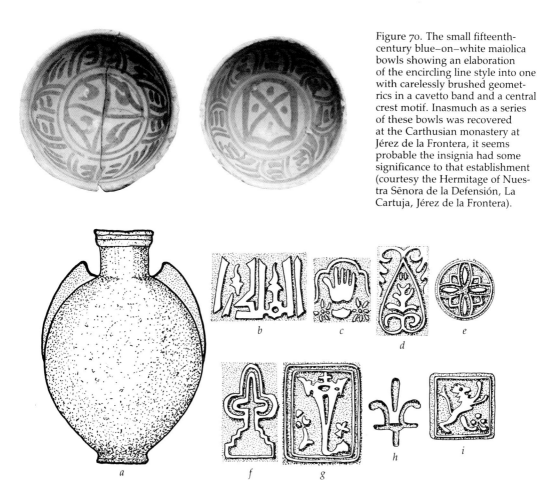

Figure 70. The small fifteenth-century blue–on–white maiolica bowls showing an elaboration of the encircling line style into one with carelessly brushed geometrics in a cavetto band and a central crest motif. Inasmuch as a series of these bowls was recovered at the Carthusian monastery at Jérez de la Frontera, it seems probable the insignia had some significance to that establishment (courtesy the Hermitage of Nuestra Sēnora de la Defensión, La Cartuja, Jérez de la Frontera).

of mass production in a preindustrial craft, which without the controls obtainable through mechanization led to a decline in quality.[260]

Their low caliber notwithstanding, these tablewares were the basic output of the Triana shops and remained thoroughly identified with them for a known two centuries, and probably longer. They and their lead-glazed companion pieces were the dishes used by the mass of commoners who made up the society, and as such doubtless reflected the prevailing poverty. Their volume must be taken as consumer demand. Next to container jars, they were the principal Andalusian ceramic export to a large part of the western Mediterranean, including North Africa and southern Portugal. A well organized means of distribution perfected over time was fundamental to this trade.

A third branch of the ceramic activity was dedicated to continued manufacture of the unwieldly *tinajas* with and without wings (Fig. 71), *pilas bautismales* (Figs. 72a, 73a,

Figure 71. Winged *tinajas*, large storage or water jars present in Andalusia from early Spanish Muslim times through the fifteenth century, often carried stamped or etched patterns that help in identifying their cultural affiliation: *b–e*, some typical Muslim motifs; *f–i*, some typical Christian motifs.

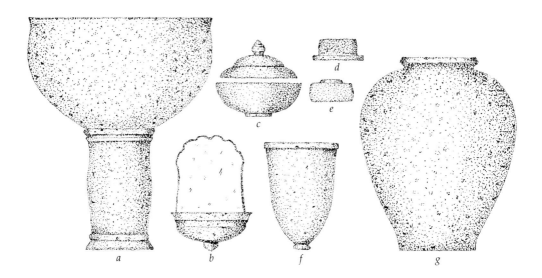

Figure 72. Some Andalusian *mudéjar* and Christian ceramic vessel forms evolved for specialized uses: *a*, large, free-standing, pedestal-based, baptismal font, *pila bautismal*, often with molded raised or incised designs; *b*, moldmade, wall-mounted holy water stoup, *pila de agua bendita*, often with religious motifs in relief; *c*, baptismal font derived from Muslim lidded bowl used for festive occasions; *d*, moldmade container with one or more depressions for sand used as pouncing agent to prevent ink from spreading on unsized paper, and also used for serving condiments; *e*, moldmade inkwell, often with one to four surrounding holes in which to insert writing quills; *f*, unglazed wide-mouthed form with basal drain hole, in which liquid cane juice was allowed to solidify into hard unrefined sugar; *g*, huge decorative jars, usually enriched with raised molded surface patterns and deep green lead glaze.

74), *brocales*, and *jarras* (Figs. 72g, 73b) that had typified the centuries associated with an unadulterated *mudéjar* era in the potting ranks. They were primarily intended for the local secular and clerical upper ranks. All were typically ornamented with some kind of plastic design, either from molding, stamping, appliqué, or carving. The last two methods were more usual at this time. Diagonal patterning on jars produced an unusual sense of excitement in this pottery. Execution of designs by cutting the surface with a broad knife point was increasingly careless. This may be a sign of a worn out tradition slowly coming to an end. Also suggesting change was a noticeable penetration of themes identifiable as Christian rather than Muslim. On *brocales* and *tinajas*, these were such motifs as grape leaves, roses, and other florals. On *pilas*, Gothic letters, monograms of Jesus and Mary, royal initials, crosses, rampant lions, small figures representing Catholic saints, shells, pineapples, and other motifs with symbolic meanings in Christian iconography were present.[261] Only the *pilas* were invariably covered with brilliant green lead glaze, and they were the main objects in this grouping to move overseas as conversion became a driving force in the American conquests. The consumers were the ecclesiastics.

A related form of the time was the heavy, stamped stand made to support a *tinaja* (see Fig. 56c). This was a flat-topped cylinder with a shaped opening in the side wall and a lateral spout to drain water that seeped from the *tinaja*. Success in fashioning these and other large, heavy, highly decorated objects was obvious and must have been owing to a class of specialists with one foot in the Muslim past and the other in the Christian future.

Cuerda seca, another distinctive kind of fifteenth-century

pottery associated with top Sevillian potters, bridged
the two principal heritages of Andalusia. Introduced first
during the tenth century at the caliphate capital, *cuerda
seca* continued to be made sporadically in Andalusia and
Morocco during the *taifa* horizon. It was known by the
Beni Hammad in North Africa, as seen on some eleventh-
century tiles; another example found at Dsira is dated
ca. 1152.[262] In the next century, with the advent of tin solutions, the style was improved by the elimination of engobe
that frequently became chalky. Furthermore, richer, more
lustrous effects were inherent in the opaque glaze. Design
entailed outlining a composition with a tinted greasy
substance to which glaze would not adhere, and then filling the circumscribed elements with colored glazes. It
was a time-consuming, painstaking task, but the materials
used cost no more than those for *alicatado* tile blanks or
for conventional tin-glazed dishes. Only two firings were
required. Therefore, beginning in the late fourteenth

a

b

Figure 73. Fifteenth-century
Sevillian *mudéjar* ceramics that
continued into sixteenth century:
a, pila bautismal; b, large jar,
jarrón. Both objects are covered
with thick green lead glaze (courtesy Museo Arqueológico Provincial, Sevilla).

Figure 74. Wooden retable panel
in Granada cathedral showing
Muslims enduring a forced baptism in 1502 by being anointed
with holy water in a *pila bautismal.*

century and continuing until well into the sixteenth century, *cuerda seca* became an outlet through which capable
Sevillian craftsmen expressed their aesthetic interests.
Perhaps one can see in the *cuerda seca* production a new
elaboration in the traditional Sevillian potting structure,
with a group of particularly talented individuals becoming
solely decorators. The pieces on which they worked were
comparable to those of the usual catalog, which suggests
the advent of a premium grade. That would have been
a new development in Sevillian ceramics. Plates, in particular, are identical to the tin-glazed series in size and have
the diagnostic central mold-induced ridge. The clay used,
however, was red, which when left unglazed made a
better definition between parts of the pattern.

The *cuerda seca* technique, not unlike modern wax resist,
had limitations. In the caliphate period the motifs were
carried by pigments without much fluxant, but glaze used
by the fifteenth century presented a problem: the method
was best employed on the uninterrupted flat grounds
offered by plates and tiles.[263] Because plates and tiles were
fired horizontally, molten glaze had less opportunity to
flow and spoil basic defining lines. It is no accident that
the majority of the known fifteenth-century *cuerda secas* are
of these two forms. Vessels worked from modifications
of a cylinder are seen, including drug jars, other jars,
finials, costrels, and pitchers, but they are not common.[264]
However, *cuerda seca* finials, spaced along flat roof lines,
became a unique architectural additive and one which has
continued to modern times.

The method was not suited to fine-lined, complex interlacements, or *lacerías*, such as were appearing on contemporary *reflejo metálico*. These make *cuerda seca* seem crude
by comparison. *Cuerda seca* patterns had to be simplified
and made bolder. Although typical Muslim radial, quartering, or other segmenting of composition was rather frequent and all-over imbrications did occur, the most
characteristic treatment was that of a large, isolated, central, figural element surrounded by a confused, casually
spaced array of geometric or stylized floral motifs (Fig.
75).[265] The figures themselves were animated long–eared
rabbits, fantastic griffins, and birds drawn from a background originally thought to be Fatimid Egyptian,[266] which
had become naturalized on Spanish Muslim pottery since
the tenth century.[267] As Italian Renaissance themes began
to make themselves known in Andalusia late in the fifteenth century, human heads in profile replaced the
assortment of eastern animals. At the same time, line work
and realistic representation were refined.[268] Westernization
was winning the day.

Figure 75. Late fifteenth- or early sixteenth-century Sevillian *cuerda seca* ceramics. Left, rare pitcher with throat modeled like human head; right, small plate with typical large, central, isolated figure (courtesy Museo Arqueológico Nacional, Madrid).

Unlike the huge impressed vessels that probably saw greatest use in public places, those bearing *cuerda seca* decoration were of sorts meant for private upper-class homes, such as the palaces of the Dukes of Alba and Medinaceli and the Pinelo family.[269] They were special ceramics when made and were handled cautiously by their users. A large number have survived the devastation of time, the elements, and human beings to come to rest in private collections and museums.[270] Their high survival rate in protected circumstances may exaggerate the amount of original production. Sevillian *cuerda seca* vessels were not commonly exported.

After *alicatado* began to lose its appeal in the first half of the fifteenth century, the *cuerda seca* method was extended to tile meant to be mounted on walls, as in the eastern manner, rather than on floors, as elsewhere in eastern Spain and Europe. Such tile seems not to have been especially popular, although some examples remain.

Cuerda seca was soon replaced by another means of tile design called *cuenca*, or *arista*. This was a process wherein moist cut tile blanks were impressed with a mold or incised mallet to create ridges, or arrises, of clay, in order to define various patterns (see Fig. 49a–b). The low spaces between the ridges of the pattern were painted with colored glazes. These zones were prevented from running during firing by the raised portions of the designs. *Cuenca* probably was regarded as a faster, cheaper way of getting somewhat the same effects as in the two previous tile techniques. Many of the same Moresque compositions were transferred to the new method. The pattern being obtained from pressure on wet clay, the method was not suitable for use on hollow ware because deformation of form would result. It can be postulated that a segregated group of potters, who formerly also made and decorated

hollow wares, now confined their energies entirely to
the decoration of tiles destined for churches and a few rich
homes. It was they and their craft descendants who,
inspired by a European energizing force known as the
Renaissance, would thrill the decorative arts world in the
upcoming century.

Once the Nasrid secret of the technology behind *reflejo
metálico* was out, it was feasible for Sevillian *mudéjares*
to have taken up its manufacture. What was lacking was
the essential financial backing that the emirate rulers
and the Manises usurper provided. Without such patronage, the venture could not have survived. So, although
a late fifteenth-century reference reported *tiendas de
dorado*[271] in Sevilla, there is no evidence as yet that lusterware actually was made there, except for a few sixteenth-
century tiles. For reasons not now understood, local
maiolica pottery was referred to occasionally as "Málaga"
pottery.

Owing to the presence of Italians in Sevilla and to their
continued connections with relatives and businesses in
their homeland, the first repercussions of the Renaissance
began to be felt in Andalusia at about the middle of the
fifteenth century. Decadence in the arts, such as was
apparent in the low-grade maiolicas, paved the way for
the successful intrusion of this new cultural vitality. Renaissance humanistic art was further popularized in a part
of Spain long under the shadow of Islam by the Catholic
Kings, who in 1484 encouraged Italian and Flemish artisans to settle there by granting them a ten-year exemption
from taxes.[272] The golden age of the Florentine artistic
explosion was in progress. Italian potters, who earlier had
borrowed from the Muslims and the Valencians, were
at the time working out procedural and design refinements
destined to influence all western European glazed earthenwares.

Three direct manifestations of Italian impact on ceramics
appeared in Sevilla during the second half of the fifteenth
century. Colossal earthenware statues were modeled
for the new cathedral. Those representing the twelve
apostles, made by the local sculptor Pedro Millán and his
disciples, were smashed when the lantern at the Sevilla
cathedral fell in December, 1511. They may have resembled a surviving set made in Barcelona by the Claperos
family.[273] Although their rendition owed much to Gothic
style, they bore witness to a new interest in representations of the human form that would be seen in thousands
of figures in the round, some of which were made of
glazed earthenware. In another venture, Millán provided
the parish church of Santa Paula with glazed relief tondos

in the Della Robbia manner (Fig. 76).[274] This was a relatively isolated interpretation and was repeated only a few other times in Sevilla, but it is evidence for rejuvenated interest in ceramic craftsmanship and for a style broken free from all traces of *mudéjar* influences. The third Italianate ceramic expression focused on that favorite of all Sevillians, tile. A tilemaker and painter from Pisa, one Francisco Niculoso, arrived in Sevilla in 1498, purchased a Triana *casa de ollería*, and introduced *pisano* smooth-surfaced polychrome tile panels. These, in time, would revolutionize Spanish tile production and make Sevillian ceramists admired in two hemispheres.[275]

With the swelling tide of Renaissance ideals washing over Andalusia came a subtle shift in popular attitude, which would culminate in an incredible artistic flowering at Sevilla. Southern Castilians somewhat reluctantly began to realize that handwork could be accomplished proudly by Christians. *Mudéjar* workmanship in the mechanical arts had continued to be admired, even though political and religious beliefs were on the point of driving these elements from Spain. It was a free Muslim who had been put in charge of continuing tile and other projects at the *alcázar* and its constellation of Alcoba, Alcobilla, and Retiro gardens. Sevillian Muslim masons were dispatched to Málaga to build a Catholic church after the Muslims there were conquered. It was Moorish craftsmen from Sevilla who were rushed to the Alhambra after its fall to undertake repairs, and it was probably Sevilla's Muslims, converted or not, who built her spectacular cathedral.[276] As the fifteenth century was ending and the medieval mentality was altering, some Christian potters for the first time since the reconquest were beginning to break class barriers

Figure 76. Tondos in Italian Della Robbia style with glazed poly-chromed reliefs of molded fruits and human figures were made in the late fifteenth century by Sevillian artist Pedro Millán for the facade of the local Santa Paula church. In the early sixteenth century they were surrounded by flat-surfaced polychrome tiles made and decorated by Niculoso, an Italian potter who had moved to Sevilla.

and social stigmas. One such artisan was Fernán Martínez Guijarro, a tiler, whose work was so widely distributed and admired that in appreciation the Crown granted him an exemption from taxes.[277] At last talent was on the brink of being as important as birth, only to be curbed in the next century by a blinding concern for purity of blood. In Sevilla, predictably, it was the tilers who prospered, rather than the makers of hollow ware.

The ceramic turn toward Italian sources of inspiration was hastened by the defeat of the Nasrids. The liquidation of the Nasridian culture and the departure of their top flight decorators brought an end to the stream of influence that for seven centuries had filtered to the western frontiers of Islam from as far away as Mesopotamia, Syria, Egypt, and Persia to reinvigorate the pottery-making craft. The remaining *mudéjares*, shortly to be transformed into *moriscos*, merged into lesser levels of the potting industry and slowly sank into mindless repetition of age-old styles.

To climax this century, in 1492 the first Andalusian pottery reached the New World aboard the Niña, the Pinta, and the Santa María.

SIXTEENTH AND SEVENTEENTH CENTURIES: MEETING GROUND OF THE OLD AND THE NEW

Historicultural Background

The history of sixteenth-century Sevilla, and by extension that of the province of Spain of which it was the capital, falls into two parts centering on mid-century. By most accounts the Age of Discovery, the first thirty years when Spaniards found, explored, and exploited new lands encircling the Caribbean, had little immediate beneficial impact upon the city. Still a frontier, the town dozed along as a slow-paced regional market with few modifications in its life style. Times were hard, with many unemployed in spite of the monopoly given Sevilla as a lifeline to the overseas Spaniards. No more than passing attention was paid the occasional parties of rash explorers or adventurers sailing from its harbor, who had anchored for provisioning within a stone's throw of the Triana potteries. The population, variously estimated at from fifty thousand to seventy thousand,[278] actually decreased because of great loss of life from virulent epidemics and the accidents and rigors of the voyage to the Americas.[279]

The society was strictly stratified.[280] At the top were a few large noble families drawing income from extensive agricultural holdings in the lower Guadalquivir Valley but preferring to dwell in town. Below them was a more unstable class of merchants, mostly foreigners or con-

verted Jews, moving with the political and commercial
tides. They were matched by members of the clergy, who
thrived on Sevillian piety. The large block of the citizenry
was made up of small tradesmen, artisans, and menial
laborers, free but destitute. At the bottom of the social
scale were numbers of Negro and Berber slaves, *moriscos*,
and a throng of riffraff unassimilated and living outside
the orbit of community life.

As the daring landing on the Mexican mainland and the
penetration of the west coast of South America slowly
changed from bloody conquest to colonization buttressed
by productive mines and *haciendas*, the pace of life in
the Andalusian port of supply accelerated. In the past the
city had been largely dependent upon the fortunes of
agriculture, but that economic base changed. The chain of
colonial events that made Spain a dominant power in
Europe transformed Sevilla into the wealthiest, largest,
most cosmopolitan and unique metropolis in the empire.
The once sleepy provincial capital became an active
administrative and commercial city, as well as a leading
money-lending market and redistribution center for the
articles of Europe. Its port complex, which included the
facilities of Sanlúcar de Barrameda and Cádiz on the coast,
was supported by a rich agricultural hinterland. New
businesses focusing on overseas trade were launched.
The years between 1530 and 1535 saw a sharp increase in
tonnage of transatlantic shipments, which coincided with
a general period of economic expansion elsewhere in
western Europe.[281] Sea loans helped stabilize this activity.
No longer were merchants themselves travelers to far-
off places. They tended to stay in the comfort of Sevilla
and put up funds for an agent, or factor, who handled
commercial affairs in the colonies. Often this was a family
member, such as a son. Revenues proved exciting. Owing
to circumstances thousands of miles away, a crescendo
of enterprise had evolved by the middle of the century to
produce a full-scale financial boom. Typically, it was characterized by quick wealth from a single shipment, or by
sudden ruin if a galleon and its cargo went to the bottom.

Additionally, the burgeoning colonial trade brought
about revitalization of Sevilla's own *mudéjar*-derived specialties, such as silk weaving, processing of fine leather,
gold smithing, embroidery, and intricate marquetry. Foreign markets were served by traders from elsewhere who
operated in the city and who were responsible for further
stimulation of craft activity. Tomás de Mercado, a Dominican traveler, in 1569 wrote that Sevilla

is on fire with all manner of business. There are great real-
exchanges for all fairs, within and without the kingdom, sales
and purchases on credit and for cash, and for huge sums, great

shipments, and *baratas* for many thousands and millions, such as neither Tyre nor Alexandria in their day could equal.[282]

The first kind of transaction to which he referred, real-exchange, was the aboveboard passing of hard cash in return for goods received. *Barata* (in Spanish meaning *cheap*) was a complicated, and often unethical, process wherein a person bought goods on credit, then immediately sold them to himself for cash at sometimes as much as twenty-five to thirty percent below market value, with the goods never having left the shop.

Behind every such commercial gamble, whether on land or sea, was the tantalizing possibility of upward social mobility. This was especially attractive to Sevillians for whom ennoblement and attached prestige were fiercely sought goals. It now was possible for formerly poor members of the society to become well-to-do and for well-to-do persons to become aristocrats.

Within a mere fifty years Sevilla's population more than doubled. The Santa Ana parish in Triana quadrupled, as laborers and artisans of all sorts flocked there to share in the new prosperity and spread out into raw areas back from the river. Such movement of workers from rural to urban locales was occurring across much of western Europe during the sixteenth century.[283] On the opposite bank the cluster of slums called the Arenal, in the lee of a tremendous hillock of refuse, bustled with ceaseless activity. Its empty lands were piled with great heaps of commodities brought from all parts of Europe to await shipment westward. The harbor, which remained just a wide stretch of the Guadalquivir above the old Almohad Torre del Oro, was clogged with ships of every description riding at anchor and with small craft freighting supplies to or from them (Fig. 77).

The changes brought by the new era served to intensify the glaring contrasts and inequalities that always had been characteristic of Sevilla. Within the ancient walls of the city proper, particularly in the Santa María *collación*, urban renewal was avidly undertaken. Palaces were erected or refurnished for those who had grown rich from the transatlantic trade. Shabby buildings from Muslim or reconquest times finally were torn down to create open spaces for central *plazas*. An elaborate city hall structure was built on one of them to replace the smelly fish market, which for centuries had been cheek to jowl with the cathedral. The bell tower of that edifice got a grandiose weathervane that could be seen for miles and balconies were added to its facade. Nearby, many new shops lined a tangle of narrow streets to become known later as the Sierpes district.

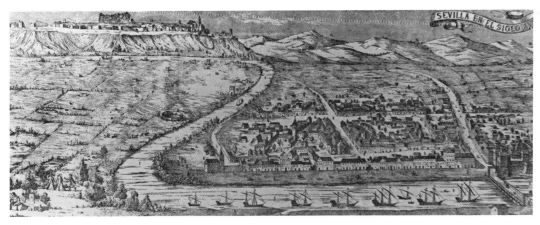

Many of these elegant facades of cut stone faced on to rutted streets strewn with filth accumulated through the centuries and with construction debris that now was left where it fell. The king was forced to issue an edict against further pollution.[284] The squalid, sunbaked mud brick houses that sheltered much of the populace might be splashed with whitewash at festival times, but they remained without improvements that would have made them more comfortable and sanitary. Everywhere the sweet scent of orange blossoms competed with the stale aromas of fried fish, rancid olive oil, old cesspools, and the rot of centuries.

The mix of peoples equalled the environmental diversity. Not only were there large communities of Italians, Flemish, Portuguese, French, and German traders jostling with local Andalusians for some of the crumbs of the commerce, there were converted Muslims and Jews left over from former times. Hundreds of slaves, who served in the homes of aristocrats, clergy, business men, and artisans, were blacks brought in by Spanish and Portuguese slavers from Africa, Muslims captured along the

Figure 77. Artist's conception of view of Sevilla and its extramural *barrio* of Triana in the sixteenth century. ABOVE: Sevilla, on the east bank of the Rió Guadalquivir. Left foreground, Triana castle and pontoon bridge; left center, Santa María de las Cuevas, La Cartuja; center front, Arenal; right rear, cathedral; right foreground, Torre del Oro at junction of Guadalquivir and Río Tagarete. BELOW: Triana, on the west bank of the Río Guadalquivir. Right foreground, pontoon bridge, Triana castle, and road leading toward the *vega*, or meadow, where some potters owned farm plots; center, houses where potteries and other small handicraft activities were concentrated, with Santa Ana parish church in their midst; left rear, Castle of Hasnalfarache, originally built by Muslims to guard the river traffic; left center on east bank, plains of Tablada.

Mediterranean during continuing pirating, and even some hapless Native Americans. All but the enslaved experienced a blatant materialism that eddied through the *barrios* like morning fog from the marshlands. Such emphasis was placed on sumptuousness that the Crown repeatedly, and fruitlessly, issued restrictions against extravagance. Illustrative of this prevalent fascination with ostentation, a late sixteenth-century listing of artisans working in Sevilla shows that the most numerous group was made up of goldsmiths and silversmiths. They outnumbered the second group, the painters, by two to one, and the third group, the potters, by more than four to one. The next six groups, in order, were carvers, swordmakers, embroiderers, gilders, gunsmiths, and knifemakers.[285]

The imbalance in the distribution of wealth steadily grew greater, even though a larger body of middlemen had some share in the rewards. While rich families lavishly supported artisans to create works for the beautification of their homes and the many local churches, a sizable segment of the populace remained on the edge of abject poverty.[286] Beggars swarmed the streets. The jail across from the cathedral overflowed with men and women who were condemned to be there for not paying debts. Robbers and ruffians were so brazen that it was unsafe to venture out at night unarmed. General lawlessness prevailed.

In the countryside also there was prosperity in the second half of the sixteenth century because of overseas demand for Andalusian olive oil and wine, which were controlled by a monopoly. As prices rose throughout the century and as the returns on crops increased, however, their real value was reduced by higher costs of services. Ultimately, in Andalusia and in Europe generally, the peasantry actually was worse off at this time than in earlier centuries.[287]

The first of the disasters of the seventeenth century, which reduced Spain to a second-rate power and Sevilla to an exhausted commercial appendage of empire, was the final expulsion of the *moriscos* between 1609 and 1614 under the reign of Felipe III (Table 3). In the one hundred seventeen years since the Nasrid defeat, efforts had been made to impose Castilian religious and social conformity upon this large minority. These onerous restrictions, heavy taxation, and a swelling popular prejudice against the *moriscos* made them openly defiant and rebellious, resulting in great loss of life and property. Finally, deep-seated suspicions of heresy and subversion and the Crown's demoralizing loss of will to attempt peaceful solutions to the problem made their exile inevitable. Many

Table 3. Spanish Hapsburgs
1516–1700

Carlos I (Charles V of the Holy Roman Empire)	1516–1556
Felipe II	1556–1598
Felipe III	1598–1621
Felipe IV	1621–1665
Carlos II	1665–1700

of those still remaining in the mountains around Granada and scattered through the Guadalquivir basin moved directly south to Moroccan shores, where for generations they continued to identify themselves as Andalusians. The effects on their former province of the loss of this cheap work force that had kept the physical labors of existence on track continue to be debated, but there doubtless were severe consequences.

As the seventeenth century continued to unfold, other troubles for Andalusia came with successive floods, droughts, famines, warfare, and uprisings. The 1649 catastrophe, a plague of unprecedented severity that took fifteen hundred or more lives—some estimate that as much as half of Sevilla's population was wiped out—caused further havoc and a pervading atmosphere of crisis from which most unstable crafts never recovered.[288] Also devastating was the bankruptcy of the nation. Braudel notes five Spanish financial crises that finally brought down the Italian money houses. He blames these disasters on a combination of factors, including dishonest Sevillian city officials and the dominance of trade by foreigners.[289] Destructive laws barring the luxurious articles typical of Sevillian handwork put large numbers of people out of work. Competition from other European factories and declining commercial exchange with the American colonies added to problems caused by increasing migration overseas. By mid-century numerous industries complained of exhaustion. Associated craft guilds died.[290] Convoys of ships departing Sevilla became more and more infrequent. After 1620 the drop in transatlantic shipping was dramatic.[291] Another setback was the sanding up of the Río Guadalquivir, making hazardous the passage of larger ships. Stores closed. Houses fell into ruin. Garbage mounted until the city gates could not be closed.[292]

The sixteenth century was a time of economic expansion throughout western Europe and the seventeenth one of contraction. Much of the beginning upturn was stimulated by a reorientation of trade from the eastern Mediterranean to the Atlantic. Industrial activity grew in an attempt to raise standards of life and satisfy an insatiable taste for luxuries. Basic to it was the flow of precious metals from the Americas to Spain, and thence to her creditors. Small-scale artisan crafts meant for regional distribution gave way to large-scale manufacturing destined to flow through international channels. This shift in emphasis entailed accelerated division and depersonalization of labor and to conflicts between employers and employees. England and the Netherlands emerged as industrialized, capitalistic states. At the same time, there was a spread of the inflationary trends of rising prices and decreasing purchasing power that troubled Spain. Costs of finished goods and wages increased by a factor of four. The years between 1623 and 1650 were years of depression, with resurgence later in the century being slow to come.[293]

Social distinctions that developed in the sixteenth and seventeenth centuries between Spain and her neighbors in western Europe, which over time would widen into an unbridgeable cultural gulf, were partially due to the wholehearted acceptance outside of the Iberian peninsula of the secular aspects of the Renaissance and the Reformation.

Pottery History and Technology

Archaeological investigation in the Spanish colonies in the Caribbean and central Mexico, together with more limited excavations in and near Sevilla, indicate a pattern of development in Andalusian pottery remarkably parallel to this history and to the great social and environmental disparities. For the first half of the century the main body of local ceramics continued virtually unchanged from its fifteenth century quality and kind. *Loza basta* and the crudely fashioned lead- and tin-glazed tablewares, with all their imperfections, accounted for most of the output. Crude, cheap, and functional, they universally were used by most people.

At the same time, as political and social inclinations tugged at the ancient *mudéjar* anchorage, there were telltale signs of that tradition's weakening hold. Manganese underglaze decorations on some of lead-glazed pieces no longer consisted of Arabic inscriptions or eight-pointed stars. The massive green or unglazed well heads, storage jars, and baptismal fonts continued to be made, but less frequently bore the eastern assortment of designs. In maiolicas there was a slide into extinction of the type with blue and purple decorations and a much corrupted Arabic phrase.[294] Simple paired blue lines around interior rims or centers of plates and bowls or around exterior rims of jars were frequent. There was the tendency to fuller, although usually careless, blue patterning on white, none of which was overtly Islamic.[295] This pattern generally was composed of hastily brushed geometrics or an occasional figural element, such as a bird. Workmanship remained casual, with typical disregard for spacing or thoughtful draftsmanship. For more monied clients, changes in pottery also were few. In tile, the *cuerda seca* technique more often gave way to *cuenca*. There was an undercurrent of alien influence expressed in some Renaissance-inspired motifs on *cuerda seca* plates.[296] For the first time since the tenth century, foreign ceramics, now wholly Italian, began to infiltrate local markets. Otherwise, it was potting as usual in what had become the tired Andalusian manner.

In Granada, the court wares for which Nasrid craftsmen had been famous for several centuries disappeared with that dynasty. Domestic vessels of types long widespread among both Andalusian Muslims and Christians continued to be produced. Some workshops functioned in old surroundings in that city, the *albaicín* sector near the Faja-lauza gate having remained a potters' district. Others are known to have been set up by *morisco* squatters in the precincts of the Alhambra palace. Kiln debris found there contains bits of red-cored white maiolica.[297] In Málaga, several Christian potters began work as the Muslims withdrew; their kitchen vessels probably could not be distinguished.[298] Large numbers of the Granadine *moriscos* were relocated in the old Sevillian *morería* and in the Triana quarter, where it is likely that the potters among them were readily absorbed into the local industry. Their expertise must have strengthened the craft, but it did not alter its basic modes.

Export of Andalusian ceramics to the New World during the first half of the sixteenth century has been substantially confirmed in the past thirty years, but the range of forms bound for the colonies greatly expanded from what had comprised the usual earlier foreign trade. No longer was it merely a matter of shipping out two or three regional specialties in certain kinds of ceramic packaging or several basic pottery shapes suitable for common table use and hoping to find a clientele in a competitive market. Now it was supplying a wide variety of objects with which sixteenth century Spaniards felt obliged to carry on their daily lives, whether at home or thousands of miles across an ocean. The latter did not have to be convinced that these were things important to their well-being; they comprised a ready-made, distant market. In the trade in glazed earthenwares for household uses, therefore, such items as candleholders, urinals, various serving bowls, mortars, and pitchers were added to the more expectable consignments of plates, bowls, and porringers. Many of the familiar unglazed ceramics also were dispatched, for the first time among them basins, water *ollas*, storage receptacles, or expendable molds to be used in sugar refining. Architectural terra cottas such as floor and roof tiles and bricks likewise filled the holds of outward-bound galleons.

In higher caliber wares, Sevillian-made *cuerda secas* only rarely left Andalusia, a clue to the lack of monied buyers in the early sixteenth century. A few baptismal fonts and *cuenca* tiles ordered for overseas churches reaffirmed both Spanish intention to stay and their dependence upon Andalusian craftsmanship.

A great expansion in kind, as well as quantity, of vessel forms came in the branch of the pottery industry devoted to making containers for comestibles and nonedible necessities. The migrant Spaniards, most of whom were determined to explore new lands and to seek their treasures, rather than to settle down to provide for themselves, continued to expect an uninterrupted Andalusian diet. As economic historians Pierre and Huguette Chanunu write, the Andalusians followed "long established eating habits at the price of veritable economic lunacy."[299] To get basic supplies and a surprising array of nonessential foodstuffs to them, it was necessary to deal with new problems. For example, there was a combination of destructive elements that previously had not posed so great a threat in the external commerce carried on with foreigners closer at hand: contaminating bilge water, weevils, rats, spoilage from excessive heat in cargo holds or exposure on deck, and rough seas that thrashed cargoes about. But potential financial gains were commensurate. Therefore, going out to the Indies were wine, olive oil, vinegar, raisins, almonds, figs, olives in brine, fish, rice, flour, *garabanzos*, honey, lard, eggplants, capers, various medicines, turpentine, gunpowder, and pitch. These were packed in earthenware containers variously described as *jarras*, *botijas*, and *cántaros* of several capacities, *botes*, and *cazuelas*.[300] Some of these terms were synonymous; others designate forms later known by other names. In this light, *cazuela* may perhaps be taken to mean *lebrillo*; *jarra* in some instances is the *cantimplora* or *ánfora*. The *botija*, today a form with two spouts, hardly plausible in the context

of sixteenth-century shipping records, probably was an
ánfora. The vessel containing special commodities such as
conserves, spices, orange cordial, and rose-flavored sugar
was called a *bote*. *Botes* and *jarros de barro* also carried
medicines. Presently, *bote* usually refers to a high-shouldered, full-bodied jar (see Fig. 25f). However, the form
most commonly found archaeologically that can be associated with known drug use is the cylindrical *albarelo* (see
Fig. 25b–c), a term that does not appear in the shipping
records. A comparable chaotic situation exists in regard to
sizes of these objects. Because the base capacity is not
positively known, neither the Castilian diminutive nor
augmentative is helpful.

One specialized product may have been shipped in
small *albarelos* 7 to 8 inches high and covered with dark
blue tin-opacified glaze. The paste and form were typically
Andalusian; the glaze color was one often seen among
Italian earthenwares.[301] It is possible that this hybrid container may have held a popular medicated treacle salve
that was a Genoese monopoly.[302] One can *speculate* about
an Italian entrepreneur in Sevilla running a business in the
redistribution of a product acquired in bulk from his
hometown, then packed in locally obtained earthenwares
meeting his specifications. A single pottery may have
supplied those drug containers. The number recovered is
not large, although the time encompassed by archaeological finds may be up to fifty years. Provocative also is
the fact that thus far they are unknown in sixteenth-century deposits in Sevilla or its environs.

Although neither this variety of goods nor containers
had been sent abroad in the centuries prior to the American enterprise, provincial traders since Muslim times
had found quickly made pottery to be more practical and
cheaper for short-term packaging purposes than leather or
fiber bags or wooden or metal boxes. Domestic buyers
often were expected to reuse such jars and jugs for transporting their purchases home. Overseas, these containers
had to be considered expendable. Doubtless their modest
cost was added into the final retail price. Moreover,
through general practice, certain other ceramic shapes had
become commonly accepted means of measuring volumes
or weights of specific produce. For instance, a *botija* was
conceded to contain 5 to 8 liters of liquid, a *cántara* of
oil some 16 liters, and a *garrafa* 20 liters, although there
was a great deal of regional variation and inexactitude was
normal.[303] Some explicit metrological standardizations
had been attempted by Alfonzo X in the thirteenth century,
and later by Isabela and Fernando in the fifteenth century,

in order to establish uniformity and to reduce fraudulent
practices. They were never universally applied. However
inconsistent, measuring vessels were accepted as usual
equipment at vending stalls in Sevillian markets. It is not
known when and to what degree such quantitative controls were applied to the colonial trade, but before the
century was out they definitely had become a fixed part of
transactions. Possibly they were regulations put in force
by the *Casa de Contratación*, or Board of Trade, after its
founding in 1503. Nevertheless, neither strict sizing of
ceramic forms nor inflexible nomenclature followed. One
might argue that such mental orderliness was counter
to the independent attitudes that had evolved along the
Andalusian frontier.

It is impossible to judge whether the volume of American commerce was sufficient to cause any appreciable
increase in the number of working potters in early
sixteenth-century Sevilla or in the country shops that may
have fed mundane vessels and other low grade objects
into that emporium. Even with augmentation of the work
force by *morisco* refugees, an increased number of names
of potters dredged from municipal and ecclesiastical files
may have been owing to greater zealousness in document-
ing all aspects of Spanish life that came during the reign
of Isabela and Fernando. Nor can one assume their total
output was necessarily greater than before; the normal
external traffic may merely have been redirected, as well
as diversified. What is seen as lack of initiative in gearing
up to meet any possible increased demand for their goods,
such as creation of a new line designed for colonial customers, was to open the door to foreign competition.

The first non-Spanish wares to reach the New World
were Italian, not an unexpected development, inasmuch as
Italian merchants in Sevilla had been granted permission
to work the otherwise closed colonial field in return for
favors to the Crown.[304] The earliest identifiable of these
earthenwares came from the Tuscan village of Montelupo,
near Florence, and likely were distributed by Pisan fleets.
Brightly colored polychromatic maiolicas or others decorated only in dark blue and datable to the first half of the
sixteenth century were so decidedly different from the
humdrum Sevillian pottery of the time that they must have
been prized as special pieces to give a lift to householders
who were having to make do in far away places. That
would have elevated their sale price. In Italy, however,
the Montelupo maiolicas were considered a cheap ware for
lower class consumers.[305]

In 1554 the taxes paid by Sevillian makers of unglazed

earthenwares were nearly nineteen times greater than
for those turning out glazed vessels. A large portion of
those taxes must have resulted from container production.
In that same year pottery making as a whole was ranked
eighth in importance in a listing of fifty-three local
occupations.[306]

About the middle of the sixteenth century the booming
economy that charged all aspects of Sevillian life also
brought changes in its pottery industry. These emanated
from two distinct sources. One was purely economic
and colonial. The other was a repeat of what happened so
often in Andalusia: an actual movement of foreign artisans
into the region. That also had economic implications.

Of greatest importance, owing to stepped up activity
and to the number of persons gainfully employed in it,
was the container trade. There were no improvements in
the ways in which these receptacles were fashioned or
in their quality. The emphasis was on quantity. That was
partly the result of scarcity of wood out of which to make
sufficient numbers of kegs or barrels.[307] Coincident with
this effort was a more regulated transatlantic intercourse
following the institution of a convoy, or *flota*, system
to discourage pirating, increased overseas population
attempting real colonization, and at home a stimulating
spirit of gain.

Because of colonial demand arising from engrained
drinking and cooking habits and official sanctions against
the raising of grapes and olives in the Indies or New
Spain, the trade in consumables changed from one supplying many articles in a half-dozen different earthenware
forms into a restricted concentration on wine and its secondary issue, vinegar, and on olive oil or, less commonly,
olives in brine.[308] These were poured into one of two
principal jar shapes. Wine became the most important of
these exports. Colonials gradually were weaned away
from cooking with olive oil in favor of oils of various New
World plants or animal fats. For wine there was no substitute, other than rum made from the introduced sugar
cane. Wine was ordered by the nobility, clergy, military,
doctors, government officials, and all others with the necessary wherewithal. In the course of the ensuing one
hundred fifty years millions of gallons of it, and lesser
quantities of the other typical liquids, went from Andalusia to the Americas. Often wine was the entire cargo.
The number of throw-away earthenware receptacles
needed to carry it from winery to imbiber reached staggering proportions. The ban against wineries and olive oil
production in parts of Spanish America, intended to bene-

Figure 78. Sixteenth- and seventeenth-century unglazed earthenware containers made to be
used for shipping Andalusian
foodstuffs to foreign markets.
Their production, running into the
millions of pieces, occupied a
large proportion of the local potting force; *a–b*, two slightly
differing versions of the *cantimplora*, descended from the pilgrim
bottle of the ancient Near East
and abandoned as a primary wine
or olive oil container about mid
sixteenth century but retained for
other uses; *c*, spheroid *ánfora*,
perhaps best known as *botija perulera* in the colonial transatlantic
trade, which continued the
regional preference for globular
amphorae begun by the Baetican
Romans; *d–e*, two variations of the
elongated tapered *ánfora*, also
ultimately derived from Roman
protoypes; *f*, elongated amphorae
recovered from beneath seven-
teenth- and eighteenth-century
Sevillian house floors, where they
had been laid as a protective
measure against subsurface seepage. All such recovered vessels
were obvious factory rejects, made
unfit for commercial purposes
by various firing accidents. None
had gone through a glaze firing
(courtesy Museo Arqueológico
Provincial, Sevilla).

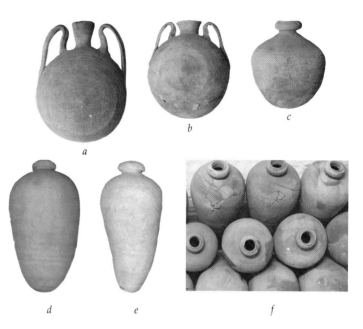

fit Andalusian agriculturalists, vintners, and oil extraction
mill operators, indirectly supported troops of Andalusian
potters as well. Everyone gained, except perhaps the
voluntarily expatriated Spaniards.

This commercialization of one kind of pottery was not
new to Andalusia, a similar development having been
seen in Roman amphorae and Muslim *arcaduces*. But the
sixteenth-century structuring of the container production
was a more gradual evolution, so that there unquestionably was an overlapping of early and late forms used for
similar functions. The *cantimplora* was replaced at some
point as the usual vessel for the purpose. It continued to
be made for other needs, as a 1590 bill of lading for merchandise bound for Havana attests (Appendix 2), and
the newly approved form to substitute for it appears in
related accounts as early as 1542 (Appendix 2).[309] The *cantimplora* handles, neck, and thin walls likely were too vulnerable in large-scale, roughly handled shipping, and
its customary capacity was limited to about 5 liters (Fig.
78a–b). Moreover, its creation may have been considered
unnecessarily involved for rapid production. In this
regard, the role of the *Casa de Contratación* needs to be
examined to determine if it played a part in the change to
other forms; it is likely, inasmuch as all aspects of the
transatlantic trade came under its authority. Perhaps
through an ordinance it promulgated, two modifications
of the traditional amphora were designed as the acceptable
shipping containers. One was a high-shouldered jar nar-

rowing to a rounded base. The other was spheroidal and round-bottomed (Fig. 78c–e). It was this form variant that had the most direct roots in Roman Baetica. Handles and necks were omitted on both kinds of jars, but thickened rings strengthened orifices to reduce breakage. They likely were stoppered with wooden or cork plugs.[310] Nominally, their size was set at from 1.25 to 1.50 *arrobas*, with half and quarter variations. However, the *arroba* in liquid measurement ranged from 2.6 to 3.6 gallons, so that an exact determination of intended volume is impossible. The larger jars seem to have been about two-thirds the size of the 26-liter Roman amphora used fourteen hundred years earlier in the same area for the same function.[311] With archaeological specimens relatively variable, it appears a limited leeway was tolerable.[312] Although such inconsistency makes it difficult for researchers to categorize a collection, it does reflect the Andalusian turn of mind that saw little value in wholesale conformity. Potters likely sized their pots visually, one by one, and did not use templates or other measuring devices. Experienced throwers on a production line were capable of reasonable replication, as shown in the uniformity of contemporary tableware.

Differences between archaic and modern terminology for Spanish vessel forms have led to considerable confusion about which jars were meant to hold which liquids. It is only academic, in any case, because that kind of invariability was not part of the Andalusian attitude. Because the elongated amphora is the one most commonly recovered in Spanish America, it probably was the usual wine jug.[313] This conforms to the documented dominance of the trade in that beverage. After the middle of the sixteenth century those same archives almost always refer to *botijas peruleras* of wine, but they also list *botijas peruleras* of vinegar.[314] That seems contradictory because *perulera* translates as *wide-bellied*, an apt description of the globular jar. In recalling that Roman practice in Andalusia was to ship wine in long amphorae and olive oil in rounder ones, the pattern may have been retained in the colonial commerce, despite occasional deviations. Another possible confirmation of the use of the rounder form for olive oil comes from finds of fragments of them associated with wrecks from the Spanish Armada dated to 1588, since wine is believed to have been carried aboard in *pipas* and barrels rather than in ceramic containers (Fig. 79).[315] Nonetheless, both forms now are known to Andalusians as *ánforas*, and to American archaeologists as olive jars.

To prevent seepage, many of these jars were coated

Figure 79. Andalusian ceramics recovered from La Trinidad Valencera, a vessel operating as part of the 1588 Spanish Armada lost off the coast of Donegal, Ireland. Left, *botija perulera*, or olive jar Middle Type B of half-*arroba* capacity; right, discolored white maiolica plate; lower center, small white maiolica drug or ointment jar, *albarelo* (courtesy Colin Martin, Scottish Institute of Maritime Studies, St. Andrews).

lightly on their interiors, and occasionally on both surfaces, with green lead glaze. Whether done out of expediency (such glaze being readily at hand) or to avoid the additional costs or tainting of pitch coating now is not known. In the case of the *aguardiente* of the Canary Islands, a specialty of that area that was bottled in Sevillian ceramics, dense green glaze on all surfaces of the jugs became a trademark.[316] In that imperviousness, which limited the growth of pathogenic bacteria, there also was possible lethal danger to consumers: lead particles tend to be released in the prolonged presence of acids, such as wine, vinegar, or brine. Certain medicines also conceivably could have reacted adversely to the lead in glazes. Copper additives used to impart green color hasten the lead release process, as does heat.[317] One can well imagine that lead-glazed *botijas peruleras* may have been stockpiled on the Guadalquivir docks for months awaiting the sailing of the *flotas*, perhaps even through torrid Andalusian summers when overseas sailings skipped a year. After being sloshed about for two or three months in the steaming galleon holds, they finally came into tropical Caribbean ports, their contents very likely already contaminated. Whether serious illnesses may have befallen thirsty colonial Spaniards as a result remains a mystery.

For several decades in mid-century, when the large-scale Andalusian wine trade was getting into high gear, wooden *pipas* and barrels containing wine were loaded onto the cargo ships. The former were said to have contained from 27 to 27.5 *arrobas* of liquid. The barrels held

from 4 to 4.5 *arrobas*. A *tonelada* was the space occupied by
3 *pipas* or 5 *botijas*.[318] The cumbersome storage casks were
accompanied by a given number of empty *botijas peruleras*.[319] Whether the unglazed examples might date from
this time cannot be determined without more field work.
The implication to be drawn from archival data is that
the jars were filled once the port of disembarkation was
reached, the casks being returned to Sevilla to be reused.
That lessened the risk of plumbism in the case of glazed
jars, while also conserving valuable imported wood
resources. There are a few notations of empty jars without
pipas being consigned to colonial traders, who must have
filled them with wine surpluses already on hand. The
jars themselves are not apt to have been a marketable item,
judging by their abundance as discards and owing to their
probable provincial manufacture to fill colonial needs.

In the second half of the sixteenth century wine merchants generally eliminated the use of wooden *pipas* and
sent the *botijas peruleras* already filled. The old merchandising method may have been too troublesome or wood too
hard to obtain, but the substitute measures greatly
increased the risks to consumers. Either the risks were not
recognized or the pressures of commerce overrode other
considerations.

In addition to containers for commodities on the commercial exchange, comparable jars were in the luggage of
outbound passengers. A mid-century listing of ships'
charges show that persons going overseas carried personal
supplies of olive oil, wine, vinegar, and water in earthenware jars variously described as *tinajas*, *botijas*, or *botijas
peruleras*.[320]

The container jars were made on the typical Andalusian
kick wheels, the thick throwing rings visible on the walls
of all of them left unobliterated because they served as
body reinforcement. The objects were formed in two sections luted together at the leather hard stage, at which
time a pulled neck ring also was added. Minor variations
in these neck rings is not a diagnostic feature, given the
unregimented work routines. It is improbable that bases
were started in a bisqued chuck on the wheel head[321]
because most specimens retain throwing rings right to the
round bottom. This suggests bases were thrown upside
down, perhaps over a mold. The tapered and round bottoms, awkward in other cultures, were accepted without
question by people nurtured in an ancient but compatible
service vessel tradition. Considering the enormous number of the vessels made, one might wonder why the workshops did not resort to vertical or other molds, which

were well known. The answer lies in the ability of the potters, who could do the job faster by the more direct throwing method. Niceties of refined finish that might have
resulted from molds were unnecessary.

The presence of a slip added to halt evaporation,
reported by some American researchers, is open to question. The insoluble white film on some surfaces more
probably was due to a chemical reaction among certain
minerals in the clay, free water when the paste was
in a plastic state, and sulphur pollutants in the firing
atmosphere.

That speed was essential to meet the demands of the
thriving overseas wine trade is clearly revealed not only
in coarse workmanship, but also in hundreds of *ánfora*
seconds recovered from beneath seventeenth– and
eighteenth-century Sevillian homes (see Fig. 78f). At some
point rejected pots of the elongated profile stacked up
around local potteries, and ingenious townsfolk began to
place them in a layer beneath floors, where they were
expected to draw moisture in an effort to cope with the
excessive humidity that had always plagued the city. This
practice was without precedent in Sevilla, although it
had been used in other parts of the Muslim world.
Recovered in impressive quantities during modern
rebuilding projects, the jars can be seen to have been articles culled from bisque firings. None are glazed, and
without exception they exhibit one or more defects that
would have made them unusable as shipping containers.
Large cracks resulting from attempted firing while still
damp and spalling of walls or entrapped air bubbles from
insufficient wedging point to too great a hurry. Their large
numbers substantiate the scope of the total enterprise of
botijería, which probably saw a contingent of Sevillian
potters spending their entire working lives making and
firing this one kind of vessel.

How much similar ceramic packaging may have been
produced in rural areas where the goods were grown
or processed is uncertain. The slight variations in clay bodies and vessel characteristics allow for at least several centers of manufacture. Promising places to search for old
farmyard potteries may be in the nearby Aljarafe to the
west of Sevilla, the delta of the Guadalquivir famous
as a source for manzanilla sherry, or the more distant
Cazalla in the mountains north of Córdoba. Considering
the persistence of custom that underlies much of the
regional culture, it is not unlikely that there was some
direct association of container makers with vineyards,
groves, and crushing mills. Evidence in support of this

suggestion is found in the continuation of the practice in
rural workshops dedicated to wine jug output in the Viceroyalty of Peru in the seventeenth century and into the
early twentieth century right in Andalusia.[322]

A third amphora form associated with these two main
container types was a much smaller cone-shaped object,
also lacking handles and significant neck. Based upon
a study of specimens in the museum at Sevilla, a particularly intriguing possibility is that they were used as torch-
holders in coastal or river navigation.[323] Similar pots are
thought to have been used by the provincial Romans, and
the practice continued into the eighteenth century. Discarded, these jars also found their way below Sevillian
floors in the continuing battle against moisture. However,
one cannot discount their probable role in the containerized trade to the colonies, where they have been recovered
in seventeenth- and eighteenth-century contexts.

Botijas glazed in white were used for the shipment of
honey. Their exact contours are undetermined.[324]

A second force for change in Andalusian ceramics in the
second half of the sixteenth century is attributable to a
new vigor accompanying both influence and craftsmen
from Italy, who were drawn to Sevilla by the exhilerating
promise of the distant empire (Fig. 80). Painters and sculptors from Italy and those trained there had been active
throughout the century in Andalusia. At last some of the
potters were catching up, owing not so much to their
example as to mercantile necessity. The influx of Italians
occurred at a very opportune time. The stimulation that
formerly had come to Sevillian potting circles from the
Nasrids had ended, and local *mudéjar* conventions had
been exhausted through endless repetition. The more
aggressive potters, perhaps unknowingly, were primed
for an aesthetic discharge. The wiser ones also saw it
as a financial imperative if they were to compete in the
marketplace.

In advance of the main body of arriving Italian potters
came a lone ceramic artisan working with tile. His name
was Niculoso. While his new neighbors routinely continued making tiles according to *alicatado, cuerda seca,* and
cuenca modes, he was showing local craftsmen works of art
made and decorated in ways he had known in his homeland. He went on to achieve a final product that is considered entirely original. Although he would not have been
regarded as an outstanding artisan in Italy, his tiles could
hardly have been more distinct from anything previously
made in Sevillian shops.[325] They were not stamped,
greased, or cut, and neither did they depend for effect

Figure 80. Map of Italy showing locations of potting industries that sent sixteenth-century wares and artisans to Andalusia, and later to the Americas.

upon interrelated geometric or calligraphic patterns or Islamic imagery. Instead, they were flowing humanistic maiolica pictures meant to dramatize wall spaces in the same way that murals or oil paintings did.

Niculoso was essentially a Faventine painter schooled in patterns derived from the grammar of the Italian Renaissance; his medium was tin-glazed earthenware. That placed him well beyond the sphere of the ordinary Andalusian potter of the early sixteenth century because it entailed capabilities in two demanding areas of expression: as a creative artist, dependent on inherent talent honed by training, and as a technician, whose skills were learned through extensive trial and error. More than a tiler, he needed not only a mastery of line, perspective, and portrayal, but also sure-handed control of the brush. The immediate absorbency of the unfired ground allowed for no corrections. Additionally, in order to obtain desired results, he had to be familiar with tile production techniques and to have intimate knowledge of chemical interactions induced by heat on certain minerals and clay. Employing no surface modification of a stanniferous ground, Niculoso depended for decoration only on a vibrant spectrum of dark blue, turquoise, yellow, orange, green, purple, and warm brown. Some of these colors required minerals not found earlier in Andalusian workshops. His central panel, composed of a number of contiguous tile blanks, some unusually large, was viewed as a background for a planned composition of a scene naturalistically rendered. Figures were darkly outlined and shadows or highlights were created by color gradations. With an eye to marketing advantages and realizing the strong religious fervor of Andalusians, Niculoso concentrated on saintly figures suitable for church adornment, which he based upon engravings. Around this central theme he placed complex borders of winged angels, garlands, fruits, grotesques, military trophies, and other motifs of usual contemporary Italian vocabularies. All were predetermined and painstakingly executed. None were original. The borders were so complex and elaborate that they almost eclipsed the principal religious scene. The spontaneity of brushwork and the imprecise rendition of minutiae usual in Muslim works were not present in his panels.

The oldest remaining Niculoso tile picture, signed and dated 1503, was installed in the Triana parish church of Santa Ana near his home. It was in that church that the potters maintained their confraternity under the advocacy of Saints Justa and Rufina. Of more fame was Niculoso's decoration of tiles and glazed figures modeled by Pedro Millán and applied to the monumental facade of the Santa Paula monastery (see Fig. 76), the altarpiece at a monastery of Santa María de Tendudía near Badajoz, and the retable of the Visitation for a chapel at the *alcázar* to be used by the Catholic Kings.[326]

Niculoso emerges from the shadow of limited ceramic archives as a rare giant figure, whose example *might* have produced an immediate stylistic revolution. So far as Sevilla was concerned, however, he was ahead of his time. Deep in the familiar stylistic tracks of Moresque conventions, local tilers remained ceramists but did not become painters. They apparently were not ready to copy his method or design mannerisms. When Niculoso died in about 1520, only his son continued making smooth-surfaced polychrome tile pictures. One of these was placed in a chapel of the Sevillian La Cartuja, which for a time housed the sarcophagus of Columbus.[327]

Nearly fifty years passed before artisans and customers

were ready to give the Niculoso type of tile a try. Behind this development was a party of newly arrived Ligurians. Their immigration was eased by contacts with the local Genoese colony, which had grown greatly because of the American trade, and by renewed privileges granted them under the regimes of Carlos I and Felipe II (see Table 3).[328] Genoa itself had supported since the fourteenth century a pottery industry devoted to green–and–brown–on–white wares comparable to those of contemporary Spanish Levantine Muslims. During the early sixteenth century, because of the city's commercial prominence and its location along routes to western Europe, mobile potters from other parts of the Italian peninsula, such as the Marches and Romagna, came there to work. They brought with them sharpened ceramic skills acquired in a florescence of maiolica-making never to be duplicated elsewhere. Among them was a Francesco da Pésaro, who in 1520 opened a factory near the Roman Gate in Genoa. He worked there for sixty years. During his lifetime he is credited with ruling a ceramic dynasty of seven relatives, including three sons.[329]

Tommaso, or Tomás in Spain, was one Pésaro son in the vanguard of artisans moving on to Sevilla about mid-sixteenth century. He had the special distinction of establishing his own workshop and potting dynasty in a house and grounds once belonging to Ferdinand Columbus, son of the Admiral of the Ocean Sea. There he found a recently constructed wooden *noria*, with its typical earthenware pots watering a small orchard. One of Tomás's

Figure 81. Polychromatic panel of flat-surfaced tiles, *azulejos*, in the potters' parish church of Santa Ana in Triana, dated ca. 1575. The overall repetitive pattern of abstracted floral motifs is characteristically Andalusian Moresque.

sons, Gusepe, took over the pottery business, operating
the Pésaro shop there until at least 1615.[330]

In the two small towns of Albisola and Savona, about
thirty miles west of Genoa on the Ligurian coast, were
other factories making identical products. Documents at
Sevilla indicate those centers as the former homes of a
dozen potters working in Andalusia from the second half
of the sixteenth century into the seventeenth century.
Among them were Pedro Antonio, Antonio and Bartolomé
Sambarino, Francisco Salamón, Virgilio Cortivas, Bernardo
Cerrudo, Bernardino Seirullo, Ghirlandi, and Ambrogio
Ottone, all of whom had dealings with Pésaro. Ottone
apparently negotiated a contract on behalf of Pésaro with
Tommaso Spirito, Giovanni Zuffo, and Benedetto Girardo,
who pledged to work in Sevilla for four years. They were
to sail from Calice or Alcantera and promised to serve
Pésaro "as it is customary of the citizens of Albisola, faith-
fully, consistently, day and night, and honestly." Some
of these men are described as tilers, some as workers on
the wheel, and others as experts in decorating.[331] Behind
their efforts were the ubiquitous design conventions of
Faenza.

These Italian artisans and a group of local potters eager
to learn from them formed a tight social and craft coterie
apparently headed by Pésaro, whose combined talents not
only brought them considerable status and perhaps a
modest income, but also helped make Sevilla the most
outstanding tile center in the realm. Beginning in the 1560s
and 1570s, five or six Sevillian churches and the *alcázar*
were adorned with lavish dados of brilliant, smoothed,
polychrome tile (Figs. 81, 82). Among the best known
were panels at the convent of Madre de Dios, 1573; Santa
Clara, 1575; Santa Ana and San Pablo, 1576; Santa Ana
and Santa María de Jesus, 1589; and an altar frontal featuring the potter saints, Justa and Rufina, executed for San
Lorenzo after 1585. For the next half century, as decoration
evolved in a Venetian-Genoese vogue, shipments of thousands of tiles went out to other European countries and
to Spanish America. A German traveler in Sevilla wrote
that the tiles were so cheap that Flemish and French merchants exported great quantities to England, France, and
the Low Countries. Many of these works remain and can
be studied in detail.[332] The city from which the tiles came
was splashed with vibrant maiolica color, for now more
people had the money to acquire them. The Almohads,
who had emblazoned several towers and minarets with
their own flashing tiles, would have liked that.

The tiles most often were used on lower walls as they

Figure 82. Border panel of polychrome flat-surfaced tiles, *azulejos*,
in the Santa Clara church, Sevilla,
dated ca. 1575. Although made
by exactly the same methods
as the panel in Figure 81, perhaps
by the same craftsman, the putti
and grotesque and the way in
which they are rendered come
from the other dominant source of
decorative influence current in
late sixteenth-century Sevillian
arts, the Italian Renaissance.

had been in earlier periods, thus differing from the Italian custom of elaborate floor tiling. They were also added to stair risers, fountain basins, garden benches, walks, counter tops, or as accents in terra cotta floors. Designs represented a fusion of native and introduced compositions. Some remained *mudéjar* interlacements, stellar arrangements, or textile motifs dependent upon juxtaposition of units of four or more tiles to complete a pattern. These orientalized compositions were combined with Plateresque grotesques and an inventive tangle of Renaissance cherubs, candelabras, baskets of flowers, scampering animals, and leafy foilage. To the delight of students of ceramics, some were dated and signed. Usual colors were a dark blue, green, black, white, amber, yellow, and a very intense orange. When it was used, the Niculoso-style central panel was reduced to a more modest medallion of saint figures. Among the popular holy characterizations were Sevilla's own patrons: Isidore, who had helped bring the Faith to the Visigoths, and the respected Justa and Rufina. Local iconography for the latter had the sisters standing erect with a palm frond of martyrdom over one shoulder, the Giralda tower with its new weather vane between them, and a few pots at their feet or in their hands.[333]

The dado panels obviously were designed as a unit and probably were painted while they were arranged together on a work table or slanting easel, so that designs could flow across them without regard to segmentation of individual tiles. A master plan for creation and installation was essential, although there are no surviving cartoons. It is assumed that engravers' books were a fruitful resource. Other tiles, which could be installed separately, sold by the piece.

The late sixteenth- and early seventeenth-century Sevillian tile production was the third and final peaking in the long panorama of Andalusian ceramics. It was the outgrowth of a peculiar merger of Islamic and European Renaissance themes and techniques, both at the time already rotting at their roots. Differing from the other two ceramic climaxes, that in the tenth-century Cordoban caliphate and that in the thirteenth-century Nasrid emirate, the names of individual artisans were preserved. Another significant difference was that it did not prosper only from the patronage of the royalty. This time it thrived as a result of capitalism in action, by providing an updated and exciting product for which the regional populace had long preconditioning and for which a potential market of buyers on both sides of the Atlantic—for whom con-

Figure 83. Late sixteenth-century polychrome plates, attributed to Sevilla, of a style borrowed from Italian models. The abstracted floral borders recall fifteenth-century Faenza maiolicas, while the heads in profile framed by floral sprays were a widely used contemporary Italianate concept. Common also were the casually brushed horizontal lines shading the background (courtesy Museo de Cerámica, Barcelona).

spicuous consumption had become a way of life—was ready.

The new rich of Sevilla acquired an eclectic taste for more luxurious tablewares than the rustic maiolicas they had used up to that time. Reflective of the prevalent cosmopolitan atmosphere, the articles available to satisfy these desires were silver pieces made by the local smiths, *reflejo metálico* of Manises, and that newest luxury, Chinese porcelain. In addition to the capricious river, which is presumed to have washed away discarded ceramics, and the lack of sufficient archaeology, the new cosmopolitan taste must be cited to help explain why relatively few examples of better caliber local pottery can be positively identified with the second half of the century. Nevertheless, it is known that Italian potters moving into the city produced superior articles in styles never seen there earlier. One result was an even sharper division in the potting ranks between makers of top and low quality wares, which for a while reflected the local distinctions between foreign and native artisans.

Such stylistic and technical improvement of better grade hollow ware came hand-in-hand with the introduction of Renaissance tile. It was apparent in new refinements of methods and in unique styles welded to well-established older concepts. No identifiable mode was transferred wholesale from Italy. A series of vessels comparable to, but less elaborate than, *pisano* tile used some of the same motifs and colors. They may have been made by the same artisans, although decorators customarily confined their efforts to one or the other. Some of these craftsmen were Italian, but within a decade others were local men. At least one Sevillian potter is documented as having engaged a Flemish decorator then working in town to teach him the methods learned from southern Italian potters who had moved north.[334]

Most of the known examples of the new Italianate type are relatively thin-walled, ring-footed plates, averaging from 30 to 39 cm in diameter and having broad flat interior bottoms, a narrow cavetto, and a horizontal brim set off by a prominent arris (Figs. 83, 84).[335] Such clear-cut definition of vessel parts had not been typical of Moresque craft in Andalusia. A milky glaze covered all surfaces. Characteristically, it was crazed, pinholed, or blemished like Spanish glazes always had been, but not to the same degree as the contemporary low-caliber domestic maiolicas. Its opaque semi-matte qualities were the result of more careful milling of ingredients and greater amounts of tin oxide added to the mixtures. There appears never to

Figure 84. Late sixteenth-century polychrome plates attributed to Sevilla, of a style borrowed from Italian sources and employing the variant motifs of a rare nude full figure and a bird. Each, on a ground line, is conventionally framed by vertical foliage elements (courtesy International Folk Art Foundation Collection, Museum of International Folk Art, a unit of the Museum of New Mexico, Santa Fe [above], and Instituto Valencia de Don Juan, Madrid [below]).

have been a transparent lead top coat, or *coperta*, as was customary in Italy. The decoration differed from past Andalusian work in its careful planning within prescribed boundaries, although it never attained the perfection of Italian models. The central obverse usually was delineated by one or more encircling lines. Within this field were laid a selected few of the hundreds of possible Italianate motifs (Fig. 85). Often a dominant element, such as a large human bust in profile or three-quarter view, a standing figure or two, or an animal, formed a centerpiece framed at one or both sides by an erect floral spray or a topiary tree. In the case of full figures, a ground line was customary. The human heads were especially interesting, owing to realistic detail of facial features and dress new to Spanish ceramic decoration. Standing figures frequently were allegorical, their occasional nudity either a clue to the presence of non-Spanish artisans or the great shedding of Islamic artistic prohibitions. Mammals and birds comprising focal elements likely came from the native background, although Italians working with ideas inspired by Ming porcelain had a fondness for similar motifs.

Using a rich assortment of blue, green, rust, brown, and bright yellow for fillers, elements typically were outlined and detailed with dark blue or brown in the Italian manner. The blue pigment was not impasto, as on some Italian examples. Shading along outer edges of human figures was common. The background of the central field often was darkened by parallel fine to medium lines of irregular lengths. Random dotting of some floral rim bands gave this style its present Spanish name of *punteada*,

Figure 85. Some commonly used design motifs or border patterns of the Gothic-Floral style developed by fifteenth-century ceramic decorators of Faenza, Italy, and adapted in various ways to sixteenth-century Sevillian and Mexico City maiolicas.

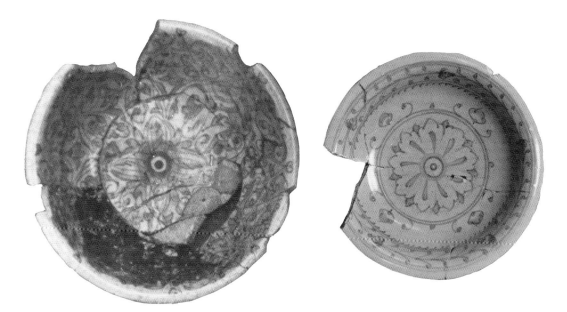

although all specimens do not conform to this description. Very reminiscent were some so-called Gothic-Floral style borders of Faenza wares of the late fifteenth century.[336]

Another indication of the transfer of Genoese mannerisms to Sevilla was an Andalusian copy of a different variety of maiolica typical of late sixteenth-century Ligurian workshops, which also varied greatly from anything made in the region previously. Although a tin glaze tinted with a small percentage of cobalt to yield a dark blue ground had covered Sevillian *albarelos* early in the century, the interiors of Italian hollow ware now were glazed in a light or grayish blue overlaid with simple abstracted foliage designs in dark blue, rarely accompanied by a touch of yellow; exteriors bore overlapping arcades (Fig. 86).[337] A rarer blue–on–white companion style also was present. It is suggested that these modes were created in the Genoa area as an exportable luxury grade substitute for a declining trade in Valencian *reflejo metálico*. Their designs appear to have been based on Turkish examples, which, in turn, drew from a Chinese bank of motifs.[338] Andalusian specimens, fired in saggars on headpins in the Italian manner, generally were small bowls, shallow plates, and modest-sized jars. They exhibit heavier line work than do the prototypes from which they were taken (Fig. 87) and lack the *coperta* top coat. Major designs were more recognizably Spanish, but a few fragments show attempts at literal translation of Ligurian coiled Damescene arabesques. For the first time in Sevillian maiolicas, bowl exteriors bore

Figure 86. Blue–on–blue maiolica made in the Ligurian area of northwest Italy during the second half of the sixteenth century and traded extensively through Sevilla to the New World: left, bowl recovered from beneath Mexico City cathedral compound; right, bowl with a yellow accent lining in center recovered in excavations in cloisters of Carthusian monastery at Jérez de la Frontera (courtesy Dirección de Inmuebles Federales, Mexico City [left], and the Hermitage of Nuestra Señora de la Defensión, La Cartuja, Jérez de la Frontera [right]).

Figure 87. Sevillian blue–on–blue mode, copying pottery with a comparable palette and styling traded to Andalusia from the Ligurian coast of Italy: *a*, fragments recovered in fill beneath Sevilla; *b*, fragments recovered in Spanish American sites; *c*, drug jar acquired in Mexico; *d*, date beneath jar handle. The jar is considered a rare Sevillian imitation of both Italian form and decorative treatment. Although the calcareous clay of Sevilla and Genoa were similar, the comparatively heavy line work and poor glaze quality point to a Sevillian source (courtesy Museo Arqueológico Provincial, Sevilla [*a*], and Carmen Pérez de Salazar de Ovando and Carlos de Ovando [*c*–*d*]).

patterning, which was a direct imitation of Ligurian arcades or encircling lines. Archaeology in Andalusia and in the American colonies, as well as shipping lists and government regulations, confirm the Sevillian manufacture of this ware.[339] It is tempting to suggest that migrant acculturated Italians may have been the producers, a situation that appears to be substantiated in a 1579 reference to copies of "Pisan" pottery being made near the Puerta de Goles, the location of the Pésaro workshop.

A variation of the blue ground style was a marbelized, or mottled, surface resulting either from swirling blue pigment over wet unfired white glaze or sprinkling it with flecks of pigment by rubbing the color-impregnated bristles of a stiff brush. Such techniques were used occasionally at the Pésaro factory in Genoa.[340]

Another Sevillian vogue attributable to Italian styling was represented in a series of plain white, broad-brimmed plates; small shallow bowls with horizontal scalloped handles; and tall-necked, often fluted-walled, two-handled jars (Fig. 88).[341] The forms and lustrous, thick white glaze lacking any further decoration are reminiscent of the Faenza all-white tradition that swept through western Europe in the late sixteenth and early seventeenth centuries. The horizontal handles, however, had been a part of a gothecized mode seen in eastern and southern Spain since the Middle Ages. The quality of the coating, with the exception of cockspur scars and pin-holing, and the more careful potting stand in marked contrast to the common white maiolicas.

Figure 88. Late sixteenth-century Sevillian top-quality white maiolica plates, showing Italian influence in refined manufacturing methods and contours (courtesy of Museo Arqueológico Provincial, Sevilla).

A parallel development was exceedingly thin, delicate, often fluted forms with tiny handles made of pure white-firing clay that was left unglazed (Fig. 89). The lack of glaze on obviously fine quality ware is puzzling, but finds do not represent bisqued vessels. This opinion is confirmed by similar Sevillian trade pottery recovered as far away as Amsterdam.[342] The shapes, thinness, and lack of glaze may have been inspired by Chinese porcelains. Perhaps these represented one kind of imitation indicated in a 1627 *tasación*.

Sixteenth-century Italian-inspired decorative styles demonstrate certain improvements of Sevilla's ancient Muslim technology in those shops devoted to such work. It is likely that the newly arrived Ligurians built their customary rectangular, two-chambered, updraft kilns, and that many Sevillians engaged in making first-caliber ceramics were sufficiently impressed to begin to take greater care in construction of their own kilns based upon the same principles (Fig. 90).[343] The usual Spanish wood-burning kiln form became the *horno quadrado*, a rectangular structure, although some country potteries clung to a domed kiln entered through a large arched door.[344] The Muslim cylindrical kilns may have been retained for bisque firing, while the new rectangular model was used for glost firing.[345]

Although atmospheres within kilns had been controlled by fires alternating between light reduction and freely burning flames, it is postulated that saggars also made their first appearance in response to Italian methods. It can be expected that they would have been used only for fancy vessels, not for ordinary table pots. Even in Italy no particular care was given to the firing of items sold in units. The typical Italian saggar, as illustrated in a 1557

Figure 89. Detail of oil painting, *Still Life with Jars* (left), by Francisco de Zurbarán, ca. 1635, that includes two examples of finely modeled white jars. Although the painting suggests a maiolica glaze, a comparable specimen (right) recovered at La Cartuja, Jérez de la Frontera, and a sherd sample from beneath Sevilla indicate an exceedingly thin ware of unglazed pure white paste. The delicate fluted or otherwise manipulated shapes point to a moldmade, rather than thrown, pottery (courtesy The Prado, Madrid [left], and the Hermitage of Nuestra Señora de la Defensión, La Cartuja, Jérez de la Frontera [right]).

Figure 90. Italian-style two-chambered updraft kiln as illustrated by Piccolpasso; the type was likely introduced to Spain in the second half of the sixteenth century. Note that in this case the firing chamber was not subterranean (courtesy the trustees of The National Art Library, Victoria and Albert Museum, London).

treatise on the potter's art and substantiated by the excavation of a sixteenth-century kiln at Genoa,[346] was a circular, bisqued clay form of several diameters, usually lacking a lid. It had holes of varying sizes in side walls and bases for better circulation of hot air. Some openings in rows up the sides of the saggars were of a size and shape suitable for insertion of small, fired clay prisms or headpins, in Spain termed *clavos*, to support stacks of similarly shaped vessels beneath their rims. This allowed them to hang freely within the protective saggars.[347] Such prisms left tiny radial marks on reverses, which were not nearly as unsightly as the three scars on obverses and reverses of vessels separated by cockspurs. Most examples thought to be representative of Sevillian wares of the late sixteenth century, other than the borrowed blue ground type, retain cockspur scars. It appears that adoption of introduced

methods was not wholehearted because some potters
unknowingly were mired in another tradition. Rim edges
and bottoms of ring feet of cylindrical shapes were wiped
free of glaze to permit vessels to be stacked one on top
of another. The use of individual support cones, or pips,
which was usual in Italian saggar loading, has not been
confirmed in Spain.[348]

Another aspect of Italian influence on equipment was
the removal of the potter's wheel from trenches in the
ground. They were installed at table height with a slanted
seat at the right of the wheel head, which usually was
attached to a work table or to the frame of the wheel itself
(Fig. 91)[349] Putting the potter farther from the dampness
of the surrounding earth was more healthful and permitted the user to change position for better light.

Figure 91. Maiolica plate from
Deruta, Italy, ca. 1530, illustrating
style and placement of the potter's
wheel believed to have been
adopted by Sevillian artisans
about mid sixteenth century and
subsequently diffused overseas.

While Sevillian *azulejo* tile was in its ascendency and
diffused Italian canons of taste were dictating evolution
of better hollow wares, there was another of the cyclic
bloomings that had characterized the history of Spanish
ceramics. It too was inspired by Italian technology and
styles and was centered in Castile. There, Toledo had stag-
nated in its worn out *mudéjar* themes and was in a state
of decline, creating a void in regional potting activity. The
new development arose at the nearby small town of Talavera de la Reina, also on the Río Tajo, where deep beds of
appropriate clays were accessible. Small-scale potting
had been known earlier at Talavera, but in the second half
of the sixteenth century it was overtaken by a vigorous
diffusionary push from several Italian sources. One source
was the nucleus of Ligurians at Sevilla who continued
their habitual ways. It now seems probable that their
immediate influence on Castile was greater than earlier
recognized. The other source was a contingent of Flemish
artisans, fellow members of the Holy Roman Empire of
Charles V (see Table 3), who moved to Castile. Among
them were Frans Andries and Jan Floris, whose families
had gone from north central Italy to Antwerp early in
the sixteenth century. These itinerant Italian ceramists
were mainly tilers.[350]

As potting activity increased at Talavera, the Crown
was sufficiently interested in its promotion to have a Sevillian master potter, Jerónimo Montero, dispatched there
to help the Castilians improve their products. He is
reported to have worked at the shop of former Sevillian
Antonio Díaz, where he tested glazes and colors, and
at that of Juan Figueroa, where he demonstrated painting.[351] Italians from a number of maiolica centers introduced, directly or indirectly, compositions and forms that

Figure 92. Two small polychrome plates believed to be representative of Sevillian workmanship in the second half of the sixteenth century or the early seventeenth century and influenced by contemporary decorative styles of Talavera de la Reina. Both carry inscriptions appropriate for ecclesiastical users at the Carthusian monastery at Jérez de la Frontera, where they were recovered: above, orange rim and central bands are framed by brown, with center inscription translating as 'Love"; below, encircling stepped pendants in orange and blue from a blue-dotted rim band, with center monogram of the Ave María framed by rayed pattern known as *estrellas de plumas* (courtesy the Hermitage of Nuestra Señora de la Defensión, La Cartuja, Jérez de la Frontera).

were assimilated and reworked to bring forth a new group of blended styles. All these channels of interest coming together at one time culminated in a Talaveran industry whose name for two centuries was synonymous with Spanish maiolica.

There were a number of reasons for the immediate success of Talaveran maiolica fashioned in several grades to serve different levels of society. Generally, it was well made and was gaily painted in ways refreshingly different from all that was associated with the Muslim past. It was truly an echo of Renaissance decorative art being popularized by the pace-setting nobility. Furthermore, although the town at one time had been in Muslim hands, artisans at Talavera were not hampered by an inbred resistance to change cultivated through century after century of experience in one particular orientation of the craft. Nor did Talaveran potters have the casual attitudes toward production methods that would allow them to accept the kinds of technical flaws seen in most Spanish Muslim earthenwares. They were eager to experiment in order to improve their wares. Also of paramount importance was royal patronage of their efforts. The Court was then establishing itself within the region at Madrid and at the Escorial slightly more than a hundred miles away, and was anxious to encourage Castilian development. One artisan was said to have been made the official potter to the king, who previously had appointed an official tiler. Another was official potter to the queen.[352] Concurrently, Manises *reflejo metálico* had degenerated to the point that, with the exile of the *moriscos* at the beginning of the seventeenth century, it rapidly slipped into folk art. When the bankrupt king of Castile issued an edict against the use of silver table services, Talaveran shops thus were in a good position to promote use of their products and so to prosper.[353] Because it was both quickly fashioned for wide appeal and more carefully executed for select customers, Talaveran hollow ware soon was to be found both in ordinary ceramic stores and in prominent places throughout Spain. Its ascendancy was furthered by hard times plaguing Sevilla, which may have curbed that city's productivity. Craftsmen from Talavera moved from their town into other areas of the kingdom, predictably bringing about a broad stylistic conformity, which ultimately diffused back to Italy in the region of Naples.[354] Potters at Puente del Arzobispo, some twenty miles downriver from Talavera, paralleled the more famous ceramic styles of their neighbors. Their works were regarded locally as coarser and so sold at lower prices.

a

b

c

d

e

Figure 93. Late sixteenth- or first half of seventeenth century vessels attributable to Sevillian manufacture but influenced by Talaveran designs; *a*, orange, brown, and blue polychromed brimmed plate of *estrellas de plumas* style; *b*, wasp-waisted drug-jar, *albarelo*, bearing arms of Unshod Carmelites in two shades of blue on shield mantled by acanthus leaves and topped by a crudely rendered crown (In the sixteenth century there were two hundred Carmelite friars in two Sevillian convents, and perhaps this jar saw use in a hospital or pharmacy operated by them.); *c*, small custom-ordered plate with polychromatic rendition of the insignia of the Jérez Carthusian monastery, consisting of two rampant lions separated by a tree of life; *d*, brown, blue, and orange pattern of S-scrolls and cross-hatching on rim band and framed basal pattern of frond wheel and quartered hub (The style is so characteristic of Talavera and Puente del Arzobispo that attribution is debatable, but comparable sherds have been identified in Sevilla); *e*, large shallow bowl decorated with central formée cross and winged angel heads and conventionalized florals spaced about cavetto (The cross was the insignia of the Trinitarians, a military religious group especially popular in Spain because of its avowed purpose of freeing Christians from captivity by the Muslims.) (courtesy the Hermitage of Nuestra Señora de la Defensión, La Cartuja, Jérez de la Frontera [*a*, *c*], and The Houghton Sawyer Collection [*b*] and the International Folk Art Foundation Collection [*d*, *e*], the Museum of International Folk Art, a unit of the Museum of New Mexico, Santa Fe).

Among the recipients of an influx of Talaveran or Puente del Arzobispo potters, wares, and influence was Sevilla.[355] So, in a roundabout way, further Italianization was to affect Andalusian pottery. Probably the full force of this particular Italianate wave did not reach the south until early in the seventeenth century. Then its decorative effect was enormous. Talaveran-inspired feathered plumes around a religious monogram or other centerpiece, winged angel heads, fronds, figural and floral themes, and a number of other modes and color combinations became standard (Figs. 92, 93). It has been suggested that the Italian emigrees working in the *collación* of San Vicente, perhaps even in the Pésaro shop, were responsible for the southern counterfeit Talaveran pieces. This opinion is based upon their familiarity with the individual elements of the styles and proven abilities in skillful brushwork.[356] They or fellow Andalusians are simply described in archives as *maestros de hacer loza de Talavera*.[357]

Even though the obvious debt to Talavera decorators was undeniable, the Sevillian potters charged with actual formation of vessels displayed far livelier imaginations. A 1627 government document indicated only three basic forms for Talavera wares, whereas thirty-two forms were noted as typical of Sevilla. In the pottery of both cities there were gradations of size. However, the Talaveran forms, consisting of plates, porringers, and jars, all were thrown. It seems probable that there were omissions

in this listing because a much greater variation is known
later. Nevertheless, the contrast with the indicated early
seventeenth-century Sevillian repertory is astounding. The
latter included the usual plates, porringers, and jars, but
also spouted jars, wall-mounted holy water stoups, wine
cups, cruets, flower vases, salt cellars, high-shouldered
drug jars with narrow bases, inkwells, candleholders,
shaving bowls, water jars, platters, snuff boxes, toys,
plaques bearing wine prices, wash basins, flasks, jardi-
nieres, spouted mortars, animal figures, and statuary.[358]
Some of these shapes affirm the frequent use of a mold
technique. Underlying such diversity in ceramics was a
sophisticated way of life for many residents of Spain's
richest city, as compared with the less complex daily routine in a Castilian small town. It also reveals a vigorous
industry at Sevilla seeking to maintain or expand its markets through innovation and improvement, such as by
making its usual variety of shapes but decorating them
in a more popular Talaveran style. If it were eventually
to lose out to the northern competition, portents of that
in the late sixteenth or early seventeenth century were not
yet evident.

Many of the objects indicated on the Sevillian ceramic
inventory formerly had been present primarily as metal
articles available to the rich or special few. Some would
have been useless to the common person. Why buy an
inkwell, for example, if one could not write? Such skill
generally had been confined to upper level males. Painters
commissioned to render portraits of administrators or
clergymen often portrayed their subjects standing by
or seated at a table on which were placed an inkwell and
plumed quill. These were symbols to tell the viewer that
here was a learned person of consequence. Thus the
appearance in the second half of the sixteenth century of
many cheaper maiolica inkwells suggests a social change.

That change was the spread of literacy into lower social
ranks, a change fostered by the necessity to record the
myriad of commercial, legal, and regulatory aspects of life
as lived in this bustling metropolis. Scribes taught simple
fundamentals of reading and writing by clerical and secular masters sat lined up at tables in official chambers and
did the bureaucratic paper work. They misspelled words,
miscalculated figures, ignored standardization, and carried
verbosity to new heights, but without their efforts our
knowledge of their time and place would be less complete.
The earthenware containers devised for the fluid of their
trade and its drying agent could have been of any size
or shape. The fact that they generally were molded forms
meant to imitate their metal counterparts once again

signals the basic conservatism of maker and user (see
Fig. 103b).

Other ceramic objects common at this time were those
meant to add pleasure to the personal lives of the segment
of society that had advanced beyond mere subsistence.
Prominent among them were various kinds of containers
for plants and flowers with which to beautify drab dwelling places. Such vessels would have found few customers
in the colder north, but in Andalusia both climate and
the Muslim legacy promoted an appreciation of gardens
and blooms. Thereafter, earthenware holders made for this
purpose remained a typical part of the output.

Another ceramic category with considerable social
implication comprised containers for holy water. These
were small slabs, usually bearing a molded or painted
design of religious significance, to which was attached
a half bowl (see Fig. 72b). They were meant to be hung
on a wall near a home altar. The religious intensity of the
period and the shadow of the Inquisition encouraged
outward display of inner conviction.

While all these advancements were seen in Sevillian
better grade ceramics destined for upper and middle level
homes, household dishes and the expectable assortment
of unglazed receptacles for the lower classes went almost
unaltered into the next century (Figs. 94–99). Little of
the prosperity of the period rubbed off on their users.
Aguadores still employed the ageless bulging jars and
drinking bowls of the past as they peddled river water
to thirsty townsfolk (Fig. 98). Street vendors still cooked
foods in timeless clay pots over portable earthen braziers
(Fig. 99). The makers of this grade of pottery stubbornly
resisted change in design or method. To them, what was
good enough in the fifteenth century was good enough
in the seventeenth.

Despite this attitude, one can detect subtle improvements among the common white maiolicas that surely
came from timid emulation of the more advanced Italian
craftsmanship. Basic forms continued, but their contours
were more carefully articulated. There was a noticeable
thinning of vessel walls. A gradual abandonment of the
poorly controlled jigger-and-jolly manufacturing methods
is evident in a growing absence of the telltale central
ridging on obverses and the trimming facets on reverses.
Ring feet replaced countersunk bottoms, and the widely
flaring horizontal brims being popularized on top quality
pieces appeared on lesser plates and shallow bowls.
Behind these modest modifications hovers the threat of
economic pressures from outside competition or of a pool
of customers becoming more discriminating. The dead

Figure 94. A range of typical
sixteenth- and seventeenth-
century Sevillian utility pottery
forms. Generally of greater size
than Muslim period counterparts,
surface elaborations and unnecessary appendages were minimized.
Noteworthy are: *a*, very large
storage jar 88 cm in height and 126
cm in greatest diameter, made in
sections; *e*, jar with elongated
neck said to have been the output
of a village industry south of
the city, many having been discovered in the vaulting of the
Jérez La Cartuja; *f*, heavy, flat-
bottomed basin, formerly often
covered with green lead glaze, but
at this time frequently covered
with tin-opacified glaze and
decorated with blue and green
linear and abstract floral patterns,
although it still was regarded as
a functional vessel for ordinary
domestic purposes (courtesy
Museo Arqueológico Provincial,
Sevilla [*a–d*, *g*, *h*], the Hermitage
of Nuestra Señora de la Defensión, La Cartuja, Jérez de la
Frontera [*e*], and the International
Folk Art Foundation Collection,
Museum of International Folk Art,
a unit of the Museum of New
Mexico, Santa Fe [*f*]).

Figure 95. Oil painting, *Marriage Feast at Cana*, by Bartolomé Murillo, ca. 1665–70. In foreground are unglazed *cántaros* of several sizes and profiles typical of seventeenth-century Sevilla (courtesy The Barber Institute of Fine Arts, University of Birmingham).

Figure 96. Examples of sixteenth-century lead-glazed commonwares uncovered beneath Sevilla: *a–b*, glaze coating is transparent honey-colored *melado* achieved by the addition of iron oxide to the dipping solution; *c–d*, clear transparent coating (courtesy Museo Arqueológico Provincial, Sevilla).

Figure 97. *Fray Francisco and the Kitchen of the Angels*, painted by Bartolomé Murillo in 1646, uses common Sevillian white maiolica plates, a bowl, partially glazed pitcher, and several unglazed *cántaros* as background accessories. The uniform size of mass-produced tableware is notable (courtesy Musées Nationaux, Paris).

Figure 98. *The Water Seller of Sevilla*, by Diego Rodríguez de Silva y Velázquez, 1622, depicting several kinds of earthenwares in common use in th early seventeenth century. The small two-handled jar and two-handled *cántaro* at the left appear to have tin-opacified glaze; the bulging, lidded, heavily-ribbed water container was the typical light-colored Andalusian *cántaro* which differed little from comparable storage vessels made centuries earlier. A fruit floats in the bottom of the glass being offered to a customer to help sweeten polluted drinking water. The water seller, *aguador*, is believed to have been an actual Sevillian street character and representative of the proud Andalusian peasant folk (courtesy the Board of Trustees of the Wellington Museum, London).

Figure 99. *Old Woman Frying Eggs,* by Diego Rodríguez de Silva y Velázquez, ca. 1618, portrays a seventeenth-century Andalusian woman using the earthenware brazier introduced to Spain a thousand years earlier to cook some eggs in a shallow earthenware *cazuela* of equal antiquity. In front of her are a typical white plate and two partially glazed, heavily ribbed pitchers. One glaze is a dark green covering highly favored by Spanish Muslim and Christian potters for commonwares; the other is a white tin-opacified lead glaze with simple cobalt blue decorations in use from the thirteenth through the eighteenth centuries. Of all the still life items shown in the scene, only the brazier and white plate with central encircling ridge have disappeared from the customary household inventory of furnishings (courtesy National Galleries of Scotland, Edinburgh).

weight of a threadbare *mudejarismo* finally was being forced off, however reluctantly.

Plain white surfaces remained typical. When decoration was applied, it was more often than not just paired lines below rims on obverses and encircling the bottom center (Fig. 100a). One variation had banded encircling lines with several of them crossed over one another in a chain (Fig. 101). Further elaboration added a central, abstracted, heavy floral decoration (Fig. 100c). Another style used freely applied scrolls and broad curved parallel lines as rim patterns combined with curvilinear floral centerpieces (Fig. 102). Some decorations were mere splotches of blue pigment on glazed surfaces, but others were simple florals, chains, and monograms (Fig. 103). The cobalt blue differed from that used earlier in its deep color and lack of speckling. It probably was purified zafre from Saxony. Closed forms, such as small pitchers and jars, were glazed on the interiors and upper halves of exterior walls only (see vessels at right center of Murillo painting in Fig. 97 and lower right of Velázquez painting in Fig. 99).

One minor change was a tin glaze darkened to slate grey or black through the addition to the solution of iron oxide or a combination of iron oxide and manganese (see Fig. 63d). Recent finds in Sevilla demonstrate this to be a true type, not merely a freak of deposition circumstances, which might have caused discoloration of the more usual white glaze. One 1590 shipping bill of lading refers especially to *loza negra*.[359]

Figure 100. Elaboration of style
on common Sevillian fifteenth-
and sixteenth-century maiolicas:
a, basic paired encircling lines
were enlivened with a rudimentary crest perhaps having meaning
to the Jérez Carthusians; *b*, basic
encircling lines increased in
number, with two sets convolut-
ing to approach a more explicit
laced motif, with addition of
a somewhat different rendition of
same crest; *c*, further enrichment
of encircling straight and wavy
lines by broadly painted floral
abstractions (courtesy the Hermitage of Nuestra Señora de la
Defensión, La Cartuja, Jérez de la
Frontera [*a*, *b*], and Museo
Arqueológico Provincial, Sevilla
[*c*]).

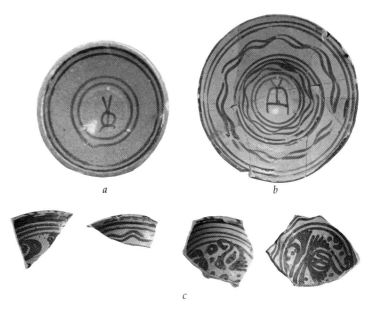

Figure 101. Three maiolica plates
from the commercialized common
tableware branch of the Sevillian
pottery industry. This style
took the paired line treatment
seen in Figure 67 one step further,
with the occasional addition of a
third line and two waved lines
around cavettos that sometimes
interlocked to form a chain.
The deeper blue of the cobalt on
most known examples of this
stylistic variation suggests a more
refined product from an as yet
unidentified source that appeared
toward the end of the sixteenth
century. There was a continuation
of the same production methods
and the same caliber of workmanship as was evident earlier.
Note raised center configuration
and triads of cockspur scars
(courtesy the Hermitage of Nuestra Señora de la Defensión, La
Cartuja, Jérez de la Frontera).

Figure 102. At top is a brimmed footless plate of probable Sevillian manufacture during the second half of the sixteenth century, decorated in a floralized style employing rim band of hooked scrolls and opposed units of parallel curved lines and curvilinear centerpiece. At bottom are potsherds of same style, executed in blue, recovered from beneath Sevilla (courtesy Instituto Valencia de Don Juan, Madrid [top], and Museo Arqueológico Privincial, Sevilla [bottom]).

a   b   c

Figure 103. Late sixteenth-century Sevillian maiolica vessels of common grade: *a*, large jar with blue monogram of Ave María framed by stylized leaves; *b*, two moldmade receptacles with blue decorations believed to be either *salvaderas*, used to hold sand or other pouncing material needed to dry ink on unsized paper, or *saleros cuadrados*, square salt cellars, such as were noted in a 1627 *tasación*; *c*, heavily ribbed, handled jar with casually applied blue decoration contaminated with a trace of green (courtesy Museo de Bellas Artes, Sevilla [*a*, *c*], and the Hermitage of Nuestra Señora de la Defensión, La Cartuja, Jérez de la Frontera [*b*]).

The most revealing documentation for the continuation of the simple Muslim-style white maiolicas well into the seventeenth century is to be found in at least thirty to forty oil paintings of the world-famous baroque Sevillian school (Appendix 1). Diego Rodríguez de Silva y Velázquez, Francisco de Zurbarán, and Bartolomé Murillo, all residents at times of the *collación* of Santa Magdalena just west of the Puerta de Triana and all considered masters of the *Siglo del Oro* of Spanish art, clearly painted contemporary dishes from local workshops being used by common people in some genre scenes, *bodegones*, or as props for more typical religious themes. That they were part of a stereotyped stage setting is apparent in repeated appearances in different paintings of the same vessel. Some renditions are of unglazed or lead-glazed objects, but most are the white maiolica domestic dishes that had epitomized Sevillian manufacture for at least two centuries. Portrayals are so realistic that the soft sheen of their glazing, the wear or imperfections of that coating, the heavy coils of their walls, the central interior ridging, and the wavering of decorative lines can be matched exactly in extant artifacts (Fig. 104).[360]

Some household earthenwares of both low and high grade were dispatched to the Americas. With the establishment of several colonial pottery industries the amount of these goods shipped steadily decreased because pottery was a cumbersome, breakable, unprofitable cargo. Sevillian tile, for which there was no serious colonial competition, was widely dispersed in the Indies, Mexico, Central America, and western South America. Some Talavera products likewise were shipped overseas, but they never matched the quantity of Sevillian shipments. Also included with Spanish wares were Italian maiolicas, principally the blue–on–blue type from the Ligurian coast, which was at its peak production at the time of greatest volume of trade to the Americas. Pisan sgraffito and marbelized lead-glazed wares have been recovered in the Caribbean, and a small number of Faenza vessels reached Mexico City.[361] These earthenwares were shipped through enterprising Italian factors in Sevilla and abroad, who competed successfully because the volume of native Spanish pottery was drastically reduced and of inferior quality.

At the end of the sixteenth century pottery making in Sevilla was the third largest craft industry, having advanced from eighth place in fifty years. This importance is apparent not so much in a traveler's mention of thirty kilns supplying fifty local retail outlets as in the figure provided by a municipal official of five thousand city residents involved in the craft.[362] The latter statistic likely included manual laborers around the workyards. If the

a

b

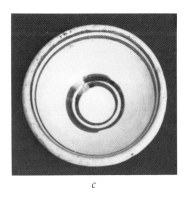

c

d

Figure 104. *The Miracle of Saint Hugh*, painted by Francisco de Zurbarán in 1629 for the Carthusian house of Santa María de las Cuevas on the west bank of the Río Guadalquivir opposite Sevilla, included three kinds of ceramics. As a testimonial to Zurbarán's accuracy, all now have been confirmed by excavations carried out at the contemporary Carthusian monastery outside of Jérez de la Frontera: *a*, coat of arms of the founder of the Sevilla monastery, Gonzalo de Mena, executed in a plaque of smooth-surfaced tiles on some extant buildings at the monastery, also appears on the two handled jars on the table; *d*, similar jar form, but with the Jérez Carthusian crest; *b*, blue–on–white Chinese porcelain rice bowl comparable to that turned upside down at left corner of table in painting; *c*, white maiolica plate with paired blue encircling lines like those on table (painting courtesy Museo de Bellas Artes, Sevilla; insets *b*, *c*, and *d* courtesy the Hermitage of Nuestra Señora de la Defensión, La Cartuja, Jérez de la Frontera).

number of these persons were to be added to those in dozens of small outlying establishments who routinely turned out pots for local consumption and who contributed to the manufacture of container vessels, it can be seen that ceramic manufacture, although of low caliber, flourished as never before in Andalusia. But the era of economic growth was nearing an end.

Under a cloud of evaporated American wealth, threatening inflation, and royal financial disarray, the national government was forced into a system of price controls early in the seventeenth century. More than three thousand individual groupings of items were covered in a sweeping 1627 regulation, or *tasación*, including the pottery then characteristically for sale in Sevilla. The variety of ceramics indicated, stemming from the focal position of the city on international trade networks, does not

yet reveal the far-reaching commerce to develop later
in English, French, Dutch, or German wares, many of
which were redirected overseas as legitimate goods and
as contraband.

Among the listed wares was one from Portugal, making
this the first record of Portuguese pottery being available
to Sevillians. The imported type is noted merely as *barros
de Portugal*,[363] implying that it was unglazed, undecorated,
coarse, and utilitarian in nature. If so, what made it sufficiently distinctive to attract buyers? Friable, inexpensive,
universal pots of this sort seldom were found much
beyond a limited radius from their place of manufacture.
Perhaps they owed their presence in the sales places
of Sevilla solely to a Portuguese trading colony of two
thousand persons residing in the Andalusian capital,[364]
some of whose members can be assumed to have dealt in
crafts of their native land. Finds have been made in Britain
and the Indies of a thin-walled, red-orange micaceous
pottery seemingly of different composition from the usual
Guadalquivir types, but associated with typical Sevillian
white maiolicas or Andalusian containers.[365] There is a
good chance that they were the *barros de Portugal* that got
cycled into the redistribution channels operating through
the Sevillian port. Alentejo or Lisbon sources have been
postulated.[366]

Other non-Sevillian ceramics considered in the 1627
tasación were those said to be white wares of Pisa. Inasmuch as the name of that town long had been popularly
synonymous with Italy and because Pisa was the outlet
through which goods of the central portion of the peninsula reached the western Mediterranean, it may be that the
ubiquitous Faenza whites were intended. No specific
examples of this finely made, snow white maiolica have
been recognized in Sevilla to date. However, some white-
slipped sgraffito wares thought to be of Pisan origin have
been recovered in the Indies and likely were also to be
had in Sevilla. The absence on the list of other former Italian styles, such as the Ligurian blue–on–blue and Montelupo polychromes on white, substantiates their demise
with the previous century.

Only three kinds of decorated ceramics were noted as
being Sevillian work, although the simple tablewares must
have been included in a *tasación* notation about *loza basta*.
None of these mentioned types were regarded as original.
They were copies, or *contrahechos*. The first duplicated
Talaveran styles, both authentic works from Talavera and
those from Puente del Arzobispo. The second was a blue
ground ware that carried on the Genoese tradition. The
third was an imitation of Chinese porcelain.[367]

The record of Chinese imitations brings up the question of the kinds and amounts of Chinese porcelains present in sixteenth- and seventeenth-century Sevilla that might have served as stylistic prototypes. The fact that almost no such porcelain presently exists in Andalusia in either whole or fragmentary state must be attributed to the same kind of disappearance of overseas riches seen in the case of American goods brought back to Europe and to a lack of archaeological investigations in potentially rewarding locales. One exception is the Jérez Carthusian establishment, where a dozen or so seventeenth-century tea cups and rice bowls have been retrieved.[368] A more indirect clue comes in several oil paintings by Francisco de Zurbarán, notable for the accuracy of secondary detail, including renditions of porcelain tableware (see Fig. 104). There are reasons to believe that porcelain was in fact an important element in urban Andalusian material life. First, there was Sevilla's prominence as an international port at a time when Portugal and the Low Countries, both with political and commercial ties to Spain, were leading agents in the distribution of millions of pieces of the ware to eager European customers. These were porcelains of expensive display grade and of a more common, less costly service grade. Second, after the instigation of the Oriental commerce via Manila to Mexico, one would assume some commodities to be shipped on to Spain. A few finds have been made in American waters of porcelains aboard sunken Spanish galleons bound for the motherland. Also, there was the prosperity of a large segment of the Sevillian society with a taste for luxuries and doubtless as susceptible as others to the seductions of fashion rages. Finally, recovered specimens such as those seen in Figures 105–107 demonstrate a forthright orientalization of composition and motifs that suggests immediacy of models rather than diffused interpretations by way of Italian or Talaveran sources.[369]

The making of the standardized types of containers for secondary agricultural products that began in the preceding century continued through the seventeenth, and, as in many previous years, was by far the most active sector of the pottery export trade. Six hundred twenty-four ships sailed in authorized *flotas* during that century, while scores of others may have slipped away without legal papers. Hamilton, however, reports a drop in seventeenth-century tonnage of about seventy-five percent compared with the first one hundred years of colonization.[370] The Chaunus note two peak trade periods, one from 1605 to 1610 and another from 1615 to 1620, with a steady decline thereafter.[371] The transatlantic exchange remained

Figure 105. Late sixteenth- or early seventeenth-century blue–on–white Sevillian maiolica plates bearing compositions and motifs believed to have been copied from Chinese porcelain prototypes, yet including some lingering Muslim concepts. The Oriental idea of the compartmentalized border was widely adopted throughout western Europe, but note that these Sevillian examples have dotted arabesque fillers in the Muslim manner and one border is based upon the highly typical eight-point Islamic star. Casual exterior designs many have been suggested by either Chinese or Muslim work, although the former never was so carelessly rendered. Their similarity suggests one factory or maker (courtesy the Hermitage of Nuestra Señora de la Defensión, La Cartuja, Jérez de la Frontera).

Figure 106. Late sixteenth- or early seventeenth-century Sevillian copies of introduced Chinese porcelain. In their more precise draftsmanship and landscaped centerpieces, these examples are less reflective of the Andalusian Muslim background than are those seen in Figure 105; these seem to have been influenced more by Italian interpretations of the Oriental model. Border patterns are known as *espiga de maiz*, tassel of corn, the corn plant having been introduced to Spain from the Americas. Similar reverse patterns on both pieces may indicate they came from the same workshop or artisan: *a*, blue–on–white, *b*, blue–orange–and–brown–on–white (courtesy the Hermitage of Nuestra Señora de la Defensión, La Cartuja, Jérez de la Frontera).

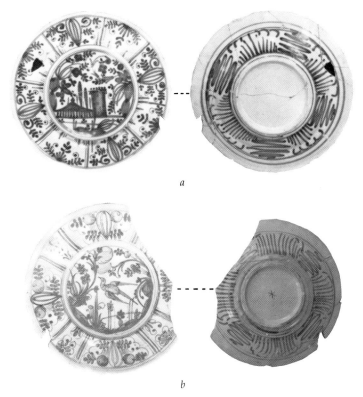

a

b

Figure 107. Two blue–on–white maiolica plates indebted to inspiration from Chinese porcelain examples. Their more casual draftsmanship may indicate a lessening hold of both Muslim and Italian aestheteic ideals on Sevillian decorators. Neither vessel bears an exterior decoration.

erratic, at best, with many years witnessing no formally recognized sailings.

Wine export during the period from 1650 to 1700 amounted to one-quarter of all peninsular foreign trade, although the volume declined toward the end of the century. Tax benefits granted to producers of the Aljarafe must have indirectly benefited the Sevillian and nearby pottery makers who provided the essential containers. Olive oil was of second importance in the external foodstuffs trade, increasing through the century as groves replaced vineyards in some parts of Andalusia. The key stretch of land for this enterprise lay between Sevilla and Cádiz. It can be guessed that products from there were funneled into the storage facilities of Sevilla for packaging in local ceramics.

The third-ranking agricultural by-product was *aguardiente*, a brandy whose export steadily increased as the century progressed. In the long term, export of this beverage was almost equally divided between the Canary Islands and the Andalusian mainland. There having been no wheel ceramic industry in the islands, the containers used there must have been made in Sevilla and shipped south to be stockpiled until needed. They are described as *botijas verdes* or *botijuelas*, with no specific volumes given.[372]

The *aguardiente* from Andalusia seems to have been put into vessels of two different configurations, one called a *frasquera* and the other a *limeta*. Both now are understood to have been squat, long-necked flasks. The former ranged from a capacity of 1.5 to 1.7 *arrobas*, almost the same as that of the *botijas peruleras*. The latter varied from .55 to 1.0 *arrobas*.[373] The carrot-shaped *ánfora* (Middle Type C in the Goggin taxonomy) does not conform to this description.[374] Nor has a constant body of such forms been recognized in archaeological ceramic materials in Spanish America. There is the real possibility of semantic distinctions between seventeenth-century scribe notations and modern interpretation, but one must also recognize that

these are at least possible hints that during the latter stages
of the period Andalusian *aguardiente* was sent out in glass
bottles.

By the middle of the seventeenth century the urban
potting industry dedicated to finer tablewares and tiles for
the upper classes stumbled. Talavera de la Reina, Talavera
of the Queen and her favors, had won the day. In the
countryside there may have been less open despair
because misery and hardship were no strangers. The trees
continued to bear fruit, and the grains ripened in the
hot Andalusian sun. Fatalistically, rural potters calmly
went about their business of keeping abreast of the simple
demands of the peasantry. It was, as it had been in the
beginning, a craft for the farmers.

Retrospective

Two and a half centuries had passed since Sevilla and
much of Andalusia had been taken back from the Muslims, yet in ceramics, as in other handicrafts, indications
of their former presence were pervasive. This came from
an introspective feeding upon the artistic ideals of the
past and a continued receptiveness to Nasridian influence.
However, an increasing divergence between the streams
of ceramic development of Christian Andalusians and
their Muslim neighbors can be detected. Its basis was to be
found in the steadily augmented participation of Andalusia in the international community of the western Mediterranean as opposed to the intensified isolation of the
Emirate of Granada, which was stranded, as it were, on
the brink of Europe.

In the branch of ceramics devoted to undecorated utilitarian earthenwares, fifteenth-century urban and rural
potteries turned out objects scarcely changed from those
made in previous centuries. They continued to function
in daily rhythms basically committed to the land and
its fruits and to an unadvanced mode of life. A presumed
greater volume of production of these articles would have
been required by resumption of agriculture in areas depop-
ulated in the plagues of the previous century or recaptured from retreating Muslims, by ameliorating circumstances as a result of more political stability, and by
expanding trade with Mediterranean partners then looking
westward to Europe's Atlantic shores.

Export of agricultural products in earthenware containers had been routine since the Roman era, but in the
fifteenth century a new ceramic commercialism based
in Sevilla appeared on the international scene. This effort
was devoted to the kind of simple, low-cost pottery that
previously had not been traded beyond a limited region

close to its source. Although the local internal market
probably was its primary target, one must assume shipping possibilities had expanded sufficiently to make export
practical. Perhaps there was some undetermined relationship between this enterprise and the shipment of foodstuffs in pottery packaging. At any rate, the new line
consisted of maiolica tableware made by the familiar Muslim methods for preliminary preparation of materials,
but with the final application of a jigger-and-jolly technique already being used by the Nasrids. This speeded up
production, while also promoting standardization. The
end products were not those intended for a Muslim clientele, however, but were to meet Christian market demand
for plates and bowls suitable for individual rather than
communal dining. Their price and purpose must have
been right, because such ware became so successful that it
continued as stock in trade for Sevillian workshops for
the next two centuries and was distributed wherever peri-
patetic Spaniards went.

    Above the subsistence level of the peasants and lower
class city dwellers served by the low grade functional
ceramics, there was an increasing complexity of life. Sevilla's heightened role as an active port, as home for a large
contingent of landed nobility and foreign merchants,
and as frequent court for the wandering monarchs brought
diversified needs and money to satisfy them. Potters
were encouraged to offer a greater variety of ceramics for
sale. Increased specialization in the fifteenth-century potting forces is indicated. One can postulate divisions
between makers of several grades of wares, between
throwers and decorators, between craftsmen operating
potter's wheels and those rolling and cutting tiles from
clay blanks. For all, a maturity of potting abilities is
obvious in some vessels of enormous sizes and in others
displaying a new degree of decorative difficulty. Among
the latter are clues to their having been made in a time of
uncertain cultural transformation, when what was old
and respected was being challenged by what was new and
novel. Traditional *mudéjar* processes and design elements
were combined in experimental ways with themes drawn
from art grammars of western Europe. Thus, *cuerda seca*
methods known in Andalusia since the tenth century now
carried some motifs popularized by the Italian Renaissance. Tiles copied the fragmented patterns of former *alicatado* by using an impressed pattern on a square form.
Castilian heraldry executed in Moresque *reflejo metálico*
accompanied polychromatic Moorish interlacements. Baptismal fonts carried a melange of repeated geometrics
and Christian symbolism. Like the society itself, the pot-

tery used in homes and places of worship was a curious
mixture of past and present.

The present was to come front and center by the mid-
sixteenth century as a direct result of the movement of
north Italians to Sevilla. Isabela may have hoped for such
a craft rejuvenation when she tried to lure these craftsmen
to the Guadalquivir, but it was the boomtown conditions
sixty years later that made it happen. Master Ligurians
set up workshops, brought in teams of their countrymen,
and proceeded to invade a promising market sustained
by an increasing flow of new wealth. At the same time,
imported Italian pottery was being offered for sale in
Sevillian markets by foreign traders, and other Italianate
works being created in Castile began to flood southward.
A bond between the ceramics of Italy and Andalusia
already existed because of a common technical Muslim
background. However, the Italians had far surpassed the
Andalusians in refining that base, as they had a mercantile
motivation that thus far had been missing from local potting circles. Therefore, new standards, procedures, and
styles were introduced both directly and indirectly into
a culturally exhausted ground facing likely extinction.
The effects were immediate, enormous, and to be seen in
the total range of pottery production activities from basic
processing of materials, to final firing of finished vessels,
to marketing the output. After seven centuries, Andalusian top-quality ceramics finally had rid themselves of
Muslimization. The exception was seen in the very important tile production that flourished because of a well cultivated local taste for such architectural embellishment.
It was stimulated to new beauty through advancement in
maiolica methods. In-glaze painting based upon the more
extensive Italian palette and freer approach to fanciful
naturalistic decoration also employed well known inter-
connected Moresque patterns that, like rich textiles, were
especially suited to great stretches of interior wall space.

The other principal source of accepted ceramic design
inspiration that revealed Andalusia's emergence from
the stranglehold of Islam into the European sphere of decorative arts was Chinese porcelain. Whether it was provided by actual pieces of Oriental ceramics in local
circulation during the sixteenth century or by a package
of ideas widely diffused among Spain's neighbors following the opening of the Canton trade is unknown. In either
case, like their contemporaries, Sevillian decorators
jumped on the Eastern bandwagon, at least in a small
way.

The fascination with new stylistic expressions did not
extend to the category of sixteenth-century common-

wares. A little more careful potting, several uncomplicated decorative modes used over and over for many years, and a few new forms to accommodate modest household improvements satisfied these potters and their customers. Change for change's sake remained the prerogative of the more monied and inquisitive.

One sub-branch of the *loza basta* industry was devoted to large-scale production of basic shipping containers for regional agricultural specialties bound for overseas colonists. The number of persons employed in this activity and the staggering quantity of vessels created out of the Guadalquivir clays suggest a substantial degree of industrialization and marketing, about which almost nothing is known. These products ended up tossed out on the far-flung junk heaps of Spanish civilization or hidden within architectural fabrics.

The sixteenth-century burst of ceramic effort was doomed to be short-lived. Within fifty or sixty years, because of economic and natural forces beyond the control of potters, creeping stagnation was apparent. The seventeenth-century record was a dismal one of diminishing quality, flagrant imitation, and decreasing output, until finally what was left was little more than the picked over bones of the once splendid Muslim craft.

PART II

Diffusion Abroad of Andalusian Pottery, Ceramic Technology, and Decorative Styles

The passage of parts or all of the Andalusian pottery complex of traits to the New World was progressive and in step with overseas Spanish expansion. From a staging area and cultural matrix prominently shared with Morocco, the diffusionary path spread southward to the Canary Islands in the late fifteenth century. There, a marketplace for exported Sevillian ceramics of all calibers evolved. Most categories were acquired for local consumption, but before the sixteenth century was out one particular kind of vessel was purchased to be used as packaging for Canarian products that were shipped further along the trade network.

Concurrently, as exploration of the Americas advanced, the same ware assemblage traveled across the Atlantic and into the Caribbean. That initial homogeneous grouping of ceramics did not vary from what was currently in use throughout Andalusia. However, about the middle of the sixteenth century, the increasing volume of overseas trade in several commodities precipitated the development of several new standardized forms based upon models well known from the very beginnings of the Andalusian ceramic continuum. Specifically made as containers for colonial commerce, they saw greater foreign than domestic use, although in both cases they served important secondary functions. Little substantial evidence exists for the manufacture in the West Indies of Spanish-style earthenwares by peninsular methods, other than construction terra cottas, such as roof and floor tiles, and bricks, and perhaps crude molds used in sugar refining.

Finally, in the Mexican highlands the Andalusian pottery that came in with colonization soon gave way in part to colonial counterparts created through application of characteristically Hispanic technology (Fig. 108). Soon, as Sevillian methods and styles refined, so did those of

Figure 108. Late fifteenth-century and sixteenth-century diffusion routes of Andalusian ceramics, technology, and decorative styles.

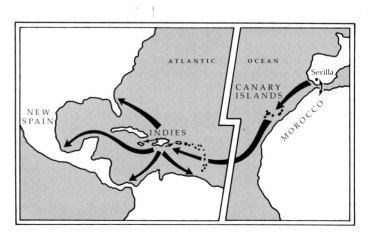

colonial artisans. These explicitly Spanish provincial wares competed on various socioeconomic levels with indigenous ceramics achieved by pre-Columbian methods and with copies of Hispanic products made by native populations using selected aspects of the introduced technology. Meanwhile, large-scale importation of Sevillian ceramic containers of foodstuffs and very limited amounts of Spanish decorated wares continued through the seventeenth century. But while local decorated wares persisted in echoing many Iberian fashions, they increasingly reflected Mexico's more eclectic milieu.

MOROCCO

Were it not for the Mediterranean Sea, today Spain and the western Maghreb, a broad shoulder of North Africa south of Gibraltar now known as Morocco, might be one nation stretching from the Pyrenees to the High Atlas. The waters posed so little barrier, in fact, that until the sixteenth century a procession of the same peoples occupied both continental extremes. Phoenicians had rounded Cap Spartel and inched their way hundreds of miles down the Atlantic coast of the African continent by about the first millennium before Christ.[1] They were followed by the Carthaginians, whose principal outlying venture was Rusaddir east of modern Tangiers. Next came the Romans, to whom the westernmost hump of the land mass just south of Baetica was known as the protectorate of Mauretania Tingitana (see Fig. 4). There they erected several important towns near the ocean and in a fertile interior valley the larger community of Volubilis, perhaps pushing aboriginal peoples even farther westward to the Canary Islands.[2]

As in Iberia, the history of Moroccan pottery essentially began with the Romans, although in the south the pattern was a broken one. Quantities of typical Roman wares confirm a regional ceramic industry related to an active agriculturalism. Because population was less, it seems not to have been on a scale comparable to that being carried on contemporaneously in the Guadalquivir Valley. When the Romans finally quit this African province, their mode of life, religion, language, and industries, including pottery making, rapidly died out. The superficial Romanization of the western Maghreb, therefore, contrasts with the cultural penetration in Andalusia, where it left behind a more deeply implanted legacy.

Vandals crossed southward out of Spain to North Africa, where in the fifth century they founded several

independent kingdoms. Apparently they did not locate in
former Roman towns, except at Tingis, or Tangiers, where
they might have absorbed artisans practicing familiar
crafts.[3] In the sixth and seventh centuries the Byzantines
moved in as part of the far-flung spread of Justinian's
empire (see Fig. 13). Because they previously had drawn
upon the accumulated technical knowledge of the Near
East, their ceramics can be postulated to have conformed
generally to those made in Byzantium. Whatever their
pottery, it was of little concern to the rude desert nomads
of Morocco who crowded in upon them. When the urban
Byzantines departed, nothing of their ceramic technology
lingered among the rural Berbers.

In 680, Berber tribes occupying most of the western
Maghreb succumbed to an Arab thrust all the way from
Egypt into southern Morocco. Enjoying a similar life style,
the Berbers felt such an affinity with the invading
Bedouins that within a very short time they had assimilated a fair measure of Mohammedan religion and Arabic
language. Just thirty-one years after this uneasy union
the two peoples together crossed the turbulent waters at
the mouth of the inland sea to plant themselves in Andalusia. One of the Moroccan points of departure is believed
to have been Qsar es-Seghir, then possibly a tiny village
at the narrowest point of the straits (Fig. 109). Thereafter it
was the Spanish Muslims, an Arab-Berber symbiosis stimulated periodically by various other Near Easterners and
all overriding a native Romano-Visigothic stratum, who
were responsible for new aesthetics in the westernmost

Figure 109. North and central
Morocco.

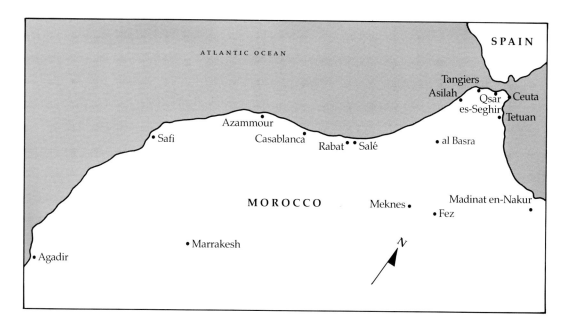

Table 4. Ruling Dynasties of Morocco.

Idrisid	788–1070
Almoravid	1090–1147
Almohad	1147–1248
Merinid	1248–1465
Wattasid	1456–1549
Saadian	1594–1654
Alouite	1666–

Note: Many of these dates are approximate; gap or overlap periods indicate times of no central authority.

corner of the Islamic world. They drew upon cultural reservoirs situated far to their east. The principal route to them stretched across the North African littoral.

During the eighth century, political and religious conflicts at the heart of Islam sent exiles streaming to the uncertain safety of new frontiers. In the far west one refugee faction was creating its own domain over older remains in the Guadalquivir basin, while in Morocco another splinter group, belonging to the Arab Idrisid family, was finding followers and haven in the unoccupied, steep valley of the Wadi Fez at the western skirts of the Middle Atlas Mountains (Fig. 109, Table 4). In this fertile spot gushing waters of many channels invited desert dwellers to stay. Nearby timbered mountains provided fuel, minerals, and game. Trails through natural passes in all directions converged upon the valley, making it an advantageous locale for the first focus in the region of urban Islamic society. Furthermore, the site was nearly the same short distance south from the Mediterranean Sea as Sevilla was to the north, thereby expediting communication between these two enclaves of western Islam.

From its beginnings the town of Fez was populated by a mixture of incoming Arabs, local Berber tribes, and a sprinkling of Jews. Within two decades after the original settlers had claimed the slopes by the river, other large bands of city dwellers arrived to join them, and so almost immediately gave the new center the character of a teeming eastern bazaar. The first to come were many families unable to endure strife in Spain. There, at Córdoba in 805, they were among Neo-Muslims involved in an unsuccessful plot to kill the emir. He ruthlessly responded by having the artisan sector of the city razed and its inhabitants expelled from the peninsula.[4] Estimates of their number range from eight hundred to eight thousand. Because of their enforced transfer to the south and the geographical proximity of the two western arms of Near

Eastern colonization, over the following epochs the same pattern of human dispersal was to be repeated time and again. Fez gradually was recognized as a traditional sanctuary for Spanish Muslims. Such a southward drift of dissidents had the effect of fostering an Andalusian hegemony there in the mechanical arts. The quarter on the right bank of the river where they congregated became acclaimed for "Cordoban" leather, gleaming copper and bronze articles, paper, musical instruments, felt "Fez" caps, intricately detailed jewelry, silken and woolen textiles and embroideries.[5]

Meanwhile, the Spanish Muslims were followed to Fez by another contingent of outcasts. These were from Kairouan in the eastern Maghreb. The Kairouanians, regarding themselves as elite intellectuals, were installed opposite the Andalusians on the left bank of the wadi. A steep incline between the two entities was left to a tumble of tanneries, mills, and dye vats. Although Fez was a single city, each of its two rival parts sought to maintain its own identity with its special mosque and markets within a walled compound. Through the succeeding centuries the wall between them was dismantled and the aesthetic and other cultural distinctions blurred. Notwithstanding, the Kairouanians' district assumed the greater commercial, religious, and social status, while in the arts the imprint of the Andalusians never was erased. And in outward appearance, old Fez resembled old Córdoba and old Sevilla.

Because Fez provided a metropolitan environment sustained by diversified, successful agriculture, pottery making was an important industrial activity carried on by Arab and Berber men who were taught the Arab methods. The craft was regulated by the same kind of informal controls as existed to the north.[6] Most of the potteries were concentrated in the Jami al Andalus, or Andalusian right-bank quarter, on a plain just inside the Bab-Khukha. Others spread over land immediately outside the walls and several burial grounds nearby. There they still flourish, although they now are jammed in among low class homes and small factories making other goods, the air about them soured by more than a millennium of ripening clay and rancid olive pressings.[7] These locations originally were chosen so that the unsightly smoky yards would not impinge upon more settled plots closer to the river. Raw materials, such as a fine-grained clay, lead, tin, copper, and olive residue could be delivered easily by donkeys. Without question, the Moroccan workyards were identical to shops in Spain following the same methods and work routines. One or more cylindrical or squared-up, domed

hornos arabes hulked in the rear of the compounds, each
morning sending columns of black smoke from burning
olive pressing residue toward the ring of surrounding hills
(see Fig. 37).[8] The usual complement of pottery-making
gear included compound kick wheels placed in trenches
(see Fig. 36).[9] Introduced at the outset of the Moroccan
industry, these wheels remain universal.

The concentration of pottery workyards in the part of
town occupied by Spanish Muslims, the known continued
intercourse between Fez and the cities in Andalusia, and a
common Near Eastern heritage underlie the belief that
most of the ceramics of the urbanized sectors of the two
regions were broadly similar. They may not have been
identical, owing to differences between the ethnic mix of
the Guadalquivir basin, which was strongly Arab-Syrian,
and that of north central Morocco, which was more Arab-
Mesopotamian. In the beginning these shared ceramics
would have consisted of the restricted number of functional shapes typical of the region since the Romans.
Those wares of better quality can be expected to have had
the simple plastic decorations customary throughout Arab-
held provinces everywhere. There was no transfer to
Morocco of the ceramic refinements of the ʿAbbasids, such
as white or luster maiolica. Instead, utilitarian objects
for storage, transport, and cooking comprised the basic
output (see Figs. 18–22, 24 for comparable examples).
Whatever Berber designs were used on handmade pots in
surrounding villages had no place in the diffused industry. In rural settings water wheel jars were another important component of the common inventory, inasmuch as
the Syrian-style vertical and horizontal *norias* and their
double-lobed jars had spread quickly south from Muslim
Spain (see Figs. 16, 17, 23).[10]

By the tenth century, as the caliphate of Córdoba
attracted a growing group of the best artisans of the Near
East, one might think that comparable ceramic elaborations would also have drifted south to merge with others
diffusing westward via Ifriqiya. At Tlemcen, Algeria,
for example, green and brown polychromes have been
recovered from a tenth-century potter's shop,[11] and a
scattering of this and other coeval advanced decorative
styles have been noted along the adjoining coastal zones.
Had such a fusion of styles occurred at ninth- and tenth-
century Fez, the ceramic assemblage would have included
manipulated surfaces covered with lead glazes, others
with black iron oxide slips bearing lightly etched designs
over unglazed bodies, brown and green patterns on white
engobe, or perhaps red pots decorated in white geometrics. The arrival of more Andalusians after the collapse of

the caliphate should have further solidified some of these modes at Fez. Only future investigations within the city can prove what seems a logical assumption. Any such early Andalusian influence likely was confined to the urban industry at the capital.

No impact of the western caliphate on local pottery can be seen in the contemporary northern Moroccan provincial city of al Basra. Located to the northwest in an interior valley and now nearly obliterated by a modern town and farms, al Basra for a time under the Idrisids assumed second importance in the region. Later it was a Fatimid provincial capital as that dynasty spread west from Tunisia to take control of much of the upper expanse of Africa; it was destroyed and subsequently rebuilt, and ultimately was abandoned by the Almoravids in the twelfth century. At its peak the town was an important way station on a long-distance trade route from the Sahara to southern Europe. This seemingly strategic prominence makes it surprising that recent probing has failed to produce ceramics that would confirm any direct awareness of the dramatic craft enrichment taking place in al Andalus.

At al Basra are the remains of combustion units of three large, nearly square, two-chambered, updraft kilns, several of which may have served in pottery production. They were located within the former city walls, but well away from concentrations of domiciles. Kiln walls were formed of sun-dried bricks and rammed earth, which hardened in use. Cross elements of brick supported the perforated floor between chambers, but sections of the floor had fallen from overheating or overburdening. Assumed to have been in operation during the time when the Cordoban caliphate was flourishing, it tells much of the modest level of cultural advancement of this rather geographically isolated center that none of the Iberian pottery elaborations was present. The only possible exceptions were a few examples of simple lead-glazed and *cuerda seca* vessels. Moreover, the mass of the plainware characteristically was incompletely oxidized during firing, indicating a lack of technical expertise, and a small percentage of vessels was fashioned by hand in the indigenous manner.[12]

A third site of contemporary age was Madinat en-Nakur, a village situated near the Mediterranean coast east of the Rif Mountains, which is of historical interest as the first settlement established in Morocco as Islam lapped toward the Atlantic. Several archaeological samplings at Madinat en-Nakur yielded a small array of utilitarian earthenwares thought to date from the eighth to twelfth centuries. They revealed no hint of the western diffusion of Near Eastern ceramic refinements or Andalusian response to them. A large proportion of Nakur wares were handmade, from which the excavators judged that the town was never sufficiently urbanized to have promoted a local commercial pottery industry.[13] Nor, it seems, did its citizens engage in the kind of trade that would have brought in specialized Spanish items.

Coming out of the western Sahara in the late eleventh century, the Berber Almoravid conquerors founded Marrakesh and moved on to claim Fez as a capital. Using that city and its environs as a depot, they campaigned as far east as Algeria, then crossed the watery gap into Iberia. Although their control of both Morocco and southern Spain was short-lived, they firmly promoted peaceful interaction between Muslims of the two territories that lasted through many later eras. In 1106 and 1126, during their drive to further the Islamization of al Andalus, they were responsible for the introduction of mozarab religious exiles and Spanish Christian mercenaries into the Maghreb.[14] One sultan is said to have had as many as twelve thousand Castilians in his army.[15] Some of these uprooted Iberians may have stayed in North Africa; whether they exercised any effect upon craft orientation is unclear. However, a community of culture makes it no surprise that ceramics recovered at Bougie and Beni Hammed in Tunisia duplicate *taifa* specimens in Spain.[16]

The next conquerors were the Almohads, considered to be the greatest of all the Berber rulers of Morocco. One of their earliest leaders was Abd el Moumen, son of a potter and founder of Rabat. That town was constructed by Christian slaves to serve as a link between the capital of Marrakesh and the seat of Andalusian provincial government in Sevilla. In the southern cities architectural embellishments, the first major ones in Morocco since the Romans, brought a stamp of limited conformity to the extensive holdings. The minaret of the Kutubiya mosque in Marrakesh, very similar in size and style to the Giralda of Sevilla, was graced with a few colored tiles, which still are in place. All three centers of Marrakesh, Rabat, and Sevilla were cogs in the same economic structure, which permitted merchants to freely commute back and forth between continents and maintain homes in both.[17] Along the coasts of Morocco the Almohads licensed Christian traders, most often Genoese, who were responsible for mixing the goods of Europe, Asia, and Africa. Saffron and lac from the Near East, indigo from India, pearls from the Persian Gulf, and musk from Himalayan deer found their way in Italian ships to ports such as Ceuta, where they were exchanged for European cotton, linen, serge, or fustian textiles, cork, or olive oil, or for African wax, ivory, gold, and slaves.[18]

Important as an operational base between the African and European parts of the Almohad empire, Fez prospered commercially. The flow to the south of Spanish Muslim personnel drawn from many ranks was responsible there for a cultural flowering with a pronounced Andalusian flavor, extending even to construction of an Andalusian mosque in 1203.[19] This was further intensified by the Turkish blockade on the eastern borders that interrupted contact with the Near East. Marrakesh also witnessed the infiltration of Spanish Muslims and Christians, but it remained more African. This southward movement of craftsmen who continually added to the complexities of Moroccan life was balanced by the northward passage of desert camel herders. In Spain their asceticism softened as they were transformed into patrons of the arts. In short, there was a very consequential commercial and technological interdependence between al Andalus and Morocco during the twelfth century.

Unfortunately, neither archival nor much archaeological documentation exists to tell of *taifa* or Almohad-style ceramics being made in Fez, Marrakesh, or smaller communities around Morocco. However, given the known extensive interplay between north and south, the fundamental sharing of basic social attitudes, and the emergence of "Moorish" art, it would have been remarkable had no comparable nuances been reflected in the two complexes. Future excavations, particularly in Fez, may reveal the same assortment of forms and decorative fashions that has been identified with eleventh- and twelfth-century al Andalus.

In the same fateful year of 1248, when the Almohads lost Sevilla to Fernando III of Castile, they also retreated across Morocco as the Beni Merin tribe advanced. As these newest rulers secured their political position, they entrenched themselves along the northern Maghreb coasts to continue harassment of the Iberian Christians, while at the same time providing aid to the new Emirate of Granada. One of their installations was the small fortified port of Qsar es-Seghir (see Fig. 109), from which it was relatively easy to disrupt sea traffic bound through the Straits of Gibraltar. Extensive excavations there in the late 1970s showed that from about 1287 to 1350 the few residents of the fort apparently were dependent for necessary domestic earthenwares on potteries in neighboring Ceuta on the Moroccan shore and for luxury wares on Málaga across the water. Predictably, both categories of pottery reflected the ceramic evolutionary stream as it had thus far progressed in the western Mediterranean.

Whether for convenience or out of necessity, about 1350
a kiln built in Qsar es-Seghir—one that may have been
operated only seasonally—took over production of most of
the required utilitarian ceramics. At the same time handmade pottery, probably supplied by nearby Berber villages, continued to be used. Contrary to usual practice, the
kiln was erected almost in the center of the walled town
instead of at its perimeter. Perhaps the location was chosen to take advantage of a large well associated with the
public bath next door. Steadily deteriorating quality of the
earthenwares produced suggests either a marginal enterprise in a state of decline, unsupportable economic and
political stresses as Merinid fortunes worsened, or a small
group of less capable potters finding employment in a
second-rate industry. Higher caliber decorated wares, such
as *reflejo metálicos*, *cuerda secas*, scratchware (in which a
panel of black manganese was etched to reveal a light
paste), and quartz inlaid redwares, continued to be
imported from Nasrid or Valencian Spain, or perhaps from
central Morocco. The Merinid top-quality styles showed
a continued adherence to plastic decorative treatments
favored by the Almohads and later by the *mudéjares* of
Andalusia. Utilitarian vessels were familiar forms from the
great bank of common wares utilized throughout western
Islam, such as braziers, well jars, basins, cook pots, water
jars, and oil lamps. The primary serving vessel was the
narrow-footed bowl with splayed walls that terminated in
a sharp vertical carination.[20]

Meanwhile, in Fez the Merinids gradually assimilated
city-based Arab culture, which led to a rejuvenation of
Muslim civilization such as was occurring in Granada.
They commenced numerous beautification projects in the
old quarters, which remained the axis of commerce. Educational houses, or *madrasas*, mosques, public baths, and
fountains were built or refurbished, and shortly the city
gained a reputation as a center of learning and culture.
A fifteen thousand-manuscript library, most of which was
confiscated from Sancho IV of Castile (see Table 2), concentrated there the learning of Muslim Spain, which
attracted European scholars south. The canyonlike alley
streets winding tightly through the market stalls remained
too narrow for any vehicular traffic, the tumble of buildings too dense to permit necessary expansion. In order to
alleviate the congestion, construction of a new administrative and military center was ordered a few hundred yards
downstream. To be called the White City, or Fez Jdid,
it was surrounded by towering double walls of rammed
earth much like those at Sevilla, inside of which were
expansive palaces with reflecting pools and manicured
gardens, barracks, and, of course, a great mosque. More

Figure 110. *Alicatado* tile panel on twelfth-century wall in the Ben Yusuf *madrasa* in Marrakesh, with stellar and terraced border patterns identical to those of contemporary Andalusia.

than any other spot in Morocco, Fez Jdid competed in the grace and elegance of its structures with the last stronghold of the Muslims in Spain.

Particularly provocative in the study of ceramics was the appearance in fourteenth-century Fez of the same complex of Persian or Seljuk Turk artistic concepts that were contemporaneously being diffused to the Nasrid Emirate of Granada. The parallel was so marked that some think Fez resembled a secondary focus of Granadine culture. The borrowed or jointly pursued ideas were demonstrated in similar ways on stucco, wood, metal, and clay.

The only tangible evidence thus far for a presumed common store of ceramic traits between Nasrid Granada and Merinid Fez and Marrakesh is found in *alicatado* tiling (Fig. 110).[21] With the full gamut of stellar and geometric patterns characteristic of coeval Spanish Muslims, panels of such tiling were used on dados and floors of most important buildings erected in Fez during the Merinid reign. Many of the mosaics still endure, but—because they are of low-fired, relatively soft earthenware—they show severe ravages from attrition. From such remains it can be observed that the process of manufacturing stanniferous glazes was well known by Merinid times and that local craftsmen were equally as skilled as their European col-

leagues in laying the tile fragments. Apparently they
remained so satisfied with *alicatado* that they never
adopted the *mudéjar* Sevillian *cuerda seca* or *cuenca* tile
methods, although the former must have been part of their
shared cultural heritage.

As for hollow wares assignable to the Merinid period at
Fez, which lasted to the middle of the fifteenth century,
one can only speculate that local potters, who likely were
joined by refugees from Andalusia, used wheel and mold
to turn out both *tour de force* and more ordinary ceramics.
Examples of lead-glazed vessels bearing impressed or
applied patterning, of vessels with dark oxide painting
over unglazed light-colored body walls or sgraffito through
dark engobe, and a variety of maiolica styles, possibly
including *cuerda seca* and *reflejo metálico*, likely existed. Ibn
Batuta earlier had written of "fine golden pottery" at
Fez, Málaga, and al Andalus.[22] If so, these special products
were primarily for use by the richest inhabitants of north
and central Morocco and did not become goods on the
transmediterranean trade routes.

After the fall of Granada hundreds of thousands of
Spanish Muslims, including the emir Boabdil, repeated a
well-established precedent and fled to various parts of
the Maghreb. Surely many Granadine potters joined colleagues at Fez, where stylistic compatability facilitated
their ready merger.

Had the Spanish Crown advanced the crusade against
the infidels into North Africa the sixteenth-century distribution of Andalusian pottery and its creators would have
been far different. This pursuit was contemplated but
was rejected because of the cost of absorbing diverse sul-
tanates. Some of the ceramic complex that was dispatched
to the Americas might well have been sucked back along
the African Mediterranean coasts, from where many of its
manifestations originally had emanated.

A notable aberration was Qsar es-Seghir, which was
captured by the Portuguese in 1458. The Muslim population was expelled and the Merinid kiln fell into disrepair.
An abrupt introduction of a group of earthenwares typical
of both contemporary Andalusia and Portugal indicated
that the European garrison was supplied from those
sources.[23] However, the distinctions between Islamic and
Christian pottery assemblages were lessened by the facts
of common background and cultural continuity. In general, sizes of some Christian vessels were considerably
larger than the earlier Muslim equivalents, but others were
of small capacities obviously meant for individual use.
The restricted number of Christian forms indicated a
greater production standardization owing to intensified
commerce.

The typical light Guadalquivir paste of many tin-glazed wares at fifteenth- and sixteenth-century Qsar es-Seghir suggests that they had been made in Sevilla rather than in Lisbon or other Portuguese shops. These included plain white tablewares typically of the mass-produced Andalusian industry, as well as others decorated in blue, black, and purple patterns. Also from Sevilla came another of its primary exports, *cuenca* tiles. They may have reached Qsar es-Seghir via Lisbon, one of the main redistribution points for this product. With Italian ships lacing the Mediterranean, it was not surprising that trade maiolicas from Montelupo and the Ligurian coast also were deposited in this North African port, as they were in Sevilla (Fig. 111).

Exactly what happened to Fez pottery between the end of Nasrid power and the last quarter of the seventeenth century, the date of a small assortment of maiolica feast bowls recovered from a locked storeroom in a Meknes palace of the sultan Moulay Ismail, is guesswork.[24] The only certainty is the unbroken continuum of *alicatado* to the exclusion of all other forms of wall tiling. At some unknown period, which might fall in this lacuna, there was a local development without significant Spanish background: roof tiles covered with a brilliant deep green glaze became customary for palaces and shrines. It may be postulated that unelaborated white maiolicas and the parallel lead-glazed series, such as was characteristic of fifteenth- through seventeenth-century Andalusia, contin-

Figure 111. Representative sample of Italian maiolicas from Montelupo recovered in sites in Morocco, the Caribbean basin, and central Mexico, datable to the first half of the sixteenth century: *a*, obverses with bold polychromatic patterns in two shades of blue, brown, and orange; *b*, obverses with etched designs in dark blue borders, with added polychromed elements; *c*, obverses with arabesques in two shades of blue.

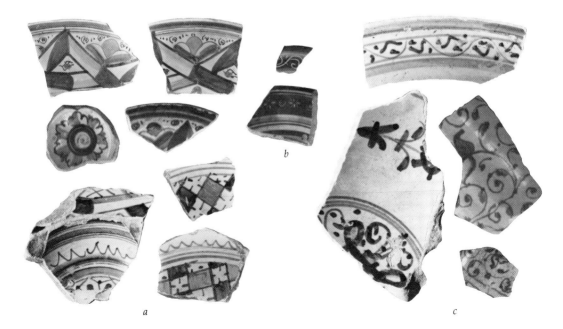

a

b

c

ued to be produced for ordinary household purposes.
A 1550 notation by a Spanish traveler in Fez of white,
green, and *melado* plates and *escudillas* being fashioned
there would appear to confirm this.[25] Inasmuch as no
Moroccan export trade in such ceramics existed, it is
unlikely that they repeated either the Sevillian commercialized jigger-and-jolly methods or the exact shapes diagnostic of that industry. Among finer hollow wares, *cuerda
secas* were almost out of fashion at the end of the fifteenth
century and are not apt to have appeared in any amounts
after that date. Tin-glazed earthenwares decorated in a
polychromatic palette became usual. Less rigid modes calling for plastic modifications beneath colorless or tinted
lead glazes that were so long an integral part of Islamic
grammar likely continued. It seems reasonable to believe
that if *reflejo metálico* had been made, it was abandoned
in Fez shops as economic conditions deteriorated toward
the end of Beni Merin supremacy. The methods by which
all commercial urban ceramics were made remained based
upon use of pit wheels and *hornos arabes,* thereby affording
modern researchers valuable insight into former practice
in Andalusia. In rural environments there probably was a
continuing reversion to the hand methods of the past,
even for some kinds of vessels formerly thrown on a potter's wheel.

It may be suggested that under religious and cultural
pressures there occurred a distillation or intensification of
traditional views of design. This would have entailed a
purging of all quasi-Europeanizations and an introvertive
concentration upon fewer abstract floral and geometric
elements. Under the mantle of purification, Gothic figural
devices, as well as those having a long history in Spanish
Muslim art, disappeared; inexplicably, so did calligraphy.
Thereafter, even through a slow reformulation of thematic
characteristics of a deep-seated, latent Islamic background,
the artistic idiom of fourteenth- and fifteenth-century
Granada was maintained in Berbería as the fundamental
language of ceramic decorative art. Quality of potting,
together with the forms of vessels and their decoration,
ossified. This was because the Moroccans not only were
cut off from Europe and sealed in the interior of their
lands, but also because the Ottoman Turks on their eastern
flank kept them from friendly Near Easterners. Hess notes
that the creative spirit of these westernmost Mohammed-
ans was unable to retain its strength after being pulled
from its Iberian cultural base. Secondly, as the importance
of cities declined, tribal power in rural areas increased
to the detriment of urban commercial pottery.[26] Thus, at
the time persuasive forces from outside Spain were caus-

ing a mounting redirection of method and decoration in Andalusian ceramics, Moroccan pottery split off from the main evolutionary trunk of western Muslim ceramic development to grow steadily more inbred and non-European (Fig. 112). Overt Andalusian stylistic affiliation dissipated just when Spanish-tradition pottery and technology were being diffused to the New World. The only minor extraneous influence on Moroccan pottery came from Chinese porcelain design. One result was that in Moroccan stanniferous wares one can observe what might have followed in Andalusian maiolica had not other Europeans introduced Spanish craftsmen to the Renaissance.

Through the nearly eight hundred-year history of the Muslims in Spain, it was not only persons and influence that flowed like a riptide back and forth across the Straits of Gibraltar, but also property. Because in a loose sense ceramics of Morocco and Andalusia are believed to have been stylistic cousins, chance finds of vessels and fragments along the northern borders of the Moroccan territory generally cannot be associated with a specific manufacturing center. That is to say, they appear Andalusian only because ceramics of that area are better known. For example, slipped or oxide-painted types recovered from upper deposits at the old Roman site of Lixis on the Atlantic may have come from thirteenth- or fourteenth-century Málaga,[27] having been brought south by the Nasrid commerce or perhaps by Italian merchantmen. They might also have been made at Fez. *Reflejo metálico* excavated from the Muslim levels at Qsar es-Seghir strongly point either to the Emirate of Granada or to the *mudéjar* shops at Manises as suppliers, but they also might have originated at Fez. Extensive excavations and physical analyses of clays utilized for pottery, neither of which have been accomplished in central Morocco, would offer some answers.

The matter of intrusive Hispanic pottery is a bit better understood for periods following the exit of the Muslims from Spain. In view of the rather considerable penetration of Morocco's coastal areas by Europeans, much more Iberian pottery ought to be scattered there than has been recognized to date. Stormy contacts between Iberians and Moroccans dating from the middle of the fifteenth century continued for most of the sixteenth and seventeenth centuries. The Portuguese built a string of strategic posts from the Gates of Hercules down the Atlantic coast. They began at Tangiers and Arzila in 1471, extended south to Mazagan in 1502, to Agadir and Safi in 1502 and 1508, and finally established themselves at Azammour in 1513. At first these installations represented a step-by-step

a

Figure 112. Maiolica vessels of probable late nineteenth-century Fez manufacture with elements of older Islamic design conventions: *a*, tapered bowl with polychrome radial pattern of lotus and 'Abbasid leaf motifs reminiscent of tenth-century Cordoban caliphate green–and–brown–on–white ware; *b*, flat-based *lebrillo* with blue dotted and hooked scrolls, abstracted florals, dot cluster fillers, and density of pattern comparable to some seventeenth-century Mexican examples, both derived from a shared design background (courtesy Oudaia Museum, Rabat [*a*], and Sultan's Palace Museum, Tangiers [*b*]).

b

exploration around Africa. Later they were necessary to
protect a growing East Indies trade and to serve as outlets
for slavers. Stray bits of Portuguese maiolica and Chinese
porcelains brought by Portuguese galleons from Canton
have been seen in surface debris around some of these settlements. Excavations doubtless would uncover other
sixteenth-century Iberian ceramics, a large proportion of
which can be predicted to have been made in Sevilla.

For their part, the Spaniards attempted establishment of
an Atlantic coast trading station for the benefit of the
Canary Islands. They put other trading and defense garri-
sons in Mediterranean sites, such as Melilla (1497), Oran
(1509–1732), Algiers (1510–1529), Bougie (1510–1553),
Tunis (1535–1574), and Tripoli (1510–1551) in attempts to
check the on-coming Ottoman Turks, whose holdings
across the North African shore and alliances with Barbary
pirates threatened Hapsburg Spain. After Portugal
regained its independence in the middle of the seventeenth century, Spain held on to Tangiers and Ceuta. One
would expect to see merchandise out of Sevilla destined
for the westerly residents of these scattered posts. Additionally, exiled Nasridians of 1492 chose Mediterranean
towns like Tetuan because of their Spanishness;[28] exiled
Jews of 1492 occupied Asilah south of Tangiers; exiled *moriscos* of 1501 converted the Atlantic port of Salé into a
corsair kingdom. In Algiers there were six thousand of
these various refugees, about half of them from southern
Spain. Another wave of exiled Spanish Muslims came
to Morocco in 1609–1614. As had their predecessors, they
moved into urban centers like Tetuan, where they continued to speak Spanish and practice many Spanish customs.[29] All the former Andalusians, who were and still are
called *andaluces*, probably had everyday pottery typical
of their time in their baggage. Indeed, a smattering of
sherds and smooth polychrome tiles recovered around the
country are signposts of the migration of Andalusians,
of piracy that brought confiscated loot to Moroccan towns,
or of outright trade with Spanish merchants. In any view,
they were anomalies in the local pottery sequence.

CANARY ISLANDS

A major event in the fifteenth-century history of Castile
was the acquisition of the Canary Islands (Fig. 113), which
would become a microcosm of mainland Spain and a
springboard for the diffusion of Andalusian culture,
including ceramics, to the New World. Located about
seven hundred miles south of Andalusia off the south
Moroccan Atlantic coast, this chain of seven craggy vol-

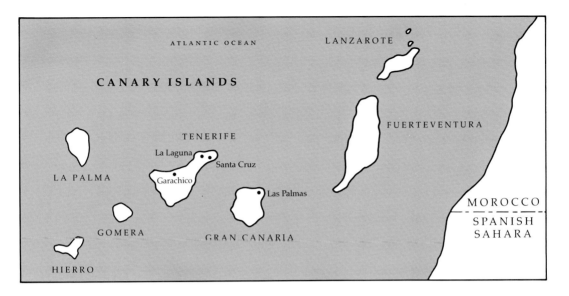

Figure 113. Canary Islands, way station enroute to Spanish America.

canic islands became Spain's first overseas colony. It remains today as the sole remnant of an empire that once stretched around the world.

The Canary Islands apparently were known in antiquity. The Greek astronomer and geographer Ptolemy, writing in A.D. 150, identified the pyramidal peak of Teide on Tenerife as Mount Atlas, commonly believed to hold up the sky. Fifteen Roman amphorae found in the waters off various of the islands and thought to date to the third century further indicate some knowledge of the islands' existence.[30] Ptolemy's book of world geography became part of a forgotten body of classical knowledge, and the Canaries for many centuries remained on the hazy boundaries of the civilized world. As Europe began to stir in the lower Middle Ages the islands were rediscovered, in the epochs bridging the thirteenth and fourteenth centuries, by the Genoese sailors D'Oria, Vivaldi, and, most notably, Lanzarotto Malocello.[31] The initial trips were followed by others from Majorca and Portugal, usually under command of Genoese pilots. Portugal laid a tenuous claim to the islands, then known as the Fortunate Islands because of their mild climate. No attempt at land exploration came until 1402, when a small garrison led by a Norman ventured onto a barren, desolate dot of land named Lanzarote after its discoverer. Castile eventually gave token backing to the colony, thus putting Spain and Portugal into contention for the island chain of which only Lanzarote, Hierro, and Fuerteventura were involved. A confused history of exploration, attempted conquest of the natives, and claims and counterclaims by private landowners and royal houses followed. This lasted until 1477, when Isabela of Castile formally took possession of the islands of Gran Canaria and Gomera. Two years later Portugal was forced to renounce its claims in the Treaty of Alcacovas. The islands of Tenerife and La Palma were not subdued until 1496, after Columbus, that most famous of all Genoese sailors, already had passed through the chain twice on his way to immortality.

The development of the caravel—two-masted, lanteen-rigged, and high-boarded—made long-distance exploration of the Atlantic a possibility, and Ptolemy's manuscript, *Geographia*, which was discovered in an Arab university and in Spain was translated into Arabic and Latin, fired the imagination of seamen. Iberian cartographers and navigators were among the best in the world at the time, owing in part to their inheritance from Islamic occupiers, who had sharpened navigational skills more than any preceding peoples.[32] During the years when the rights to the Canaries were in dispute, Portuguese sailors, motivated and trained by Prince Henry the Navigator, slowly groped their way down the west coast of Africa in a search for a way to the east. They passed by or through the Canaries. On their return voyages coastal currents forced them into a wide arc out to sea, which eventually led them to the virgin Azores. Those tiny specks of land in the immense waters of the Atlantic were destined to become the last port of call for many vessels returning home from the Americas. At the same time, other vessels and their crews were sailing out of the Gates of Hercules or down the Guadalquivir into the Atlantic, bringing back gold, ivory, slaves, and tropical products for the markets of Sevilla and Lisbon. The Cape Verde Islands south of the Canaries and Madeira to the northwest soon were known to the European world. Genoese farmers introduced sugar cane from Cyprus and Sicily first to Portuguese Madeira and then to the Spanish Canaries, from where it was sent to the Indies.[33]

Most of the aboriginal population of the Canaries was killed off, setting a pattern to be repeated as the empire expanded. Then the land was divided and resettled primarily by a mixture of men from Andalusia, Estremadura, and Genoa. The town of La Laguna, situated on Tenerife in the healthier highlands overlooking the sea, served as capital of the colony. Down at the port the village of Santa Cruz grew with a motley group of fishermen, seamen, slavers, and a few surviving native Guanches. In the sixteenth century Las Palmas came into being on the island of Gran Canaria, the government official residence being located in a district called Triana.

Administration of the colony and its supplies came directly from Sevilla, making it inevitable that the earthenwares in which foodstuffs were packed and shipped and

those essential in every Spanish household or farm would
be included in outbound cargoes. This commerce must
have included amphorae and other jugs of varying capacities and various articles for domestic and storage purposes. A form not needed earlier by Andalusian users, a
wide-mouthed inverted cone with a basal drip hole, called
a *horma*, was evolved to serve as a mold in which juices
squeezed from sugar cane hardened into crude sugar (see
Fig. 72f). Household pottery included tableware, candleholders, chamber pots, and cooking pots. Although the
island colony population remained small, its requirements
likely supported a segment of the late fifteenth- through
seventeenth-century Sevillian craft. This would have been
particularly significant for makers of earthenware containers when Canary vintages, especially the famous
Canary Sack or *malvasía*, were dispatched to the Indies
or when they became popular in Europe. Again, proof
is woefully limited by the absence of applicable data.
The Fortunate Islands have not been so fortunate for
archaeologists, since they have been plagued by a variety
of natural disasters in the form of tidal waves and volcanic
eruptions, which in occupied areas wiped out the cultural
record.

A few lines of prose continue.

The Canary Island colony remained poor, with little
extravagance apparent in its public and private buildings
other than *mudéjar* wooden ceilings, balconies, and trim.
The fact that a few Sevillian tiles remain here and there
suggests the possibility of more elaborate architectural
ceramics having been present formerly. Among the riches
of churches on Tenerife, La Palma, and Gran Canaria
are five typical Sevillian *pilas bautismales*. They are the
large, deep bowl-on-a-pedestal style bearing the usual
elaborate relief decoration and either green or amber lead
glaze coating. Gestoso suggests dates for their manufacture from 1479, when the Catholic Kings ordered
the council of Sevilla to send men and money to secure
the islands and to build monasteries, to 1539, when the
islands had become a mandatory victualing stop for all
Spanish vessels bound for American waters.[34]

A small collection of potsherds recently made below a
retaining wall along the shore at Garachico, Tenerife (see
Fig. 113), an important port in the overseas trade before it
was swallowed up by lava at the beginning of the eighteenth century, includes examples of the same common
sixteenth-century lead- and tin-glazed ceramics that have
been observed in the environs of Sevilla. Local archaeologists and antiquarians report having seen similar ceramics
from time to time, but their whereabouts presently is
unknown. Even so, there is no doubt but that the islanders and men passing through ate from the same kind

of dishes and used the identical sort of utility vessels as those back in Andalusia. Inasmuch as no Spanish ceramic industry of any kind ever developed in the islands and the few remaining Guanches were incompetent potters, the customary earthenwares needed to serve most settlers would have had to have been imported from the nearest source: Sevilla.

By the end of the fifteenth century this first step in the diffusion to America of Spanish ceramics unquestionably had been taken, but the spread of Andalusian pottery-making methods had not yet begun.

THE INDIES

After early mass on August 3, 1492, Columbus, with his fleet of three ships and their complement of ninety mismatched renegades, sailed at ebb tide from the small fishing village of Palos de la Frontera. Crouched on the windswept shore west of Sevilla, *frontera* signified the town's placement on the ancient borderland between Andalusian Muslim and Christian. It was a name with even deeper prophetic meaning, given the awesome frontier toward which it looked across the brine lapping at its piers. On board the bobbing vessels, the provisions for the voyagers consisted of wine in casks, hard biscuits, salted fish and meat, lentils, *garabanzos*, and olive oil. The containers in which most of those supplies were stowed surely were the tapered and flat-based *ánforas* and *cántaros* of several sizes typical of southern Spain. On most ships of the time a sandy cooking pit and a brick oven were on deck for use by the crew, who were responsible for their own meals (Fig. 114).[35] It can be assumed that the utensils and dishes from which they cooked, ate, and drank were minimal in number, but also of the sorts found in most Andalusian homes.

Running down south-by-west across the choppy entrance to the Mediterranean Sea to the rugged Canary Islands, where Castilian conquest already was almost secured, the expedition paused to repair one of its ships, took on additional food and water, and set forth into the unknown. South of the Canaries the northeast *alisios* billowed the carrack and caravel sails to carry the fleet for thirty-three days across the mysterious Atlantic. First it encountered the Mar Tenebroso, rumored to be filled with horrible monsters, and then pushed on into the vegetation-tangled eye of the North Atlantic current system, called the Sargasso Sea. Finally it came to a fateful landfall in the Bahamas on October 12. The first person to sight land was Rodrigo de Triana, his name taken from his

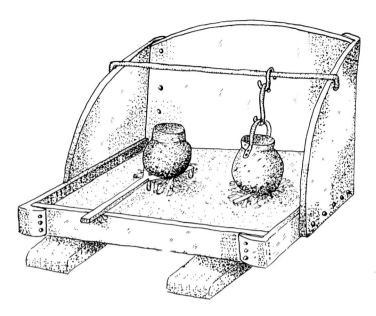

Figure 114. Cooking hearths aboard Spanish sailing vessels consisted of a metal-covered wooden framework, in the bottom of which was a thick bed of sand. The arrangement was known to sailors as the "island of the olla". Cooking pots resting on trivets or suspended from a rod likely were both earthenware and metal (after Martínez Hidalgo 1966).

hometown, as was customary.[36] The name of the street in front of the Santa Ana church in Triana honors him.

During the second day of this initial Spanish *entrada*, October 13, 1492, Andalusian pottery found its way to American shores for the first time. Glass beads, brass rings, red caps, and hawk's bells were the truck taken as gifts for friendly native peoples Columbus hoped to meet on his trek to Cathay, but it was quickly learned that almost anything novel to the aborigines would induce them to part with some of their own accoutrements. Columbus noted in an October 13 journal entry:

But all that they [the natives] do possess, they give for anything which is given to them, so that they exchange things even for pieces of broken dishes and bits of broken glass cups.

On October 17 he wrote:

And here I saw that some boys from the ships exchanged some little pieces of broken dishes and glass for their spears.

This was followed on October 22 by:

They brought spears and some skeins of cotton to exchange, and they bartered these with some sailors for bits of glass from broken cups and for bits of earthenware.[37]

There was a fourth similar remark on December 22 as the Spaniards landed on the north shore of an island they named Hispaniola.

Here are documentary clues that somewhere on San Salvador (Watlings Island), Fernandina (Long Island), Isabela (Crooked Island), and Hispaniola (Haiti) there may be scattered fragments of Andalusian ceramics left behind

in 1492. Exchanges included sherds of the traditional
Sevillian maiolica *platos*, *tazas*, and *escudillas*, which ultimately mixed with Native American trash. In addition,
emptied jars not put to other uses likely were discarded as
the ships reconnoitered the islands, thus becoming the
first Spanish litter in the New World. To distinguish them
from what was tossed away by other Spaniards during
the next fifty years would be impossible now, because
stylistically they remained virtually unchanged.

So that his sponsors would not accuse him of cheating
the natives, Columbus put the use of pottery as truck
in a different light in a letter to Isabela and Fernando by
explaining:

They [the natives] are content with whatever trifle of whatever
kind that may be given to them, whether it be of value or value-
less. I forbade that they should be given things so worthless
as fragments of broken crockery, scraps of broken glass and lace
tips, although when they were able to get them, they fancied
that they possessed the best jewel in the world.[38]

After the cumbersome Santa María flagship went
aground on Christmas Eve on the part of the northwestern
coast of Hispaniola now known as Haiti, the galleon was
dismantled to build quarters (named Navidad) for an estimated thirty to forty men left behind while their com-
mander returned to Sevilla for reinforcements. Jars with
remaining foodstuffs must have been dragged ashore;
their shattered remains likely lie buried deep beneath
drifts of water- and windborne soil accumulated in the
more than four and a half centuries since local Arawaks
rose up against the stranded Europeans, wiping them out
to a man.[39]

On his second voyage to America Columbus came
prepared to settle in and exploit his findings. In the process *hispanidad* was firmly implanted, but that was not
his immediate intention. The Hispaniola colony he envi-
sioned was to be essentially an Italian-style trading factory,
whose personnel frequently rotated. Nevertheless, the
second expedition, outfitted during five feverish months
by way of Sevilla and finally dispatched from Cádiz, comprised twelve to fifteen hundred men representing a cross
section of fifteenth century Spanish male society. Together
with foodstuffs, tools, seeds, and domestic animals, they
were loaded into a wild assortment of seventeen dissimilar
sailing ships. This time Columbus led his party far south
of the Canaries, where the fleet was caught up in the
westward-flowing equatorial current and favorable winds
that propelled them across the ocean to the Dominica
Passage between the Leeward and Windward Islands of
the Lesser Antilles. This established a westward route

from Spain to America that was to be used for the entire colonial epoch. From the Lesser Antilles it was a relatively easier voyage up the Caribbean past Guadalupe and Puerto Rico to Hispaniola.

The journal written by Columbus during this second voyage has been lost. That the practice followed earlier of giving truck including potsherds to the aborigines was continued is verified by a letter from the physician in the party, Diego Alvarez Chanca, to the Sevilla council three months after the successful crossing. He is quoted as saying:

These Indians barter their gold, provisions, and everything they bring with them, for tags, nails, broken pieces of darning needles, beads, pins, laces, and broken saucers and dishes.[40]

Exactly where that pottery was scattered is uncertain, but it probably was in the vicinity of Navidad or en route as the ships made their way along the north coast of His-paniola in search of a suitable halting spot. Logic tells us it is still there amid the debris of ancient middens or refuse mounds.

The first Spanish settlement of any permanence was placed on the same northern shore of the island as was the ill-fated Navidad colony (Fig. 115). Named Isabela after

Figure 115. The Indies.

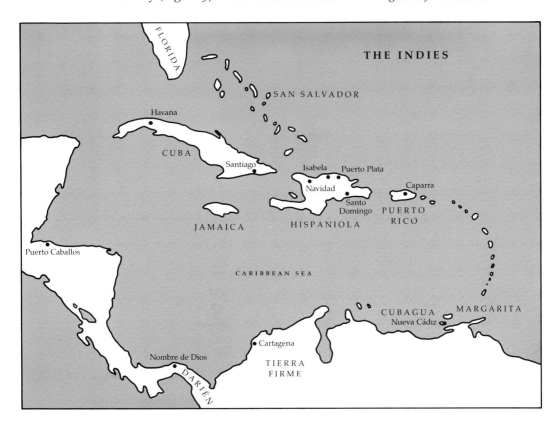

Figure 116. Modern view of site of Isabela, the first Spanish settlement on Hispaniola in 1494.

the queen, its founding came on January 2, 1494, exactly one year to the day after Columbus first quit the island to return to Spain to announce his discovery to the Catholic Kings, and two years after the same sovereigns witnessed capitulation by the Nasrid emir at Granada. The locale selected was a unique choice: an open roadstead in a hurricane path (Fig. 116). But water for drinking and for operating grist mills was provided by two streams, a deep forest and potential farmlands lay behind the settlement, beds of clay suitable for roof tile and construction lined an arroyo, and—most important to conquerors with auriferous dreams—goldfields were allegedly to be found in a nearby central province. A stone church, a fortress with circular tower, and a house for the Admiral soon were built on a flat terrace back from the sea. A square *plaza*, streets, and aqueduct within a walled enclosure were laid out in accord with medieval concepts. The remainder of the dwellings, some two hundred according to an Italian in the party,[41] were of thatch or jacal, which quickly disintegrated and rotted in the humid climate.

Nearly all accounts of this insecure occupation mention that artisans of various kinds were in the group, but there is no indication that potters were among them.[42] In all likelihood the artisans were those with construction skills, such as masons, who may have set up a workyard in the neighboring wash where they formed and baked the curved terra cotta roof tiles usual in southern Spain. In view of the turmoil within the colony, dishes would have been of little concern. Each man continued to use whatever he had in his original baggage or replaced it from the one or two shipments of goods from Sevilla that managed to get through. As objects broke or were discarded they formed the second deposit of Andalusian ceramics to come to rest in the Western Hemisphere.

It was not long until tropical illnesses, incapacity or lack of motivation for physical labor, internal and external strife, and pervading disillusionment led to the demise of the town. In just two years plans were made by the Admiral's brother, Bartolomé, to move what was left of the settlement to the south shore of the island at the mouth of the Río Ozama. There it would be protected from the severest storms and at the same time be closer to the sea-lane from Spain. By 1500 Isabela had become a ghost town, home only to rebels or stragglers.[43] Two decades later Father Bartolomé de las Casas reported the ruins to be haunted by ghostly figures of well-dressed courtiers who took off their heads when they doffed their hats. As a Dominican prior in the northern coast town of Puerto Plata, a squalid port that became the jumping off place for the voyage back to Spain, Las Casas also wrote that he and others took stones from the original settlement to reuse elsewhere.[44]

In 1498 Columbus undertook his third voyage. He swung farther south of the Canary Island stepping stones than on either of his earlier trips and came into Caribbean waters just off the island of Trinidad and mainland Venezuela. In this way he discovered the continent of South America. He failed to recognize the potential of pearl beds in the vicinity, which within a few years led to active Spanish exploitation, but he did take notice of gold objects worn by the natives he met. The greedy appreciation of this metal prompted an amusing incident involving *reflejo metálico* ceramics. Fernández de Oviedo relates how some of the sailors broke such a lusterware plate with shiny metallic decorations and gave the fragments to unsuspecting natives with whom they were bartering in exchange for the genuine article.[45] To Columbus also goes dubious credit for first mentioning the *bacín*, or chamber pot, in the Americas. Apparently he showed one aboard his flagship to hesitant natives in an effort to entice them to come closer.[46]

That the practice of pleasing the natives by gifts of pottery was continued as Spanish explorations touched the American mainland is shown in an account by Juan Días, a member of the Juan de Grijalva party of 1518 to Yucatan, who wrote:

Our men gave the Indians in the canoe certain cups and other utensils from the ships to make them happy, for they were people of good will.[47]

The Admiral was followed in the southern Caribbean by the Hojeda-Vespucci expedition and that of Peralonso Niño. These groups sailed among the islands of Trinidad, Curacao, Bonaire, and Aruba, and the Paria area of Vene-

zuela and her offshore islands of Margarita and Cubagua.
Pearls and emeralds were found, which together with
large numbers of Native Americans to be taken as slaves,
led to prolonged ravaging of the Pearl Coast for some
years. About 1500 a camp called Nueva Cádiz grew up on
an arid point of land on Cubagua (see Fig. 115). In the
next forty years it became a large town, with solid public
buildings, churches, and a white population determined to
enrich itself as rapidly as possible with the labors of native
slaves brought from the mainland and from as far away
as the Bahama Islands, and then to depart to enjoy an easier life in some other place.[48]

The promise of the Pearl Coast led to a voyage of exploration by Rodrigo de Bastidas further westward along
the Colombian coast, soon to be termed the Tierra Firme
or Spanish Main, the harbor that became Cartagena, the
Gulf of Urabá, the Isthmus of Panamá or Darién, and
the Bay of Retrete near the later site of Nombre de Dios.
At least eleven so-called Andalusian voyages led by various seamen ensued, in order to begin reaping the harvest
of the pearl beds.[49]

Columbus's fourth voyage, from 1502 to 1504, completed the exploration of the southern mainland fronting
on the Caribbean. He sailed in from the north along the
Mosquito Coast of Honduras and down the Veragua area
of Costa Rica and Panamá, where he left one of his worm-
eaten galleons at the site of Portobello. During the first
decade of the sixteenth century, exploration inland was
attempted from small settlements on the coasts. Best
known among the settlements were Santa María la
Antigua del Darién and Aclá, the first two Spanish villages
on the American mainland, both located in a rain-
drenched malarial forest.

For the first eight years of this era of exploration the
only substantial Spanish occupation was confined to Hispaniola. A string of fifteen villages spread up through
the fertile interior and at key port positions along all
coasts. Thereafter, a restless population more interested in
chasing illusions of quick riches than in creating new
homes in the wilderness drifted out to adjoining islands.
Puerto Rico and Jamaica in 1509 and Cuba in 1511 came
into the Spanish fold. The peninsula of Florida was
probed.

By 1519 the first phase of the Spanish adventure in the
New World was completed. Some conquistadors for the
first time took up residence on the west coast of America at
Panamá Viejo. Others stood at the gates of Tenochtitlán
in the Mexican highlands. The Florida Passage and the
Gulf Stream became the standard eastward route for the

carrera de indias. In twenty-seven years the indomitable
men from Iberia had perused the lengthy coastline of the
Americas, presumably from Maryland to Argentina.

Few ceramics directly attributable to these many expedi-
tionary forces have been found. This may appear surprising when one reads of the very large numbers of men
in the various parties, which often spent years on the
trail. For example, there were two thousand men with
Pedrarias in Darién, six hundred with De Soto in Florida,
one hundred fifty with Valdivia in Chile, seven hundred eighty-five with Nicuesa in Castilla del Oro, three
hundred with Hojeda in Tierra Firme, and three hundred
with Velázquez in Cuba. There is no question but that
a few drinking and eating bowls would have been tucked
in their packs, or that various communal containers of
foodstuffs and beverages would have been included in the
company gear. If these explorers left a trail of broken
pots behind, they now would be found or identified
merely by chance. The expedition routes are not precisely
known, the vegetation cover and often rugged terrain
conceal any such small stray bits and pieces of evidence,
and what was in use then was exactly what was in use a
half-century later.

Otherwise, Spanish pottery was present wherever
homes or even semipermanent quarters were established
up to 1520, regardless of whether the population was
entirely male or included peninsular or native females, or
whether indigenous earthenwares were available. Such
non-Indian wares have been recovered from surface glean-
ings and a few excavations from the rubble of Caparra in
Puerto Rico, from under the *ayuntamiento* in Santiago
de Cuba, from fill dirt beneath Sevilla la Nueva, Jamaica,
from scattered *rancherías* now drowned by waters behind
the locks of the Panama Canal, from the mangrove
swamps of Santa María la Antigua in Darién, and from the
windswept pearling stations off the Venezuelan coast.[50]
Predictably, the concentration is heaviest in the area until
then most intensely occupied by Iberians, the island of
Hispaniola. Spanish pottery also has been unearthed in
many Caribbean or Floridian Native American villages of
the contact period. It probably had been acquired by the
natives as gifts, through raids, or from scavenging abandoned towns or shipwrecks. The humble potters hunched
before their wheels in the dreary humid shops of Triana,
who likely had never traveled more than a few miles
from home, would have been dumbfounded had they
known of the far-flung, exotic fate of their wares.

All the pre-1520 Spanish sites of the Caribbean basin
have yielded exactly the same complex of shapes and

kinds of pottery, although not all known types were present everywhere. Most abundant were coarse-grained, plainware storage or shipping receptacles and cook pots (see Figs. 55, 58). These represented the complete definitive package of full-bodied, wheel-turned forms identical to specimens known in southern Spain for centuries. Next in frequency were the characteristically Andalusian partially or totally lead-glazed flat-bottomed basins, wide-mouthed *ollas*, round-bodied bowls with narrow rims, and cylindrical chamber pots (see Fig. 56). Most typically they were made of red-burning clay. Also made of the red paste, because of its strength, were heavily potted *tinajas* covered with green lead glaze, and enormous, mold-enhanced, green-glazed baptismal fonts sent for church use (see Fig. 72a). Of all the ceramics diffused to the Americas with the Spanish colonization, fonts had the most positive connection to Muslim al Andalus, reaching back in time to tenth-century Córdoba. In the next century (1671) earthenware fonts would be banned by church authorities in favor of more substantial and more costly stone duplicates in greater harmony with the new phalanx of impressive ecclesiastical structures then being raised in the New World.[51]

Made of the diagnostic light-colored Guadalquivir clay body were the small plates with countersunk bases, small carinated drinking bowls, and porringers with and without horizontal lobed handles that had for several hundred years been the mainstay of the Sevillian commercial inventory (see Fig. 57a, g–i). With them were larger bowls with concave or flat bases, single-handled pitchers, and drug jars in several sizes of rounded or cylindrical profiles. In their completed state, these forms either were coated with a thin lead or tin-opacified glaze. Some of the lead-glazed plates carried unstructured manganese patterning beneath a clear shiny coating. In addition to the plain white tablewares, there were blue–on–whites and blue–and–purple–on–whites that already had typified Andalusian workmanship for as long as several centuries and would, with minor refinements, continue in fashion for another hundred years (Fig. 117b,e,g).[52] A few blue cylindrical drug jars may have resulted from Italian trade in a Genoese medicant packaged in ceramics made to special order in Sevilla (Fig. 117f). This was the only ceramic type in the initially diffused group of wares that had no former history in Andalusian ceramics. It was the glaze color that was new. In Spain, the form it covered dated from the fourteenth century.

Such homogeneity of the pottery reclaimed from the pre-1520 Spanish occupation in the Indies resulted from

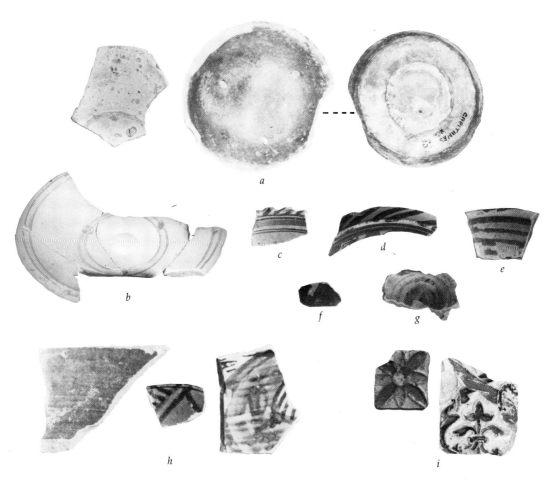

Figure 117. Some types of six-teenth-century Sevillian glazed earthwares recovered in the Indies: *a*, plain white commercial-ized tableware; *b*, blue–on–white plate; *c*, orange rim band defined in brown; *d*, heavy basin rim with rim slashes; *e*, encircling blue lines beneath plate rim; *f*, plain dark blue, probably from a drug jar; *g*, blue–and–purple–on–white bowl bottom; *h*, lead-glazed fragments, plain or bearing simple brown patterns, from bowls or jars; *i*, blue, orange, and brown *cuenca* tiles of several sizes.

the fact that all American traffic was outfitted at Sevilla; other Europeans had not yet begun to probe the Caribbean basin. There was, in fact, a monotony to the ceramic assemblage because extraneous wares were screened out through trading restrictions and because the same monot-ony also prevailed in Sevilla. Shops engaged in producing the tableware and service pieces commonly used by the regional populace were within sight of the quays where the preparatory activity for overseas exploration took place. If such supplies were needed by seamen or passen-gers, they were easily obtainable at a low cost. In the initial decades of the sixteenth century there was no ceramic trade coming to Sevilla from elsewhere, except for a limited commerce in luxury items executed in the *reflejo metálico* technique at Manises. That meant that local mer-chandise had no competition. What went overseas was exactly that in use in Sevilla, with one questionable excep-tion. What appears to be an inordinate number of bisqued table vessels lacking the finishing glaze suggests that suppliers on occasion may have shipped cheaper ceramics

out to the early colonists. Intentional shortchanging is
known to have occurred with other goods.[53] The poor of
Sevilla may have eaten from similar unfinished pottery,
but bisqued tableware has not yet come from Sevillian
excavations in sufficient quantity to verify this. However,
a large market for *cachacarría*, or coarse crockery, spread
along the trashy Arenal by the Río Guadalquivir, and
one group of peddlers garnered a meager living from sales
of factory wasters. These factors lead one to believe that
poorer citizens, whether at home or abroad, were treated
equally in the matter of dishes.

   In addition to the furnishings taken across the ocean by
the colonists and adventurers, which must account for a
high percentage of the discarded household ceramics
now being unearthed, there were a number of business
transactions in the pre-1520 period involving the export
from Sevilla of consignments of pottery. Unfortunately,
records of less than a dozen such transactions have been
found for this study. The earliest was a lot of two hundred
forty cartons of white maiolica sent in 1508 to Francisco
Niño in Santo Domingo by a Sevillian-Genoese merchant,
Lucas Pineolo (also found as Luco Pinelo).[54]

   The next year, in the twenty-ship convoy that took
Diego Columbus to his governor's post in Hispaniola, nine
naos carried orders of pottery to be sold in Santo Domingo.
Alvaro de Briones, Diego Fernández de Morón, and the
Genoese Bernardo Grimaldi had consignments of such size
as to suggest they were setting themselves up as merchants selling pottery. Some bills of lading merely note
containers of pottery, but others specify green *tinajas*,
green *pilas bautismales*, *cántaros*, *ollas*, *albornías*, and *tablas*.
Casseroles, mortars, and fifty figurines could have been of
earthenware, although they might have been of brass or
wood. In all, there were six hundred ten packages of
pottery of unknown size, two baskets containing earthenwares, nine boxes of *loza de Valencia*, which must have
been *reflejo metálico* that required special handling in stur-
dier wooden crates, and one hundred thirty pieces of
other earthenwares. Of particular interest was wall tile,
doubtless the *cuenca* type or types made by the same
impressed method but bearing *alicatado* patterns. These
have been recovered archaeologically in the Indies in
limited amounts (Fig. 117i).[55] One intriguing notation
mentions Dutch tiles, their precise number not given. The
presence of tiles and lusterware highlights a desire for
objects beyond those necessary for daily routine.[56] This
was noted by the monarch, who in the same year issued a
pragmatic to the colonists against expenditures for luxury
goods.[57] If this considerable 1509 shipment of earthen-

wares can be regarded as typical for the transatlantic fleets, it is obvious that Sevillian pottery in all grades from the costliest to the lowliest was plentiful in this American center of early sixteenth-century Spain.

The remaining records for shipment of pottery in the years prior to 1520 are two. One referred to a Sevillian merchant, Francisco López, who included seven crates of pottery with other goods destined for Santo Domingo in 1511; the second, dated 1514, notes two glazed baptismal fonts going to Jamaica.[58]

The traffic in pottery was a sellers' market; no salesmanship was necessary. Consumers apparently were eager to acquire familiar household items in order to carry on their lives with as little disruption as possible. Although no figures are available on the cost of exported wares until late in the sixteenth century, it can be assumed that colonials paid an elevated price. The restricted amounts that could be sent in the confined ships, the distance and difficulties of transport, customer demand, and human avarice would have been underlying reasons for revising costs upward (Fig. 118). Middlemen were now taking their share, too, whereas in Sevilla it had been possible to deal directly with the potter.

The question arises as to why, after nearly three decades, the overseas Spaniards were not making their own dishes. The local pottery-producing natives had been reduced in number—in some areas virtually eliminated— and one would expect the migrant Spaniards to have an aversion to using indigenous goods unless absolutely

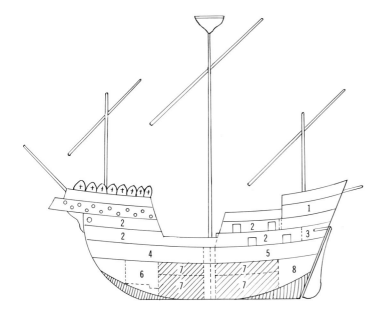

Figure 118. Diagrammatic cross section of a Spanish sailing vessel of four hundred tons, with two bridges, and carrying a complement of one hundred fifty men: *1*, quarters of officers and pilot; *2*, seamen's quarters; *3*, pilot house; *4*, passengers' quarters; *5*, soldiers' quarters; *6*, storeroom for general supplies; *7*, cargo and ballast hold; *8*, storeroom for officers' supplies (after Etayo 1971).

necessary. Surely Spanish earthenwares of these everyday sorts were troublesome and, even with increased prices, not very profitable as cargo. Although Sevillian records may have been ethnocentric, the answer lies in the mobile, restive nature of the occupation; to the Crown's alarm, the occupation was not self-sufficient but instead was almost totally parasitic. An illustration of this bizarre situation is the sending to the Indies of such basic construction materials as bricks and roof tiles. The Diego Columbus *flota*, for example, carried 22,900 roof tile and 35,500 bricks, some of which were consigned to Governor Columbus and some to Alcalde Mayor Marcos de Aguilar. In 1508 and 1512 another known 18,000 bricks were loaded on the galleons in Spain, with an additional 6,000 bricks directed at an unspecified date to the Santo Domingo monastery and 16,500 to the government administration of the capital.[59] Probably drains, water tubing, sewer lines, and downspouts also were brought from the motherland. This traffic occurred even though eye witnesses, among them Las Casas, commented on the fine beds of clay available in Hispaniola for such purposes.[60] Obviously there also was some local production, since building far outstripped shipping. One justification for transporting these terra cottas at all may have been that they served as ship ballast to be sold in the Indies, with rocks substituted for the return trip. Two notations of glazed tile being carted to Panamá must represent special products for particular needs. Many of the bricks aboard the galleons were sent in the name of the ships' masters, reaffirming their use as salable ballast.

The most conclusive evidence of the dependent nature of the early sixteenth-century colonization was the exportation from Sevilla of a large volume of foodstuffs that were Andalusian specialties. The use of earthenware shipping containers was a continuation of an Andalusian custom that had been followed without interruption since the Roman era. Now, however, the variety of commodities traveling along the transatlantic sea-lane far exceeded that of previous trade. This was because overseas Andalusians were loathe to give up their usual diet, which, thanks to the Muslim legacy, was rich in sweets, spices, and fruits unusual in contemporary Europe and not yet available in the Indies. Even more puzzling was the sending of fish products to an insular world whose surrounding waters abounded with delectable seafood. That has to be chalked up to an absorbing passion even among humble fishermen for bigger profits. Scribes who recorded this one-sided commerce used a number of names for containers of these goods, which may indicate that their contours were varied.

The 1509 fleet carried 3,190 pottery containers, the term
jarra being most frequently noted. Slightly less than half,
or 1,459, were filled with olive oil. Next most numerous
were containers of honey (406), wine (353), vinegar (297),
olives (126), and raisins (121). The remaining 428 pots
held almonds, figs, flour, *garabanzos*, dried fruits, quince
meat, pitch, shad, lard, unidentified dried fish, and rice.
There were 354 *botes* in the 1509 cargo, of which 190 contained unspecified medicines. They were consigned to
a person merely indicated as *el boticario*, perhaps the only
pharmacist in Santo Domingo at the time. Another 103
botes held *azucar rosado*, and 57 were filled with conserves.[61]
  The custom of pottery packaging worked to the benefit
of the colonial buyer because such ceramics could be
put to a multitude of secondary uses once the original contents were consumed. This was an important consideration in a society still struggling to get established. One
secondary usage of pottery was in construction. Sevillian
masons brought to Santo Domingo to work on new buildings planned for Castile's capital abroad incorporated
the large empty container jars and fragments available
in local trash deposits into the fabric of church and other
large edifice vaulting. Hence, a favored Andalusian custom dating to the time of the Romans was transferred
to the Western Hemisphere, where it seems to have
died out with the decline in importance of the insular
holdings.[62]
  The next thirty years witnessed the growth and spread
of plantation economy from Hispaniola to the neighboring
islands; with it came a more stable, perhaps better
described resigned, attitude. Here and there a seasonally
operated country pottery workshop may have begun
to provide the usual assortment of Andalusian-style utilitarian crocks and jars that the residents expected, with
the adoption also of an indigenous form tentatively identified as a manioc griddle. Provincial potters may have
formed some crude earthenware molds used in the sugar-
refining process, broken specimens also having served
as construction fill.[63] However, a 1505 reference at Sevilla
noted that a resident potter there, also participating in
the Indies trade, committed himself to supplying a thousand such forms to an unidentified purchaser,[64] who
may have placed the order because no colonial pottery
industry yet existed.[65] Records of an *ollero* from Sevilla,
Diego Fernández de Morón, shows him to have sent such
a substantial order to himself in Santo Domingo that he
obviously had gone into the retail ceramic business rather
than opening up an overseas workshop, although it was
he who produced the sugar molds.[66]
  Nor is there convincing evidence anywhere else in the

Greater Antilles for any attempt during the colonial era to inaugurate a viable Hispanic pottery enterprise proposing to turn out better caliber earthenwares. Therefore, the merchants of Sevilla routinely continued to include pottery in outbound cargoes destined for Santo Domingo. Extant documents for 1523 show that candleholders, chamber pots of two sizes, small spouted jars, and basins, as well as an unitemized entry for containers of pottery, were shipped from Sevilla.[67] In the latter order there may have been a variety of earthenware cooking utensils. A Sevillian *tinajero*, Fernando Olmedo, sold two large glazed baptismal fonts to the bishop of Tierra Firme, Father Luis de Berlanga, in 1534.[68]

Not all the pottery reached its intended destination. There are two reasons for a wider distribution of Sevillian wares than normally would have occurred. Foremost were all-too-frequent shipwrecks resulting from badly constructed craft, poor seamanship, and travel in one of the world's hurricane spawning grounds. It was not uncommon for entire fleets to be sunk; to the bottom went sailors' property and cargo. Salvage operations and underwater archaeology have brought up barnacled, salt-impregnated Sevillian earthenwares off the coasts of Texas, Florida, and various West Indies islands (Fig. 119).[69] Another agent in the shuffling of the ceramic record was the French, Dutch, and English pirates who infested Caribbean waters and preyed upon Spanish shipping. They confiscated, used, and threw away loot, often in places where no occupation, Spanish or otherwise, had occurred.

Fortunately, archaeological excavations, principally those conducted as part of a massive program by the government of the Dominican Republic to restore the colonial quarter of Santo Domingo, have yielded great quantities of

Figure 119. Fragments of Andalusian ceramics, salt-impregnated and discolored, recovered from 1554 shipwrecks off Padre Island, Texas (courtesy Texas Antiquities Commission, Austin).

1520–1550 ceramics to verify the legitimate trade (Fig. 120).[70] Other assortments have come to light in similar projects in Concepción de la Vega, Dominican Republic; Sevilla la Nueva, Jamaica; and in municipal undertakings such as the construction of a new city hall in a former Cuban capital or the renovation of colonial buildings at the heart of Havana.[71] None of these efforts was more than mere retrieval of artifacts, but they were informative and confirmed data from sounder scientific projects. Additionally, a few known cargo lists refer to ceramic candleholders, chamber pots, and *botijas*, the latter either empty or filled with such things as vinegar, mustard, *garabanzos*, or wine being forwarded to the colonists. Basically, these and other plainwares, and lead-glazed and tin-glazed ceramics recovered from the 1520–1550 horizon are identical to those of the pre-1520 period. One change noted was the somewhat fewer examples of *mudéjar* maiolica bearing the lingering but totally debased Arabic calligraphy executed in blue and purple, which at the same time was disappearing in Andalusia (Fig. 117g). Further, the refinement of potting techniques evident on some coeval maiolicas known in Sevilla and attributable to the infusion of Italian expertise and taste appeared in these ca. 1550 colonial specimens. Such attributes as ring feet, thinner walls, and more carefully formed parts became usual. Large, heavy basins, which earlier had been covered on interiors with a green lead glaze often were treated instead with a white tin-opacified glaze decorated with blue or an occasional combination of blue and green motifs (Fig. 117d). *Cuenca* tile was giving way to flat surfaced *azulejos*, or *pisanos*. Some burnished and etched redwares were further enhanced by minor feldspar inlays in a style developed by the Muslims.[72] It is possible that some of this

Figure 120. Modern view of San Francisco church, Santo Domingo (left), begun in 1544, and of the garden area behind the church, where trenching revealed quantities of sixteenth-century Sevillian potsherds.

pottery had been brought to Sevilla by Muslims relocated there at the end of the fifteenth century or by Christian soldiers returning from the campaigns against the infidels. Or perhaps it had continued as a village craft in the mountains near Granada, and from there reached Sevilla and, in turn, the colonies. The late American archaeologist Charles Fairbanks suggests its colonial Panamanian manufacture at a slightly later date, inasmuch as a few fragments were found associated with a late sixteenth- or early seventeenth-century kiln site in Panamá Viejo. The brick-red clay available there would have been well suited to that style. Generally, the feldspar inlaid vessels were tiny jars, saucers, water jars, or plates. One example is a flat, unflanged, knobbed lid of the style used by Sevillian *mudéjares* to place over water jar mouths. Another is a molded figurine.

Andalusians had little familiarity with handmade pottery, although they surely were prejudiced against it, as they were prejudiced against its American Indian makers. Nevertheless, the unreliability of the colonial supply system forced them to use it. No doubt to their surprise, it was not all bad. Many pieces were well engineered for storage and some culinary purposes. There were no forms for individual usage, which had become part and parcel of Spanish ways, and there were no more-or-less matched sets. The major drawback, however, was lack of glaze. This allowed the liquid in braised foods, a fundamental of

Figure 121. Representative sample of Italian Ligurian maiolica recovered from sites in the Canary Islands, the Caribbean basin, and central Mexico, datable to the second half of the sixteenth century: *a*, obverses of blue–on–blue mode, with exception of top fragment, which also bears a yellow accent; *b*, reverses of blue–on–blue mode; *c*, blue–on–white style.

the Spanish diet, to sweat through vessel walls or, particularly in the case of hot foods, to be absorbed into the clay. The food then took on an unpleasant muddy taste. Consequently, the Spanish housewife likely added native pottery to her long list of little annoyances that made overseas life trying. Still, from kitchens in Cubagua to Cuba American Indian pottery served many supplemental needs and in most occupations comprises a high percentage of the pottery now recovered. Also present in some areas was a handmade pottery believed to have been made by African slaves brought into the Caribbean settlements after about 1515.[73]

Beginning about the middle of the sixteenth century, the first substantial amounts of non-Hispanic maiolicas began to reach the colonies. Most were Italian, and most numerous among them was the blue type of Liguria that had been introduced to Andalusia at about the same period (Fig. 121 a–b).[74] There was also a companion blue–on–white type from the same source (Fig. 121c). They frequently were accompanied by Sevillian derivatives (see Fig. 87). Also present were boldly patterned maiolica polychromes from Montelupo and lead-glazed sgraffito and slip-marbelized types from Pisa, two potting centers in Tuscany (see Figs. 111, 122d,e).[75] Both were active in the production of what in Italy were inexpensive ceramics for the middle and lower classes. Some of the Montelupo styles were most characteristic of the first half of the sixteenth century, but the other types were primarily of

Figure 122. Representative sample of sixteenth-century Italian maiolicas recovered in colonial Spanish American sites: *a*, Faenza all-white style; *b*, Faenza polychrome *compendiaro*; *c*, Faenza polychrome *istoriato*, with notable use of very dark blue (To date, Faenza trade pottery has been identified only from excavations beneath Mexico City.); *d*, Pisa white-slipped fine-lined sgraffito covered with lead glaze; *e*, Pisa slip-marbelized lead-glazed style (To date, Pisan types have been more commonly recovered in the Indies than on the mainland).

the second half of the century, perhaps extending into the early decades of the seventeenth century. The design style on the Ligurian maiolica, however, was that typical of the sixteenth century, rather than the naturalistic foliage and landscapes used after 1600.[76]

In theory, all merchandise bound for Spanish markets in the Americas was to be Spanish. That was an impossible regulation to which to adhere because Spain shortly proved unable to cope with colonial demands. More enterprising dealers at work in the bustling redistribution center Sevilla had become saw to it that Genoese, Pisan, and Venetian merchantmen brought Italian goods to the Guadalquivir docks for reshipment westward on Spanish galleons. Haring would have five-sixths of the cargoes then destined for the New World being supplied by foreigners.[77] The pottery does not reflect that volume of non-Spanish trade, but it is nevertheless evident that in the Indies Genoese factors were active. They had special permission to reside and engage in commerce there because of their many financial favors to the Spanish monarchy and most of the early explorers.[78]

The containerized trade continued unabated, now more concentrated on three or four products in several standardized forms (Fig. 123). Scattered Sevillian documents note 26,750 such ceramic receptacles shipped between 1542 and 1580, another 3,758 having been sent from the Canaries in 1551 and 1567. New household articles dispatched with shipments of foodstuffs were glazed tiles. They were identified as *tejas vidriadas*, but more than likely they were floor rather than roof tiles.[79]

After 1550 Santo Domingo became a quiet backwater with a population of less than a thousand. The *flotas* from Spain sailed directly to Cartagena (Tierra Firme), Puerto Caballos (Honduras), or Vera Cruz (New Spain), with only occasional shipments proceeding directly to Hispaniola. Out of thirty-one entries gleaned from the incomplete records of the Archives of the Indies in Sevilla for shipments of pottery leaving Sevilla or the Canary Islands for America between 1550 and 1600 (all in the years of 1551, 1583, 1590, and 1592–1593), only eight were addressed to Santo Domingo. Earlier, all known consignments of pottery from Sevilla had been directed there. Two went to Tierra Firme, one to the island of Margarita off Venezuela, six to Panamá, two to Honduras, five to Vera Cruz, and six were held for delivery in Havana. The Cuban town was an obligatory stop on the return leg of the voyages, which by this time avoided going as far east as Hispaniola in favor of a more northerly course to the Florida Straits.

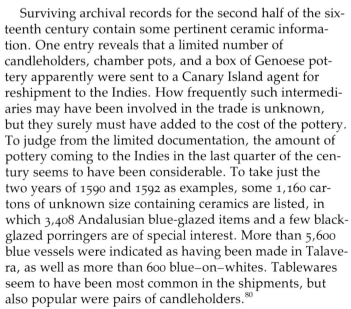

Figure 123. Containerized commerce with the American colonies was typified by heavy duty earthware jars such as these, variously known as *ánforas*, *botijas peruleras*, or olive jars. Although representative of a preindustrial ceramic effort of enormous proportions, each jar was thrown and sized individually. Consequently, each shows slight variations, which cannot yet be conclusively demonstrated to have temporal significance. Example *b*, however, may represent the Late Style B (post 1780) of the Goggin 1964 taxonomy, indicated in a slightly more pronounced shoulder angle, and example e may be in the same category, owing to a somewhat thinner orifice ring and a thin interior glazing that appears to have been tin-opacified. Several show the whitish surface scumming that has erroneously been interpreted as an applied slip. Examples: *a*, acquired in Sevilla; *b*, acquired in Guatemala; *c*, acquired in Yucatan; *d*, acquired in Mexico, a leather covering still in place over the mouth; *e*, acquired in Mexico, possible owner's or maker's initials stamped at orifice (courtesy Spanish Colonial Arts Society Inc. [*a*], International Folk Art Collection [*b*, *e*], The Houghton Sawyer Collection [*c*], and School of American Research Collection [*d*], all housed in the Museum of International Folk Art, a unit of the Museum of New Mexico, Santa Fe).

Surviving archival records for the second half of the sixteenth century contain some pertinent ceramic information. One entry reveals that a limited number of candleholders, chamber pots, and a box of Genoese pottery apparently were sent to a Canary Island agent for reshipment to the Indies. How frequently such intermediaries may have been involved in the trade is unknown, but they surely must have added to the cost of the pottery. To judge from the limited documentation, the amount of pottery coming to the Indies in the last quarter of the century seems to have been considerable. To take just the two years of 1590 and 1592 as examples, some 1,160 cartons of unknown size containing ceramics are listed, in which 3,408 Andalusian blue-glazed items and a few black-glazed porringers are of special interest. More than 5,600 blue vessels were indicated as having been made in Talavera, as well as more than 600 blue–on–whites. Tablewares seem to have been most common in the shipments, but also popular were pairs of candleholders.[80]

Archaeology confirms the continued commerce in Sevillian white maiolicas suggested by the documents, some with more refined decorations than before, executed both in polychromes and in blue. Blue maiolicas bearing darker blue and, rarely, yellow accented patterning were present. Among plainwares was one with a distinctive orange paste incorporating flecks of mica that was made into small, thin-walled, handled bowls or saucers.[81] Portuguese origin is postulated for this pottery, although it was exported through Sevilla.

Increasingly after the sixteenth century merchandise for the colonial trade was from European countries other than Spain. As economic conditions deteriorated in Sevilla, its ceramic production, with the exception of containers, seems to have dropped to the point where there was little for export. The slack was partially taken up in the Indies by Mexican ceramics then being made in volume. Interisland traffic dealt in these wares in such quantity that during the seventeenth and eighteenth centuries Mexican pottery became relatively commonplace. In the far south of the Caribbean, pottery was supplied for a short while by a factory set up toward the end of the sixteenth or early in the seventeenth century in Panamá Viejo on the Pacific coast.[82] Whether there was some other operation in the area making a hard-paste maiolica as described by Council awaits further research.[83] From his descriptions, these examples appear to have been over-fired specimens and perhaps were another example of shipping inferior quality goods to the colonists. Finally, throughout the Caribbean the declining contacts with the motherland, which became a fact of life after 1620, forced considerable dependence upon contraband dishes and utensils from Dutch, French, Portuguese, English, and even Oriental sources.[84]

Although not geographically a part of the Caribbean basin, the southern North American Atlantic coast from South Carolina to Georgia to northern Florida saw the establishment of a number of tiny Spanish settlements and missions that were culturally and temporally allied to the Indies. One was Santa Elena on Parris Island, South Carolina. Occupied from 1566 to 1587, it was a civilian town associated with three military installations known as San Salvador, San Felipe, and San Marcos. The latter were deemed necessary to curb the French expansionism that threatened Spanish colonies and shipping. Also founded for the same purposes was the smaller *presidio* of San Agustín (St. Augustine), Florida, begun in 1565. Unlike Santa Elena, it was not abandoned; in fact, it accepted the Hispanic and some American Indian occu-

pants of that town when they were ordered to move. With
many hardships, San Agustín and some outlying fortifica-
tions endured as a Spanish outpost until 1763. During
most of that time it was a crown colony entirely dependent
on an annual government cash allotment and supplies
from Havana and New Spain. These two connections
brought in Mexican ceramics as they became available and
European articles transmitted through Cuba. For twenty-
one years between 1763 and 1784 San Agustín was under
British control, and then was returned to Spain until the
loss of her American holdings in 1821.

Over the past thirty years sufficient identifying and
descriptive information has been compiled about Andalusian ceramics in the Indies to permit archaeologists to
use this data base in pursuit of new lines of inquiry
designed to answer broad anthropological questions about
cultural processes. Cases in point are recent orientations
of investigations undertaken at the two Atlantic sites
of Santa Elena and San Agustín and at the sixteenth-
century town of Puerto Real in northern Haiti (occupied
1503–ca. 1580). Using the record of diffused Spanish tradition ceramics, together with other data, attempts have
been made to gain meaningful insight into Spanish colonial adaptation to a set of circumstances of which their
Iberian forebears would never have dreamed.[85]

The Atlantic coast towns were small, with populations
comprised of persons of very modest or low incomes.
They were situated on the outermost fringe of the Spanish
New World, where seaborne contact was infrequent.
Although sharing the same island as the capital city of
Santo Domingo, Puerto Real likewise was removed from
the main communication and trade networks, but its
citizens were better fixed to provide for themselves; this
apparently was attributable to more natural resources,
including a good harbor, and a lifestyle not given over to
soldiering. At all three settlements the complex of Andalusian earthenwares typically was restricted to six or seven
decorated types and comparably limited kinds of plainwares, in the case of San Agustín incorporating several
presumed to be of Mexican origin. The number of excavated fragments is unimpressive when compared with
many other Spanish sites. On the other hand, when con-
trasted with the English settlements that soon were to
appear to the north of the Atlantic coast outposts, the solid
integration of pottery into many aspects of daily Iberian
life is reaffirmed. Statistical analyses of the empirical
record provided through carefully monitored excavations
of Spanish and American Indian materials, including
pottery, have suggested complex patterns of personal

interactions. Some were among the Spaniards who found themselves on an isolated, often ignored borderland or a hurricane-wracked island. Others were between them and native peoples, who were drawn, through marriage, labor, missionization, or other means, into the Hispanic sphere of influence. The stresses and adjustments to stress of which these data speak are the essence of life itself. Their identification provides a platform for understanding the common connectors of a society that generally eludes the social scientist dealing solely with event-oriented history on a grander and more political scale.

As to the pottery, these studies have revealed that in some circumstances Andalusian earthenware acquired a new dimension: amid the disruptive cultural vibrations attendant on moving from one world into another, it had been converted from a necessity into a status symbol.

If investigations were undertaken in appropriate Sevillian sites, theoretically it should be possible to use pottery, together with other artifacts, to distinguish rich from poor households. For instance, a family with money might have had some tiled dados in its house and broken *reflejo metálico* or *cuerda seca* bowls in its trash. City and village dwellers might have discarded varying percentages of tin- and lead-glazed dishes that could be clues to financial worth. Ethnic affiliations of former users could not be inferred so easily, because there were all degrees of wealth in each of the three principal components of Spanish society, although Muslims tended to fill the lower ranks of labor.

In the colonial situation there were sharper societal distinctions to be mirrored in material possessions. To Iberian settlers, who over the centuries of confrontation in the peninsula had acquired a deep sense of superiority, Spanish was best. Therefore, in the overseas cultural climate, possession of even the crude white plates used by the Guadalquivir peasantry proclaimed a readily visible Spanishness. Through that came an affirmation of a desirable economic, social, and ethnic status. It was not so important that behind the scenes cookwares, as well as the cook, were products of the adopted environment. In the stratified social structure, the group below the peninsular or creole Spaniards was that arising from racial interbreeding. Persons in this grouping may have desired Spanish pottery either for practical or prestige reasons but, because of economic factors, had to settle for fewer imported and more local pieces. Probably with no regrets, the Native Americans at the bottom of the scale relied only on their own handicraft, although it sometimes was modified by introduced influences. If it is justifiable to take

pottery as a signpost, it is no surprise that the democrati-
zation that might have resulted from fresh beginnings
in a new land had not materialized.

The historically dated Caribbean and North American
Atlantic coast sites yielding Andalusian pottery have
been of critical importance in providing some finite substantiation for its sixteenth-century chronological evolution, evidence that still is lacking in Spain. These data
have been expanded through a statistical formula (Mean
Ceramic Date Formula) proposed by American archaeologist Stanley South for dating collections of similar maiolica
from occupations of unknown historical date. Tests of
the formula made at Santa Elena, where a brief occupation
is well documented and where, therefore, statistical controls could be tighter, showed it to be a sensitive, promising tool that may help place some sites and the maiolicas
they contain in their proper temporal niches.[86] Crossfinds
of those maiolicas elsewhere can then be fitted into the
time framework and so merge archaeology with history.

A footnote to the distribution of Andalusian ceramics to
the Indies came on the Virginia coast at English Jamestown, founded in 1609. Excavations there in the 1950s
unearthed fragments of four or five of the decorated and
plainware types in use to the south at the period spanning
the sixteenth and seventeenth centuries. There had been
trade to the enemy.[87]

In the process of colonization, spearheaded as it was by
a dominant proportion of men and women from southern
Spain who equipped themselves there for their lives away
from home with familiar food, drink, and household
furnishings, the earthenware products of Andalusia had
been diffused en masse to this first Spanish stronghold in
the Americas. But, so far as is presently known, the potting technology and ceramic aesthetic evolved in Spain
had not made the trip.

NEW SPAIN

Once the Aztecs were vanquished and their capital
razed, groups of treasure-seeking Spaniards poured onto
the Mexican highlands from the Caribbean insular colonies
and from Spain itself. It soon was obvious to many that
not all riches in the new land were of the golden variety
with which the followers of Moctezuma had dazzled the
first conquistadors. An acceptance of the hard realities and
tangible opportunities of frontier life began to prevail as
men applied for land grants and set about to create homes
and businesses.

From the beginning a new stability combined with the scope of the endeavor and its location deep in the interior of the craggy country to promote a greater need for independence from the motherland in basic material goods. There is no indication, for instance, that architectural terra cottas were supplied to the mainland settlements as they had been to the Caribbean ports. Rather, in order to commence reconstruction of the capital as soon as possible, workyards to make these items were set up in places nearby where suitable deposits of clay existed. A Spanish overseer directed the labors of Mexican Indians working under *repartimiento* arrangements.[88]

Of less pressing importance were earthenwares for daily use. The first settlers relied upon indigenous pottery to supplement whatever personal pieces they happened to have brought with them. This was no hardship, inasmuch as most of the central Mexican Indians were skillful, prolific potters with an even longer familiarity with the craft than the invading Spaniards. The staggering variety of sizes, shapes, and decorations of the native pottery, sometimes even verging on the grotesque, must have astounded the conquerors, who were then accustomed to wares of far less artistic merit. Made in a number of ways but without the potter's wheel, the local pottery was found to be satisfactory for many purposes around the kitchens; some specialized shapes had evolved for the preparation of particular native foods adopted by the whites. Native American cooks and wives in the homes of the Spaniards were used to them.

In Spanish eyes, negative aspects of the indigenous Mexican pottery were the same they had seen in Antillean pottery, namely a lack of glaze coatings, few shapes or sizes appropriate for individual use, and none for specialized household purposes. Probably then, as now, Spanish cooks were convinced that clay pots of particular shapes and finish were best for certain foods. These factors, added to the hold of custom, prejudice against tableware that was not white, and the prestige value that colonial attitudes had attached to Hispanic objects of all kinds, may have prompted early orders for Spanish ceramics.

To the despair of municipal authorities but to the good fortune of modern archaeologists, the casual disposal of rubbish typical of Sevillians at home continued in the colony.[89] The citizens of Mexico City made it a habit to toss their trash, larded with fragments of friable dishes and utensils, into the canals that laced the city. If such waterways were not immediately at hand, they dumped their refuse among debris of dismantled Aztec structures at the north end of the main *plaza*, or they simply discarded it directly outside

their own doors. Later occupation covered and preserved
these remains. If we interpret this silent record correctly, it
would appear that within a short time the importation
of customary crockery was begun either from reserves of
Spanish materials in the Indies or from Sevilla.

From the 1520s to perhaps the late 1530s, all the kinds
and shapes of earthenware storage containers, cook pots,
and eating vessels, the latter commonly packed in dozen
lots by contemporary Sevillian shops, appeared in local
marketplaces. Present were *tinajas*, *botijas peruleras*, *botes*,
and *jarras*, which brought to Mexico the same variety of
Andalusian olives, grains, wine, fish sauces, raisins,
almonds, olive oil, medicines, or cheeses that went to the
Indies. This was the part of the ceramic trade that survived through the seventeenth century and was responsible for millions of Andalusian earthenware containers
in the Western Hemisphere.[90] Once the contents were consumed, the handy receptacles were put to varied supple-
mentary uses. Andalusian footless plates; lug-handled
porringers; carinated drinking bowls; bulbous, single-
handled pitchers; expansive, flat-bottomed basins; wasp-
waisted drug jars; tall candleholders; square, molded
inkwells with holes for quill pens; and cylindrical, broad-
brimmed urinals found ready customers. They were partially or totally lead- or tin-glazed (Fig. 124). So far as
is presently known, only one variety of imported Spanish
earthenware was made in a place other than Andalusia.
It comprised a few examples of Manises *reflejo metálico*,
which may have graced the residences of Cortéz, the arch-
bishop, or some other dignitary. The Italian Montelupo
polychromes in deep bowl and plate forms were included
with the early complex of Sevillian types, as they had
been in the Caribbean (see Fig. 111).[91]

After several decades a hopeful surge of prosperity was
beginning to be felt at the colonial capital, the echo of
which would shortly reach Sevilla. Times were not good,
as widespread vagabondism among Spaniards and deci-
mation of the natives continued, but optimism was being
felt for a better future. Ranches in the countryside proved
profitable. The fabulous silver mines of Zacatecas and
Pachuca had or were about to be opened. In the city, new
palaces in Spanish Renaissance style were rising along
the streets of the *traza*, or restricted European zone. Scores
of small retail shops were stocked with foreign merchandise as commerce, long an anathema to Castilians, became
an acceptable occupation. Craftsmen of all sorts, who
up to this period had not migrated in numbers because of
the need for them in Spain as a consequence of the departure of Jews and Muslims, began moving in. They also

Figure 124. Representative sample of sixteenth-century Sevillian tin-glazed ceramic types recovered beneath Mexico City: *a*, plain white commercialized tableware; *b*, blue-banded type with added central motifs; *c*, blue–and–purple–on–white type with debased or pseudo Arabic inscriptions; *d*, unstructured blue designs on white ground; *e*, base glaze darkened to black or gunmetal color; *f*, fine quality blue designs on more refined white ware; *g*, fine quality white tableware. Examples *a–d* date to the fifteenth to mid-sixteenth century, at least, with probable earlier beginnings for some styles; *e–g*, probably date to the second half of the sixteenth century (courtesy Instituto Nacional de Antropología e Historia and Dirección de Inmuebles Federales, Mexico City).

had been slow to move because of the expenses involved in the preliminaries of administrative licensing. More Spanish women arrived steadily to set up housekeeping. In this atmosphere of promise, one or more colonial pottery industries emerged.

To meet local demands at the capital, tin- and lead-glazed vessels identical in form and style to the earlier imports were copied by resident Spanish potters. Customers would have been hard pressed to distinguish between local and Andalusian pieces. The slight divergences that did occur are attributable to differences in raw materials utilized.[92] Nevertheless, the same kind of ceramics, the same kind of workmanship, the same kind of technology used for large-volume production of low-

quality objects with identical imperfections leave no doubt
of the indebtedness of the provincial effort to a Sevillian
donor craft still strongly linked to a Muslim foundation.
Among plainwares, which must have come into production as early as, if not prior to, the glazed types, such
a definitive association is not as clearly evident, owing to
the widespread distribution of this kind of earthenware
throughout southern Spain. A number of contributors
were available upon which overseas models might have
been based. Logically, the two branches of the initial
colonial industry arose from a common background.

Aside from the virtual monopoly of Sevillian earthenwares in the early Spanish transatlantic commerce, there
was another explanation for the overriding impact of
that region upon the diffused activity. It has been estimated that to the mid-sixteenth century more than sixty
percent of all classes came to New Spain from Andalusia.
Boyd-Bowman places the sixteenth-century number of
persons emigrating from the province of Sevilla at 12,566.
Among female immigrants arriving in the formative period
before 1560, fully one-third specifically claimed the city
of Sevilla as home. One-third of the merchants also were
from there.[93] Such a regional coloration to the young colonization provided a firm basis for the first dispersal anywhere outside Spain of Andalusian medieval ceramic
technology and style. Maiolica production in colonial Mexico, therefore, preceded by many years a similar activity
in Europe north of the Alps.

Behind this spread to the Western Hemisphere of Sevillian pottery-making methods was a fifteen-hundred-year-
old pattern of evolution on three continents. As with
most aspects of colonial life, it was a case primarily of
resuming an old craft in a new environment for the benefit
of migrant Spaniards, not of diffusing it to a new people.
In a real sense, it was just a territorial transfer. The Sevillian system—complete with compound potter's wheel;
enclosed, two-chambered, updraft kiln; and glaze finishing
and in-glaze decoration—was, and to a large extent
remained, independent of Mexican Indian practice in the
same art, which aboriginally incorporated none of these
refinements. Actually, some of the European technology
was deliberately kept secret,[94] although a few clergymen
tutored their neophytes in unfamiliar aspects of the craft.

Through ensuing years in New Spain, as accommoda-
tion of the two opposed cultures increased, there was
inevitable reciprocal interaction on many different levels.
For economic reasons, natives sometimes imitated Spanish
forms, motifs, and even some methods in order to make
sales to the whites. Less purposefully, native ability and

taste seeped down through hybrid generations to cause mutations of Hispanic wares. The Spanish example diversely affected Mexican Indian pottery through selective adoption of new techniques. Kilns and lead glazing met a rather general acceptance, the former being used even when the latter was not. Some Aztecs outside the Valley of Mexico did not make use of lead glaze until nearly a century after the conquest and a new set of economic needs had arisen.[95] Kilns were altered in many ways to suit Mexican Indian purposes, from circular, single unit, rock-lined pits in the ground to two aboveground chambers generally left open at the top. Pots frequently were stacked with the protection of sherds, as they had been in pre-Conquest times. The potter's wheel, which required a new set of motor habits, was ignored unless it was found to supplement, rather than to replace, traditional methods.[96] As *mestizos* constituted the mass of the

Figure 125. Sixteenth-century Mexico City *traza*, surrounded by four Indian *barrios*. The suggested location of the potters' district was on the northwestern edge of the island on which the city was located.

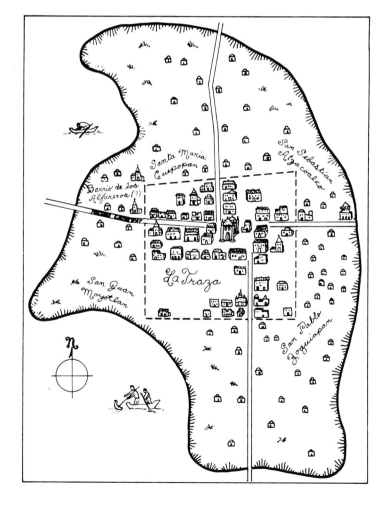

artisan force, they took over workshop production of utilitarian plain or lead-glazed wares with a combination of
techniques. At Puebla they are said to have made Spanish
forms on the wheel and pre-Columbian objects in ancient
molds. Similarly, the Andalusian contributions to the
craft diffused to New Spain diluted as men from other
parts of Iberia and colonial artisans of mixed blood filled
the potters' ranks and as a flood of Oriental porcelains
reached Mexico, bringing in a stylistic and commercial
stimulus absent in Spain.

The earliest records of potters in Mexico City so far
encountered are dated 1537 and 1538. In those years allot-
ments of land went to Francisco de la Reyna and Francisco
de Morales, described as *olleros*.[97] This was a generic term
in Sevilla for potters that in Mexico changed to *loceros*.
It is not at all certain that Reyna, Morales, or their associates took up their old means of livelihood at once. Because
the conquest allowed an upheaval of usual societal roles,
artisans engaged in low-paying, low-status work often
tried to better their lot. Having failed, many then resumed
their former trades. It is not certain that these potters
were Old Christians. The Muslim element still formed a
substantial substratum in Andalusian potting circles and
could have spread abroad in spite of on-and-off official
curbs.

Nor is the location of their land known. Because later
potteries and the potters' confraternity were situated
there, it may be that the district of Santa María Cuepopan
became the potters' quarter as early as this period. The
locality was at the western side of the island on which
Mexico City was placed and was close to access roads from
the mainland over which raw materials could be brought.[98]
In the sixteenth century it was a district not unlike Triana,
in that it had a mixed lower class population (Fig. 125).

Preparation for a low-level workshop designed to produce a series of uncomplicated vessels for a homogenous
Spanish clientele was not difficult (Fig. 126). The necessary
wheels and kilns were of simple design, so familiar to
Andalusian artisans that they could have been constructed
even by those with minimal experience. Without much
doubt, wheels were still entrenched in workroom floors
and kilns were the elliptical to squared, domed Muslim
style. Local natives knew of adequate deposits of service-
able red-burning clay, which they and their ancestors
had used for centuries.[99] Grinding pits and soaking tanks
were dug and operated by such helpers. Lead for glazes
and, when desired, copper and iron oxide to give them
color were plentiful. Wood fuel or *zacate* for firing
abounded, although within the century serious deforesta-

Figure 126. Almost seventeen
hundred red-slipped moldmade
bowls of this type have been
found in the muck beneath Mexico
City. They represent a secondary
potting activity unrelated to
the wheel industry; it may have
been carried out by Indian neophytes under direction of the
clergy. All bowls have a raised
insignia in the obverse center.
They are believed to have been
made for various religious houses
for the express purposes of
feeding the poor who thronged
the sixteenth-century capital. Why
so many were discarded unbroken
is puzzling (courtesy Instituto
Nacional de Antropología e
Historia, Mexico City).

tion threatened the Valley of Mexico. Fuel was not the
trimmings of olive trees or olive residue as in Andalusia,
because the growing of those trees was prohibited. In
short order modest establishments of a potter or two could
begin operation. Although neither documentary nor
archaeological evidence is yet available, it is certain that a
cluster of such shops came into existence in or near sixteenth-century Mexico City in order to keep the European
residents supplied with their preferred domestic utensils.
Eventually they might have evolved into factories with
a number of workers, but this surely did not happen at the
outset, owing to a comparatively small user population.
When expansion did come, the basic procedures and
products remained unchanged.

To produce the maiolica ware that in New Spain
remained an exclusive part of the Spanish tradition, the
artisans had to demonstrate more ingenuity in adapting to
local conditions. First, a clay was desired that fired to a
lighter color than usually was seen in the regional Mexican
Indian pottery. Not only would such a chalky body
require less tin in the lead-fluxed glaze bath in order to
conceal the core, but it would shrink in cooling so that the
glassy coating would not crack excessively. Moreover,
Sevillian maiolica pastes, the standard against which early
colonial potters worked, were pale buff. The fact that
that kind of calcareous clay had become traditional in Sevilla for tin-glazed domestic vessels originally was based
upon the same rationale: the whiter the paste, the less tin
and crazing. Back in Sevilla, a light-firing clay was common in the Guadalquivir basin and had long been used for
vessels that were not tin-glazed. Determined to have a
similar light-firing material, the sixteenth-century Mexico
City potters were forced to go outside the Valley of Mexico
to get it. The exact source is unknown, but transporting
it to the city would have been little problem, owing to a
virtually unlimited supply of native labor. Perhaps several
kinds of clay were mixed to take advantage of particular
physical properties of each.[100] This might have resulted in
a more plastic, stronger, finer-textured medium and a
bleached, lightweight finished product.

Mexican maiolists benefited from a search for sources of
tin commenced immediately after the shooting at Tenochtitlán had stopped, in order to be able to cast new bronze
cannons for defense of the outnumbered invaders. These
efforts were so successful that just a year later a tin mine
was opened in the hot country of Guerrero.[101] This and
other deposits discovered later, as well as occasional drifts
of nodules washing down streambeds, met the requirements of arms makers, sculptors, and potters. A mid-

seventeenth-century document records the exchange of
some Mexican earthenware for Peruvian tin, but this
was not a common practice, as trade restrictions existed
between the two viceroyalties.[102]

The third substance needed to promote the fluxing
action of the glaze was sodium. In all likelihood the quest
for this material was initiated because it was essential
for refining gold and silver. However, pottery, glass, and
soap production profited when it was learned that a native
plant growing along the marshy lake shores would produce soda ash when burned. The scrubby plant promptly
was called *barrilla* after a different plant used for the same
purposes in Sevilla.[103]

Tequesquite, a rocky material embedded near the shores
of the saline lakes of the Mexican interior highlands, was
found to be a more abundant source of sodium. The salt
flats around Lake Texcoco in the same valley as the capital
became the most convenient source. *Tequesquite* was broken into chunks and hauled by burro trains to the city
to be used by makers of dyes, gunpowder, fireworks, salt-
peter, soap, and, finally, glazes.[104]

Lastly, cobalt, *polvo azul*, for minimal painted decoration
was brought from Spain. It had been sent there from the
Near East in cake form. The unrefined processing of the
Muslim cobalt produced an unstable grayish blue color
that remained typical of Old and New World maiolicas
throughout the sixteenth century.

While the pottery-making enterprises were getting
organized in Mexico City, a few potters set themselves up
in businesses in other parts of the country in villages
with sufficient Spanish population to support their work.
Perhaps they hired a native helper or two and gradually
taught them the trade. The rural inventory concentrated
on tableware, cook pots, and furnishings, such as candleholders and urinals, considered essential in European
homes. Lead glazing was customary for many articles,
although only one known sixteenth-century reference specifically discusses its introduction.[105] The total output
was comparable to those of rural potteries in southern
Spain.

It soon was seen that small Hispanic country shops in
Mexico did not have the importance they had in Andalusia. One reason was the availability of large quantities
of indigenous pottery. The Mexican Indian hand-building
and mold techniques generally did not allow as rapid
manufacture as the potter's wheel, but native potters were
content to work for less profit and often undersold their
white competition.[106] The range of Andalusian forms
was not resumed to its full extent, therefore, but native

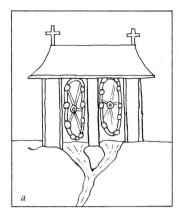

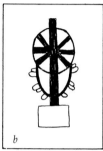

Figure 127. Spanish-introduced water wheels as illustrated in two sixteenth-century Mexican codices. Although in both instances the wheels are shown as vertical, it is probable that the *noria de sangre* was intended. The artists omitted the complexity of the horizontal gearing wheel. Example a from Codex Osuna, 1565, showing water lifts in use during construction of the Mexico City cathedral; example b from Codex Aubin, 1576, showing water lift used in a garden behind an unidentified church (after Dibble 1963; Mexico, Instituo Indigenista Interamericano 1947; Toussaint 1924).

contributions made for a greater overall variability. Another factor in abandonment of some traditional vessel shapes was the difference in Mexican agriculture from that of Andalusia. Because water wheels were not widely used for irrigation, there was less need for suitable jars. However, small drawings in the sixteenth-century Codex Osuna and the Codex Aubin show that water lifts with ceramic jars were employed for some purposes (Fig. 127).[107] *Ánforas* or *botijos* were not required for the shipment or dispensing of wine or olive oil. Nevertheless, similar containers likely were made in rural environments for the export of some Mexican natural and processed products, such as cacao, medicines, lard, soap, or flour. For example, the 1554 Cortez fleet sailing from Tehuantepec to Callao, Peru, had in its cargo 167 *cántaros* of pitch and another mixture of pitch, grease, resin, and oil.[108] Some of the pitch may have been used as jar lining by potters, but its most important use was in shipbuilding.

In addition to the usual assemblage of unglazed or lead-glazed pots of elementary contours, some attempts were made in predominately Spanish peasant communities to make tin-glazed dishes along the lines of those being sold at the capital. One such village maiolica industry is suggested by finds beneath Mexico City of remains of poorly made vessels that did not conform in paste, finish, or variety to what are regarded as the contemporary urban products. They did repeat some design motifs seen on common grade city types. It is suggested that they were made elsewhere by persons of journeyman ability to be used locally and were brought into the capital's markets to undersell the standard ceramics.[109]

Up to about the middle of the sixteenth century, in Mexico City as in Sevilla, all those who could afford European-style tablewares ate from virtually the same dishes, regardless of which city had produced them. At that time new wealth in some sectors of the populace and hope for more to come brought a small body of skilled Italian craftsmen to Sevilla. Their example—and, one must believe, their financial success—forced a larger local community of passive potters, who formerly were content with the status quo, into a program of improvement. In Sevilla, as we have seen, that led to a refinement of techniques and a new design ensemble that produced a series of prestige wares for the well-to-do. The age-old, coarse white series, although also improved, still comprised the archetypal second-quality dishes for the masses because the grasp of the long Islamic tradition remained firm among the more conservative potters making that caliber

of tableware. There was little common ground between
these categories of domestic vessels, underscoring the
great social and economic distinctions between their users.

In Mexico City, by contrast, two more similar grades
of tablewares for different groups of consumers came into
being. In most respects the top quality equalled that of
Sevilla, but the lower category differed markedly from its
Spanish counterpart. In Mexico City the *mudéjar* coarse
wares were discontinued and, by inference, so were the
outmoded pit wheel and beehive kiln. The pottery was
replaced by another second-quality grouping that superfi-
cially resembled the concurrent top grade, but that was
made to sell at lower cost by certain modifications: it bore
a less opaque glaze with reduced tin content and a careless
patterning in a *contrahecho* blue derived from a mixture
of copper oxide plus zinc, rather than cobalt, or, more
commonly, copper green and iron brown. Even with these
differences, lower class housewives could feel satisfied
that they were in style. Did the technical similarities
between the two calibers arise from some unsuspected
leveling agent in the colonial society, or were the makers
less constrained by the Muslim past and less conservative
in their attitudes? The latter is more probable.

In both categories of the urban Mexican maiolicas that
appeared in the second half of the sixteenth century,
shapes were more sharply delineated than formerly. Walls
were thinned. Plate rims were flattened horizontally. Ring
feet became standard. All-white schemes predominated.
The top grade styles with suitably shaped rims were fired
suspended in saggars by headpins to avoid cockspur
blemishes. This was the only time in the four hundred
fifty year history of Mexican maiolica production that
headpins would be used. When these types ceased to be
made, the use of those devices terminated because they
were a lightly accepted adjunct of an introduced technology. Headpins were discarded in Sevilla also. Design
motifs, composition, and polychrome format on finer decorated pieces faintly recalled Faenza or Genoa, but as
seen through Andalusian eyes.[110] The fact that explicit
Talaveran styling was not so evident must be due to influence from that potting center not having come so early
in the sixteenth century. Difficulties in controlling cobalt
pigments not present in Spanish prototypes appear in
colonial efforts. Otherwise, the similarities in the peninsular and provincial Mexico City best hollow wares are striking. As more research is accomplished in southern Spain
and in Mexico, these are becoming increasingly apparent
(Figs. 128–130).

Figure 128. Representative sample
of maiolica styles made in Mexico
City during second half of sixteenth century and, in several
cases, into the seventeenth century: *a*, top grade polychrome
of two shades of blue, with
occasional touch of yellow (upper
left sherd bears scar on reverse
surface of headpin used in firing);
b, top grade blue-banded and
centerpiece floral pattern; *c*, top
grade polychrome of blue, yellow,
and orange; *d*, common grade
blue–on–cream type that broadly
duplicated simpler designs of
contemporary top grades (courtesy Instituto Nacional de Antropología e Historia and Dirección
de Inmuebles Federales, Mexico
City).

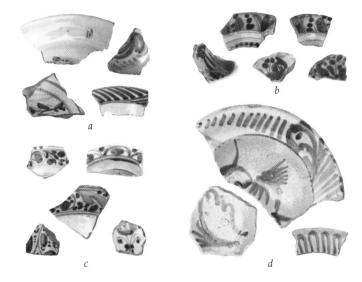

Figure 129. Perhaps the earliest,
longest, and most heavily used
Mexico City maiolica style featured a palmette motif. Executed
in greyish blue with frequent
accents of orange, it was a design
element with ancient Near Eastern
ancestry: *a*, shallow bowl recovered beneath Mexico City;
b, late fifteenth- or early sixteenth-
century pitcher from Granada,
with palmette in brown, illustrating contemporary Andalusian
familiarity with the design element; *c*, obverse and reverse
of small Mexican plate of
unknown derivation (courtesy
Instituto Nacional de Antropología
e Historia, Mexico City [*a*], Casa
de los Tiros, Granada [*b*], and
Carmen Pérez de Salazar de
Ovando and Carlos de Ovando,
Mexico City [*c*]).

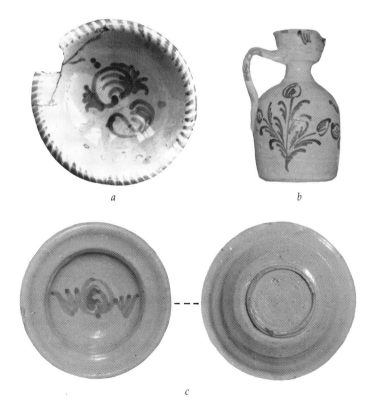

Tile making also appears to have imitated Sevillian modes of smooth-surfaced *azulejos*, although the oldest surviving Andalusian examples so far known in Mexico are of early seventeenth-century date (Fig. 131).[111] In Mexico the colors and some motifs were those of the coetaneous pottery. Although the direct contributor of this tile-making trait was Andalusia, the original idea of polychromatic flat-surfaced tile and many of the design elements were Italian.

The technical improvements in the late sixteenth-century maiolicas of New Spain likewise can be attributed to the same Italian impetus operating in Sevilla. It occurred at more or less the same time, but was interposed into a distinctive cultural environment. The Italianization could have been transmitted in one of three ways, or by a combination of them. First, a considerable amount of Italian maiolica from Liguria, Romagna, and Tuscany found its way to the Mexican highlands during the second half

Figure 130. Reconstruction of composition of mid sixteenth- to mid seventeenth-century Mexico City blue–on–white maolica style.

a

b

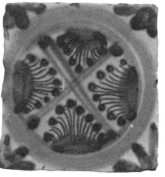

c

d

Figure 131. Sixteenth-century *azulejos* believed to have been made in Mexico City. Although stylistically similar to Sevillian models, the colors and brushwork correspond closely to contemporary Mexican maiolica styles: *a–b*, polychrome tile facing in crypt area uncovered in Mexico City cathedral compound; *c–d*, ind..idual polychrome tiles repeating contemporary top grade hollow ware maiolica design styles (courtesy Instituto Nacional de Antropología e Historia, Mexico City [*a, b*], and Carmen Pérez de Salazar de Ovando and Carlos de Ovando, Mexico City [*c, d*].

of the sixteenth century. Its increased volume over the first
half of the century points either to greater traffic to the
Spanish Americas and a heightened exchange or to a
mounting inability of Spanish suppliers to meet colonial
orders with Spanish goods. Probably both factors were
involved. There also was a significant presence of Italians
in the colony.[112] More affluence and sophistication among
colonial consumers are behind the scenes in this commerce. In any case, the novelty and superior caliber of Italian pottery made it prized. In order to compete, local
artisans may have been compelled to attempt refinement.
Secondly, finer Sevillian and Talaveran maiolicas, at the
time based upon Italianate styles, were shipped to New
Spain. They would have provided prototypes, but provincial ability and taste altered the regional results. Here,
the records of transactions are exceedingly skimpy.
Between 1565 and 1600 fourteen authorized convoys,
composed of varying numbers of ships, sailed to New
Spain. Only four entries regarding pottery are known, all
in the 1590s. They shed no light on the importation of
either fine Sevillian or Talaveran pottery; three were shipments of ordinary candleholders and the fourth was one
hundred bundles of low-grade utility objects.[113] Thus
far, known archaeological or museum Sevillian specimens
of maiolica brought to Mexico in this era likewise are
not plentiful. Or thirdly, Sevillian potters and decorators
conversant in the new Italianate methods and styles
worked out in Andalusia arrived to merge into the colonial
work force. Such an extenuated diffusion diminished
likenesses to the original items.

Very early in the Spanish occupation of central Mexico
there was a divergent line of ceramic diffusion involving
Andalusian earthenwares unlike any known to have
occurred elsewhere. Specifically, this was a kind of handmade ware in a plain white-slipped, lead-glazed version
and a companion slipped, engraved, polychromed, lead-
glazed style. The brick-red clay utilized and the method
of shaping and finishing vessels from it were aboriginal.
So too were many of the motifs, such as the sacred native
corn plant. Mexican Indian craftsmanship is indicated.
However, the typical basin and broad-brimmed plate
forms, the use of a thin white slip and transparent lead
glaze on the most visible surface, and the engraving of elements filled with green and/or amber colorants came
from European influence. Oddly, the decorative technique, while basically Islamo-Byzantine, was not practiced
in Andalusia. It must have come to the Mexican Indians
from an Old World source other than southern Spain. One
suspects its introduction to central Mexico by clergymen

from Italy, where the mode was used on cheaper ceramics
at such places as Pisa. Very probably this red-bodied,
handmade ware was a native product designed to compete
in the Spanish market by supplying preferred shapes
of utensils with white, glazed surfaces at a lower cost
than the traditional Iberian ceramics. The amount of this
pottery recovered from beneath Mexico City reveals its
success, which, however, may not have survived the devastating epidemics late in the sixteenth century, which
wiped out enormous segments of the Mexican Indian
communities.[114]

When Spanish intercourse with the Indies faltered,
Mexican dealers in ceramics quickly jumped into the
breach. Although it is likely that plainwares made in Mexico were distributed either as containers or as pottery to
be used domestically, this has not been satisfactorily demonstrated as yet.[115] Because of outward similarities, physical tests of clays are needed to distinguish New World
utilitarian objects from those of the homeland.

Several of the top-grade Mexico City maiolica styles
seem to have been made in small quantity and not to have
been traded much beyond the capital. Neither did friable
commonwares reach distant users. Two of the more abundantly made fine-grade maiolicas, one with an isolated
blue and yellow/orange palmette centerpiece and another
with a banded abstracted floral decoration in blue, did
spread through the Caribbean area from Venezuela and its
offshore islands of Cubagua and Margarita in the south
to Cuba in the north (Figs. 128b, 129a, c). From there they
reached Florida, and in the opening eras of the seventeenth century were taken on to Darien Bluff in Georgia
and Jamestown in Virginia. Also in the early seventeenth
century, after colonization and missionization were commenced along the Rio Grande in New Mexico and in
north central Arizona, occasional vessels of these maiolica
types were dispatched north with supply caravans to
such remote, scattered places as Casas Grandes in Chihuahua; Abó, Quarai, Gran Quivira, Puaray, Santa Fe,
Pecos, and Hawikuh in New Mexico; and Awatobi in Arizona.[116] It should be noted that although finished Mexican
maiolicas were widely dispersed, the methods of their
manufacture were not. They must have been considered
luxury articles on the frontiers, most likely comprising
a few altar furnishings or special dishes for festive occasions. Only later would maiolica plates be typical tablewares in outlying presidial posts.

The pottery-making endeavor at Mexico City retained
its momentum through the sixteenth century in part
because that city remained the apex of Spanish colonial

life. Then, in a curious repetition of disasters that were
ending Sevillian dominance in the craft, the Mexico City
business also slowed. Floods, epidemics, and malaise
at the capital seem to have caused a desertion of the potting ranks.[117] Perhaps also the necessity of obtaining a
light-firing clay from an unknown source outside the
Valley of Mexico was too inconvenient.[118] Potters left at
Mexico City lost their spark and, quite unconsciously,
remained committed to an older point of view. From then
on the local efforts in maiolica, which continued into
the eighteenth century, produced characterless tablewares,
smooth-surfaced tiles, or a few simply designed, better
quality pieces that often listlessly copied fashions being
made popular at a new center of activity. Plain or lead-
glazed utility vessels may have continued to be made in
unchanging styles. Toussaint, prominent Mexican art
historian, found the names of seven such Mexico City potters in seventeenth-century archives dating from 1626 to
1653. There surely were many more workers, since a
guild, having as its patron saints the Sevillian sisters Justa
and Rufina, was organized during that century.[119]

Meanwhile, in 1531, across the mountains from the
Valley of Mexico a Spanish town named Puebla de los
Angeles had been founded by forty settlers in a temperate
valley on the road between the capital and the Caribbean
port of Vera Cruz. It was conceived as an industrial center
where uprooted Spaniards could find employment in a
number of enterprises to supply European-style goods for
the settlers of New Spain. Even though there was a large
Native American population in the vicinity, the locale
selected for the settlement was unoccupied. This permitted
the authorities to lay out a grid-patterned town of rectangular blocks and straight streets crossing each other at
right angles with no obstructions.[120] The heart of the original plan of Puebla still survives.

The location of Puebla was a wise choice. The climate
was mild, the soil fertile, and there was an enormous
supply of native labor. In addition to town plots, small
acreages of land were granted to foot and mounted soldiers who had participated in the conquest, turning them
into New Spain's first farmers. Gradually, larger *estancias*
spread throughout the area. These recreated Andalusian
cortijos in a new setting. Before the end of the sixteenth
century the Puebla and nearby Atlixco valleys had become
the richest agricultural region in the viceroyalty, known
for wheat, fruits, and great herds of sheep and cattle.[121] In
the early seventeenth century large *haciendas* came into
being, their lore permeating many aspects of colonial life.
The landed gentry, however, preferred to live in town

as it had in Sevilla. There, the people adopted the trappings of an aristocracy with sufficient funds to underwrite
advancements in the arts and beautification of their hometown. They erected palatial homes filled with the best
the country could supply and were eager to acquire more.
On a commercial level, more than three dozen textile
mills, a glass factory, a soap factory, many metal works,
and other urban commerce were building a thriving economy.[122] Little wonder that potters were drawn to this
locality when conditions at the capital worsened.

Pottery making at Puebla was possible because in the
environs there were extensive beds of suitable clays of several types and deposits of the *tequesquite* essential for
glaze preparation. In fact, the white calcareous clay used
in Mexico City maiolicas may have been transported from
near Puebla,[123] although it is not certainly known that
colonial clay sources prior to the eighteenth century were
the same as those used today.[124] The first potters are
recorded as being at work in the village shortly before the
end of the sixteenth century. They brought with them
the technological advancements that had accrued to that
time.

It was prophetic that the first of these Puebla potters,
Gaspar de Encinas, was singled out in archival papers as a
tiler because in the next one hundred years Puebla not
only became the tile capital of New Spain, it outstripped
Andalusian devotion to these architectural additives.
The kind of ceramics made by nine other sixteenth-century
potters was not stated.[125] Encinas might have been one
connecting link between pottery making at the capital and
that at Puebla. In 1602, twenty years after he is noted as
a resident of Puebla, he signed a contract with the purchasing agent for the first cathedral in Mexico City for
twelve hundred large *azulejos* and six hundred *cintillos*,
narrow border tiles, to be used on the main altar and in a
chapel.[126] That 1525 structure was still in use during construction of a replacement and was renovated, beginning
in 1585. In the early 1980s explorations south of the modern Mexico City cathedral revealed burial crypts of the
first church decorated in the same polychromed tiles identified in fragments recovered from the fill beneath adjoining structures.[127] These *azulejos* duplicated a popular
Sevillian mode of the last few decades of the sixteenth
century, but the actual colors of the pigments utilized and
noticeable nuances of decorative technique indicate imita-
tive colonial workmanship directly related to several of
the local fineware maiolicas (Fig. 131a, b). If these tiles
were in fact the work of Encinas, it suggests first that he
was well schooled in Sevillian tile making, and second that

he likely continued at Puebla a vogue begun in the Valley
of Mexico. The other sixteenth-century potters who moved
there also can be expected to have pursued their familiar
styles, most likely those of the capital. If this were the
case, especially the two leading maiolicas of the Valley of
Mexico (San Juan Polychrome and San Luis Blue–on–
White) continued in the Puebla valley for an overlap
period during the evolution of new styles.

Nothing indicates that a potters' quarter was specifically
defined when the town was laid out. Nevertheless,
because there were no earlier conflicting structures or
streets, it was an unusual opportunity to put idealized city
planning to work. Therefore, beginning with the first
records of potters in Puebla, the location of two of the
workshops was shown as being restricted to the northwest
quadrant from the central *plaza*. One was along the road
west to Cholula, where ironmongers already were busy,
and the other was some ten blocks northwest from the
plaza in what must still have been an undeveloped area.[128]
Most likely the village first had grown toward a small
river that coursed along its eastern boundary, leaving land
empty in the opposite direction. It was a suitable spot
for potting activities because a main road came into town
through the district, a spring and intermittent stream
were available for additional water if needed, and prevailing wind currents may have blown fumes away from settled areas. Seventeen specific pottery workshop locations
can be plotted for the seventeenth century, all in the
northwest quadrant but closer to the center of town (Fig.
132).[129] All potteries were concentrated in the same district
until the late nineteenth century. It was there that participants in the craft were born, grew to maturity, worked,
married, died, and were buried. The Puebla potters'
quarter thus emerged as a paradigm of a form of medieval
structured craft regulation carried out with stricter conformity than had been feasible, in most instances, in
mother Spain.

The names of one hundred ninety-one potters or
apprentices are known for the seventeenth-century Puebla
industry. By that time most had been born in Mexico,
either being *criollos* or *mestizos* (see Glossary). Three are
known to have emigrated from Spain, two of those serving
their apprenticeships in Puebla. They obviously brought
no acquired ceramic ability from home. In the middle
of the century a master craftsman came from Cádiz in
Andalusia, but he would have had to conform to procedures and styles already crystallized. The appearance
of some Italians may have been especially important in the
formative stage of the endeavor, inasmuch as one was

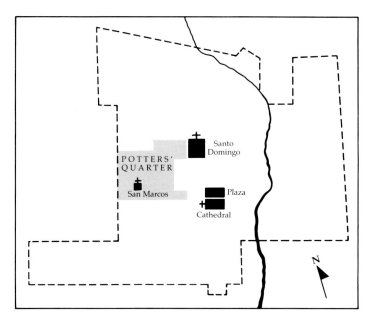

Figure 132. Potters' quarter in seventeenth-century Puebla, northwest of the main plaza.

Francisco de Pésaro (or Pézaro), son of the eminent Sevillian Ligurian potter, Tomás de Pésaro, and thus was conversant with an impressive pottery-making patrimony. Arriving before the end of the sixteenth century, at Puebla he was regarded as a master of white wares, that is, maiolicas.[130] He was followed some years later by Juan Pizón, a potter who moved to Puebla from Savona.[131] The skill and ideas of these and other unknown Italians in the colony doubtless would have made significant contributions to the nascent craft activity.

It has been commonly reported that the success of the Puebla enterprise came about because potting priests were brought to New Spain by their Dominican brothers from seventeenth-century Talavera de la Reina in Castile.[132] There is no tangible evidence whatsoever to support this theory, although the linkage of the two industries was so fixed in the public mind that Puebla-made maiolicas became known as Talavera de Puebla. That was a popular association of the best in Spain with the best in New Spain. A single potter was named Roque de Talavera, which might appear suggestive of Castilian derivation. However, this man, who did not work in Puebla until the middle of the seventeenth century, came from Jalapa, Mexico, and learned his craft in his adopted home. Expect no more success in tracing a Sevillian source in three men named Sevilla and two named Sevillano; all appear to have been native Pueblans.[133]

Some time early in the seventeenth century, as urban potters slowly congregated in Puebla, two contrasting

diffusionary streams of ceramic knowledge from opposite
sides of the world came together there. In different ways
they helped give birth to an exceedingly active pottery-
making industry that was to contribute immensely to a
regional distinctiveness that continues today.

In addition to the basic craft fundamentals and an
assortment of tried-and-true forms, from Spain came an
overwhelming infusion of Moresque taste that would have
great impact on maiolicas for many years. Could it have
been a coincidence that the *morisco* expulsion from Spain
had just taken place? Toussaint did not think so.[134] He
believed that despite fluctuating prohibitions against their
coming to the New World, enough *moriscos* did slip
through to leave behind in the Puebla region in particular
a pageant of *mudéjar* decorative arts, including carved
and inlaid cedar ceilings, worked stone portals, embossed
leather, latticed screens, stirrups, carpets, plaster confec-
tions, and brightly colored tiles interspersed with brick to
enliven wall spaces. The number and variety of these
works makes likely the actual presence of artisans steeped
in this perspective, rather than a more remote restatement
drawn from the Andalusian experience after a lapse of a
century or more.

As might be expected, overt Muslimization of hollow
wares came in superficial decoration. Composition of field
and treatment of elements had deep, ancient roots in
Islam. Because such relatively little fine pottery was coming from Spain to New Spain, these new colonial decorative modes had no basis in marketplace competition,
but were expressions for sensual pleasure only. Moreover,
comparable *mudéjar* qualities in contemporary Andalusian
pottery design, as in architecture and lesser crafts, had
long since dried up. The great diffusionary tide that for
centuries had welled up out of western Asia and rolled
relentlessly toward the setting sun came at last to its final
resting place at the foot of Popocatepetl.

A second but profound undercurrent stimulating the
new Puebla ceramic endeavor came from the opposite
direction, the Orient. This was the only time in the history
of ceramics prior to the modern period that East affected
West across the Pacific Ocean. While lasting technical
improvements resulted, the principal impetus for borrow-
ing was economic. Uncharacteristically, in their desire
to become established and solvent, money was speaking
louder to potters than was artistic satisfaction. This was
because since the arrival of the first Manila Galleon in 1569
provincials had become enamoured of Chinese porcelain
(Fig. 133).[135] Even though much of what got to New Spain
was considered inferior by its makers, porcelain was a

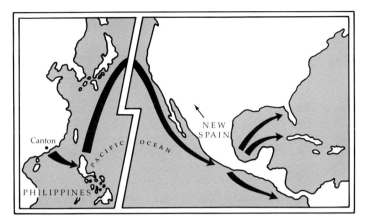

Figure 133. Distribution, during late sixteenth through seventeenth centuries, of porcelains from China to the Americas. New Spain received and retained the bulk of these shipments, but secondary dispersal to South America, the northern borderlands of New Spain, the Indies, and Florida occurred. The volume of reship-ment of porcelains to Andalusia is unknown.

wondrous kind of ceramics to those reared in the Spanish earthenware tradition. In order to compete with it, or perhaps to replace it after the Chinese trade began to taper off in the post-1620 eras,[136] colonial potters wisely realized that it was imperative to make certain refinements in their own products, a need to which they had previously paid little heed. This they did through more careful prepa-ration of raw materials and production methods. Although a light-colored clay was desirable for maiolica, the need to match white-bodied porcelain made such material even more essential. How much search was entailed is unknown, but the Pueblans did achieve a more consistent-ly white-firing, fine-grained clay body than had been used earlier. In this instance, no admixture of any iron-bearing, red-burning clay was made. They threw this material in untypically thin-walled vessels with elegantly proportioned Eastern shapes. Later guild ordinances stip-ulated that body thickness not exceed that of a *real* coin.[137] A thick, satiny, completely opaque, white glaze covered these vessels, upon which designs were painted in brilliant pigments freed of the impurities that formerly had yielded disappointing results. Care was given to the critical firing stage, so that unsightly blemishes would be reduced or eliminated. The admired translucence of porcelain remained elusive, but it is unknown whether the potters recognized that this difference resulted from base materials and firing methods used. With this attention to the Chinese example, it is curious to note that the ingrained allegiance to Spanish Muslim design grammar remained so entrenched that for a number of years there was no attempt to imitate unfamiliar Chinese motifs or to rely on their limited one-color, two-value palette.

As Puebla's decorated maiolica production evolved, there emerged two grades aimed at different kinds of con-sumers. The lowest grade was *entrefino*, or middling fine.

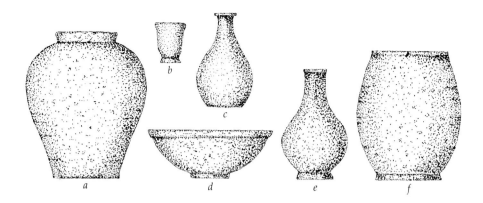

Figure 134. Some forms of Puebla maiolica ceramics that were influenced by Chinese export porcelain examples: *a, tibor; b, cup, pocillo; c, e,* pear-shaped bottles; *d,* hemispherical, ring-footed bowl; *f,* barrel, often with reinforcing applied rings.

This was restricted to tableware, which to a large degree reflected Chinese form inspiration (Fig. 134). There were small, ring-footed plates with direct rims; saucers; little cups, with and without handles and with orifices that expanded slightly outward; and footed, hemispherical bowls with gently flared rims. Chinese tea cups and rice bowls must have been very much in mind.

The tea cup, in particular, mirrors the crosscultural forces at work in the colony. It was a small, ring-footed object called a *pocillo,* a Mexican term not diffused to Spain. On occasion in both Mexico and Spain the cup was known as *jícara,* the name for an American calabash gourd used as a drinking vessel by Native Americans and Europeans living in reduced circumstances in New Spain. The shape obviously was inspired by the Chinese tea cup, although the use of tea never became popular in Mexico or the motherland. Instead, it was employed for serving an indigenous beverage of sweetened, vanilla-flavored chocolate and milk. In eighteenth-century Spain a moldmade, oval or leaf-shaped, individual tray outfitted with a securing gallery to steady the cup became an elite object for social imbibing of this luxury drink. The tray, or *mancerina,* named for the Marques de Mancera, was not adopted by colonial Puebla potters.[138] In Mexico an associated Eastern vessel form used for holding ginger became a container for cacao beans.

As the pottery industry matured, more Spanish forms that formerly had been glazed in white and left undecorated were pulled into the decorating rooms for added treatment. These were such familiar articles as cylindrical drug jars, molded octagonal or rectangular inkwells, saucer-and-shaft candleholders, and two-handled, tubular chamber pots. Among Puebla maiolicas, this group of *entrefino* ceramics is that most frequently found archaeologically. It was made in quantity by most maiolists for the domestic needs of a growing body of people with the necessary cash to acquire it. Moreover, the delicacy its makers strove to attain made it very vulnerable, with a resultant high rate of breakage. It is suspected that the very top levels of society were not its typical users, since by then they were able to indulge themselves in more status-enhancing articles of porcelain or native silver.[139]

In the initial period of Puebla maiolica production the top quality *fino* grade focused principally upon large basins, some from 45 to 50 cm in diameter, with broad flat bottoms and steep, slightly flared walls terminating in a thickened or narrow horizontal rim. They had come into the Spanish grammar via the Muslims, but to that time in Spain had remained undecorated, other than being glazed or treated with a frame line or two. In a repetition of the Nasrid elevation of the common winged amphora to an enriched object of special beauty, the Mexicans saw in the formerly utilitarian shape a similar challenge. To them, the form offered a good field for painted pattern, a centerpiece in the bottom with the vessel walls forming a frame. The basins were so particularized that distribution generally was limited to churches or their hospitals, where they were not subjected to rough everyday usage. Thus, they today comprise a high proportion of the extant museum or collector specimens of the types.

As colonial lifeways grew more complex and the industry reached full stride, other forms entered the *fino* complement of shapes. Many of these were taken from Oriental sources. Most prominent were bottles with pear-shaped bases and long, narrow necks; full-bodied, often strapped, flat-topped barrels; and high-shouldered, narrow-based, large jars with brief vertical necks (Fig. 134). The latter, called *tibores*, frequently were outfitted with lockable metal lids, as were the so-called ginger jars they imitated. Being of commodious, often stupendous, size, the *fino* vessels generally were heavy, thick-walled, and made of a sturdy red-burning clay.

Turning to surface design, the two early *mudéjar* modes were polychrome. One style, for convenience now known to archaeologists as Puebla Polychrome, made primary use of black and blue pigments against a creamy white ground, with an occasional yellow or green accent. The other, named Abó Polychrome for a mission site in New Mexico where several nearly whole pieces were recovered early in New World maiolica research, bore such colors as blue, green, yellow, orange, and brown on a comparable white glaze.[140] These palettes, contemporaneously being used in Sevilla and Talavera, often are regarded as Italianate. Actually, some of the earliest tin-glazed pieces in Mesopotamia had been decorated in the same colors, but all were not combined on one object. Both Spaniards and Italians ultimately were indebted to that innovation.

The main element of the Puebla Polychrome style was an interesting adaptation to pottery of a lace pattern. With the sixteenth-century love of richly finished clothing and money to spend on it, lace making had become an important occupation in both Sevilla and Talavera. Behind these Spanish efforts were exports to Andalusia and Castile of bobbin and guipure laces from Albisola on the Italian Ligurian coast.[141] Whether pottery decorators in each of the two Spanish potting centers were simultaneously inspired by that material or whether one group was copying the other remains an unanswered question. An outside guess is that there also was some Portuguese contribution to this new theme, since a few seventeenth-century objects there carried similar designs.[142] Concurrent with the peninsular interest in lace patterns, decorators in Mexico wholeheartedly adapted them in their own inimitable way and clung to them long after they had lost favor in the homeland.

Spanish artisans strove to capture the delicate nature of lace with exceedingly fine black lines, the scalloped lace edges providing a border pattern. Elements within the hatched weblike lace were small open florals of a central dot and surrounding dots. On plates the lace framed a centerpiece composed of a Renaissance theme, such as a putti, sun face, or allegorical figure (Fig. 135b). On cylindrical forms and some plates fanned lace tips were arranged as encircling bands, a figural motif then being eliminated (Fig. 135a). Often the lace was laid over a broad yellow line in order to highlight its implied sheerness,

Figure 135. Lace patterns on two seventeenth-century maiolica vessels attributed to Talavera de la Reina. Typically, the motif was executed as a border in fine black lines: *a*, footed pitcher with molded handle and spout inspired by a metal prototype (blue bands separate lace passages and line handle, rim, and spout); *b*, plate, with blue band encircling centerpiece of a sunface drawn in yellow with black detailing (courtesy Instituto Valencia de Don Juan, Madrid [*a*], and Museo Arqueológico Nacional, Madrid [*b*]).

a   *b*

a   *b*   *c*

with blue confined to a frame line defined by narrower black lines at the rim or around the central element.[143] A good deal of the white ground was allowed to remain visible as contrast. In total, the style, as it was worked out in Iberia, was a fusion of homegrown and Italian concepts.

   Similar fine-lined execution of the lace, combined with a central naturalistic medallion, apparently was used in Mexico only on a few of the *fino* grade *lebrillos*. Almost as if the Mexican decorator was declaring his independence from Spanish pacesetters, the accompanying elements on two of the finest extant examples were an American turkey and a female bust (Fig. 136a).[144] To these were added floral sprays and background fillers, all borrowed from the companion Abó Polychrome package of motifs. These two specimens were painted in black only, that bicolor treatment being uncommon. In all the above ways these particular basins were unlike the run-of-the-mill Puebla Polychromes and may have survived thanks to extra care given them because of their distinctiveness. Certainly the work of someone familiar with the Spanish manner, could they have come from the shop of the Hispano-Italian, Francisco de Pésaro?

   Otherwise, decorators working in the lace-embellished style exuberantly converted an essentially restrained European mode into a flamboyant neo-*mudéjar* one (Figs. 136b, 137). Gone was any trace of Renaissance imagery or the lightness of touch seen on Spanish prototypes. In colonial hands the lace gimp, which was the skeleton of the fabric, was indicated by broad, boldly executed, unframed, luminous, deep blue lines that delineated the pattern. The refined quality of the cobalt pigment that yielded the clear, intense color and allowed the decoration to rise slightly in low relief above the glaze surface was distinct from that used in the sixteenth century in Mexico City. A new source of raw material is evident. Records indicate that the mineral was purchased packed in boxes in dry powder

Figure 136. Lace motif as used by seventeenth-century Puebla maiolica decorators: *a, fino* grade basin, *lebrillo*, 43 cm in diameter, with decoration executed in black only, making it most like Spanish workmanship of any known Mexican specimens; *b, entrefino* grade plate, 20 cm in diameter, with a heavier and more *mudéjar*-influenced interpretation of lace and a center dot motif borrowed from a design ensemble more typical of the multicolored companion style Abó Polychrome (The inscription translates as "the use of the infirmary."); *c, fino* grade basin, 48 cm in diameter, showing a combination of lace and naturalistic motifs and an aberrant color scheme of blue and yellow with black defining lines (courtesy Carmen Pérez de Salazar de Ovando and Carlos de Ovando, Mexico City).

Figure 137. An exceptionally fine
lebrillo, 53 cm in diameter, made in
Puebla ca. 1650. It is covered
with a creamy crazed glaze, and
its obverse bears an intricate
lace pattern of heavy blue gimp
lines and fine black filaments
in a decidedly Moresque manner.
The border inscription translates,
"I am for washing the purificators
and no more," indicating it was
commissioned for church use
(courtesy the Metropolitan
Museum of Art, New York. Gift of
Mrs. Robert W. de Forest, 1912).

form, a marketing procedure that may have been followed
by suppliers other than the traditional Muslim ones.[145]

The lace filaments were drawn in black, but only in
some scalloped borders did they approach Spanish fine-
ness. Their intersections were dotted to indicate thread
knots, and no effort was made to keep patterns within the
lace small. The pigment utilized must have been manganese, since it often fired to a characteristic purplish tone.
Rather than being restricted to bands, the lace pattern
was densely spread over the entire field of decoration,
leaving little exposed ground. Some arrangements were
seemingly unstructured, the gimp lines running amok
over the field. Others were eight-part radials or were
worked in a balanced format from a central floral medallion. This was a Muslim approach to composition. On
still other vessels the lace patterns on walls were compartmentalized by vertical dividers in an idea borrowed from
Chinese porcelains by most European designers. Rarely,
elements other than lace were used, such as balloonlike
dots on a string taken from the coeval motif assemblage of
characteristically Abó Polychrome renditions. Custom
orders from religious houses required appropriate inscriptions lettered in black, for which space was allowed.[146]
Examples are known with a yellow ground beneath the
black lace pattern, or with green or yellow gimp or rim
banded lines. Perhaps these were the kinds of deviations
from the established format that the 1682 guild ordinance

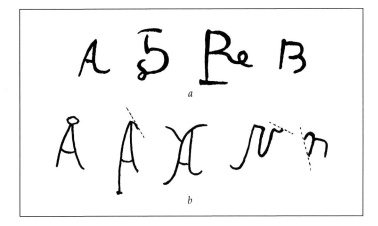

a

b

Figure 138. Some makers' marks painted before firing on the reverses of seventeenth-century Puebla maiolica ceramics. They were not as restricted to type as this study assortment might imply: *a*, Abó Polychrome; *b*, Puebla Polychrome.

amendments attempted to eliminate. One reason behind a desire for conformity was a desire to stop substitution of cheaper copper green pigment for cobalt blue, for fear that this would lower the quality of the entire type. The overall flat, decorative effect of the Mexican product was one of complex interlacements or spatial fracturing as expressive of the Muslim approach to design as were the Alhambra's *alicatado* friezes.

The companion style of many colors and featuring naturalistic elements as centerpieces was made in the same shops by the same group of craftsmen. This is proven by the 1682 guild ordinance amendments and by the physical characteristics of the pottery, including in some cases identical maker's marks (Fig. 138).[147] The shapes and sizes of vessels, the clays, and the base glaze were duplicated in the two types. It would be strange if the multi-colored version also did not exhibit some Moresque features, even though the Mexican potters themselves considered this type to have Talaveran leanings. Indeed, there were *mudéjar* overtones. First was a compacted allover decoration leaving little undecorated ground, reflecting the horror vacui typical of much Islamic decorative art. Second, floral sprays used as fillers and large-scale mammal or bird elements isolated as principal motifs were readable as such, but were not literal. The size of the figural elements dominating the field and their animated portrayal carried over from tenth-century Cordoban treatment (Fig. 139b). Filling the outlines of living forms with random dotting was a Muslim concept dating back to the ninth century in the Middle East (Fig. 140). Finally, there is a strong relationship between Spanish Muslim tile work and *cuerda seca* styling on the one hand, and on the other in the way in which the Mexican decorators treated color as unrelated, unshaded, solid patches. This was totally foreign to Italian or Talaveran work.

Figure 139. Seventeenth-century
multicolored Puebla maiolica style
with naturalistic motifs, many
of which had roots in the Italian
Renaissance: *a, fino* grade basin,
55 cm in diameter, with a scene of
the baptism of Christ and winged
cherubs combined with conventionalized solid color floral
abstractions; *b*, small *entrefino*
plate, with dominant bird motif
from old Spanish grammar,
recovered at base of Cholula pyra-
mid outside of Puebla (This is a
less complex version of the
expression seen in example *a*.);
c, parallel tile facade at the *pocito*
of San Miguel el Milagro near
Puebla, built in 1631, which in its
lightness reflects a drawing
away from the *mudéjar* Andalusian
concept while retaining the
connected patterning (courtesy
Carmen Pérez de Salazar de
Ovando and Carlos de Ovando,
Mexico City [*a*], and Instituto
Nacional de Antropología e
Historia, Mexico City [*b*]).

a   *b*

c

As in the case of the lace-patterned polychrome, few
fino basins showed a recognizable European touch tem-
pered by colonial mannerisms. One such specimen carried
a stylized central scene of the baptism of Christ (Fig. 139a).
An angel floated overhead and to one side was a token
depiction of an architectural device. On the surrounding
walls, interspersed with clusters of abstracted florals composed of swirls and dots that were diagnostic of the type,
were winged cherub heads. Pomegranates were incorporated in the wall design; these had symbolic meaning
in Christian art, but in Spain they became a hallmark of
the town of Granada, whose name means pomegranate
tree. The exterior bottom of the vessel carried a letter M,
a maker's mark theoretically required in the second half of
the century.[148] The draftsmanship was more controlled
than on many related examples, suggesting that perhaps
an itinerant Italian potter at work in Puebla might have
been responsible for this special piece. Was it Pésaro?

a

b

c

d

e

f

The unadulterated styles apparent on the *entrefino* objects of the two decorative modes came from peer-regulated, mutually agreed upon formats and components that to some extent reverted to an ancient cultural seeding. These were formalized in the guild regulations after the middle of the century. Theoretically, no deviations in colors, forms, or motifs were permitted artisans making this kind of ware. Combinations of the two principal design complexes were not uncommon on *fino* articles, however. For example, one basin is known that has a large eagle (?) as a centerpiece surrounded by floral sprays, both taken from Abó Polychrome motif inventory (Fig. 136c). On the walls are an Abó turkey, three other birds, and the same florals, but they are separated by four simplified lace dividers from the Puebla Polychrome set of motifs. The colors used were blue, three hues of yellow, and black.[149]

These variations between grades of the same style can be accounted for by observation of present shop organization. The main body of decorators turned out the *entrefinos*. These were the artisans. There were not more than one or two such workers in any one establishment, but there were many shops operating simultaneously. The workers were given a model to follow, probably drawn by the shop owner or *maestro*, but they were allowed to copy

Figure 140. Varied uses of dot fillers for animal motifs, perhaps suggested to Muslim ceramic decorators by niello elements on bronze articles, were copied by decorators of Chinese Ming porcelains and Mexican Puebla ceramics. Although the spotted deer on Mexican ceramics may have been borrowed directly from Chinese sources, other dotted figures used by them quite surely came from the Muslim background: *a*, western Persia, ninth to tenth centuries; *b*, Egypt, eleventh century; *c*, Mallorca, tenth to eleventh centuries; *d*, China, late fifteenth century; *e–f*, Puebla, Mexico, late seventeenth to early eighteenth century (after Allan 1971; J.A. Pope 1956; Ovando Collection; Rosselló Bordoy 1981).

it freehand according to their own abilities. This produced
small differences within a basic uniformity in a batch of
finished vessels. Today in Mexico women and girls fill this
level of the decorator ranks; in the seventeenth century
it was an exclusively male sphere. The master designers
undertaking the finishing of *fino* maiolicas were few in
number. These were the artists. They may have worked
only in selected shops. Their assignments required more
time, and the number of vessels completed was comparatively small. Respected as persons with special talent
and expertise, they were allowed to create more fanciful
ceramics within the limits of commonly accepted vogues.
This they did by picking and choosing colors and motifs
from the two fundamental style packages and combining
them to their individual tastes. Needless to say, this practice can confound the modern student, who would like
to reconstruct the past ceramic evolution with the aid of
neatly defined, mutually exclusive stylistic entities.

By the middle of the seventeenth century, Puebla
maiolists were succumbing to the allure of the Oriental
complex of motifs and a blue–on–white color scheme. A
flood of pagodas, phoenixes, coolie figures, flowers, rocks,
waves, and cloud scrolls washed over Puebla ceramics.[150]
All were rendered with an unschooled artlessness that
clearly showed the designers' disregard for the realism,
the precision, and the tonal contrasts that typified the
Chinese ceramic art they sought to emulate. Although the
results had their own charm, it was obvious that there
was no desire to slavishly copy minutiae to which the
Spanish colonials did not relate.

The extraordinary *tibor* illustrated in Figure 141 reveals
this unique fusion of East and West, which was more
explicit and complex than what had occurred at Sevilla,
owing to the direct substantial nature of the colonial Oriental trade. The vessel form and the format of the decoration on the jar were sufficiently Chinese to have pleased
provincial customers. However, in spite of the virtuoso
skills demonstrated in throwing and finishing, there were
technical flaws resulting from the bisque firing and subsequent glazing that would have prompted immediate rejection by Oriental craftsmen. For example, a large crack
had opened at the base, the area within the ring foot had
slumped, sand from the shelving had adhered to the
jar bottom, and the glaze was pinholed and crazed. These
blemishes were acceptable to both makers and consumers
familiar with the Spanish Muslim tradition. Furthermore,
dissection of the individual elements of design shows
them to be a fascinating melange of suggestions, rather
than the realistic presentation one would have seen in

Figure 141. Four views of *tibor*, 46 cm in height, made in Puebla in the second half of the seventeenth century. Its form and much of the composition and elements of blue design were meant to imitate Chinese porcelain. The heavy casual brushwork, the motifs drawn from local or Hispanic experience, and the lack of literalism suggest a subtle Muslimization (courtesy The Houghton Sawyer Collection, Museum of International Folk Art, a unit of the Museum of New Mexico, Santa Fe).

Chinese work. Within the four panels created by foliated diapered netting are disarrays of human, faunal, floral, and architectural designs that fail to coalesce, in position or scale, into an organized landscape scene. Animated human figures are shown in both silhouette and outline. The former perhaps were inspired by children-at-play themes found on Ming blue–on–whites, but their seemingly baggy clothing could have been that of Mexican peasants as well. The latter can be identified as Oriental only by the presence of a queue, Chinese facial features likely not striking the Mexicans, with their strong strain of Mongoloid blood, as distinctive. The clothing on this figure is indicated by dot fillers within an outline, a trick of rendition borrowed from the ancient Muslim technique of portraying animals. The use of dots carried over into floral renditions, which became a common, typically Mexican mode. Dot fillers are scattered profusely through the background in the Muslim manner. Most of the architectural motifs seem to be churches, such as those that

Figure 142. Puebla blue–on–white maiolicas, *fino* grade, inspired by Chinese porcelain but converted into an expression of *mudéjar* decorative art through the use of some traditional Spanish forms, a dense massing of unrealistic pattern, background fillers, and motifs such as scampering animals and dotted hooked scrolls with a long history in Spanish Muslim art: *a*, basin; *b*, large jar; *c*, plate, obverse and reverse; *d*, bowl, obverse and reverse (courtesy The Houghton Sawyer Collection, Museum of International Folk Art, a unit of the Museum of New Mexico, Santa Fe).

crowd Mexican vistas, but none are topped with crosses. Other gabled structures could be teahouses. The upper and lower encircling frames also appear architectural and were widely used on much of the Chinese-inspired colonial maiolica. They have no known parallels in either Chinese or Muslim decorative art. As for animal figures, the flying birds with long plumage likely were suggested by the phoenixes and other birds on porcelain, but the long-eared rabbits, long-necked fowl, and even antlered stags were deeply embedded in Spanish Muslim art, although they formerly were more often expressed on Valencian than on Andalusian ceramics.

Deep-seated Andalusian moorings are evident on other Chinese imitations in a massing of flat, repetitive pattern that virtually obscured the ground and lost individual elements in a bewildering maze, in unrealistic portrayal of speckled or silhouetted naturalistic motifs, in a variety of extraneous space fillers, or in dots laid profusely over a netted or washed background (Fig. 142). Exterior porcelain decorations, if used, were comparable to those on obverses or were simple encircling lines at rim or foot. Mexican decorators made some use of exterior lining, but large designs consisted of a half-dozen or so hastily brushed motifs spaced around the pot, which differed little from early Muslim Near Eastern treatment or that on later Spanish Muslim *reflejo metálico* (see Fig. 52). These continued manifestations of the ancient Muslim theories of beauty once again point to the conservatism that had characterized the Andalusian complex from its beginnings. However, an aesthetic torque was created by the two conflicting approaches to design—originally from opposite sides of Asia—that imparted a uniqueness to Puebla maiolica unmatched in either hemisphere.

At the same time these decorated maiolicas were being identified with Puebla, other groups of artisans were engaged in making two lesser wares. A variety of typically Spanish forms, such as drug jars, deep plates, chamber pots, candleholders, and bowls, were glazed with a solution containing a third less tin than the better pottery. Generally they were left plain, although some for clerical buyers were adorned with the appropriate emblem (Fig. 143). In addition to convents, users included hospitals, taverns, and lower class homes. Although the numbers of such pieces must have been great, their low caliber dictated that they be used until broken and then tossed out with the trash. Typically, they did not survive to reach modern collectors' hands. For that reason, and because of their nondescriptness, the usual impossibility of knowing

Figure 143. Plain white service vessels, *loza común*, made throughout the seventeenth- and eighteenth-century history of Puebla maiolica: *a–b*, bowls; *c*, handled jug; *d*, drug jar (courtesy International Folk Art Foundation Collection, Museum of International Folk Art, a unit of the Museum of New Mexico, Santa Fe).

b

a

c

d

whether white sherds are from otherwise decorated types
or plain vessels, and the lack of archaeological work in
appropriate sites, the *loza común*, as this ware category was
called, has not been studied. Similarly unstudied is a
third grouping, utility plainwares termed *loza amarilla*.[151]

While orientalization seemed about to swamp Mexican
decorated maiolicas, the European Renaissance urge for
statuary exposed another tangled weft in the fabric of
colonial culture. As the Sevillian shops had done before
them, those in Puebla produced a number of moldmade,
glazed, saintly figures in earthenware. They must have
been the work of the artists in the group, although they
had a decided popular quality. Daily on view from the
potters' quarter were blond, white-skinned angels wearing
nothing more than a blue sash across one shoulder and
standing a meter tall around the cupola of the neighboring
Capilla del Rosario.[152]

In tile, it can be seen that the Islamic love of color met
its match in the tastes of Mexican Indians, whose blood
had merged with that of the conquerors to produce the
artesanado of Mexico. Tile work that resulted from colonial
racial and cultural hybridization burst forth into a bouquet
of brilliantly glistening works. Employing many passages
of interdependent units, repeated self-contained designs
that paralleled those appearing on contemporary hollow
ware, or tiles of single colors, colonial structures were
transformed in manners both indigenous and derived.
Particularly distinctive was the way in which brick and tile
were combined in checkerboards, chevrons, or diagonals
on Puebla facades and church domes; spires were paved
with specially shaped, glazed terra cottas. A latent Muslimization is inherent in these displays because those two
architectural materials also were joined in medieval Persia,
where, too, mosque domes were covered with tiles.[153]
For unknown reasons, the westward diffusion of these
particular tile usages had not taken firm hold in Spain,
although the Almohads combined brick and tile on some
edifices. The cultural mechanisms by which they resur-
faced stronger than in any previous Hispanic experience
halfway around the world from the place of their introduction and over an abyss of time are unfathomable.

Home folks and customers farther afield alike
applauded the incongruous mixture of *mudéjar* tile, Renaissance figures, and Chinese-like and Muslim-like pottery
that had also absorbed Italian and Spanish attributes.
In their own ways, the individual parts of this ceramic
package aptly reflected the heady maelstrom of colonial
life. Some time in the late seventeenth century, Vetancurt

wrote with civic pride that Puebla pottery was finer than
that of Talavera and could compete with that of China.
This chauvanistic attitude jibes well with a grand description of seventeenth-century Mexico attributed to Balbuena:

In thee Spain and China meet, Italy is linked with Japan, and
now ultimately a world joined by treaty and authority.[154]

Any honest assessment finds the Vetancurt statement
to be incorrect: as had always been true of Spanish Muslim
earthenwares and of the ceramics based upon them, technical flaws were many. Furthermore, there was a rapid,
unplanned execution of suggestive design, as opposed to
the mathematical precision of literal Oriental work or the
shaded narrative painting copied from engravings often
favored by the Talaverans.[155] The facts notwithstanding,
others must have felt as Vetancurt did, because at the turn
of the century Puebla pottery enjoyed a tremendous wave
of popularity throughout New Spain and beyond. At the
root of this success was the abiding appreciation for
ceramics among all ethnic elements of the society. Added
to that was a greatly increased colonial population, a
level of prosperity among potential user classes, an
expanding urban artisanal body, and an enviable dominance of maiolica manufacture that was almost a monopoly. As the seventeenth century was drawing to a close,
Puebla pottery production was reaching its artistic and
economic zenith.

From small Hispanic settlements in the Guatemalan
highlands on the south to the east coast of Florida, *poblano*
ceramics were well known. They ranked next to wheat
in volume of export to Venezuela. In the Caribbean, while
contraband and legitimate trade were bringing in more
western European goods, Mexican tablewares continued
in demand. In a Chihuahua mission dating from 1660
to 1686, all three main seventeenth-century types of Puebla
wares were present. To the north, Spanish settlers driven
temporarily from New Mexico left behind in abandoned
haciendas and mission churches a scattering of fragments of
seventeenth-century Puebla pottery (Fig. 144). On the
west coast, a limited trade in several Puebla styles may
have reached northern Sonora or southern Arizona before
the end of the seventeenth century.[156] A well organized
trade distribution network on land and sea made this
extensive commerce possible. Predictably, middlemen and
cartage costs greatly increased prices at the frontiers.

At the height of the Puebla industry a third New Spain
maiolica ceramic focus evolved in the Audiencia of Guatemala at the isolated capital of Santiago de los Caballeros

Figure 144. Sample of Mexican
maiolica recovered in seventeenth-
century Indian villages in New
Mexico. All are small plates
of *entrefino* grade that probably
served as altar furnishings in
churches established in those
pueblos: *a*, Puebla black and blue
lace-patterned style (Puebla
Polychrome) recovered at Pecos
pueblo, reverse with maker's
mark; *b*, blue–on–white abstracted
floral style (San Luis Blue–on–
White) recovered at San Gregorio
de Abó, believed to have been
made in Mexico City; *c*, Puebla
blue, yellow, orange, green, and
black naturalistic style (Abó
Polychrome) recovered at San
Gregorio de Abó.

a

b   *c*

(modern Antigua). In terms of quality and quantity it
remained a secondary effort, but one with probable ties to
Andalusian sources. The colony was geographically
removed from the active Mexican center of Spanish colonial life and its eclectic setting. Although Puebla ceramics
have been recovered at Santiago and earlier Sevillian
and Mexico City types may lie buried beneath numerous
wrecked structures, its most direct contact with the outside
world was through Puerto Caballos, Honduras, and a
cadre of Cádiz merchants. These agents are postulated to
have imported the earthenwares of Sevilla. The pottery
made at Santiago, with neither *morisco* nor Oriental overtones, may well afford a clearer picture of some seventeenth-century Sevillian styles than anything in Mexico
(Fig. 145). If that is the case, traditional post-1550 manufacture methods were followed; in this tradition, a green–
brown–on–cream color scheme was used to present large
faunal or floral depictions across obverse centers, leafy
abstractions around cavettos or rims, and encircling lines
zoning the format.[157] From the prominent use of green
it can be concluded that cobalt was too expensive or not
available. The quality of potting and very thin glaze coatings that permitted a red-firing clay to show through
confirm a low-ranking industry on the sidelines of empire.

Retrospective

The sixteenth-century instigation in Mexico City of a pottery-making enterprise designed to supply Hispanic settlers with simple domestic goods brought in an ancient Middle Eastern technology, a rhythm of operation, and a structure of workers new to the Western Hemisphere but identical to those of contemporary Andalusia. These facets of the craft were to continue to dictate the fundamental work orientation to the present. Moreover, throughout the century the connection between the motherland potting industry and that of its overseas counterpart remained so unshaken that as refined methods and decorative styles modified at home under a wave of Italian influence they passed rapidly along the transatlantic diffusionary pipeline. In Sevilla and in Mexico City, potters making earthenwares for Europeans were two sides of the same coin.

Because of an evolving social, economic, and racial environment that steadily moved the colony away from the bonds of the past, stylistic distinctions began to emerge in the provincial output. The gap between original and branch industries widened markedly after the focal point of pottery manufacture in New Spain shifted to seventeenth-century Puebla. There, from an aesthetic matrix shared with Spanish craftsmen, an artisan body

Figure 145. Assortment of maiolica ceramics made at colonial Santiago de los Caballeros, Audiencia de Guatemala. Where decorations occur, they are rendered in yellow, green, and brown. The dating of these objects is uncertain, owing to an unbroken stylistic continuum and little stratigraphically controlled archaeology, but some examples likely date to the seventeenth century: *a–d, i–j,* small plates and saucers; *e,* two-handled jar; *f,* candleholder; *g,* small pedestal-based bowl; *h,* small ring-footed bowl; *k,* chamber pot (courtesy Virginia and Edwin Shook, Antigua, and Luis Luján Muñoz, Guatemala City).

growing increasingly independent worked with a mysterious last burst of *mudéjar* creativity merged with a powerful
but naive orientalization. When 1700 came around, a
ceramic complex had resulted that was based upon Hispanic experience, but which more authentically registered
the unique cultural exposure of colonial New Spain.

An eighteenth-century postscript should be added.
Market saturation of earthenware pottery imitating
Chinese porcelain ultimately was reached. By then mude-
jarism also had vanished. When in the mid eighteenth
century colonial potters once more began to march in step
with European colleagues, the shared fashions called for
Rococo molded shapes based upon metal prototypes,
some light-hued polychromatic palettes in addition to the
blue–on–whites, and dainty, highly conventionalized
floral arrangements. Bourbon Spain was directing yet
another ingredient into the colonial melting pot, this one
French. By then, the peak years for the Puebla pottery
industry had passed.

PART III

The Potters:
Their Work and
Social Roles

Until the Industrial Revolution, when labor gained a voice, the great mass of workers throughout western Europe who toiled in generally miserable circumstances to produce the material things necessary to sustain life and trade remained the shadowy foundation of society. Their names and deeds went unrecorded, although at times their products were prized. This was especially so in hierarchial Andalusia, where the parasitic nobility had a taste for rich possessions but considered the handwork necessary to produce them beneath their social position. Any concept of the working classes, of the physical and psychological demands of their trades, or of their social and economic situations now has to come from inferences winnowed from scrappy documentation of local happenings, from knowledge of comparable artisan benefits and hazards elsewhere, from assumptions of continuity in attitudes as well as procedures, and from a few surviving relics. What follows, then, is an attempt based upon such inadequate evidence to at least partially understand the potters responsible for the humble earthenware craft of Andalusia, a craft that bridged both time and continents. It also is an effort to make archaeologists working with elements of the ceramic complex at home or abroad aware of interpretive inferences to be drawn from them.

Place and Routines of Work

For the Andalusians, pottery making was not an industry in which large numbers of craftsmen labored shoulder to shoulder in a sweatshop atmosphere. Whether in Spain or overseas, pottery was produced in a complex of small family workshops, all making the same kind of wares at any given period but with no defined quotas. Surprisingly, perhaps, in a society increasingly ordered by the monarchy, there were no state regulations over them other than taxation, possible guidelines for containers set by the *Casa de Contratación*, and unknown guild ordinances. In Sevilla it had not been possible to have these workshops concentrated in one particular district, since long practice of the craft under a variety of conditions had allowed dispersal throughout the town. Although potteries likely were confined to one part of Mexico City, they may not have been close neighbors, owing to the continued presence of aboriginal structures. In the planned settlement of Puebla, however, such grouping, which also coincided with a single parish church, was strictly enforced for three centuries. It had no known relevance to any comparable spatial organization of crafts that may have existed in the region prehistorically, nor should it have, since this was to be a Spanish community working only for Spanish

interests. In that sense, therefore, there was official control.

The rigidly structured geographical pattern of the
Puebla potters' quarter had obvious administrative benefits
when it came to collecting taxes and keeping private enterprise repressed. Its application to the many trades making
up the economic and political whole, added to parallel
religious enclaves, inevitably promoted and perpetuated
social fragmentation. In a damaging way, the concept
was a throwback to the Middle Ages philosophy of
unyielding segmentation of the populace. Most amazing,
it was put into place at a time when most western European societies were moving into egalitarianism. Whether
intended or not, peer pressure arising from the constant
observation that came with close daily association effectively curbed social and aesthetic deviation from established norms. A case in point is the censuring of one
master potter for failing to use saggars for glaze firings,
a regulation which although on the books seems seldom
to have been observed by anyone.[1] What were the personal reasons behind this attack, and would they have
been publicly expressed if he had worked in a more isolated location?

Did the potters passively acquiesce in this clustering
system for reasons of mutual support, for camaraderie, for
the purpose of sharing facilities or stocks of raw materials,
for exploiting a market not available otherwise? Did they
see it as a way to maintain their Spanishness against a
riptide of cultural dilution? Did they unhesitatingly accept
the arrangement because it was customary? Or had they
no choice if they wished to make a living at urban pottery
making? Most likely, all of these considerations were
involved to some degree. In any event, the artisans were
not apt to have resisted the *cabildo's* authority.

Typically, wherever it was found, the pottery establishment was a structure of one or two stories with an open
courtyard in the center, wherein many of the daily work
activities and social affairs of the residents were conducted
(Fig. 146). A central well provided essential water. Doors
of living and work rooms opened to galleries surrounding
this inner yard. There was a single entrance from the
street as a means of protection from the rampant lawlessness of the times. A 1314 document recorded such a pottery *corral*, to give its Sevillian designation, as an *ollería
con sus fornos [hornos] e con sus palacios e con una torre que está
a la entrada*. It was said to be in the extramural *barrio* of
Triana.[2]

Pottery workshops required a fair amount of space to
accommodate the many steps of manufacture. Within

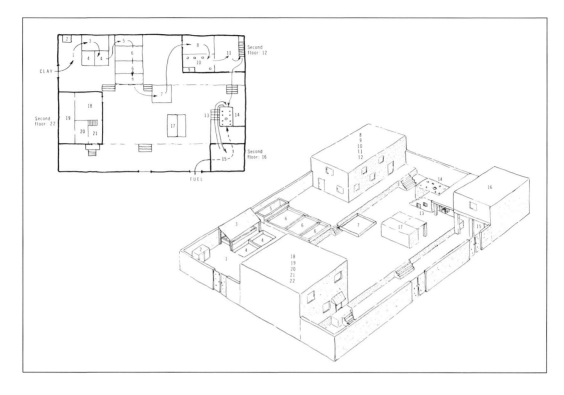

Figure 146. Diagrammatic plan
and elevation of Spanish potter's
workshop, based upon extant
traditional factory in Granada.
Arrangement varied according to
space available, but in all cases
there was an organized traffic pattern to facilitate successive craft
operations. The numbers in
the drawings correspond as follows: 1, clay storage; 2, well;
3, grinding wheels; 4, ground clay
pits; 5, water tank; 6, soaking
backs; 7, wet clay drying floor; 8,
prepared clay; 9, wedging table;
10, potter's wheels; 11, greenware
drying; 12, bisqueware storage
(second floor); 13, calcination kiln;
14, kiln; 15, kiln fuel; 16, glazing
and crude decoration (second
floor); 17, tool shed; 18, fine
decoration; 19, finished product
storage; 20, sales and packing; 21,
office; 22, living quarters (second
floor).

all of them in Sevilla or New Spain the physical arrangements and routines of operation were much the same
and could be duplicated in hundreds of localities in the
homeland and in lands occupied by Muslims.[3] Despite a
chaotic appearance, these cluttered home factories actually
featured a reasonably well planned traffic flow from arrival
of raw materials to exit of completed pots. First, there
were necessary stockpiles of clay, the basic ingredient of
pottery. The clay was taken as hard, jagged clods from pits
or caves cut into deposits that were usually nearby. These
were sacked and transported by muleteers to the workshops, where they were dumped inside the enclosure near
open air work surfaces and soaking backs.

Two kinds of clay typically were used in Andalusian-
style earthenwares, each with distinct physical properties
appropriate for certain items. Clay that fired to a red color
was most common in both Spain and Mexico. What it
lacked in plasticity was compensated for in greater
strength and ability to withstand heat, thus making it the
best resource for bricks, roof tiles, cooking pots, and
heavy objects. The red-burning Sevillian clay was extracted
from pits in the Triana or Tablada meadows or from an
island in the river. Light-firing calcareous clay came from
along the river banks or from near Castilleja de la Cuesta,
although today that village is best known as the supplier

of the yellowish sand spread in bullrings. The assumption
is that the pits were considered the property of all, since
at one time the potters protested to Sevillian municipal
authorities about outsiders taking "their" clay.[4] It was this
light-firing clay, which was used from Roman times for
common earthenwares, that became the favorite of those
engaged in making all stanniferous wares except *cuerda
seca*. Probably because it was on hand, the same light clay
went into the formation of lesser products, which were
left unglazed or were coated partially on one or all surfaces
with lead glaze. Because it was more plastic than the red
clay, throwing was easier. Its relatively fine texture produced smoother surfaces, its high shrinkage rate meant
less crazing of glazes, and its light color permitted a
reduced amount of tin in glazes. Vessels of this clay also
tended to be of lighter weight. There is no evidence that
grog was added to the light clay, but it may have been
added to the red-firing clay.

Sixteenth-century artisans of utility wares in the Valley
of Mexico made use of the same red-burning clay deposits
that had been worked since Preclassic times by the
natives. Light-firing calcareous clay more suitable for
better quality maiolicas came from an undetermined
source, which may have been at some remove.[5] Perhaps a
fundamental reason for establishing a ceramic industry
near Puebla was that there were accessible deposits of both
kinds of clay.[6] An indication of the mixing of clays is
contained in the seventeenth-century Mexico City guild
ordinances, which specified ten baskets of white clay to
twelve baskets of gray clay in order to "strengthen the clay
body and receive the colors with perfection".[7]

For shops in both hemispheres, the first step in making
either of the clays usable was to crush it in a pit with a
pounding mortar, or *pilón* (Fig. 147). The pulverized material was then sieved, poured into a tank, and soaked.
Laborers frequently worked the mass with their feet. After

Figure 147. Initial pulverizing
of dry raw clay (after Piccolpasso
1934).

any extraneous inclusions had sunk to the bottom, the
clay in liquid state was directed into a series of tanks in
succession for decanting. The resulting material was then
spread out like frosting over a work surface to stiffen.
The preparation surface may have been plastered or
bricked to keep the clay in clean condition and to hasten
drying. Fired, unglazed, and hence porous tubes or very
large bisqued potsherds may have been implanted in the
layer to more rapidly draw off excess moisture. When
the clay was sufficiently hardened but still pliable, it was
cut into blocks to be stored in a cool dry place in order
to ripen and increase its plasticity. A resting period of several or more months was believed necessary. The storeroom was adjacent to or was the same area where potters
worked. Typically, both were dark, humid, shedlike
rooms opening to the *corral*, the reserve clay making the
air heavy and sour. As clay was needed, apprentices
or journeymen took blocks to nearby stone shelves or
tables where they carefully wedged them to release air
bubbles and enhance workability. Then they rolled up
balls of suitable size and placed them near the potters, one
of whom may have been the proprietor of the *ollería*.
Prior to the mid sixteenth century, potters engaged in
throwing worked at wheels in a shallow trench sunk about
2½ ft deep in the dirt floor; later, the apparatus was placed
at table height (Figs. 148, 149e, f). Potters worked in a
semi-erect position slightly to the right of the wheel head
and were supported by a wooden seat. Their hand tools

Figure 148. Compound kickwheel
at table height popularized in
Andalusia after the middle of the
sixteenth century by emigrant
Italian potters, and then diffused
to New Spain (after Piccolpasso
1934).

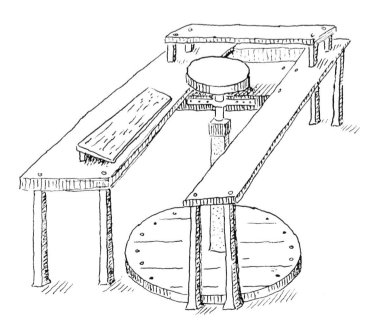

Figure 149. Scenes of modern Fez potteries offer probable insight into the ancient Spanish Muslim craft in Andalusia: *a*, open yard of workshop with layer of moistened clay in foreground, bisqued roof tiles stacked at rear; *b*, donkeys bringing in basketloads of raw clay, with oily smoke of kiln fires in background, a stack of fuel resting on top of an unused circular kiln at right rear, and many pottery bases and sherds used in wall and kiln construction; *c*, freshly thrown pots firming up in the sun before the open door to potter's dark throwing room to the left of a circular kiln topped with fuel supply; *d*, taking finished pottery to market on donkeys past one of Fez's cemeteries, beyond which is a shrine with typical roof of green glazed tile (note blanket of sherds covering foreground); *e*, pit wheel in use in its customary position to left of potter; *f*, "throwing off the hump" (note bowl of slurry inset in dirt in front of potter and pile of excess moist clay removed in throwing process); *g*, freehand decorating. The holes observable in the ring feet of these plates are now customary, so that objects can be hung on walls of houses typically without cupboards.

Figure 150. Potter's hand tools
(*a–e*, workyard implements; *f–n*,
tools for formation process):
a, wooden mallet for crushing
clay; *b*, metal hoe on wooden handle for stirring moist clay;
c, two-pronged wooden fork for
stoking kilns; *d*, metal scoop
on wooden handle for drawing
molten material from calcination
kiln; *e*, fiber broom to sweep
out kiln; *f*, chamois to wet and to
compact rims and wipe freshly
thrown pots; *g*, cord between rods
to slice newly thrown vessel
from wheelhead; *h–i*, shaped
wooden ribs used to contour pots
being thrown; *j*, *l–n*, bamboo
section and shaped wooden tools
for finishing or decorating moist
pots; *k*, shaped iron for trimming
excess clay from leather hard
vessels.

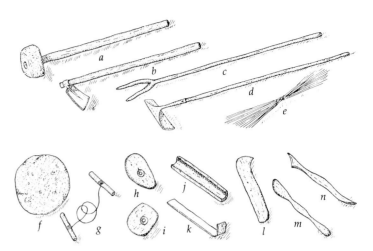

consisted of a few wooden ribs of various contours for
shaping, some shaped irons for trimming, a length of cordage or wire to slip beneath a finished vessel and cut it
from the wheel, and a scrap of leather with which to wipe
rim edges in order to smooth and compress them (Fig.
150). Close by was a bowl of water or slurry with which to
lubricate their hands. If tiles were being made, the men
stood before long tables or benches where the clay could
be flattened and cut. They used rollers over boards of
equal thickness and a form around which to shape the
desired tile blank. Metal or wooden stamps served to
impress patterns in the case of *cuenca* tile.

Once the articles were formed, they were placed on
long boards. These were carried to some spot away from
the center of activity while they firmed up through loss of
moisture. If they were to have appendages added, to be
decorated through some sort of pressure or engraving, or
to be trimmed and smoothed, they received necessary
attention at the leather hard stage, when the walls were
relatively inflexible but not hard. Following that, it was
important to set the objects aside until they were thoroughly dry. A shed with shelving usually was provided
for the purpose. The prevailing humidity of Sevilla
required more drying time than was necessary in highland
Mexico. Some Mexican maiolists today claim to allow a
drying period of up to three months, but it is questionable
whether such an interlude between throwing and bisquing
would have fit primitive conditions.[8]

Kilns often were situated in the midst of a complex of
flimsy workrooms without regard to noxious fumes, great
heat, and potential fire hazards. No known records tell
of probable disasters as a consequence of this arrangement, but they must have been recurrent. An initial bisque
firing took place when enough vessels had accumulated

to fill the upper kiln chamber and sometimes a shelf
around the inner walls of the lower chamber. In Sevilla, if
a potter's facility did not have a kiln, space could be
rented in a neighboring yard. This fostered an important
interaction among the artisans. Before the adoption of
Italian methods, interior surfaces of kiln roofs apparently
were not coated with lute. Such a solution, usually formed
of fine sand or fire clay, ashes, donkey dung, and iron
scales scraped from anvils, helped prevent loss of heat by
sealing the surface and filling joints between the bricks.
Handling the fragile greenware cautiously, the stacker
arranged it in the kiln, nesting pieces together if convenient, occasionally placing them rim-to-rim to reduce
stresses. A closely stacked kiln was desirable so that the
heat would flow from pot to pot by combustion, although
it was imperative to leave the heat vent holes between
the chambers unblocked. A load of similarly shaped
objects greatly facilitated setting the kiln. Proper alignment
was so important that in Sevilla experienced stackers
frequently moved from kiln to kiln in the community
devoting themselves to that one task. Their mobility was
another factor in equalizing local output. A comparable
practice is not recorded for colonial Mexico.

Fuel was stored under shed roofs adjacent to the firing
unit of the kiln. Ideally, this was close to an access gate.
After the fuel chamber was stuffed, it was ignited and
kept burning until a practiced eye peering through a peep
hole told the stoker the right temperature had been
achieved. For the bisque firing, that probably was no more
than 600° to 800°C., or just enough to drive out the moisture. Most of a day was devoted to this firing. The kiln
was allowed to cool slowly before being unloaded, so as to
reduce thermal shock to the pots. Stackers worked at
drawing, or unloading, the kilns for a flat fee per load. It
was the owner's task then to cull the results for defective
vessels, often as much as half the load being rejected.
There is little concrete evidence that serious efforts were
made to improve methods in order to reduce these losses.
The wasters, *cascajo*, were cast aside to be carted off later
to a suitable dump spot. In Sevilla this was thought to
be the banks of the Guadalquivir, which obligingly cleared
away the debris periodically. In Mexico City it likely was a
nearby canal or the watery channel between the island
on which the city stood and the mainland. In Puebla it was
an open area at the westernmost edge of town.[9]

The first step in glaze preparation was the calcination of
lead and tin, lead serving as a flux and tin as an opacifier.
The plan of the calcination kiln, or *padilla*, was the same
as that employed for firing the vessels, but was on a much
smaller scale. Abū'l Qāsim, a fourteenth-century Persian

potter who wrote the earliest known treatise on the making of maiolica ceramics, described the method that doubtless was followed in Spain and its dependencies.

Another such kiln is used for breaking up the tin and lead. This is done as follows. One takes three parts of good white lead and a third of a part of tin, or if one wants a better and finer mixture up to half of tin. First they put the lead into the kiln for a time, and then they throw the tin in on top of it. They mix them at a high temperature until they are well melted. When [this mixture] brings up an earthy substance on its surface it is completely ready. They then make the fire smaller and seal the furnace door with mud. The earthy substance which collects on the melt is taken off with an iron shovel until in half a day it had all gradually changed to earth.[10]

The Sevillians still call the shovel an *almijarra*, a corruption of an Arabic word.

The six-to-one ratio of lead to tin indicated by Abū'l Qāsim was a standard not always observed. It was not uncommon to reduce amounts of the expensive metal for glazes to be applied to lesser items, and to increase it for greater opacity on finer wares.[11] The four-to-one ratio said to be characteristic of modern Sevillian maiolica was quite surely lower in the period of mass production of coarse dishes.

The second stage in glaze production was the preparation of a massicot, or frit, described by Abū'l Qāsim:

They take 105 parts of *skukār-i sang* [quartz] which has been powdered, beaten, ground, and sifted through silk, and 100 parts of *shakhār* [soda ash] in lumps the size of hazelnuts or almonds, and mix them and put them in a kiln, technically known as *barīz*. The pungency or weakness of the *shakhār* varies depending on the place. . . . This is cooked over a slow fire, and is stirred from morning till night with an iron ladle made as large as the diameter of the kiln until it is well mixed and is become one, like molten glaze, and this is the material for glass vessels. After eight hours they take out the brew by the ladleful. Below, in front of the oven, is a pit full of water, into which they put the glass frit. When water and fire meet there is a great noise and roaring like thunder, which for all the world could be real thunder and lightning. The craftsmen call this mixture *jawhar* and store it, until the time comes to compound it, in a broken up, powdered and sifted form.[12]

The silicate of potash resulting from this procedure was important in decreasing the solubility of the lead, imparting a high coefficient of expansion to the glaze, and helping to toughen it. It also reduced the temperature at which quartz melted.

Abū'l Qāsim's source for soda ash was a plant native to the Persian deserts, probably *Salsola kali*, which had provided alkali for soaps, medicines, and glazes for at least five millennia. In Sevilla the plant used was *Salsola soda L.*,[13] locally called *barrilla*, which is found throughout

the great waterlogged marshes of Coto Doñana. Had
not such a handy source for carbonate of soda been available, the potters could have followed the practice known
in other areas of making use of tartar present in calcined
wine lees. *Barrilla* probably was gathered by a special
group of laborers, was left to dry for a period of several
weeks, and then was burned in pits in the countryside,
owing to its objectionable sulphur odor when heated. It
cooled overnight, during which time it hardened into
a rocklike substance. Chunks were calcined in a special
small kiln as needed and then stored.[14] Colonial artisans
made use of a comparable saltwort found near Lake Texcoco, or of the native deposits of *tequesquite*.

A shortcut method for fritting, which may have been
fairly common, was use of ground glass slag, which,
in addition to reducing the toxicity of lead, also aided in
the melting process. The discovery of a close association of
a glass factory and a pottery with bins of glass cullet in
Fostat, Egypt (destroyed in 1168), suggests a symbiotic
relationship between the two crafts.[15] Perhaps it is significant that glass making had been an occupation in Muslim
Sevilla, which gained new prominence in the fifteenth
century. At the later date the factory was on an alley called
El Vidrio, meaning glass. Twisting through the part of
the old city between the Moorish and Jewish quarters, this
locality was not immediate to known potteries, but it
was not far removed.[16] Similarly, a glass factory was
opened in 1542 in what became the potters' quarter of
Puebla. This shop operated until the beginning of the
eighteenth century.[17]

When the glaze minerals and frit had been calcined and
remelted with some quartz sand, they were placed in a
large mill, a *tahona*, to which a draft animal was attached
(Fig. 151). As the beast plodded around and around the
outer circumference of the mill, the materials were crushed

Figure 151. Grinding of clay or
glaze minerals by means of geared
wooden wheels turned by a
draft animal (after Piccolpasso
1934).

Figure 152. Sieving lumps and
extraneous matter from glaze
ingredients (after Piccolpasso
1934).

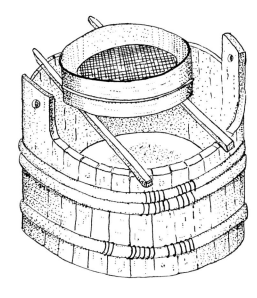

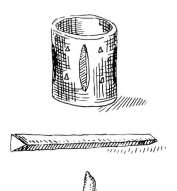

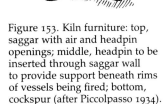

Figure 153. Kiln furniture: top,
saggar with air and headpin
openings; middle, headpin to be
inserted through saggar wall
to provide support beneath rims
of vessels being fired; bottom,
cockspur (after Piccolpasso 1934).

to a fine powder between revolving stones. They were
sieved, blended in proper proportions, dissolved in water
to produce a creamy liquid, and poured into wide-
mouthed earthenware containers (Fig. 152). This was the
stanniferous glaze. The silica content of the quartz sand
helped to promote a glassy finish and to decrease thermal
expansion. The unfired color of the glaze probably was
light gray to white, but in modern Granada it is an unusually dark slate color.

Those objects to be glazed were taken to an interior
workroom, where they were dusted to remove any particles of foreign substances before being plunged into the
liquid glaze. This coat was quickly absorbed by porous
body walls. In dealing with low-grade types, the potter
took care of his own decorating. If better pieces were
being made, after about the mid sixteenth century the vessels were passed on to decorators for application of
needed pigments, which previously had been finely
ground, mixed with fluxant, and worked into solution.
The decorators may or may not also have acquired throwing skills. If the room were too dark or cold, it was not
unusual for the painters to move their stools and donkey
or horse hair brushes and paint pots outdoors. Elaborate
patterns occasionally were faintly indicated by means
of pouncing a dark powder over a stencil. Simpler designs
were drawn freehand as a decorator held the vessel on
his knees or set it in a tow of straw inside a fired earthenware or wooden bowl. In modern practice, honey sometimes is added to pigments so they will flow more easily
over the dry glaze. No records report this method earlier,

and because the honey would have burned out during firing, it cannot be detected easily.

Stacking kilns for glost firing was tedious, often taking several days, depending on the load. It was imperative that vessels not touch. If they did, the molten glazes would fuse them together as they cooled. To separate stacks of vessels of similar shapes and sizes, tripods of fired clay were used (Figs. 153, 154). In Sevilla they were called *atífles*; in Mexico they were *vicoles* or *caballitos*. In Sevilla the long ceramic rods, or *birlos*, typical of Muslim practice quite possibly were used as shelving until the middle of the sixteenth century. Confirmation of their diffusion to Mexico awaits further research. There is no

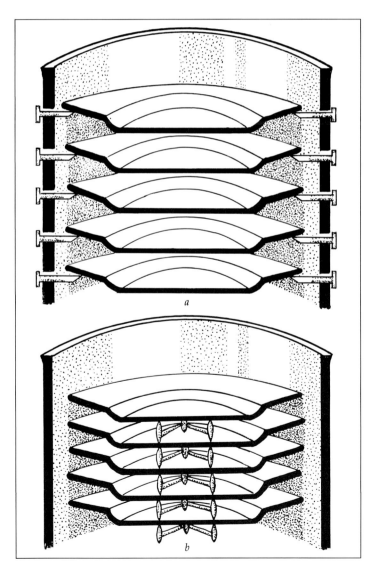

a

b

Figure 154. Methods for separating similar vessel forms during glaze firings: *a*, headpins, an Italian tool adopted in Talavera but used in Sevilla and Mexico City only in the second half of the sixteenth century and only for imitations of Italian styles; *b*, cockspurs, traditional devices used throughout the continuum of Andalusian pottery making in Spain and New Spain.

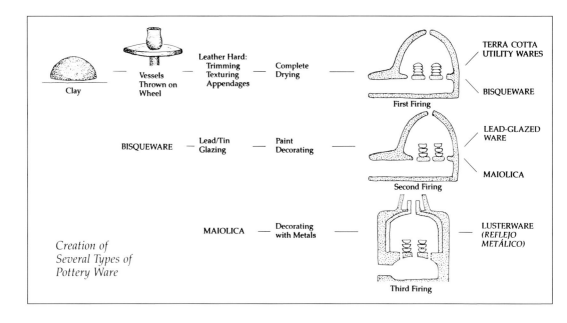

Clay — Vessels Thrown on Wheel — Leather Hard: Trimming Texturing Appendages — Complete Drying — First Firing — TERRA COTTA UTILITY WARES / BISQUEWARE

BISQUEWARE — Lead/Tin Glazing — Paint Decorating — Second Firing — LEAD-GLAZED WARE / MAIOLICA

MAIOLICA — Decorating with Metals — Third Firing — LUSTERWARE (REFLEJO METÁLICO)

Creation of Several Types of Pottery Ware

Fig. 155. From raw clay to finished vessels of different categories. In right column, upper box indicates ware completed at that stage. Maiolica is completed at second firing, unless mineral overglaze decoration is desired, which requires third firing in a reducing, rather than oxidizing, kiln atmosphere.

evidence for saggars in either area until just before the middle of the sixteenth century. It was not unusual for some greenware or pigments to be fritted to fill empty spaces in the load.

Glaze firings generally took longer than bisque firings because it was necessary to reach temperatures ranging from about 1000° to 1100°C. in order to mature the glaze. Thirteen to twenty hours of constant attention to the actual firing was followed by a twenty-four-hour cooling period (Fig. 155).[18]

The firing of a kiln was an event cloaked in superstition and apprehension. No matter how many times it was witnessed, there remained an element of mystery. Few handicrafts, other than glass-blowing and ironworking, were subjected to the test of fire; few exhibited such strange, often unpredictable, transformations. Labors of hours or days could be ruined in this one critical phase of production by a variety of possible accidents. Vessels could warp because of uneven temperatures or placement. They could crack because of excessive or abrupt expansion. Through some unplanned movement, they could tilt, be pushed together, or fall over. Pigments and glazes compounded under haphazard conditions often behaved in unanticipated ways. In the attempt to circumvent these and other mishaps and to insure successful firings, Muslim potters typically recited prayers at all the various stages of production and sprinkled sand ceremoniously in the kiln. Most Christian shops included a small shrine near the kiln before which a brief prescribed ritual was performed at the lighting and the opening of each load. Today shrines, religious pictures, and blessed palm crosses are more in evidence in Mexico than in Spain, perhaps because of the native fervor still pulsing through Mexican Catholicism. Even with hoped-for divine intervention, unsophisticated and careless methods produced a high percentage of less than perfect results. In Sevilla, at least, all was seldom lost. There, a group of peddlers known as *almalluqueros* made a business of acquiring pottery seconds or discards for sale to the city's poor.

Although improper proportions of the basic glaze ingredients and variable firing procedures led to many imperfections, few of them were sufficiently objectionable to the potters themselves to cause the pots to be considered as wasters prior to the mid sixteenth century. Furthermore, little effort seems to have been expended to upgrade fundamental methods in order to correct these flaws. Crazing, pinholing, and crawling of glazes were typical. The common maiolicas were further damaged by poor original potting, uncontrolled drafts during drying and within kilns, and unsteady stacking, which encouraged frequent warping of vessel walls. Bits of sand, twigs, and other debris were allowed to fall on pots either before or during firing, thus blemishing vessel surfaces. The most universal blemish was the scarring caused by cockspurs.

After about 1550 both the maiolicas made in Sevilla and those made in Mexico City greatly improved, both technically and artistically. Another concerted drive for refinement was evident in the seventeenth-century industry at Puebla. Behind peninsular and colonial programs of bettering the typical tin-glazed ceramics were basic economic pressures, rather than sheer desire to raise standards for aesthetic reasons. Severe competition engendered by Italian wares and Italian potters at Sevilla and by Chinese porcelains in Mexico (the presence of Oriental artisans is unlikely) provided the necessary incentives for upgrading. But even with new methods, sharpened skills, and careful workmanship, many of the flaws that had typified Spanish Muslim ceramic art from its beginning continued.

Once firing was completed, some finished items were moved to a room next to the street where the master often maintained a small store to offer his products for sale. He accepted special orders, particularly if he specialized in tiles. It is likely, too, that a personal clientele may have formed through a potter's career. The same room, or several adjoining rooms, served as the living quarters for the family, which on occasion expanded to include one or more young apprentices, unmarried journeymen and laborers, and maybe a slave. The bulk of the finished pottery was packed in saddle bags, baskets, or bundles to be taken to local markets or to be transported elsewhere. The canvas-sheeted sailing vessels or cumbersome, large-wheeled carts of Sevilla, the camel caravans of Morocco, and the *recuas* of native bearers and burro trains of Mexico were a few of the carriers of the fragile merchandise.

In addition to the large constructions requisite to the trade, scattered about the pottery was an untidy congestion of baskets, *esparto*, and other packing materials, scales for measuring minerals, shovels, sledges, hammers, cockspurs, planks for carrying freshly thrown pots, bats, wasters, and general trash (Figs. 149, 156–158).[19]

Because of the constancy of the physical attributes of the Andalusian pottery craft, whether in Spain or its detached overseas communities, the archaeologist working with Spanish medieval or American colonial horizons has the enormous advantage of being able to bank on relatively little change through time in procedures or tools.

Figure 156. Scenes from modern rural Morocco offer insight into various aspects of the craft as it may hae been practiced in ancient Spanish Muslim Andalusia; *a*, hauling finished pottery to market on camels; *b*, present Moroccan version of the ageless amphora, still with tapered base; *c–d*, earthenware braziers and assorted unglazed cooking and storage wares for sale in a country market; *e*, the water seller makes his rounds by donkey, his stock carried in amphorae stoppered with wads of palm fiber; *f*, bowls on graves once held offerings for the dead.

Figure 157. Scenes from a Moroccan rural pottery in a remote village still strongly allied to the tribal past. They show partial acceptance of the introduced Islamic technology: *a–b,* potter's pit wheel being used to thin and finish a base vessel formed by a paddle over a suitably shaped rock, with no throwing involved (The location of the wheel in the hot sunlight differs from more formal workyards, where shade and humidity are essential to keep clay at proper consistency.); *c,* keyhole pit used for firing pottery is shaped like the combustion unit of a kiln, but in this instance accomodates both fuel and pots with no second baking chamber above; *d,* a load of pots in the firing pit merely covered over with fragments of broken pottery. It is interesting to note that some rural Mexican potters accepted this same kind of modification of the kiln.

The spatial arrangements of workshops, as diagrammetically suggested in Figure 146, were not invariable. All the indicated work stations and tools were essential, however, and would have been present in some form or position in a functioning shop. This means that if several such features are found associated, diligent search for others that may be less obvious, such as clay preparation platforms or pits, should be undertaken in order to more completely verify the former presence of a pottery-making endeavor. Similarly, remaining traces of certain raw materials, such as particular minerals, soda ash, glass cullet, or kiln fuel, can be interpreted in the light of known manufacturing methods recorded for the fourteenth century.

Ethnicity of Potting Work Forces

At the time of the Spanish opening of the New World and dispersal of the first European ceramics and the secrets of their making to the Western Hemisphere, the potter force in Sevilla was racially and culturally mixed. To what degree is uncertain, owing to an exceedingly muddled record. The roster of some seventy known names of fifteenth-century individuals and another two hundred living in the sixteenth century who were involved in some way in pottery making reads like a muster role of any other group of typical Castilians.[20] But the Spanishness of appellations like Pedro Chavez, Bartolomé García, Juan Gómez, or Martín Valiente might not necessarily translate into Old Christian personages. This was because under the mounting social and religious conflicts of

Figure 158. Scenes from a Granada pottery workshop notable for continuation of Muslim technology: *a*, pit wheel in use; *b*, levigated clay being allowed to stiffen, with porous bricks in paving and bisqued tubes helping to absorb excess moisture; *c*, calcination kiln, with scrap metal being weighed in front; *d*, earthenware glaze vat with supply of bisqued bowls to be dipped; *e*, kiln baking chamber loaded with tiles, saggars and fired earthenware rods serving as supports and shelving (floor holes open to subterranean combusion chamber); *f*, fired earthenware rods used as kiln shelving; *g*, supply of cockspurs waiting to be baked; *h*, kiln roof with port holes covered by inverted pots when not in use.

fifteenth-century Spain and the pall of fear spreading out from the Inquisition housed in the Triana castle, some neighborhood infidels found it expedient to at least nominally embrace Christianity. To seal their conversion, they assumed common names of their associates, sometimes those of the Christian potters who served as their godparents. Muslim potter Abdalla turned into Juan de

Toledo.[21] Perhaps nothing had really changed in his private life, but in the public record he became untraceable. It can be expected that there were a dozen other Castilians with the identical name.

Not all the local Muslim potters were intimidated, however, so that their cultural roots remain clearly recognizable in late fifteenth-century references to Aguja, Abad, Ali, Zaida, or Alfaqui, many of whom continued plying their trade in the part of town that had been the ancient *morería*. They sold pots to the church authorities for closing the vaults of the towering Catholic cathedral. They laid up brilliant panels of mosaic tiles in the palaces of the Catholic nobility, and when the Catholic Kings chose to refurbish the Alhambra they were selected to do the job. Their craftsmanship in a variety of decorative arts, if not their mores and religion, was a source of pride to Andalusians. Intellectual ability also was recognized in the case of one who was selected to serve as the scribe for the potters' confraternity dedicated to Justa and Rufina. He was respected for the fact that he could write. This put him a step above most of his colleagues, Christian or Muslim, who were illiterate.

Hamete de Cobexi illustrates the confusion resulting from the practice of taking new names from thin air. Hamete was a free Moor who lived in Triana and earned a living as a maker of hollow ware. He was a prominent member of the community, for a time during the reign of Fernando and Isabela being in charge of some projects at the Sevilla *alcázar*, where their Majesties resided when in town. He was always addressed by the informal title of *maestre* (*maestro*), or master, and his wife was respectfully called Doña Haxa. When the enforced conversion of all Muslims was ordered in 1502 he became Juan Fernández. His wife conformed to the demands of the times and became one more Isabel Rodríguez, there probably being many other Spanish women of the same name. Her son followed suit, taking the name of Jerónimo Rodríquez. He then married a Muslim convert who earlier had assumed the same alias to become María Rodríguez.[22] Rodríguez plus Rodríguez may have produced other Rodríguezes. That did not erase the blood line; it merely confused accounting.

Whether a Sevillian potter of the period called himself Miguel or Mohammed, his craft in all its aspects was that of the Muslims who happened to reside in Spain. Even though by the end of the fifteenth century Andalusia had been reclaimed by the Castilians for two and a half centuries, the remarkable unbroken continuum in regional pottery from the time of the Cordoban efflorescence to the era of Columbus allows for no disruption such as would have occurred had Muslim potters moved out following the reconquest to make room for Christian potters with a different artistic bias. Instead, what must have transpired was a slow infiltration of the pottery ranks by a dribble of Christian artisans. They may have previously absorbed Muslim conventions through the permeable border between the two major entities jointly occupying the peninsula. Outnumbered and with less expertise, they followed the lead of the Muslim potters who chose to stay on after the Almohad defeat. By the end of the fifteenth century the Christian potters may have attained numerical superiority, but, with few exceptions, they had not yet gained prominence in the craft.

It was not until the middle of the next century that the non-Muslim sector of the Sevillian pottery *artesanado* came to the forefront and the recognizable Muslim designations disappear from the record. Then, under stimulation from other Catholics who had settled among them, principally Italians and Flemings, some of the local workers adopted procedures and ornamental phrases that at least partially freed them from the Islamic hold over their occupation. Nonetheless, a major constituent continued to produce the same old pots in the same old ways. It is in this amorphous and generally anonymous group that the substantial *morisco*, or converted Muslim, element likely was to be found. One known exception was Luis García. He was described by his contemporaries as a specialist in imitating Talaveran styles and may have been engaged in the American trade.[23]

After the fall of the Nasrid dynasty, many of the residents of Granada who did not flee from Spain were transferred to Sevilla. There, some took refuge in confined little *adarves*, communal quarters secluded in narrow alleyways of the inner city, shared by earlier refugees from Málaga and captured hamlets in the former emirate. Most settled among the former *mudéjares* of Triana. From 1568 to 1570 their number was augmented by four thousand uprooted persons following a suppressed rebellion in the Alpujarras.[24] The prohibitions forced upon them included the bearing of arms, entrance into taverns, and living more than two to a house. They paid special taxes and wore distinctive clothes.

When the exodus of the *moriscos* finally came, between 1609 and 1614, some seventy five hundred of them departed Sevilla.[25] Without question, an important block of this unassimilated community had functioned in the ceramic industry for which their ancestors were responsible. Whether by then they were a despised group, owing to jealousy and religious intolerance on the part of their Christian colleagues, cannot be surely determined, but it is probable. By the time of their final farewell their artistic importance in the local output had so diminished that their leaving caused only a depletion of the ranks.

Meantime, archaeological delving beneath Mexico City demonstrates that the Muslim pottery technology naturalized in Andalusia over many centuries was diffused to New Spain well before the middle of the sixteenth century. A few men could have been responsible, but their ethnic background is unknown. The likelihood of an early sixteenth-century overseas extension of some of Sevilla's *moriscos* cannot be ignored, however, even though the names of the only two potters known to have been in the colony at that time are orthodox Castilian.[26] To enhance overseas migration, bans against movement to the colonies of Jews and Muslims actually were dropped in 1511, but sons and grandsons of infidels were forbidden to hold office or share in *repartimientos*. In 1543 another royal *cédula* again prohibited Muslims from moving abroad. If such Muslim elements were behind the initial colonial ceramic industry, they would not then have been subjected to as much prejudice as later on. Viceroy Mendoza was known to have had the blood of heretics in his veins. When he and Bishop Zumárraga presented a plan to the monarch for Granadine *moriscos* to come to central Mexico to set up a silk-raising enterprise, it was approved.[27] Although never consummated, this official proposal confirms a tolerant attitude toward the possible emigration of the defeated minority. At the beginning of the seventeenth century, policies had hardened to forbid such movement, but clandestine travel from Spain to New Spain remained a possibility. Understandably, data are lacking for such activity. Nevertheless, some of the thousands driven out of Sevilla and Granada, for example, might well have bribed their way across the Atlantic. By that time their outward physical appearance was such that, once in the New World, they easily could have blended in to become indistinquishable. In a colonial haven they may have found their fellow Spaniards more ready to close their eyes to social deviations in order to profit from respected artistic merit. According to Santiago Cruz, some guild ordinances restricted Muslims and other non-Christians from attaining the top rank of master.[28] If this statement is accurate, *morisco* presence among the colonial artisan class was acknowledged. It surely was engulfed in a wave of hybridization that in several generations created a new race.

Pottery workshops were manned by a limited number

of trained persons, often two generations of a single family. One or several individuals worked at the wheels, perhaps another one or two were before the paint pots, and
another was learning one or both aspects of the operation.
These were the Spaniards, *moriscos*, and, within a generation or two in the colony of New Spain, Mexican *mestizos*.
Engaged in other heavy tasks of the endeavor were those
men generally considered inferior by Castilians, some
of whom were slaves. Their heterogeneous ranks in Andalusia included Negroes from sub-Saharan Africa, mulattoes, captured Muslims from the western Mediterranean,
resident *moriscos*, and a few Native Americans. They
remained outside the main core of the craft. In Mexico the
laborers were Mexican Indians, Negroes, Chinese coolies
who came to the colony on the Manila Galleons, mulattoes, and young Spanish or *mestizo* waifs drawn from
the streets of the settlements. By 1681 revisions to earlier
guild restrictions allowed these various racial mixtures
to participate at all levels of the industry, except the
elected position of Inspector, or *Veedor*. That was to remain
in the hands of Spaniards or *mestizos*.[29] This was the final
admission that the craft had become too big to be exclusive
and had in actuality absorbed more diverse racial strains
than was the case in Spain.

Women had no role in the manufacture of commercial
ceramics. This is in sharp contrast to the present, as
women now comprise the main body of decorators in
Spain and in Mexico. Two known exceptions were a Sevillian woman described in a 1561 listing as a potter and
another said in 1571 to be a painter of pottery.[30] Under
guild regulations formulated in seventeenth-century
Puebla and Mexico City, widows of potters had the right
to their husband's business. They did not participate
in the actual forming of wares, but likely saw to their
sale.[31]

Social Perception of Potters

The haze of time makes it hard now to judge how
potters as a group were regarded by the society at large
or how they perceived themselves. In the urbanized artisanal Muslim economy, producers as a class were respected
as vital cogs in the machinery, and works of artistic merit
were appreciated. It has been said that for Islam creativity
was next to godliness. That may have been behind the
occasional marking of Nasrid *reflejo metálico* with the maker's initial. According to one writer, guilds in Algiers
had distinctive clothes, diet, education, and even ways of
worship.[32] That would suggest a degree of status. On
the other hand, Glick feels the Muslim artisans were of

such low status that they often turned to mystical move-
ments to find emotional reinforcement.[33] One can only
speculate about how the individual potter may have been
viewed, when even his name was not important enough
to have been recorded. Goitein states that in medieval
Jewish enclaves within a larger Muslim context, wherein
many attitudes of that body were shared, there were
certain despised professions. Among these were street
sweepers, sewer cleaners, dyers, cobblers, and potters.[34]
Scorn for potters must have grown after Biblical times,
because none of the references to the craft in the Bible
conveys this feeling. In these writings pottery is a frequent metaphor for the fragility of the human spirit, and
potter's field refers to an exploited land suitable only
for wretched burial.

   Castilians admired and attempted to perpetuate *mudéjar*
handicrafts, but they considered their production appropriate only for the Muslim sector of society, not for their
own kind. This feeling merged with an abhorrence of
physical toil and is commented upon by a courtier writing
to Felipe II in 1558:

So great is the love of ease, so advanced Spain's perdition, that
none, whatever his state or condition, will hear of working at any
craft or business.[35]

The antipathy toward *oficios mecánicos* intensified for those
dirty ones such as pottery making. This was true even
though the ceramic industry brought needed revenues into
the region. Therefore, potters had low social standing,
only slightly above that of the companion occupations of
forming and laying bricks and terra cotta roof and floor
tiles. Pike calls the entire artisan group a submerged
majority and points to the absence of members of this
social stratum in the literature of the period as proof of the
disdain with which they were viewed by the more fortunate.[36] Yet as the sixteenth century waned, social change
was in the air. Incipient industrialization was making
room for previously ignored artisanal ranks, but not as
effectively in backward Spain as in her more aggressive
neighbors.

   The pottery itself is an enlightening compendium of the
fundamental underlying attitudes and preferences the
potters brought to their craft: in it one finds the grandiose
and massive, with appreciation for proportion and line;
the dramatic impact of vibrant, bold color and incessant
repetitive pattern to appeal to the eye, as well as tactile
manipulations to appeal to the touch; the joyousness of
some spirited motifs and the austerity of others; the concern with making the earth's materials work for basic

human needs and enrich the environment; the inflexible
constancy of form and style over great stretches of time;
the disinterest in tedious secondary detail and refinement.
These qualities invoke the spirit of Hispanic culture in
two worlds that produced great artists, writers, architects,
musicians, and adventurers, but few scientists or jurists.

Even with the adverse feelings about handicraftsmen,
it is not likely that the individual potter was psychologi-
cally downtrodden. The long centuries of living and surviving on a warring frontier had made the Andalusians
a self-reliant, confident breed quite cognizant of its worth.
The many of them who faced the uncertainties of the New
World with such remarkable courage and inner strength
attest to this. Their poverty did not set them up for ridi-
cule, because poverty was a condition common not only
to most artisans but to lesser nobility. Nor did it diminish
their inherent dignity. Quite unique in such a stratified
society as Spain was, there existed an astonishing democratic ease of intercourse among classes and a courteous
manner that transcended social barriers. The humblest
could address the mightiest and look him squarely in the
eye. Whether a potter with his hands caked in mud or
a genteel *caballero* astride a blooded steed, all were united
by a code that glorified the Spanish soul. It should be
added that no *hidalgos* are known to have taken up careers
in the making of clay pots. Potting priests, such as those
suggested to have emigrated to Puebla, would have been
entirely out of character for the usual Castilians of
position.[37]

A potter could consider himself an independent man
who, within certain limitations, was responsible for his
choice of occupation and master of his own income from
it. That made him a capitalist by most definitions of the
term. Generally he had come into the craft through birth,
though that was not an inflexible precondition. He had
grown up in the workshop of his father, uncle, or some
other male relative, had played amid the potting activity
and tools, and quite unconsciously had been drawn into
various aspects of the work as he aged. He learned
through observation and imitation. By the time he had
reached early manhood he was actively engaged in acquiring necessary technical, mechanical, and artistic skills.
When his pots were included for sale with others from the
shop, he knew he had attained a professional level and
could work as a journeyman, or *locero oficial*, for his parent
or some other potter making the same sort of wares. He
was totally unaware of being a vital link in the perpetuation of his craft or a leveling agent in its stylistic evolution,
although he was both of these. Contemplation of marriage

and the attainment of master status, or *locero maestro*, often
came at more or less the same time in a potter's life. Then
he was free to go out on his own. In Andalusia the ties
of custom were so strong that unquestioningly he continued to live and work near others who spoke the same
craft language and to marry into the same social class. In
Puebla this amalgamating tendency was reinforced by
official regulation of a prescribed potters' quarter. If the
potter were Christian, he attended the same masses and
fiestas as his colleagues. Until 1502, if he were a Sevillian
Muslim he went to the same mosque on Fridays and
observed the same rules of conduct as the other Muslims.
In both cases he expected his male children to continue
his example. In the event of his death, he knew his widow's rights to his property would be honored and that
young male heirs would be accepted by fellow potters as
apprentices. He willingly entered into *compadrazco* relationships with other potters, so extending a network of
mutual interest and support throughout the potting community. This further reinforced the stylistic conventions
and social attitudes he had inherited from his predecessors. He wore the same kind of clothes as his peers. During the fifteenth century these were a wide, frequently
patched smock or jerkin, full bombast-stuffed knee
britches borrowed by all commoners from the Muslims,
soft-soled slippers or laced sandals, and a brimless round
crowned hat.[38] Brown was his color, black garments being
reserved for the gentility. Later, Eastern styles were
dropped.

Occupational Hazards

The physical drawbacks attached to the craft were
many, even in a time when illness was commonplace and
accepted with resignation. Pottery making was customarily carried out in poorly lighted, damp surroundings necessary to maintain the raw clay and finished greenware in
optimum condition. Even in sunlit Andalusia or central
Mexico a chill could creep through a thinly clad figure
seated in a trench in the ground. A sixteenth-century Italian doctor interested in diseases associated with different
categories of workers described his country's potters in
graphic terms that might as well have applied to their
Spanish contemporaries:

Since they constantly handle moist clay and spend their days in
damp places, they are usually sallow, pale, cachectic, and nearly
always sickly. Those who sit at the wheel and turn it to shape
the vessels become subject to vertigo if they suffer from some
previous weakness of the eyes; moreover, from excessive fatigue
of the feet they are often subject to satiatica.[39]

He might have added the possibility of headaches, dizziness, nausea, dermatitis, depression, skin discoloration, silicosis, rheumatism, pneumonia, and eye strain.

Of more devastating danger was lead poisoning from ingestion of lethal compounds into the system through handling raw lead and then rubbing eyes or mouth, of absorbing particles through the mouth or body pores when lead was in solution, or of inhaling noxious vapors. Of this terror the doctor wrote:

There's scarce any City in which there are not other Workmen, besides those mention'd above, who receive great Prejudice from the Metallick Plagues. Among such we reckon the Potters; for what City, what Town is without such as practise that Ancientest of all Arts? Now, the Potters make use of burnt and calcin'd Lead for glazing their ware; and for that end grind their Lead in Marble Vessels, by burning about a long Piece of Wood hung from the Roof, with a square Stone fasten'd to it at the other end. While they do this, as well as when with a pair of Tongs they daub their Vessels over with melted Lead before they put 'em into the Furnace; they receive by the Mouth and Nostrils and all the Pores of the Body all the virulent Parts of the Lead thus melted in Water & dissolv'd, and thereupon are siez'd with heavy Disorders. For first of all their Hands begin to shake and tremble, soon after they become Paralytick, Lethargick, Splenetick, Cachectick, and Toothless; and in fine, you'll scarce see a Potter that has not a Leaden Death-like Complexion.[40]

It had been an old problem, of course, ever since the first lead glazes were concocted. How soon it was recognized remains unclear. By the time Muslim potters took up the use of such glaze, however, they knew of one method for coping with the danger,[41] although the Italian doctor apparently did not consider it effective. They fritted the lead solution in a process described earlier. This usually caused the resultant material to become insoluble and nontoxic.

Even the precaution of fritting was not a foolproof protection against plumbism. Under certain conditions some lead glazes remained subject to slight softening in the presence of acids such as were to be found in various fruit juices or wine, particularly if they were stored for a long time in warm places. These glazes were thinly applied solutions fired at the high range of earthenware temperatures for a longer time than was actually necessary for maturing the coating. Kiln atmosphere also played a part in greater lead release. Moreover, chemical studies have shown that the addition to the glaze of copper colorants, very popular with Muslim and Spanish potters, actually promoted the dissolution of lead particles.[42]

Low-level chronic exposure to lead is an insidious hazard because of its cumulative nature. A buildup in the human body can affect the nervous system, gastro-intes-

tinal tract, and blood-forming tissues. In addition to the
results colorfully described by the sixteenth-century Italian
doctor, an afflicted person can lose strength and coordina-
tion in his fingers, hands, and wrists and his sight can
be weakened. A potter's ability depended to a large extent
upon those faculties. Also at risk were the users of plum-
biferous ceramics.

To some extent the external conditions of pottery making at Puebla were an improvement. The town was considered clean by contemporary standards and less subject
than Sevilla or Mexico City to the floods that rotted scattered garbage or the pollution of eons of human occupation. The hazards inherent in the craft itself remained
undiminished.

Economics of the Pottery Craft in Sevilla

Pottery making was not a craft that required a great
capital investment. Other than original acquisition of a
simply constructed wheel or two and some hand tools, all
of which could be fashioned by the artisan himself, the
only expenses were in wages of helpers, support of con-
tracted apprentices, and replenishment of raw materials.
Locally obtained clay, iron, *barrilla*, and fuel probably were
not costly. Imported items such as tin and cobalt were
more expensive, but these were required only in relatively
small amounts.[43] In some cultures the considerable investment of time in mastering various techniques, usually
lasting through an entire juvenile stage of life or a lengthy
apprenticeship, would have been of consequence. Not
so for Sevillians and their associates, who felt time to be a
commodity of little importance, except when working
hours kept them from more pleasurable pastimes.

The pottery business was primarily a family affair carried on by a man, his sons, sons-in-law, and perhaps
a parent. Partnerships with outsiders occasionally were
formed under strict contracts. An instance of such an
alliance was that of a two-year agreement between Sevillian potters Alonso Garrobero and Juan Pérez Carrasquillo
signed in May, 1552. Garrobero was to provide the pottery
shop, located next door to the house of Niculoso's widow,
and the necessary raw materials. Pérez Carrasquillo would
work at the potter's wheel. The wedging, stacking, and
firing duties would be shared by the two men, as would
the labors of building a vault roof for the Italian-style
kiln and a partition in the quarters where Pérez Carrasquillo would reside. Pérez Carrasquillo would pay Garrobero 4500 *maravedíes* annual rent. The profits from sale
of the ceramics and any unsold pieces would be divided.[44]

The making of ceramics was not lucrative. Even after
years of training and occasional long working hours,

few Sevillian potters could expect much profit from their
work. In the Andalusian point of view, pottery was a
cheap substitute for other kinds of receptacles made of
more precious materials. This did not prevent high taxes
from being slapped on all phases of the industry, from
purchase of resources, to igniting the kilns, to selling and
shipping the output.[45] The *alcabala* and *diezmo* were duties
on consumption or commercial transactions; the *aduana*
and *almojarifazgo* taxed import and export; the *montazgo*
and *portazgo* were charges levied against distribution or
circulation.

At the beginning of the sixteenth century the actual
monetary returns from sale of pottery are difficult to ascertain. Elastic standardization of currency, inconsistent and
fragmentary inscriptions, as well as little precise knowledge of prevailing costs of living at the time, make com-
parisons tentative at best. One source of information
is a household ledger kept from August, 1544, to February,
1545, for the canon of the Sevilla cathedral. It notes prices
paid during that time for ordinary supplies and services
(Tables 5, 6).[46] As a basis for judging the relative price of

Table 5. Comparative prices of some common commodities for sale in Sevilla in 1544–1545.
(Extracted from Wagner 1972:119–30)

Ceramics	Mvd.	Housewares	Mvd.	Foodstuffs	Mvd.
drain pipes	2–2.5	caldron	10	veal	
tiles	2–7	broom	2	1 lb.	14.5
cook pot	1	writing paper		goat	
oil cruet	2	1 sheet	1	1 quarter	13
small olla	3	ink	4	chicken	
small olla & jar	3.5	glass flask	15	1 piece	17
larger olla	4	mortar	3	sardines	
chamber pot	6	candle	2	100	7
basin	4	charcoal		egg	2
porringers & plates		1 lb.	1.5	olive oil	
1 carton (6?)	18	soap		1 qt.	6.5
porringer		1 lb.	6	milk	
from Valencia	8.5	*Clothing*		2 pts.	5
Medicines		shoes	35	sugar	
pills		cap	85	1 oz.	2
1 oz., type unknown	51	breeches	40	lettuce	1
unguent				onions	
2 oz.	25	*Liquor*		1 handful	5
violet oil		white wine		asparagus	
1 oz.	7	¼ lit.	2	1 handful	3
waters (mineral?)		red wine		pears	
½ lit.	34	¼ lit.	3	1 lb.	8
		aguardiente		grapes	
		½ lit.	20	1 lb.	1

Table 6. Comparative prices of common services in Sevilla,
1544–1545.
(Extracted from Wagner 1972:119–30)

	Mvd.
scribe	
will	680
power of attorney	102
copy of papers	40
mass and communion	34
grinding of *fanega* of wheat	17
consultation with doctor	136
barber	
shave	34
bleeding	17
toll on bridge to Triana	2

earthenware, it is interesting to note that most foodstuffs
were similarly low priced. Clothing, medicines, and services were priced sufficiently higher to make one wonder
how the artisans managed.

To be sure, not all of them did. It was not rare for a
down-on-his-luck Sevillian potter to end up in the over-
crowded local jail because he could not meet some debt.
There he might have encountered Cervantes in confine-
ment for the same reasons. An eviction of one Fernán
Sanchez for non-payment of rent is recorded for posterity.
Another destitute *ollero* saw his millstone, stone mortar,
two potter's wheels, hoe, roller, and molds sold at auction
in order to pay off a creditor. That action would have
put him temporarily out of the potting business.[47] Others,
who for one reason or another were taken prisoner by
raiding Muslims, rotted away in prison in Algeria because
they did not have the wherewithal to be ransomed.

Some Sevillian potters were more fortunate. A rich
source of information about their general financial condition is the scattered but painstakingly detailed testaments
filed before death by persons who seem to have had more
than the average potter's income. The cost of the testa-
ment itself, at 680 *maravedíes*, would have been prohibitive
to many. Most revealing in these documents are the indicated sizes of dowries. Before the middle of the sixteenth
century these ranged from 15,000 to about 35,000 *maravedíes* in estimated value. Later, sums double those amounts
were more common, but whether they reflected inflation
or actual increased wealth is not clear. Dowries generally
were issued in the form of a promissory note, and were
composed of a combination of cash, clothes, jewels,
household goods, and sometimes the tools or products of

the potting trade. As a dowry of 20,000 *maravedíes* was considered just above the poverty level,[48] and the great majority of the potters listed no dowries at all, the financial state of potters seems one of near destitution, even for the most successful. Several daughters needing such backing would have meant a considerable drain of limited resources.

Further records of the number and kinds of real estate dealings, bequests and endowed benefices to the church, gifts to children, contracts with apprentices, and arrangements for widows represented continual outlay of funds. Most potters did not own their own establishments, but instead rented them from the monasteries of Santa Clara, Santa Paula, San Jerónimo, and San Clemente, or from the parish church of Santa Ana in Triana. The Carthusian Order at Sevilla, in a *comunidad* on the same bank of the river as the principal potters' quarter of Triana, was the largest landlord of the *casas de ollería*. Rents were low, but tenants were expected to take care of upkeep. Better off potters did have legal title to their houses/workyards, often to several, and there was a good deal of shifting from one locale to another. As Triana expanded following the opening of America, a new sector called the Barrio Nuevo attracted a group of potters from elsewhere in the crowded, confined city. Perhaps such moves were made because greater space could be encompassed within the compounds. Many artisans also owned tiny salesrooms in the *alcaicería de la loza* on Salvador Street in Sevilla, where their own pots were offered for sale. Besides these residences and shops, a number of potters acquired a small patch of *tierra calma*, undeveloped land, in the Triana meadow where a garden, vineyard, and a few olive trees and other fruit trees were planted. One potter who owned such property reported a profit in 1555 of 24,000 *maravedíes* on the grape harvest from three such vineyards.[49] Once the wine trade to the colonies boomed, the price of this grape-growing land increased accordingly. That put it out of the reach of less prosperous individuals and made profits for earlier speculators.

Some Sevillian potters invested in slaves purchased at the flourishing market held next to the cathedral. To the elite class, with its passion for servants, slaves were further ostentation. For the artisans, they had the practical advantage of added hands and backs to keep the shops functioning in good times; in leaner periods they could be sold.[50] Their cost was considerable, ranging from 30 to 100 *ducats*, or 11,250 to 37,500 *maravedíes*. This was the yearly wage of most journeymen.[51] At least one local potter, the Italian Tomás de Pésaro, owned a Mexican Indian.[52]

Riots of frustrated, desperate artisans were not uncommon in Sevilla. A serious one took place in 1521, at a time of great food shortages.[53] Strangely, few demonstrations seem to have swept through Triana or to have involved potters.

At the watershed period in the middle of the sixteenth century, when Spanish colonization started to yield big dividends, Sevillian potters stood on the threshold of a potentially better future for their craft, in terms both of the products themselves and of the monetary returns they would bring. With centuries of experience behind them, a large contingent of trained workers at established workshops, a pottery-using clientele with money to spend, and a steady influx of foreign craftsmen bringing a healthy stimulation of refined procedures and new ideas, parts of the local activity reached an unfamiliar level of excellence. It was, unfortunately, not enough to stifle the nascent endeavor at Talavera. In accomplishing that, it would have siphoned off Talavera's royal patronage. Despite the craft rejuvenation that commenced at the top and filtered down and despite the control of the colonial outlets being firmly in Sevillian hands, Andalusian potters did not exploit overseas trade. They did not make more varied or refined forms with elaborated decorations to appeal to colonial customers or to compete with containers of other materials. Except for makers of disposable containers, potters did not anticipate *flota* shipments with large stockpiles of the usual wares for provincial users, even though sailing times were reasonably firmly fixed.[54] With an eager body of consumers waiting, there was no industrialization. The amount of domestic wares turned out slowly fell behind even regional requirements, until either Mexican or non-Spanish ceramics controlled the colonial market. Few Andalusian potters even took advantage of the chances open to them to move up the social and economic scale by becoming overseas traders of their own merchandise. It was not so much the odium attached by Castilians to retailing as it was dearth of enterprise. One example of this was the fact that only a fraction of the masters solicited the right to rent the various taxes, which meant they could take a share for collection.

The reasons behind the missed opportunities were as complex as the multi-strained history and cultural composition of the pottery-making group. Underlying the matter was the dead weight of the threadbare Muslim artistic tradition and its satisfaction with superficial decorative effect, rather than with technical perfection. It must have been too difficult for many to change lifetime mental attitudes and concentrate on facets of the production that, until then, had seemed unimportant. Moreover, the

Table 7. Prices in *maravedíes* set by 1627 *tasación* for ceramics sold in Sevilla.
(Extracted from Gestoso y Pérez 1903:305–7; Pescador del Hoyo 1965:245–60)

		Talavera		Puente del Arzobispo		Sevilla Talavera copies		Sevilla Chinese copies		Sevilla Blue	Italian
		Plain	Decorated	Plain	Decorated	Plain	Decorated	Plain	Decorated		
Plates	Small	10	24	8		10	14	28		9	20
	Medium	24	40	20				50			40
	Large	40	68	36				84			60
Porringers		10	24	8		10	14	28		9	20
Jars	Small					10					
	Medium	24	40	20		34		50		32	40
	Large	40	68	36		68	102	84		28	60

pattern of small familial cottage industry rather than aggressive commercialism, the mounting governmental interference, the lack of capital, and the absence of mercantile wisdom all undercut any eager adoption of change. Perhaps even the warm sunshine and blue skies for which Andalusia is famous sapped human energies. Even more detrimental was a baffling lack of self esteem among makers of hollow wares. For so many centuries they had identified themselves as makers of coarse tablewares that there seemed to be no confidence left in their innate abilities. Some of them actually were so skillful that modern experts cannot always distinguish Sevillian copies from Talaveran originals, although surface finish of the Castilian vessels usually was superior. A 1627 *tasación* demonstrates that Sevillian hollow wares sold at lower prices than did all competing commodities (Table 7). That brought less money into local pockets and little prestige to local producers.

For another thing, although the potters may not have felt their occupation to be ignoble and were resigned to being poor but proud, they were not prodded ahead by the drive known nowadays as the work ethic. Time for pleasure, plentiful for the aristocracy they longed to emu-

late, was the ultimate aim of most of them. To illustrate
how well they succeeded in attaining this goal, it is estimated that at least half of a potter's normal year was taken
up by personal, civic, and religious celebrations. Some
participation was enforced, but love of festivals and a gre-
gariousness erased any rare resentment. Also, when on
the job, normally sunup to sundown, lengthy breaks
for meals and *siesta* reduced the working hours by a
third.[55] Every Sunday and Monday were days of rest.
Night work was forbidden, except in some kiln firings,
because such activity was not "good or loyal."[56] All that
time away from the job and the periods of illness to which
all were subject meant a low rate of yield. A further handi-
cap to any large-scale accumulation of stock for sale was
the fact that reserves for the future were foreign to the
usual Sevillian artisan mentality. Providing for today was
effort enough; tomorrow would take care of itself.

To further depress the Sevillian pottery market, inflation became excessive in Spain in the second half of the
sixteenth century. Prices for raw materials and finished
goods spiraled upward. Hamilton estimates that prices in
the quarter century between 1601 and 1625 were three
times what they were from 1501 to 1525.[57] Due to the small
sums involved, these changes were less obvious when
considering pottery than in the more sumptuous articles
for which Sevilla became famous. Nevertheless, prices
for ordinary household objects, such as plates, bowls,
urinals, and basins, also seem to have at least tripled over
what they had been at the beginning of the century. Even
with that rise such ceramics represented a comparative
bargain. Bills of lading for overseas shipments in the 1580s
and 1590s, with prices that are presumed to be greatly
advanced over what would have been charged in Sevilla,
itemized white maiolica porringers and plates at 6 *reales*
a dozen (36 cents), candleholders at 15 *reales* a pair
(90 cents), blue maiolica objects of unspecified forms at 4
reales a dozen (24 cents) and common lesser wares also at 4
reales a dozen (24 cents) (see Appendix 2). What are
believed to have been large utility vessels, perhaps water
or storage jars, cost 17 *reales* ($1.02) if lead-glazed, 13
(78 cents) if only bisqued. The 1627 *tasación* reaffirms such
low returns to the men in the pottery shops who threw
and decorated pots (Tables 7,8). Foreign earthenwares of
high quality eventually flooded into Sevilla's warehouses
and stores to drive local decorated maiolicas virtually off
the shelves. By this time there was little traffic in ceramics
outbound to the colonies, other than that in containers.
Only the ordinary domestic crockery needed to continue
daily routines was made in any important amounts.

Even the specialty of the city, its tiles, were cheap.

Table 8. Prices set by 1627 *tasación* for Sevillian ceramics
imitating those of Talavera de la Reina.
(Extracted from Gestoso y Pérez 1903:307–8; Pescador del Hoyo 1965:245–60.
Computed at 1 *maravedi* equalling ⅙ cent; 34 *maravedíes* equalling 1 *real*; 1 *real*
equalling 6 cents.)

figurines, painted green/yellow	16 rl.	(96¢)
platter	6 rl.	(36¢)
shaving bowl	6 rl.	(36¢)
inkwell	5 rl.	(30¢)
water cooler, painted green/yellow	4 rl.	(24¢)
water jar, spouted	24 mvd.	(4¢)
jar, spouted	50 mvd.	(8¢)
jar, spouted in imitation of Chinese form	60 mvd.	(10¢)
work box (?)	3 rl.	(18¢)
drug jar, urn form	3 rl.	(18¢)
drug jar, urn form, small	24 mvd.	(4¢)
drug jar, *bote* form, small	24 mvd.	(4¢)
drug jar, *bote* form, ¼ size	14 mvd.	(2¢)
drug jar, *bote* form, ⅓ ht.	1½ rl.	(9¢)
drug jar, *bote* form, ½ size	20 mvd.	(3¢)
drug jar, *bote* form, 2 oz. cap.	10 mvd.	(2¢)
snuff box	3 rl.	(18¢)
planter, medium	3 rl.	(18¢)
planter, small	2 rl.	(12¢)
flower vase, handled, pair	2 rl.	(12¢)
flower vase, large	100 mvd.	(17¢)
flower vase, medium	56 mvd.	(9¢)
jardiniere on pedestal base	2½ rl.	(15¢)
candleholders imitating silver forms, pair	2½ rl.	(15¢)
jar for religious order, large	2¼ rl.	(14¢)
jar for religious order, medium	50 mvd.	(8¢)
cadenete (?)	2¼ rl.	(14¢)
cadenete, blue (?)	42 mvd.	(7¢)
mortar, spouted	2 rl.	(12¢)
flask	2 rl.	(12¢)
cup, *bernegal* form	¼ rl.	(1½¢)
cup for wine, small	24 mvd.	(4¢)
cup for priests, medium	24 mvd.	(4¢)
salt cellar, two-part	1½ rl.	(9¢)
salt cellar, square	34 mvd.	(6¢)
salt cellar, ordinary	20 mvd.	(3¢)
bottle, for 1 lb. conserves	24 mvd.	(4¢)
bottle, for 2 lbs. conserves	1 rl.	(6¢)
bottle, for 3 lbs. conserves	1½ rl.	(9¢)
chamber pot, white	14 mvd.	(2¢)
chamber pot, blue	12 mvd.	(2¢)

Table 8. *continued*

holy water stoup	50 mvd.	(8¢)
oil cruet, pair	34 mvd.	(6¢)
plaque with wine prices	16 mvd.	(3¢)
sauce dish, either plain white or with painted decoration	6 mvd.	(1¢)
toy, small	8 mvd.	(1¢)
owl figure	3 rl.	(18¢)

Square *azulejos* with polychromatic patterns were priced at
12 *maravedíes* (2 cents) each, the small *olambrillas* used
for insets in walls and floors at 4 *maravedíes* (½ cent) each,
and handcut mosaic fragments at 16 *maravedíes* (3 cents)
each. The fees paid the tile decorators likewise amounted
to very little. For painting 100 *olambrillas* a worker received
2½ *maravedíes* (¼ cent), for 100 *azulejos* 6 *maravedíes*
(1 cent).[58] At these prices, quantity sales were essential in
order to survive. Church and government officials obliged
to such an extent that most monuments were splashed
with vivid tile dados and trim, and sizable orders went out
to western Europe and Spanish America. The stars of
the regional potting world were tilers like Bartolomé Sambarino, Hernando de Valladares, and Cristóbal de
Augusta, who continued a tradition begun a century
earlier by Niculoso but whose income from that activity
remained modest. After their deaths, Sevillian tile making
faded into oblivion.

The greatest effort by the highest percentage of the
estimated five thousand persons in Sevilla involved with
production of earthenwares at the end of the sixteenth
century[59] went into turning out thousands of identical containers to carry regional food products across the Atlantic.
Had Sevillian merchants not had a monopoly on the trade
in those commodities, which the colonists were forbidden
to raise or process themselves, it is probable that that
branch of the ceramic business also would have died.

The end result of a lack of initiative combined with a
Spanish economy that steadily weakened as the century
wore on was that potters, other than exceptional tilers, did
not share proportionately in the general prosperity that
for half a century had blessed many of the citizens. That is
not to say, however, that there was no bettering of conditions because of raised wages. Records show an increase
in the amounts of dowries pledged by potters for their
daughters and the further acquisitions of meadow land,
worldly goods, and perpetual masses for their souls. Some
of the potter force also accumulated enough cash to contribute to the decorations for the parades on Corpus

Christi and for the arches erected by the potters' confraternity, to acquire fancy clothes of richly embroidered
textiles for celebrating royal visits to their city, and to treat
themselves to feasts and wine whenever the occasion
allowed. In these ways they were imitating their peers and
their superiors. At all levels of sixteenth-century Sevillian
society the thirst for pleasure, the gambling spirit, the
widespread affluence, and the elevated prices so warped
money's value that immediate self-indulgence was universal. Visitors from more thrift-conscious nations often
were shocked at the lavish display of finery on everyone,
but most especially on humble artisans who strutted the
streets as gloriously as any grandee.[60] An amazed traveler
in 1603 wrote:

As for the small handicraftsmen, unable to do anything else but
work for their living, they do it as a matter of form. Most of
the time they sit disdainfully outside their shops and, for two or
three hours in the afternoon they parade up and down wearing
swords. If they manage to amass two or three hundred *reals*,
they suddenly become noblemen. There is no reason for them
to do anything until, having spent it all, they have to go back
to work to earn more money to enable them to show themselves
off again.[61]

Craft Guilds of Sevillian Potters

Sevillian potters, and most other urban craftsmen,
comprised corporate groups within the larger community
structure. One possible basis for such ordering of the
work forces of Andalusia may have resided in inherited
Muslim practice, wherein participants in crafts were infor-
mally distinguished as being masters (*mu'allim*), journeymen (*sani'*), and apprentices (*muta'allim*).[62] The same three
levels of competence were recognized by the later Christians. The Muslim artisans enjoyed some self-government
through an appointed official from the ranks, the *amin*
or *arif*, who served as intermediary in any disputes
between the municipal administration and them. He also
was an arm of the market police in guarding against fraudulent practices among the artisans. There was an overall
observer of the market, the *almotácen*, who controlled
weights and measures, assigned trade positions, collected
taxes, and enforced rules against dishonest acts. The
craft bodies had a set of bylaws and offered some assistance to their fellows in cases of misfortune. Their exact
kind of involvement in devotional life is uncertain.[63] There
were no restrictions against Christian or Jewish presence
in the craft structure, and in fact the latter are known
to have had sodalities of their own within Muslim towns.
It is more probable that the model for the structuring of
Andalusian craftsmen as it evolved during the fifteenth
century came most directly from eastern Christian Spain.

There, the craft guild is thought to have grown out of the confraternity, or *cofradía*, a religious-beneficent group, the idea for which may have come into Spain as a result of Cluniac influence along the Santiago de Compostela pilgrimage route. The medieval propensity for organizing societies into clearly differentiated groups with fixed roles found fertile ground in Spain through Catalonia, Aragón, Asturias, and the Biscay coastal regions. This distribution would seem to support the view of confraternity diffusion from France. These lay federations associated themselves with a particular church or chapel, adopted a patron saint, urged upon their members an active role in religious observances, and undertook various kinds of charitable services, such as caring for the ill, the dead, and surviving members of a deceased craftsman's family. On occasion the confraternities supported measures to retrieve Christian captives in Muslim hands. Some of them also may have had secondary economic functions in the protection of craft goods. One variation of the concept concerned itself rather exclusively with matters of work, while at the same time never totally divorcing itself from religious matters. It was this sort of basically secular grouping that provided the most demonstrable foundation of the Spanish craft guild.

The guild, as such, appeared first in the kingdom of Aragón during a twelfth-century burst of commercial vigor. The unsettled economic and social conditions of the times made attractive the security and guidance of a formalized group response. A corporation was deemed a desirable shield against non-Spanish competition. Its other functions were in determining proficiency of craftsmen and their progression from apprentice to master ranks and in maintaining product quality. Although the expressed purposes of such federations of artisans were temporal, the deep-seated religious passions of the Spaniards furnished a vitality lacking in other contemporary European guilds. Conversely, the religious bodies were increasingly involved in political matters, because Church and State had become two facets of one large governing organism. For this reason both confraternities and guilds periodically were banned by the monarchies, which suspected them of being a threat to their authority.

Because there was less need to control the artisan and peasant classes than in more populous Aragón, guilds apparently were not organized in Castile, including Andalusia, until late in the fifteenth century. When Isabela assumed the throne in 1474, she and Fernando, ruler of Aragón, launched upon a massive program of institutionalization of the chaotic economic life of the western kingdom. The full-blown guild framework of Aragón, with

its faults as well as its virtues, was introduced. Guilds
were seen as a useful means for ordering and stimulating
the backward economy, for bringing national uniformity
to techniques, prices, and policies that for centuries had
suffered from localism, for conserving public calm among
the masses, as well as for administration of the growing
volume of taxation and bureaucratic documentation. It was
not a case of outright coercion from the top imposing a
guild superstructure over an unyielding *artesanado*, but
rather a matter of persuasion through the extension of
both tangible and intangible advantages. Occasional special recognition of individual craftsmen and the granting of
franquesas—for example, that to the Sevillian tile decorator
Fernán Martínez Guijarro[64]—carried an unstated message
of service to the nation enriched by group association.
The actual initiative to organize was left to the artisans
themselves, working through local authorities who were
directly responsible to the Crown.

So, at a time when the rest of Europe was beginning to
enjoy an atmosphere of free enterprise and when Spain
desperately needed strong industrial diversity, as well
as a greater body of workers infused with eagerness and
a sense of challenge, Castile shifted into a reverse course.
This took her to the precipice of economic strangulation
as, in the name of cultural homogeneity, the Catholic
Kings and their Hapsburg successors wove a retrograde,
entangling web of legislative minutia. In the end, this
action either killed initiative or promoted circumvention of
the law as a viable mode of conduct.

Before the end of the fifteenth century various Castilian
cities were encouraged to grant guild ordinances. Sevillian
officials as early as 1470 had drawn up codified regulations
in which seventy incorporated trades were recognized.
It is strange, indeed, that pottery making, known to have
been a leading local activity, appears not to have been
listed.

Once a trade took steps to become organized, obligatory
membership of all persons pursuing that line of work,
rank examinations, and heir privileges were accepted
from the Aragonese format. To this primary foundation
the Catholic Kings added exhaustive regimentation,
which became a deeply ingrained method of operation for
the Crown, Cortés, counsels, and even those who had
the most to lose, the artisans themselves. Second, an
insidious racial qualification reflective of the national tor-
ment was thrust into the economic realm. All guild appli-
cants had to produce baptismal records to prove purity
of blood.

Therein is one possible reason that Sevillian potters of
the late fifteenth, and perhaps most of the sixteenth,
century chose not to unite. Their ranks still were composed of a large body of the Muslim minority, who, under
the current ground rules, would have been ineligible for
guild membership and hence forbidden to work. Pragma-
tists understood that it was their widely appreciated artistic finesse that brought revenues to many non-Muslims
engaged in the craft. To blackball them would have far-
reaching and disastrous effects. Moreover, other Europeans, even though they were Catholic Christians in religious belief, also were excluded from participation in the
Castilian guild corporations. Even with the lure of a ten-
year exemption from taxes, Italian artisans coming to Sevilla may have found the prospects of extraguild status
so uninviting that they prevailed upon influential intermediaries to resist the formation of a guild. Whatever the
reasons, the earliest oblique suggestions of Sevillian pottery guilds do not appear until the middle of the sixteenth
century, or some eighty-five years after the first of the
city's ordinances was issued. Even then, neither their
composition nor regulations were specifically outlined.[65]

Within the craft the hair-splitting specialization required
in some trades seems not to have been applied to pottery.
The two traditional groups of makers of finewares and
makers of commonwares possibly may have had distinct
organizations. The lower category included both those
fashioning lesser caliber maiolica tableware and those producing unglazed utilitarian objects. Among the latter
there may have been segregation based on forms, such as
the containers *botijas peruleras*. The upper ranks might
have been composed of throwers, decorators, and tilers.
The presumed requirement for the marking of pots by
makers to prevent counterfeiting was not enforced,
although Gestoso thought the schematic outline of the
Giralda a possible guild insignia.[66] A lackluster federation
may have continued into the next century, but if so it
expired long before all Spanish guilds were outlawed in
1834.

The traditional relationship of craft guild and confraternity made the duality of community life inescapable.
The former oversaw one's occupation, the latter one's
attentiveness to religion. In spite of the lack of information
about potters' guilds, there is little doubt but that the
social and medical aid proffered by the Sevillian potters'
confraternity, the associated hospital, and the ideal of
brotherhood had appeal for the poorest artisans. Overt
manifestations of piety among all strata of the society

became ever more mandatory. Guild and confraternity members alike were pressured through peer approval to take active part in church festivities, with consequent loss of work time, and to assume extra expenses for all the elaborate accessories such demonstrations demanded.[67] The same participation in civil functions was required of guilds. As detrimental as the resulting drains on time and money were, these group activities had some positive qualities. They compensated for a scarcity of pleasures available to the lower classes, while at the same time helping to formulate a badly needed sense of community.

Taking the format of known guilds as a model, potting members of such a federation would have been given the right to annual meetings for the purpose of discussing mutual interests and naming members to police their trade (*veedores*) and to serve as intermediaries in dealing with the authorities (*alcaldes*). Unlike the more democratic situation in Aragón, they had no place in municipal government. They were granted power to fix terms of apprenticeships and advancements through the grades, to guard quality of raw materials and finished goods, and to decide upon the kinds of punishment for disregard of the *reglas*. Streams of pragmatics continually imposed more and more regimentation on all crafts. Inasmuch as only the sanctioned methods and even broad decorative styles could be followed within any trade, technical experimentation and original artistic expressions of all types were discouraged, although obviously some growth was allowable. Anachronistic procedures tended to be perpetuated. In the absence of guild records, the extent to which ancient Muslim technology was still officially acceptable remains unknown. The anti-capitalistic viewpoint of the monarchy instituted strict price regulation and enforced cooperative marketing, which meant that incentives for personal gain either were dampened or eliminated.[68]

Economic Status of Colonial Potters

Thus far no archival material has been found to afford a specific idea of the economic condition of the sixteenth-century potters who found their way from Andalusia to central Mexico. In all likelihood, the new environment did not eliminate the familiar near-poverty. Although wages for unskilled laborers, such as would have been employed for the manual chores of the pottery workshop, rose four hundred percent owing to epidemics that caused a severe shortage of workers, the cost of living increased apace.[69] A low standard of living for common craftsmen remained universal. In Mexico there were the same drains on time and money for participation in group pleasures as in Andalusia.

Reading between the lines of the limited archival resources available for seventeenth-century Puebla, it appears that financial conditions for potters were on an upswing. Probably this was reflective not only of the emphasis on low-level industrialization that characterized the city's growth, but also of the fact that the importation of Chinese porcelain, for which the upper classes had developed an appetite, may have been declining. Four landlords of rental property in which to set up potteries were churches and ten were ordinary citizens. With the locations being in the potters' quarter, there is a good chance that private owners were other potters. In some of these cases, rent was shared by two persons who must have been business partners. Other artisans owned their shops, houses, and some empty lots with gardens.

The most prosperous of these owners was Diego Salvador Carreto, who in 1671 left his heirs two *haciendas* in the province of Tlaxcala and three houses in Puebla, one of which quartered his pottery. The street in front took the name of Baño de Carreto (now Calle 5 Norte 600). Its name derived from a bathhouse on the premises established after Carreto received a *merced* of water in 1649. These holdings indicate a substantial investment for a craftsman. That he was successful is shown in his being selected by his peers to serve on a committee of four to draft the 1653 guild ordinances.[70]

Impressive inventories of equipment, raw materials, and completed stock were recorded for some shops. For example, in the assortment of paraphernalia in a shop belonging to Roque de Talavera (on a street that is now Avenida 6 Poniente) there were five kilns. One was of large size, one medium, one reserved for *ollas*, one reserved for saggars, and the fifth for calcination of minerals. The number of these constructions emphasizes what one must believe was an active and profitable career with a rather surprising specialization.[71]

Several Puebla men carried a military title, which may have entailed some income in addition to that made through their craft. Most prominent was Lieutenant Juan Gómez de Villegas. Identified as a superstar, or *maestro mayor de locero de lo fino*, he was said to have been one of the best decorators of the era. Inasmuch as he trained sixteen apprenctices over a twelve-year period, not only was much of his skill presumably passed on, but a considerable expense was involved. A better than average income is implied.[72]

There is no information available about the actual number of people working in any one Puebla shop or, consequently, whether one complex was appreciably larger or more productive than another. Many of the twenty-nine journeymen in the seventeenth-century archives probably worked for wages in the shops owned by masters. There likely was some movement in this group from employer to employer, which served to homogenize and equalize the ceramic community's output. Only three or four slaves, another indicator of financial reserves, are known to have been owned by seventeenth-century Puebla potters.

No prices of seventeenth-century Puebla raw materials or wares are known. Nevertheless, considering the great public enthusiasm for their products and what must have been a steadily increasing demand for all grades of hollow ware and tile for home consumption and export, it seems reasonable to believe that the potters enjoyed more individual security than any of their Spanish or Mexican predecessors. Only seventeenth-century Talavera could rival their monetary success; this would apply primarily to the maiolists. The growth in colonial population and its domestic needs and the thriving Puebla economy would also have contributed to the coffers of the lower potting ranks. Since urban pottery making was not an industry affected by the great decrease in available native labor, it may not have suffered from that circumstance. Potters certainly continued to do well financially through most of the eighteenth century, although stylistic exuberance declined after about 1750. Nevertheless, through the colonial era masters were limited to having one outlet for their pottery, prices were controlled, taxes were many and high, and free enterprise was discouraged. With all on a comparable footing, there was little competition among masters, although the work of some was recognized as superior to that of others. Commercial traders acquired large orders of pottery for resale, no doubt adding to the price charged at the workshop.

Not unexpectedly, the restrictive patterning inherent in the potters' quarter concept, which permitted only a thirty-two-block residential and work area, together with the traditional hereditary participation in the craft accounted for a tight network of interlocking family ties among Puebla potters. Records reveal forty-one fathers, sons, and brothers in the seventeenth-century ranks. Intermarriage among potting families was common, thus multiplying the familial bonds.[73] In a number of instances these extended in a dynastic manner over several centuries, during which time the large potting families occupied the same workshops.[74] Blood kinships were further reinforced by *compadrazco*, or the relationships between parents and godparents of a child.

Potters' Confraternity in Puebla

Another agent binding Puebla potters together was the confraternity, which had its seat in the San Marcos parish church in the potters' quarter (Fig. 159). The original building began in 1538 as a hermitage in the open land west of the plaza. As the town expanded, the hermitage became an interior chapel of a larger church constructed

Figure 159. Modern view of the San Marcos parish church in the Puebla potters' quarter. It was here that the colonial era potters' confraternity was housed.

between 1578 and 1606, which was remodeled during
the middle of the seventeenth century. The modern facade
is emblazoned with late eighteenth-century tiles.[75] Very
probably some of the seventeenth-century potters lie
buried in its small cemetery, but the actual date of initia-
tion of the confraternity is unknown.

Guild confraternities were quasi-religious in nature,
imposing some obligatory church activities, but they also
were temporal bodies with social and recreational aspects.
Members celebrated saints' days with masses, candles,
costumes, food, and parades. Such interaction on a social
plane surely furthered craft continuity. The good fellow-
ship excluded some of the work force, however, in spite of
regulations calling for all guild members to join the confraternity: in 1688, Negroes, mulattoes, and Mexican Indians
were forbidden to participate.[76] A more positive side to
the confraternity was a *montepío*, or public assistance fund,
to help its members in times of illness, accident, or death.
The money came from donations, alms, fines for ordinance infractions, examination fees, assessments, and
dues. The adoption of these organizations in seventeenth-
century New Spain is another example of a medieval
institutionalization of artisan life that had been adandoned
or outlawed in contemporary Spain.[77] Although no anthropological investigation has been made, there is little to
suggest that any Native American response was behind
the *cofradía* movement. It seems improbable because the
entire urban pottery complex in New Spain remained
exclusively Hispanic in technology, patterns of work, makers, and markets. Such circumscribed craft orientation
would have carried over into sociological realms.

Potters' Craft Guild in Puebla

As sufficient numbers of artisans arrived in New Spain,
they unhesitatingly grouped themselves together by trade
and petitioned the authorities for guild status, as was
customary in Andalusia. It reveals much about the expa-
triates that the first craftsmen to gain a federation were not
the scores of masons needed to direct native laborers in
building the capital city from the rubble left after the
frightful destruction of Tenochtitlán, or the many others
involved in the essential business of clothing, feeding, and
protecting the white populace, but silversmiths (1524),
silk workers (1542), and embroiderers (1546). By the end of
the sixteenth century there were one hundred fifty-three
colonial guilds in New Spain, most of them producing
goods for Spanish residents of Mexico City and Puebla.
There may have been a comparable number of parallel
native groups making the same kind of merchandise for

the same users and organized according to the European plan, which resembled their own preconquest work structure.[78] The Native American guilds were in potential conflict commercially with the white men, because they often made items of better quality and sold them at lower cost.

All this arranging of colonial life notwithstanding, potters were not among the sodalities of either the white or Native American factions of sixteenth-century society. Maybe their numbers remained too few and their importance to economic health too insignificant. Or maybe the independent spirit they carried from Andalusia to New Spain led them to feel that such structuring represented little benefit and much interference.

Fifty years later trade guilds were rapidly becoming anachronistic in Spain, but at that late date Puebla potters selected four of their number to draft and present proposed ordinances under which such a body could be instituted. Mexico City potters soon followed suit, but little else is known about that industry.[79] The Puebla potter ranks had swollen from a few pioneers to several hundred active participants. Other than earthenware containers, which continued to be imported in quantity, their works had nearly replaced imported wares from Spain and other European sources, and in tablewares and architectural embellishments they had far outstripped all other provincial efforts. Throughout the viceroyalty Puebla pottery was coming into use and bringing needed monies to the treasury. Having accomplished this without the support of a formal organization, why was there a move to an outmoded corporation such as a guild? One thing is certain: it was yet another reflection of the ultraconservative acceptance of a rigid societal management already witnessed in the potters' quarter and the confraternity.[80]

The success of the Puebla pottery complex was so substantial, even to the point of culminating in a distinctive regional architectural style, that the attitudes of potters toward their work and themselves must have been greatly enhanced. The caste system within the potting community did not disappear, however. As the guild documents show, participants in the fulltime potting industry, as opposed to supporting day laborers, were formally segregated into the existing three-level hierarchy of apprentice, journeyman, and master. A steady progression through these ranks during the course of a working lifetime was assumed. Under the guild organization, it was to be through oral and demonstration examinations witnessed by selected peers. Three broad categories of wares were recognized: plainwares, common grade maiolicas, and fine grade maiolicas. A man could make only the kind of ware

in which he had passed the examination, which conceivably could be all three if he fulfilled the test requirement.
Although licensing may have been desirable for reasons
other than allowing government to exact more fees, class
distinctions were implicit in the categorization of labor.

The master rank encompassed throwers and decorators.
No persons were identified specifically as tilers, but in
Puebla they surely comprised a large portion of the decorators. Inventories of finished ceramics in some shops
included tiles of various sizes, as well as hollow ware,
making it obvious that the same persons applied designs
to both kinds of objects. Master potters were men apparently respected in the community as proprietors of small
businesses, teachers of the young, and skilled in their
occupation. Most of them in seventeenth-century Puebla
were literate, or at least could sign their names.

The master potters brought credibility to their proposed
guild ordinances, which admirably seemed to be aimed
at quality control. Stipulations were put forth regarding
raw materials, ratios of minerals in glaze solutions, firing
methods, and approved decorative modes for the mid-
seventeenth century. No updating occurred later, even
though the guild was operative through the entire colonial
period. Many facets of the production process were not
addressed. Some of those that were considered were
elementary. Was it necessary to remind capable potters to
use clean clay and to center it on their wheels so that
vessel walls would be of uniform thickness? Did the inclu-
sion of these simple procedures, which would have been
the first steps learned by any apprentice, mean that
untrained novices were turning out poor pottery that
threatened the reputation of the industry? Other areas
where laxity in fine wares seems to have been disturbing
were use of what were regarded as inferior decorative
pigments, variation from a set style, innovations in size,
and reliance upon cockspurs rather than saggars to separate objects. The masters seem to have felt unsettled by
some nonconformists and hoped to force compliance
through regulation.

Much attention was given in the suggested ordinances
to social and economic matters, giving rise to a suspicion
that these also prodded the clique of master maiolica
potters into action. They understandably wanted to protect
their privileges. They proposed to do this in two ways.
One was by employing what had become customary Spanish racial discrimination, which would provide a kind of
social insurance in an ethnically plural society, there being
divisions of labor along the lines of ethnic separations.
The other was through the skill examinations that would

afford economic safeguards and eliminate unwanted competition. They hoped that no one could make pottery in
Puebla unless he were a guild member, and he could not
attain that status without approval of the elite body that
ran the guild. The masters also wanted to make sure
they were neither misrepresented to prospective clients
nor undersold. Pots were to carry fired-on maker's marks,
which could not be forged without heavy fines. Only
persons who had earned a *carta de examen* could operate
home sales shops to market their products or sell those
products in public stores.

How strictly these new ordinances were observed when
enacted through approval of the city and viceregal admin-
istrations is problematical. Only a small percentage of
pieces were marked, design idiosyncrasies continued, and
the saggar ordinance was doomed to failure because their
use was considered a time-consuming nuisance.[81] They
also were not part of the traditional technology. If craft
examinations were not merely a way to keep undesirable
elements out of an exclusive group, they would have been
one means of maintaining mutually agreed upon standards. Unfortunately, there is no way of knowing how
seriously the examinations were conducted. They did
require fees, which some workers probably could not pay,
even with the threat that unexamined artisans could neither employ others in their shops nor sell their own pottery. One of the surviving documents concerning guild
infractions suggests that lack of funds to meet the fees was
an issue. Six makers of kitchen wares, the lowest grade
of pottery, were censured because they had no examination papers.[82] In spite of obstacles to becoming a master,
there is no hint that those already at that level necessarily
felt secretive about their methods or motifs. They were, in
fact, obliged to allow inspectors to examine their shop
operations.

In an era of early death and debilitating diseases, proposed social considerations charitably concentrated upon
the welfare of widows and young sons of deceased potters
and apprentices, who usually were orphans. The former
were given assurances of full rights to continue their
spouse's business, and sons were extended a three-year
learning period before required examinations. Trainees
who failed such tests were to be offered further instruction
at their master's expense in order to gain self-sufficiency.

Apprenticeship in the Pottery-Making Craft

An important element of past custom was formally
structured in the guild regulations. That was apprenticeship. Under potters' ordinances, the obligations of master

and apprentice were clearly enumerated, and legally binding contracts were signed by both parties. The artisan
agreed to feed, house, and clothe his charge and to care
for him in times of illness. He was to educate the apprentice in all or selected facets of the craft, to set a good moral
example, and to provide instruction in the Christian doc-
trine. Upon completion of the term, the apprentice was to
receive a new set of clothes or the equivalent in money.[83]
In essence, the master took on the responsibility of surro-
gate father. For his part, the apprentice had to promise
to work diligently to learn the trade as instructed, to be
loyal to the family but not to intrude on its privacy, to aid
in case of fire or flood, to be respectful of the master, to
take care of his tools, and not to attempt to desert.[84] The
term of apprenticeship among potters varied from one to
five years, three to four being most common. Instruction
occasionally was to be limited to either use of the potter's
wheel or decorative techniques, but usually both aspects
of production were involved.

Apprentices came from several sources. Sometimes they
were sons of daughters or sisters of potters who had
married a man of another trade, or sons of unrelated persons who for unknown reasons chose pottery making
as a suitable future occupation for their offspring. Sons of
slaves found their way into apprentice ranks. Most frequently, however, the apprentices were male orphans
ranging in age from about twelve to eighteen years.
Assumption of their care was not charity, because a return
in the form of labor was expected. Still, it was a humane
means of providing a home and purpose where none
might have been available otherwise, while at the same
time being an investment in the potter's own future.

There are extant records of only thirteen pottery
apprenticeships in sixteenth-century Sevilla, although the
practice is believed to have been much more common
than these archives indicate. Only one artisan, the comparatively prosperous tiler Pedro de Herrera, is indicated
as having trained two such youngsters.[85] One overriding
reason that likely restricted the practice was the cost
involved in another mouth to feed and body to dress at a
time when many craftsmen could barely care for their
immediate families. An apprentice was a gamble that
might not pay off, since there were no guarantees of compliance or aptitude. In the more flourishing seventeenth-
century industry at Puebla, seventy-nine apprenticeships
are documented, with many masters assuming the burden
of more than one.[86]

As in the case of a potter's own sons, instruction was by
example rather than through any verbal communication.

A period of trial and error ensued. Acknowledgment
of final success came only when a learner's efforts sufficiently matched a model to be included with the regular
issue from the workshop. Sometimes specific daily
amounts of certain forms were stipulated. The neophyte
potter tended to repeat the works that had been deemed
satisfactory, rather than to improvise and risk rejection.[87]
Just at that point the basic conservatism of potters took
hold. In this lengthy apprenticeship, which depended on
mutuality of interest and respect, another avenue for
perpetuation of the technology and its stylistic modes was
assured.

Retrospective

In the preindustrial Spanish world, the potter's life was
hard. The work was dirty, unhealthy, exacting but tedious, and subject to physical forces beyond his limited
means of control. It was seen as a disgusting occupation
by many contemporaries, and seldom was it profitable.
The resulting earthenware output remained cheap and,
except for Muslim lusters and maiolica tile, had little prestige value. Typically, it was viewed as a substitute for
something of higher quality. As soon as Andalusian customers could afford objects of more costly materials, they
turned away from use of lead- or tin-glazed pottery. Sometimes the change was based on practical considerations
such as durability, but often it was for the sake of ostentation. In either case, it cut into potters' revenues.

Surprisingly, in the seventeenth century the potter's lot
appears to have gradually improved, although Spain
then hovered on the borderlands of the expanding Mediterranean economic world rather than comprising its
axis. On the peninsula it was Talaveran artisans rather
than their Sevillian colleagues who benefited. Overseas it
was the maiolists in Puebla who enjoyed security. A rising
prosperity in that area, abetted by an informal ceramic
monopoly, a drop in maritime trade with Spain that
opened intra-provincial exchange, and perhaps an untypi-
cal mercantile astuteness in sizing up a potential market
hungry for something even vaguely Oriental made the
regional success possible. It cannot now be determined to
what extent financial gains elevated the potter's status,
since available municipal records deal only with intermediary activities between local authorities and selected guild
officers acting on behalf of their fellow members. Whether
these men had a say in community affairs beyond those
matters involving their own occupation, or whether they
received more personal recognition because of public
appreciation of some of their works remains unknown,

although both were perhaps likely. Regardless, it is quite clear that, even with a somewhat higher standard of living, colonial urban potters shared the same marginal class position accorded those in Spain, with little chance of achieving anything better.

In an expanding colonial industry, whose forward-looking participants gradually formulated recognizable *poblano* styling for domestic wares and tiles, there is a puzzling contradiction. Archival data seem to suggest a retreat on the part of Puebla potters to sociological orientation more in tune with the fourteenth and fifteenth centuries than with the emerging Age of Enlightenment. Even with presumed greater material rewards and personal recognition there must have been deep-rooted attitudes that fostered a slower relinquishment of anachronistic practices than was true in coeval Spain, a country itself rapidly sinking into withdrawal. As a class, Spanish potters have been shown to be conservative, but whether quiet acceptance of guild, confraternity, and potters' quarter was also an indication of narrow-visioned provincialism, maybe even of a previously unsuspected strain of indigeneity, is a question neither present historical nor anthropological research can satisfactorily answer.

With the many drawbacks, one wonders why men chose the trade of pottery. Most probably were absorbed into the craft as unquestioning youths following in parental footsteps. They were not awed by the miraculous possibility of combining earth, water, and fire to create a totally new substance. To them the making of pottery was a stable, though poorly paid, means of livelihood in a society dependent upon its products. For most, that was what it remained throughout a working lifetime. For those with special talents there must have been gratification in creativity, even though that was curbed by convention. In that kernel of aesthetic release is seated the incongruity between a potter's unrewarding personal place in his culture and the enduring objects of beauty he left behind.

Epilogue

The evolution of the Andalusian pottery craft has been reconstructed from before the time of Christ to that of the Bourbon kings of Spain. The premise that historical facts could be used to explain archaeological ceramics and, conversely, that pottery could bring some of those facts down to commonplace levels and even suggest some social conditions not recorded, in our opinion, has been validated.

The undercurrent of Andalusian pottery from its earliest commercialized appearances has been shown to have reflected the agricultural orientation of the province. It is no accident that a preponderance of earthenware forms were those designed to store, ship, manipulate, or dispense liquids. Not only did the local climate and that of areas from which successive invaders came make the control and utilization of water of primary concern, but the major crops sustaining the economy from Roman into Christian times yielded liquid end products. Associated with the varied containers for fluids was a restricted assemblage of domestic articles appropriate to unelaborated rural or township lifeways that continued relentlessly across temporal segmentation imposed by larger events. When portions of this pottery inventory assumed a role in international trade, they were designed for consumers sharing a similarly unadvanced, modulated rhythm of life.

Meanwhile, at periods when history notes that Andalusian political tides brought increased importance of upper social classes having more complex patterns of behavior, concurrently there appeared luxury grade ceramics drawn from elite cultural reservoirs characteristic of the particular time. Whether or not alien influences from outside Andalusia were part of the drives behind these cyclic rises of special elements of the regional society, the pottery associated with them was expanded beyond mere functionalism. It disappeared when those persons, along with their worldviews, vanished from the local picture. However, some of their cluster of associated pottery traits became layered within the artisan knowledge to reappear periodically in various mutations. Examples of the overlay of more ephemeral specialized styles upon the fundamental ceramic stratum are the molded, mythologically interpreted *terra sigillatas* of the Romans, the polychromes with boldly executed naturalistic motifs under clear lead glaze of the Cordoban caliphate, the technically and artistically intricate *reflejo metálicos* of the Nasrids, and the colorful, uncompromising *cuerda secas* of the late fifteenth-century Sevillians. In their own times, each mode reflected the current sociopolitical circumstances of Andalusia and the prevalent canons of cultivated taste, but it had no real relevance to the routines or possessions of the mass of contemporary commoners. The passing modes were superfluous in a broad overview of the mainstream ceramic evolution, but were essential in more discrete cultural dissection.

By the end of the fifteenth century, when the New World lay before the intrepid Iberians, Spain was approaching, but had not crossed, the threshold of a new era. Economically and philosophically the country lethargically hung back in the darkened corners of the Middle Ages, even though glimmerings of the modern world system were beginning to be seen. The Andalusian pottery and the technology of its making, both at home and in the new overseas settlements, precisely parallel this situation: they were, in the main, the long familiar remnants of a Muslimized craft that had become lifeless, even though some designs on display pieces indicated an awareness of the Renaissance. Because of a group of apathetic journeymen potters, this pottery remained the primary interpretation of earthenware manufacture to be had by the bulk of peninsular Andalusian society well into the seventeenth century.

It proved impossible during this study to fully ascertain the processes of that manufacture through either archival or artifact analyses, although both were informative. Unfortunately, there had been no eyewitness accounts of the inner workings of the occupation that for a thousand years had turned out characteristically Andalusian ceramics. Nor had a workshop been excavated. In the sphere of methods, on-site observations made possible by the remarkable technological continuity of the craft were called upon to supplement more academic data. A network of small traditional pottery-making industries fortunately still functions throughout the province. Those in and around Granada retain the highest percentage of survivals from the past, such as potter's wheels in floor pits and grinding mills turned by draft animals. Even more significant to total understanding is the urban potting activity that continues in modern Morocco. There, except for use of some commercially refined pigments, the entire endeavor and the men who perpetuate it seem encapsulated in a Muslim medieval atmosphere, providing a living exhibition of what the potting scene had been in Triana and other Andalusian centers until the middle of the sixteenth century.

At that time, accelerating forces that were to culminate in the Industrial Revolution combined with American riches to pull Spain briefly from the periphery to the center of a new European economic alignment. Enterprising Ligurians, always ready to capitalize on international financial trends, are documented as having greatly increased their numbers in Andalusia during the sixteenth century. They previously were believed to have devoted their energies principally to commerce and banking, but earthenwares recovered in Andalusia and the transatlantic provinces now corroborate their active participation in local pottery production. They are thought to be directly responsible for a revitalization of the nearly moribund tableware branch of the ceramic craft, having introduced improved techniques and equipment that replaced those introduced at the beginning of the Muslim occupation.

The changes the Italian potters wrought in Sevilla soon migrated across the Atlantic to central Mexico. Not only top but lower calibers of urban dishes were affected. The hold of the initial outdated methods and decorative modes proved to be more tenuous in the invigorated colonial work places.

At what became the leading pottery center of New Spain, better wares steadily moved away from Sevillian models in a cultural climate enlivened by fresh *mudéjar* and Oriental design mannerisms, as interpreted by a body of craftsmen absorbing native preferences and aptitudes. More accurately than many contemporary handicrafts, these ceramics mirrored colonial Mexico's unique position as a place where East and West did, in fact, meet. In this instance, pottery registered a social phenomenon suspected of having been purposefully omitted in official written records. It was only in tantalizing, elusive ways that the potting *moriscos* banished from Spain revealed themselves for the final time in the maiolica ceramic arts of seventeenth-century Puebla.

Appendix 1

Notable Seventeenth-Century Paintings
by Sevillian Masters
Depicting Local Ceramics

DIEGO RODRÍGUEZ DE SILVA Y VELÁZQUEZ
Two Men Eating, ca. 1616–17, Wellington Museum, London;
  white maiolica plates, partially lead-glazed pitcher, lead-
  glazed *cántaro* with an orange in the throat to sweeten water.
The Luncheon, ca. 1617–18, Hungarian Museum, Budapest; white
  maiolica plates.
The Maid Servant, ca. 1617–18, Art Institute, Chicago; white
  maiolica plates, white maiolica bowls, partially glazed white
  maiolica pitcher, two-handled white maiolica jars.
Christ at Emmaus, ca. 1622–23, Metropolitan Museum, New York;
  white maiolica plate.
Old Woman Frying Eggs, ca. 1618, National Gallery of Scotland,
  Edinburgh; white maiolica plate, partially glazed white maiolica pitcher, partially lead-glazed pitcher, lead-glazed bowl,
  earthenware brazier.
Jesus in House of Martha and Mary, ca. 1618, National Gallery,
  London; plates with gunmetal maiolica (?) glaze, partially
  lead-glazed pitcher.
The Water Seller of Sevilla, 1622, Wellington Museum, London;
  small and large two-handled white maiolica jars, unglazed
  single-handled *cántaro*.
Still Life, ca. 1620, Rijkmuseum, Amsterdam; white maiolica
  plate.
The Forge of Vulcan, ca. 1630, Prado, Madrid; white maiolica
  pitcher.
The Topers, ca. 1629, Prado, Madrid; white maiolica bowl.
Menippus, ca. 1637–40, Prado, Madrid; single-handled unglazed
  cántaro.

BARTOLOMÉ MURILLO
Rebecca and Eleazer, ca. 1650, Prado, Madrid; single- and two-
  handled unglazed *cántaros*.
Marriage Feast at Cana, ca. 1650–70, Barber Institute of Fine Art,
  Birmingham; two-handled unglazed *cántaros*, one-handled
  jars.
The Meal of the Old Woman, ca. 1650–60, Sammlung Carstanjen,
  Munich; pitcher with partial maiolica glaze, white maiolica
  bowl.
Saints Justa and Rufina, undated, Chapter Room, Sevilla Cathe-
  dral; white maiolica plates, bowls, jars.
Saint Justa, undated, Stafford House, London; white maiolica
  bowl.

Saint Rufina, undated, Stafford House, London; two white maiol-
ica jars.
The Saints Justa and Rufina, ca. 1672–76, Museo de Bellas Artes,
Sevilla; white maiolica plates, bowls, pitcher, jars.
Fray Francisco and the Kitchen of the Angels, 1646, Louvre, Paris;
white maiolica plates, bowl, pitcher with partial white maiolica
glaze.
Moses and the Pain of Horeb, undated, La Caridad, Sevilla; white
maiolica jars, bowl.
Saint Diego Feeding Poor Boys, undated, Academia de San Fernando, Madrid; white maiolica plates.
Jacob Blessing Isaac, undated, Hermitage, Leningrad; two-handled
unglazed *cántaros*.
Boy Delousing Himself, undated, Louvre, Paris; two-handled
unglazed *cántaro*.
Saint Justa, undated, Los Angeles County Museum; maiolica
bowl, jar.
Saint Rufina, undated, private collection, Caracas; two dimpled
and handled white maiolica jars.
Cure of the Paralytic at the Pool, undated, National Gallery, London; white maiolica jars, bowl, unglazed *cántaros*.
Saint Justa, undated, Meadows Museum, Dallas; white maiolica
bowl, unglazed *cántaro*.
Saint Rufina, undated, Meadows Museum, Dallas; two dimpled
and handled white maiolica jars.

FRANCISCO DE ZURBARÁN
Santa Rufina, ca. 1641–58, Fitzwilliam Museum, Cambridge;
white maiolica plates and bowls.
Santa Rufina, ca. 1641–58, National Gallery of Ireland, Dublin;
white maiolica pitcher and jar.
Santa Rufina, ca. 1641–58, Cathedral, Sevilla; white maiolica
plates and bowls.
Santa Justa, ca. 1641–58, private collection, Paris; white maiolica
plates and bowls.
Still Life with a Basket of Flowers, ca. 1660, private collection,
Sevilla; two-handled white maiolica cup.
Still Life with Oranges, ca. 1633, Norton Simon Museum, Los
Angeles; two-handled white maiolica cup.
Still Life with Jars, ca. 1635, Prado, Madrid; two-handled white
maiolica (?) jars, red jar.
The Virgin as a Child, with Saint Joachim and Saint Anne, c. 1631–40,
private collection, Florence; two-handled white maiolica cup.
The Miraculous Cure of Blessed Reginald of Orleans, c. 1626–27,
Church of the Magdalan, Sevilla; two-handled white maiolica
cup.
The Virgin of the Annunciation, ca. 1658–64, Juan March Founda-
tion, Palma de Mallorca; two-handled white maiolica jar.
The Adoration of the Shepherds, ca. 1625–30, private collection, Bar-
celona; two-handled jar with partial white maiolica glaze.
The Adoration of the Shepherds, 1638, Museum, Grenoble; white
maiolica plate, two-handled jar with partial white maiolica
glaze.
Christ at Emmaus, 1639, Academy of Fine Arts of San Carlos,
Mexico City; white maiolica plates, pitcher with partial white
maiolica glaze.
Christ at Emmaus, 1631–40, Private collection, Madrid; white
maiolica plates, pitcher with partial white maiolica glaze.
The Adoration of Saint Joseph, ca. 1629, private collection, Geneva;
white maiolica plate, two-handled jar with partial glaze.

The Virgin Suckling the Child Jesus, 1658, Pushkin State Museum of
    Fine Arts, Moscow; small two-handled white maiolica jar.
The Virgin as a Child, Praying, ca. 1631–40, Metropolitan Museum
    of Art, New York; small white maiolica two-handled (?) jar.
The Miracle of Saint Hugh, ca. 1633, Museo de Bellas Artes, Sevilla;
    white maiolica plates, two-handled jars with escutcheon of
    Gonzalo de Mena (Bishop of Sevilla, who had founded Car-
    thusian Chapter of that city in 1400), Chinese porcelain cup.
Saint Dominic, ca. 1641–58, University, Sevilla; small, handled
    white maiolica jar.
Saint Benedict, ca. 1641–58, Convent of the Capuchin Nuns,
    Castellón de la Plena; small, handled white maiolica jar.
Saint Benedict, ca. 1641–58, private collection, New York; small,
    handled white maiolica jar.

Appendix 2

Sixteenth-Century Spanish Shipping Records Containing References to Ceramics and Architectural Terra Cottas

DIEGO COLÓN FLOTA FROM SEVILLA, 1509
(Otté 1964: 482–88, 490–93, 495–502)
Destination: Santo Domingo [Dominican Republic]

Santa María; Alonso Pérez, Captain
El Señor Gobernador: 4500 *tejas*
Alonso Gorjón: 3 *jarras de vino*; 10 *jarras de vinagre*; 3 *jarras de pasas*
El Escribano: 2 *jarras de almendras, pasas, e higos*
El contramaestre: 7 *jarras de pasas e higos*
Juan de Castellanos: 2 *jarras de higos y pasas*
Orozco: 1 *jarra de pasas*
Gorjón: 7 *jarras de vino*
Fernán Lorenzo: 7 *jarras de pasas*; 13 *jarras de vino*
Francisco Robledo: 171 *jarras de vino*; 10 *cantaritas de aceitunas*
Ortíz: 4 *jarras de berenjenas y aceitunas*
Alonso de la Palma: 4500 *ladrillos*
Diego Márquez: 3 *botijas de aceite*
Alonso Martín: 1 *jarra de harina*; 1 *jarra de vino*; 1 *jarra de garabanzos*
Bernardo Grimaldi: 2 *cajas con 36 botes de conserva de Valencia*;
  azulejos de holanda

Santa María Antigua; Diego Rodríguez, Captain
Diego Fernández de Morón, *ollero* (one of guarantors): 400 *vasos
  de loza*; 140 *seras de azulejos*; 40 *tinajas verdes*; 100 *morteros*;
  2 *pilas verdes*
Juan Cristóbal: 100 *jarras de miel*
Diego Rodríguez: 90 *jarras de vino*; 80 *jarras (de media arroba) de
  pasas*
Maestre Gonzalo Rodríguez: 6 *jarras de vino*
Alonso de Baena: 2 *jarreticas de aceitunas*

Santa María Magdalena; Diego Díaz, Captain
Diego de León y Alonso de Burgos: 13 *jarras de aceitunas*; 50
  arrobas (en 100 botijas) de aceite; 6 *botijas (de media azumbre) de
  miel*
El maestre Díaz: 52 *jarras de aceitunas*; 1500 *ladrillos*
Pedro de la Palma: 1500 *ladrillos*
Briones: 2000 *tejas*
El maestre de la chapinera: 1500 *tejas*

San Juan; Cristóbal Valles, Captain
Briones: 6000 *tejas*; 6 *seras de azulejos*

Juan de Burgos: 30 *botijas (de 1 arroba) de aceite;* 229 *botijas (de media arroba) de aceite;* 89 *botijas (de cuartilla) de aceite*
Un pasajero: 8 *botijas (de media arroba) de vino*
El maestre Cristóbal Valles: 3 *jarras de pasas*
El contramaestre: 2 *jarras de pasas*
Pedro Méndez: 5 *jarras de fruta y salgas*
Cristóbal Sánchez: 8 *jarras de vino;* 3 *jarras de fruta*

Santa Clara; Juan Gutiérrez, Captain
El jurado Nicolás de Durango: 5 *jarras de aceitunas*
El maestre Juan Gutiérrez: 8 *jarras de vino*
Alonso Gutiérrez: 31 *jarras de vino;* 23 *botijas de vinagre*
Rodrigo Remolar: 2 *jarras de pasas*
Briones: 3000 *tejas*

Santa María; San Juan de Solórzano, Captain
El contado Diego Méndez: 2 *jarretas de aceitunas;* 1 *jarreta de vinagre*
Lorenzo de Ahumada: 20 *jarretas de alquitrán*
Hontiveros: 3 *botes de conservas*

San Telmo; Diego Vicente, Captain
Jurado Durango: 5 *cántaros (4 de cobre, 1 de barro) con almendras*
El escribano: 40 *vasos de loza*

Santa Ana; Diego Sánchez Colchero, Captain
Piloto: 2 *jarretas de sábalos*
Juan de Valencia: 1 *canasta de loza*
Briones: 2000 *tejas*
Diego de Ocaña: 4 *botijas de aceite;* 1 *jarro de manteca*
Diego de Zayas: 2 *botes de conservas*
El alcalde mayor: 2000 *tejas;* 2000 *ladrillos;* 3 *botes de conservas*
Bachiller Serrano: 5 *botijas de aceite;* 2 *botijas de aceitunas;* 5 *cazuelas de carne de membrillo*

Santa María; Bartolomé Rodríguez Tiscareño, Captain
Bernardo Grimaldi: 8000 *ladrillos;* 9 *cajas de loza de Valencia*
Juan Díaz: 100 *botijas (de 1 arroba) de aceite*
Antonio Catalán: 2 *jarretas de aceitunas;* 103 *botes de azucar rosado*

La Trinidad; Juan Ortíz, Captain
García de Sorbe: 12 *botijas de aceite;* 6 *botijas de vinagre*
Juan de Jérez: 1000 *ladrillos*
Miguel de Vanar: 10 *jarretas de aceitunas*
Francisco de Fuentes: 1 *jarreta de vino;* 5 *botes de conservas*
El secretario del almirante: 2 *jarras de aceitunas*
Villaverde y Alonso de Soto: 2 *botes de conserva*
Domingo de Atienza: 50 *imágenes esmaltadas de color* [possibly earthenware]
Gómez Díaz: 1 *bote de naranjada*
Juan Fernández, barbero: 18 *botijas (de media arroba) de aceite*
Sotomayor: 2 *botes de conservas, azafrán, pimienta, y canela*
Juan de Mesa: 4 *botijas (2 arrobas en total) de aceite;* 1 *jarra de aceitunas verdes*
Sebastián Marro: 1 *botija de aceite;* 1 *botija de vinagre*
El licenciado Carrillo: 3 *jarretas de vino*
Juan de Porras: 30 *botijas de aceite*
El alcalde mayor Marcos de Aguilar: 21 *botijas (de 1 arroba) de aceite;* 48 *botijas (de media arroba) de aceite;* 1000 *ladrillos*

Santiago; Juan de Jérez, Captain
Diego Méndez y el secretario del almirante: 16 *botijas (de 1 arroba) de aceite;* 2 *botijas (de cuarta) de aceite*

Francisco García Mondragón: 46 *botijas (de media arroba) de aceite*
Pedro Arana: 7 *botijas (de media arroba) de aceite*
Francisco de Cuenca: 1 *jarra de almendras*; 2 *jarras de pasas*; 4 *jarras
de aceitunas*
El maestre Juan de Jérez: 5 *jarras de pasas*, 3 *jarras de aceitunas*;
4000 *ladrillos*

San Miguel; Manuel Cansino, Captain
El boticario: 60 *botes medianos en que van las medicinas*; 105 *botes de
barro en que van las medicinas*; 12 *albornías*; 26 *tablas*
Luis Ramírez y Juan de Villegas: 2 *botijas de aceite*; 2 *botijas de miel*
Cristóbal de Sotomayor: 2 *jarros de miel*

Santiago; Pedro Grande, Captain
Juan de Nájara: 20 *jarras de vinagre*; 24 *botijas (de 1 arroba) de
vinagre*; 7 *jarras de aceitunas*; 70 *botijas (de cuartillo) de aceite*
Domingo de Atencia: 40 *botijas (de cuarta) de aceite*; 2900 *tejas*
Alvaro de Briones: 170 *vasos de loza blanca*
Juan de Villoria: 1 *cesta de loza*

Santa María del Antigua; Lope Sánchez, Captain
Miguel Criado: 5000 *ladrillos*
Alonso de Salina: 40 *cazuelas* [possibly earthenware]
El prior de Magazela: 2 *botes de conservas*
Alvaro de Briones: 8 *cántaros*; 2 *ollas*
Blas Méndez: 2 *jarretas de harina*; 3 *botijas de miel*

Santa María de Consolación; Pedro González Romero, Captain
Alvaro Sandoval para el tesorero Miguel de Pasamonte:
4 *jarretas de vinagre*; 1 *jarreta de aceitunas*; 2 *botijas de miel*
Bernaldino de Isla: 99 *botijas (de media arroba) de aceite*; 92 *botijas (de
cuartillo) de aceite*; 31 *botijas de vinagre*; 29 *botijas (de media arroba)
de vinagre*
Alonso de Gumiel: 101 *botijas (de media arroba) de aceite*; 150 *botijas
(de cuartillo) de aceite*
Pedro González Romero: 1000 *ladrillos*
El contramaestre, el escribano, y 3 marineros: 2000 *ladrillos*

Santo Domingo; Juan de Medina, Captain
Pedro de Jérez: 1 *jarrilla de conserva*
El piloto: 41 *jarros de miel*; 1 *jarreta de aceitunas*;
Morales, maestre: 2000 *tejas y ladrillos*
Juan Suárez: 47 *jarros de miel*; 1 *bote con 1 arroba de alcaparras*

Santa Catalina; Diego Bernal, Captain
Bernaldino de Isla: 130 *botijas de a cuarta de aceite*; 90 *botijas de a
media arroba de aceite*; 74 *botijas de vinagre*

Santa María; Pedro de Balzola, Captain
Alonso de Santa Clara: 6 *botijas de aceite*; 2 *jarretas de aceitunas*

Santa María de la Victoria; Tomás Sánchez, Captain
Juan Jiménez de España y compañeros: 8 *jarras de pez*
Tomás Sánchez, maestre: 3000 *ladrillos*; 203 *jarros de miel (de hasta
1 azumbre)*; 7 *jarras de arroz*

SHIPMENTS IN 1523 FROM SEVILLA
(España, Archivo General de Indias, Contratación 1079)
Destination: Santo Domingo [Dominican Republic]
Juan Rodríguez de Bastidas to himself: 3 *seras de azulejos*
Alonso de Jérez to himself: 10 *candeleros*
Bartolomé Sánchez to himself: 50 *vasos de loza*
Francisco Alvarez to himself: 68 *bacines*, 11 *bacines blancos grandes*,
13 *vasos de jarricos e pequeños*, 12 *jarros de pico blancos*

Beatriz Alvarez to Inez de Escobar: 22 *vasos de jarricos*, 10 *vasos de escudillas*
Gabriel Baitan to himself: 150 *vasos de loza*

SHIPMENTS IN 1542 FROM SEVILLA
(España, Sevilla, Archivo de Protocolos 1932(2): 134, 139; (3): 58, 60–61, 66, 68)
Destination: Tierra Firme [Colombia]
Alonso Pérez to Fernando de Jérez and Juan Martínez: 5000 *tejas*
Pedro Rodríguez Quintero to Sebastián Ruiz and Alonso Martínez: 20 *botijas peruleras por cada de 35 pipas de vino*

Destination: Nombre de Dios [Panamá]
Clemente de Santana to Fernán Pérez Jarada: 6 *toneladas de botijas*
Cosme Buitrón to Luis Alvarez: 400 *botijas peruleras*
Alonso de Illescas and Fernán Sánchez Dalvo: 12 *pipas de vino, cada con 22 botijas peruleras vacías*
Juan Ortíz to Alonso de Illescas and Fernando Sánchez Dalvo: 400 *botijas peruleras vacías y 20 pipas de vino*
Pedro Milanes to Gonzalo and Gaspar Jorge: 25 *botijas peruleras por cada uno de 20 pipas de vino*

Destination: Puerto Caballos [Honduras]
Lorenzo García to Antón López: 6 *toneladas de tejas*; 150 *botijas peruleras*

SHIPMENTS IN 1546 FROM SEVILLA
(España, Sevilla, Archivo de Protocolos 1932(3): 89, 94–95, 113, 122)
Destination: Tierra Firme [Colombia]
Diego de Quesada to Juan Galvarro: 10 *pipas, cada con 7 botijas peruleras vacías*

Destination: Nombre de Dios [Panamá]
Tomé de la Isla to Pedro de Sanlúcar and Martín de Flores: 38–40 *pipas, cada con 15 botijas peruleras vacías*
Cristóbal Martín to Pedro Días de Baeza: 150 *botijas peruleras vacías*
Andrés Pérez to Gonzalo and Gaspar Jorge: 16 *pipas cada con 70 botijas peruleras vacías*
Juan de Azcora to Ruy Díaz de Gibraleón: 6 *pipas y 100 botijas peruleras*

SHIPMENTS IN 1548 FROM SEVILLA
(España, Sevilla, Archivo de Protocolos 1932 (3): 126, 132, 134–35, 138)
Destination: Nombre de Dios [Panamá]
Cosme Rodríguez Farfán to Diego Montesinos and Juan Rodríguez: 20 *pipas, cada con 15 botijas peruleras vacías*
Cosme Rodríguez Farfán to Juan de Montesdoca: 15 *toneladas de vino, cada con 15 botijas peruleras vacías*
Cosme Rodríguez Farfán to Ruy Díaz de Gibraleón: 15 *toneladas de vino, cada con 18 botijas peruleras vacías*
Francisco de Vallejo to Luis Sánchez Dalvo: 40 *pipas, de vino, cada con 15 botijas peruleras*
Lorenzo de Villarreal to Juanes de Saucedo and Alonso Díaz de León: 10 *pipas de vino, cada con 20 botijas peruleras*

Destination: San Juan de Ulua [México]
Tomé de la Isla to Diego and Pedro Caballero: 100 *pipas y* 3 *toneladas de botijas peruleras*

SHIPMENT IN 1549 FROM SEVILLA
(España, Sevilla, Archivo de Protocolos 1932 (3): 155)
Destination: Vera Cruz [México]
Gomez Hurtado to Gonzalo Ruin de Córdoba: 80 *arrobas de aceite
en botijas*

SHIPMENT IN 1549 FROM SEVILLA
(España, Sevilla, Archivo de Protocolos 1935: 210, 216, 219)
Destination: Nombre de Dios [Panamá]
Sebastián González to Alonso Cabezas: 30 *pipas de vino, en cada
una* 17 *botijas peruleras*
Lorenzo García to Diego y Pedro Caballero: 50 *pipas de vino, en
cada una* 15 *botijas peruleras vacías; cuatro toneladas de botijas llenas
de vinagre*
Francisco Galdámez to Francisco de Sanlúcar: 40 *pipas de vino,* 100
botijas peruleras vacías; 10,000 *tejas vidriadas*
Juan de Nápoles to Fernán Pérez Jarada y Fernán Pérez de la
Fuente: 24 *pipas de vino, con cada una* 22 *botijas peruleras*

SHIPMENTS IN 1550 FROM SEVILLA
(España, Sevilla, Archivo de Protocolos 1935: 269–70, 292)
Destination: Nombre de Dios [Panamá]
Juan López to Gaspar de Cazalla: 50 *pipas de vino, y en cada con*
20 *botijas peruleras vacías; una tonelada de botijas de vinagre;
una tonelada de botijas de aceitunas;* 50 *arrobas de aceite en botijas*
Juan Olines to Diego y Pedro Caballero: 40 *pipas de vino, en
cada una* 18 *botijas peruleras*
Alonso Pérez to Fernán Núñez y Gonzalo Mostrenco: 60 *pipas de
vino, y con cada una* 20 *botijas peruleras vacías;* 3000 *tejas vidriadas;
por el millar de tejas que llegasen sanas* 6000 *maravedíes*

SHIPMENTS IN 1551 FROM SEVILLA
(España, Sevilla, Archivo de Protocolos 1935: 343–4, 347, 385,
409)
Destination: Nombre de Dios [Panamá]
Martín García to Gaspar de Cazalla: 50 *pipas de vino, y con cada una*
20 *botijas peruleras vacías*
Martín García to Gaspar de Cazalla: 50 *pipas de vino, y con cada una*
20 *botijas peruleras vacías*
Alonso de la Barrera to Gómez de la Fuente: 30 *pipas de vino,*
500 *botijas peruleras*
Diego Rodríguez Morzillo to Diego y Pedro Caballero: 40 *pipas de
vino, y con cada una* 18 *botijas peruleras vacías; cinco toneladas
de aceite y vinagre en botijas*
Alonso de Bolaños to Luis Sánchez Dalvo: 66 *pipas de vino, y con
cada una* 20 *botijas peruleras*
Domingo de Ancheta to Luis García: 35 *toneladas* of merchandise,
including wine and unspecified number of *botijas peruleras
vacías*

SHIPMENTS IN 1551 FROM SANTA CRUZ DE LA PALMA,
CANARY ISLANDS
(Morales Padrón 1955: 320–37)
Destination: Nombre de Dios [Panamá]
Ship: *Santiago*
400 *botijas peruleras vacías;* 40 *botijas peruleras de vinagre*

Destination: Santo Domingo [Dominican Republic]
Ship: *Santo Espíritu*
415 *botijas peruleras;* 1 *serón que lleva* 3 *vasos de calderas,*

12 *candeleros y* 15 *basinicas de cámara;* 35 *botijas de aceite;* 150
botijas de ½ a [arroba]

Destination: Puerto Rico
Ship: *San Bartolomé*
    75 *botijas peruleras de vinagre;* 23 *botijas peruleras de vino;*
    7 *botijas de vinagre*

Destination: Puerto Rico and Santo Domingo [Dominican
Republic]
Ship: *La Concepción*
    6 *botes de azafrán (7½ libras)*

Destination: Unnamed
Ship: *Santiago*
    20 *botijas de miel (herreña);* 37 *botijas de vinagre;* 1 *caja de loza de*
    Génova

SHIPMENTS IN 1567, ONE FROM SANTA CRUZ DE LA PALMA, THREE
FROM SANTA CRUZ DE TENERIFE, CANARY ISLANDS
(Morales Padrón 1955: 320–37)
Destination: New Spain [México]
Ship: *Santiago*
    425 *botijas de vino;* 70 *botijas peruleras de vino*
Ship: *San Sebastián*
    100 *botijas peruleras*
Ship: *Nuestra Señora de la India*
    230 *botijas peruleras de vino;* 220 *botijas peruleras;* 149 *botijas*
    peruleras; 90 *botijas peruleras de vino*

Destination: Cartagena de Indias [Colombia]
Ship: *Nuestra Señora de la Encarnación*
    1000 *botijas peruleras de vino;* 7 *botijas peruleras de vino;*
    199 *botijas de vino;* 60 *botijas peruleras de vino*

SHIPMENTS IN 1572 FROM SEVILLA
(España, Sevilla, Archivo de Protocolos 1932 (1): 403, 404, 406,
    407, 408)
Destination: Tierra Firme [Colombia]
Juan de Ribera to Melchor de Ledesma: 400 *botijas peruleras*
    llenadas
Juan de Ribera to Tomás Convergel: 1000 *botijas peruleras llenadas*
Vincencio Garullo Centurión to Pedro de Vargas: 2000 *botijas*
    peruleras llenadas
Miguel Ramírez to Juan de la Barrera: 700 *botijas peruleras*
    llenadas
Rodrigo González to Juan de Baeza: 1000 *botijas peruleras llenadas*
Antón Manzera to Hernando de Cantillana: 300 *botijas peruleras*
    llenadas

SHIPMENTS IN 1574 FROM SEVILLA
(España, Sevilla, Archivo de Protocolos 1932 (1): 415)
Destination: New Spain [México]
    Vicente Centurión to Hernan Pérez Roldan: 500 *botijas*
    peruleras

Destination: Honduras
    Vicente Centurión to Diego Almonte: 15 *toneladas de botijas*
    peruleras

SHIPMENTS IN 1580 FROM SEVILLA.
(España, Sevilla, Archivo de Protocolos 1932 (2): 222, 302, 385,
    394, 398, 413, 446)
Destination: Tierra Firme [Colombia]
    Lorenzo Bautista Escoto to Juan de Palacios and Gabriel de
    Herrera: 100 *botijas peruleras*
    Pedro Martínez de Oñate to Juan López de Solis: 300 *botijas*
    peruleras llenas de vino, las 150 de Cazalla de la Sierra y las otras
    de Manzanilla
    Alonso Pabon to Lope de Tapia: 340 *botijas peruleras llenadas*

Destination: Cartagena [Colombia]
    Juan Bautista de Medina to Jerónimo de Hojeda: 15 *botijas*
    peruleras

Destination: Santo Domingo [Dominican Republic]
    Alonso Pabon to Estéban Pérez and Francisco de Ribero:
    600 *botijas peruleras llenadas*; 600 *vasos de loza*

Destination: Campeche [México]
    100 *toneladas de pipas y botijas*

SHIPMENT IN 1583 FROM SEVILLA.
(España, Archivo General de Indias, Contratación 1080)
Destination: Tierra Firme [Colombia]
    García de Azaoz to Pedro Rodríguez: *escudillas dos docenas a*
    16 reales, 1088 maravedíes
    García del Covedo to Pedro López Treviño: *caja quintaleña que*
    lleva 17 docenas de loza blanca y azul hecha en Triana a 5 reales
    docena, 2890 maravedíes; cajón tosco en que van 8 docenas de jarros
    blancos y 12 escudillas hecho en Triana a 4 reales docena, 1088; caja
    de a vara lleva 9 docenas de loza a 4 reales docena

SHIPMENTS IN 1590 FROM SEVILLA.
(España, Archivo General de Indias, Contratación 1089, 1090,
    1091)
Destination: San Cristóbal de la Habana [Cuba]
    Pedro de Carvajal to himself: 6 *cantimploras a 10 reales, 3040*
    maravedíes
    Andrés de Allura to himself or to Antonio Bermúdez Manso:
    10 *vaso de loza de Triana en 80 reales, 2720 maravedíes*
    No sender given: *una caja de loza blanca de Sevilla en 22*
    ducados, 8250 maravedíes
    Gaspar Tamayo to Rodrigo Madera: 200 *vasos de loza blanca de*
    Triana, costo a 34 maravedíes cada vaso

Destination: Santo Domingo [Dominican Republic]
    Francisco López Olivos to Salvador de Baeza: 12 *pares de*
    candeleros de Sevilla a 12 reales, 4896 maravedíes
    Francisco de Bivero to Juan Beltran de Caizedo: 12 *esendillas*
    [escudillas?] *negras a real cada una, 408 maravedíes*
    Baltasár de Riberos to himself: 12 *cajas en fue van 419 docenas*
    de platos y esendillas [escudillas?] *azules de Talavera, costo cada*
    docena 2 reales y medio, 1047 reales; 2 cajas de loza de Talavera
    azul y blanca 53 docenas fue costo cada docena una con otra a
    4 reales, 212 reales; 200 vasos de loza de Triana costo cada vaso a
    24 maravedíes, 141 reales
    Fernando Laynez to Luis de Benavides: 52 *docena de platos*
    chicos y tazas de 12 en docena a 3 reales y medio la docena, 6188
    maravedíes

Destination: New Spain [México]
   Francisco de Santa Cruz [consignee not given]: 8 *pares de
   candeleros de Sevilla a 15 reales el par*, 4080 *maravedíes*
   Francisco López Olivos to Juan López de Ribera: 20 *pares de
   candeleros sevillanos a 12 reales*, 8160 *maravedíes*
   Gaspar Pérez to Pedro Fernández de Torquemada: 11 *pares de
   candeleros de Sevilla a 15 reales el par*, 5610 *maravedíes*

Destination: Isla Margarita [Venezuela]
   Jerónimo de Velasco, in name of Antonio Hernández
   [consignee not given]: 100 *vasos de loza de Triana a real vaso*,
   3400 *maravedíes*

SHIPMENTS IN 1592 AND 1593 FROM SEVILLA.
(España, Archivo General de Indias, Contratación 1099, 1100)
Destination: San Cristóbal de Habana [Cuba]
   Bartolomé Bernal to himself: 50 *vasos de loza basta de Triana*

Destination: Santo Domingo [Dominican Republic]
   Esteban de Ulloa to Alonso de Ulloa de Toro: 11 *cajones
   quintaleños marcados con* ℞* ; *los cajones llevan* 102 *docenas de
   loza azul hecha en Sevilla a 4 reales la docena;* 15 *docenas de loza
   blanca hecha en Sevilla, todos platos y escudillas, a 6 reales la
   docena;* 4 *cajones quintaleños marcados tambien con* ℞* *llevan* 36
   docenas de loza azul hecha en Sevilla a 4 reales cada una

Destination: Coban de la Verapaz [Honduras]
   Pedro de Mendoza to Convento de Santo Domingo: 6
   candeleros de Sevilla a 14 reales y medio el par

Destination: Puerto Caballos [Honduras]
   Agustín de Nolique to Dalmacio Martín: *tres cajas con* 150
   docenas de loza azul a 4 reales cada docena, 20,400 *maravedíes*

Destination: Vera Cruz [México]
   Agustín de Nolique to himself: 100 *vasos de loza basta en*
   100 *reales*

Notes

Notes to History of the Craft

1. Almagro Basch 1946:13–133; Blanco Freijeiro 1979:91–2; García y Bellido 1946a:137–98.

2. García y Bellido 1946b:199–300; Malaquer de Motes et al 1957:599–765; Nicocini 1974:162.

3. The *kabal* used in southern and eastern Mexico differs from a slow wheel in not being pivoted. It is merely a wooden disk, often waxed on its under surface, resting on a board on the ground. It is a turntable revolved by the potter's feet, sometimes very rapidly. However, it cannot move under its own momentum. There is no known historical connection to any pre-wheel device in the Old World, as the *kabal* appears to have been a pre-Columbian invention. For detailed discussions, see Foster 1959a:53–63; 1959b:108; Shepard 1956:61–2; Whitaker and Whitaker 1978:36, 80, 83.

4. Mata Carriazo 1973:474; Scheufler 1968:2. Foster 1959a:61–2 argues that as few as sixty revolutions per minute are sufficient for throwing, but most modern potters prefer higher velocities. Foster 1959b:109 outlines an evolutionary sequence from unpivoted turntable, to pivoted turntable, to simple (single) wheel, to double (compound or kick) wheel.

5. Arribas 1964:166–7; González Martí 1954:29; Hispanic Society of America 1938:105. For in-depth discussion of the evolution of kiln types, see Hodges, H. 1970:67; Scheufler 1968:3; Scott 1954:391–7.

6. García y Bellido 1946a:137–98; Nicocini 1974:158–62.

7. Ortíz Muñoz 1973:37–44.

8. Forbes 1965c:128 discusses Roman exploitation of Spanish tin deposits. Dayton 1971:49–70 reports Spanish tin in the Levant as having been exploited as early as Troy II trading times, or ca. 2500–2300 B.C.

9. Sutherland 1939; Wiseman 1956.

10. Bonsor 1931:17, 21, Figs. XIII, XIV, XXI, XXII.

11. Beltrán Lloris 1978:Pls. LXVII, LXVIII, and Peacock 1974:232–44 provide the best descriptions of Spanish Roman amphora use. Rothschild-Boros 1981:79–89 describes high sensitivity sequential chromatographic methods used to determine former contents of a sample of amphorae recovered in Italy. Such analysis is made possible because of absorption by unglazed walls of retained organic residue.

12. Forbes 1956:663–94.

13. For sample of such stamped seals, see Hernández Días et al 1939(3):Fig. 37. For painted inscriptions, see Callender 1965:19–22.

14. Bonsor 1931:60; Hernández Días et al 1939(2):111; Hispanic Society of America 1938:108; Peacock 1974:232–44.

15. Torres, P. 1982.

16. Bonsor 1931:60. James 1985:41 notes the mass of amphorae were periodically covered with layers of quick lime to reduce the foul odors of rancid olive oil.

17. Numerous examples of the incorporation into the haunches of vaulted structures of whole earthenwares have been noted in Rome and its port of Ostia after the second century. Fifth- and sixth-century Byzantine masons continued this practice in their capital of Ravenna and elsewhere (Anderson 1927:37, 82; Arslan 1967:Fig. 324; Blake, M.E. 1973:91, 99, 103, 179, 242, 256, 278; Fletcher 1961:Fig. 285D; Grace 1956:Fig. 68). Both groups followed similar methods in their colonial buildings in Spain, examples having been observed in Catalonia and the vicinity of Granada (Guasch 1963:Figs. 2 [1–2], 4 [1–2]; Puig i Cadafalch 1927–31:114). Callender 1965:30 notes the use of Baetican amphorae as urinals in Hadrian's wall in Britain.

18. Sotomayor 1972:263; Sotomayor et al 1976:113–42.

19. Sayas Abengochea 1957:707–11; Taracena 1946:168–72; Zozaya 1969a:134.

20. Richter 1956:273.

21. For that reason, whether the wheels were balanced by lead weights, as is known from Roman shops elsewhere, cannot be determined (Matson 1955:38).

22. Bonsor 1931:Fig. XXIII; Callender 1965:19–22; González 1951:400; Hernández Días et al 1939(2):71, 108; Hispanic Society of America 1938:108–9; Taracena 1946:168–72. Peacock 1974:232–44 discusses the evidence for seafood containers, noting the light clays of the lower Guadalquivir in contrast to jars from elsewhere along the southern Spanish coast with different physical composition.

23. Daumas 1969 (1):231.

24. Hodges, H. 1970:Fig. 172; Richter 1956:Fig. 237.

25. Pope, E.M. 1956:Fig. 282.

26. Hernández Días et al 1939(2):Fig. 29.

27. Daumas 1969 (1):233.

28. Pope, E.M. (1956:297) describes Roman kilns in general. Sotomayor et al. (1976:113–42) note Spanish kilns in Andalusia, but no kiln designed exclusively for the manufacture of *terra sigillata* is mentioned. These authors are in disagreement over Roman use of saggars, but cockspurs are recorded in instances where glaze ware was being fired.

29. Bonsor 1931:31; Bosch Gimpera et al 1935:344.

30. Richter 1956:273, Fig. 255.

31. Blanco Freijeiro 1979:167–9; Davillier 1949:409; Delaney and Tobin 1961:639; García Rodríguez 1966:231–4; Morgada 1887:28–35.

32. Thursdon and Attwater 1963(3):145.

33. Payne 1973(1):9.

34. Zozaya 1969a:134; 1981b:38.

35. Torres Balbás 1957:656, 658, Fig. 451; Zozaya 1969a:133–4.

36. Zozaya 1969a:134.

37. Thompson 1969:16.

38. Dozy 1978:146.

39. Lewis, A. 1978:8.

40. Glick 1979:55–6.

41. Ibid:29.

42. Forbes 1965a:1–79 sees a Persian origin for the *noria*. Torres Balbás 1940:197 provides a relevant description of water wheels on the Guadalquivir.

43. Rodinson 1973:1, 51.

44. López and Raymond 1970:30–8.
45. Payne 1973(1);18–9.
46. Barraclough 1976:14–20; Pirenne 1937:4–5.
47. Zozaya, pers. comm. 1983.
48. Although a forbidden drink for faithful Muslims, wine continued to be produced for Jewish and Christian consumers; it was legalized for Muslims by 'Abd al Rahman II in the ninth century (Glick 1979:80; Lévi-Provencal 1957:161).
49. Lewis, H. 1978:8fn.20.
50. There were 5,000 thirteenth-century *norias de sangre* in the Córdoba area. A very large *noria de vuelo* was on the Guadalquivir beside a dam, some mills, and an aqueduct. The extant ruins date from the Christian period, but a similar ninth-century complex existed on the same spot. Although both types of wheels made use of earthen jars, the vertical model more often was equipped with wooden receptacles (Glick 1979:75; Torres Balbás 1940:203). Supplemental data appear in Lévi-Provencal 1957:Figs. 32–3, and Smith, N. 1976:13–4, Fig. 3.
51. Typical specimens of a later horizon measured at the Museo Arqueológico Provincial de Sevilla varied from 41 to 48 cm ht., 20 to 23.5 cm diam.
52. Glick 1979:239.
53. Redman 1983:374–5; Zozaya 1969a:135, Fig. 45; 1981b:37; however, photograph on 40 of suggested Berber introductions shows obvious wheel-turned vessels. It is possible, as in parts of modern Berber Morocco, that handbuilt vessels were finished on a pit wheel and were fired in a rudimentary kiln consisting of a single subterranean fuel pit, with vessels to be baked merely covered with potsherds (see Fig. 157).
54. Pope, E.M. 1956:290 discusses compacting clay to prevent cracking. For discussions of forms possibly made during the early Muslim era on the borders of modern Andalusia, see Duda 1972:Pls. 67–92; Zozaya 1983:430–516.
55. Daumas 1969 (1):364.
56. Ainaud de Lasarte 1952:Figs. 29, 126–8, 213–4.
57. Amiran 1965:240–7; Hodges, H. 1970:65–6; Kingery 1980:598–600; Singer et al 1954 (1):199.
58. Charleston 1968:13–4.
59. See Grabar 1976:69–88 for discussion of influence of classical Rome and Byzantium on early Islamic manifestations in Syria.
60. Smith, R.M. 1965:43.
61. Chejne 1980:114; Payne 1973(1):25.
62. On the unity of all medieval culture under Roman Catholicism, Greek Byzantine Catholicism, and Islam, see Deutsch 1967:247–60.
63. Lewis, A. 1978:20.
64. Singer et al 1954(2):770–1 lists twenty-six different technologies that spread from China to the West.
65. Chejne 1980:110–33; Glick 1979:22; Needham 1949:135–45.
66. Torres Balbás 1947:446.
67. Payne 1973(1):25.
68. Lévi-Provencal 1957:182, 235.
69. Ibid:242.
70. Duda 1972:345–432, Pls. 67–92; Gómez Moreno 1951a:Figs. 376f–g, 377a–b; Pavón Maldonado 1972:Fig. 495; Torres Balbás 1957:773–4.
71. Lévi-Provencal 1957:139. Into the sixteenth and seventeenth centuries, *azumbre* in Mexico remained a term for a liquid measurement of four pints (Carrera Stampa 1949:5–6).

72. Pope, E.M. 1956:300.
73. Lane 1937:33.
74. Stevenson 1954:89. See also, Philon 1980:59, Fig. 128 for a fragment from North Africa with yellow glaze.
75. Grabar 1976:78.
76. Torres Balbás 1957:564, 700. Zozaya 1969a:136 states that Byzantine potters were present, but gives no supporting documentation.
77. Singer et al 1954(2):753–76.
78. Pavón Maldonado 1966; 1967:415–37; 1968:206–19; 1972:191–227.
79. Zozaya 1981b:38.
80. Lerner 1978:Fig. 38.
81. Charleston 1968:14.
82. Grube 1976:59.
83. Charleston 1968:102, Fig. 302c; Copplestone and Myers 1970:27, Fig. 34; Pavón Maldonado 1967:415–37, 457–8; 1972:Figs. 1–7, 9–11; Talbot Rice 1965b:199, 203–4; Zozaya 1981b:42–5.
84. Talbot Rice 1965b:Fig. 8.
85. Allan 1971:11, Fig. 6; Grube 1976:64; Pavón Maldonado 1972:Fig. 256; Santos 1952:401–3; Torres Balbás 1957:778.
86. Torres Balbás 1957:Figs. 652, 655, 657–9.
87. Rosselló-Bordoy 1981:271–6.
88. Gómez Moreno 1951b:374; Pavón Maldonado 1972:Figs. 20–6; Rosselló-Bordoy 1981:271–6; Torres Balbás 1957:780, Figs. 652, 655, 657–9; Zbiss 1956:Figs. 10–3, Pl. IV.
89. Grube 1976:64.
90. Zozaya 1981b:39.
91. Gómez Moreno 1951a:313; Llubiá 1967:Fig. 26.
92. Pavón Maldonado 1967:415–47; 1972:415; Zbiss 1956:Figs. 10–13.
93. Gómez Moreno 1951a:34; Llubiá 1967:Fig. 12; Pavón Maldonado 1972:Fig. 12; Torres Balbás 1957:724.
94. Zozaya 1981b:40.
95. Ainaud de Lasarte 1952:Fig. 384; Charleston 1968:145; Gómez Moreno 1951a:323; Lane 1937:32; Llubiá 1967:Fig. 46; Torres Balbás 1957:782.
96. Gómez Moreno 1951a:323; Torres Balbás 1957:Figs. 662, 663; 1959:221–34.
97. Ainaud de Lasarte 1952:Fig. 381; Frothingham 1951:2, 6–7, Figs. 1–2; Gómez Moreno 1951a:314; Hispanic Society of America 1938:112; Lane 1958:6; Pavón Maldonado 1972:195; Torres Balbás 1957:781; Velázquez Bosco 1912:Figs. XLIX, L, LI, LII; Wilber 1968:22. Ettinghausen (1954:133–56) identifies one Spanish fragment (Fig. 35c) as having a motif of a camel bearing a litter, or 'otfeh, with possible zodiacal meaning, and sees a similarity to a complete specimen now in the Detroit Institute of Art.
98. Hill 1976:143; Talbot Rice 1965a:42; Wilber 1968:22; Zbiss 1956:Fig. 4.
99. Jenkins 1968:119–26.
100. Iamuddin 1965:114; Velázquez Bosco 1912:73.
101. Torres Balbás 1957:710–13.
102. Wilkinson 1973:179. Glass had been made opaque through the addition of tin oxide long before the method was adopted by Mesopotamian potters (Pope, E.M. 1956:301).
103. Charleston 1968:73–5. Grube 1976:35–7fn.2 provides a complete listing of finds of Samarra ware made in imitation of the Chinese ceramics. See also, Kramers 1970:66–78. Plumer 1968:195–200 identifies the Chinese porcelain found at Samarra as

Yueh ware made on a lakeshore near Ningpi in Chekiang Province [Ningbo in Zhejiang Province].

104. Torres Balbás 1957:776.

105. Grube 1976:37, 121, Fig. 77 is in error in stating that such pottery reached caliphate Spain. His identification of a single maiolica sherd recovered in Cairo as being from Umayyad Spain also is open to question. Goggin 1968:5 also erroneously said maiolica was known in Spain before the eleventh century.

106. Lane 1937:32.

107. Piccolpasso 1934:15–6; 1980(2):28–9.

108. Frothingham 1944a:90; Williams 1908(2):176.

109. Whitehouse 1971:14.

110. Foster 1960:91; Llorens Artigas and Corredor Matheos 1970:148–51.

111. Lister and Lister 1975a:291, Fig. a; Myers 1984:71. The modern industry at Safi has adopted the table-high wheel.

112. Ronsheim 1977:32; Rye and Evans 1976:19, 117; Willis, M.D. 1977:36; Wulff 1966:155. These known occurrences of the pit wheel lead one to suspect the survival in arabized environments of an old tradition ultimately related to the ground level turntables and hand propelled wheels of the ancient Middle East. For examples, see Hodges, H. 1970:Fig. 55.

113. The position of wheel head to a potter's left side also is confirmed in Piccolpasso's drawing (1980[2]:47). There is no indication of past or present wheel heads being slightly tilted to permit a thrower to have a better view of the lower portion of any vessel being formed, although that kind of angle has been observed in other Muslim potting industries. See Caiger-Smith 1973:Fig. 186. The off-center position of the Spanish tradition apparatus offers a potter the same advantage.

114. Caiger-Smith 1973:32; Scanlon 1965:19fn.15; Whitehouse 1971:15.

115. González Martí 1944(1):18, Fig. 5; Lister and Lister 1982:Fig. 5.2; Torres Balbás 1934:387–8.

116. González Martí 1944(1):18.

117. Whitehouse 1971:15.

118. Lister and Lister 1975a:219, Fig. 31b; Redman 1983:358, 360, 364; Ronsheim 1977:323.

119. Manises muffle kilns for the third firing of *reflejo metálico* were equipped with a low chimney that could be dampered for reduction (González Martí 1944[1]:323, Fig. 413). Myers 1984:53 reports chimneys on some modern Moroccan kilns.

120. Lister and Lister 1975a:292.

121. Frothingham 1951:197.

122. Examples excavated at *mudéjar* Manises were small chambers attached by means of a horizontal tunnel to a domed combustion unit (González Martí 1944[1]:25–6, Figs. 8–9). A similar chamber built adjacent to the main kiln to take advantage of its brick wall is used today in Granada.

123. Allan 1973:111–20.

124. Caiger-Smith 1973:212fn.; Frick 1971:238; Frothingham 1951:197; González Martí 1944(1):21, 248; Pope, E.M. 1956:300.

125. González Martí 1944(1):29, Fig. 12.

126. Long, tapered clay pegs reportedly extending inward from interior kiln walls, some of sufficient length to have made a complete grid, have been described from twelfth-century Nishapur (Wilkinson 1973:xxxix), and at fourteenth-century Tabriz, and from Sirāf and Takht-i-Sulaiman in the same region (Whitehouse 1971:15), where they are assumed to have been supports

on which vessels being fired were set. Abū'l Qāsim, in describing fourteenth-century Persian methods, wrote, "For each vessel is made an earthenware case with a fitting lid. These are placed in the kiln . . . This is like a high tower, and inside has row upon row of fired earthenware pegs, each an *arsh* and a half long, fitted into holes in the wall. The vessels are placed on them and fired for twelve hours with a hot even fire" (Allan 1973:111–120; see also E.M. Pope 1956:Fig. 282). Modern oldtimers in Iran (ancient Persia) report that kilns formerly used there had ceramic shelves resting on clay pegs projecting inward from kiln walls (Wulff 1966:160). Myers (1984:118) reports that in modern Tangiers construction bricks occasionally are used in stacking.

127. González Martí 1944(1):110.

128. Pope, E.M. 1956:301.

129. López de Coca Castañer 1980:13–44; Ortíz Muñoz 1973:410.

130. Jackson 1972:32; O'Callaghan 1975:151.

131. Heer 1961:191.

132. Blum 1970:22–3; Pirenne 1937:110–5.

133. Glick 1979:49, 131.

134. O'Callaghan 1975:286.

135. See Zozaya 1981a:277–86 for typological discussion of *taifa* period ceramics.

136. Lévi-Provencal and García Gómez 1948:137.

137. Zozaya 1981a:43 suggests it was a marmite used for making cheese. He places its introduction in *taifa* times.

138. Frothingham 1941a:104, Fig. 5.

139. Llubiá 1967:Fig. 71.

140. España. Museos Arqueológicos Provinciales 1945 (7):Pl. IV; Specimens on exhibit in Museo Arqueológico Nacional, Madrid, and Museo Arqueológico Provincial de Sevilla.

141. Imamuddin 1965:114. Another *brocal* recovered at Ceuta bears a date equivalent to 1190 (Torres Balbás 1949:64).

142. See Collantes de Teran and Zozaya 1972:258 and Vince 1982:137 for light paste; Zozaya 1981a:275–86 for red micaceous paste.

143. Gestoso y Pérez 1918:20, 76–94. Torres Balbás 1949:55 notes that the Giralda had been decorated with black ceramic convex tiles in the arches over the balconies, the Torre del Oro (built 1200–21) with white and green glazed tiles, and the Santo Tomás tower with green glazed ceramic disks.

144. Goitein 1967(1):111.

145. Krueger 1933:377–95.

146. An interesting philological approach to the question of the impact of the Muslims on domestic wares is provided by Glick 1979:298, Table 6, quoting Neuvoven. In the years 711–1050 it was found that 8 percent of the total number of arabisms in Castilian Spanish related to these articles. That percentage fell to 4.8 between 1050–1200 and to 3.1 between 1200–1300. These data can be interpreted either as a diminishing Muslim contribution, or, more probably, as a steady loss of Arabic terminology. However, as late as the early twentieth century Gestoso y Pérez noted many Arabic semantic survivals in the ceramic craft at Sevilla, including the word for potter, *alfarero*. Other arabisms retained were *alpetije*, wooden tool used for trimming; *alpanata*, piece of chamois for smoothing and compacting freshly thrown rims; *alaria*, fettling tool; *almijarra*, iron ladle in which oxides were secured during calcination; *almajena*, an earthenware vat

containing liquid glazes; *almajo*, saltwort burned to obtain soda
ash for tin glazes; *almalluque*, waster; *almártaga*, litharge (Gestoso
y Pérez 1903:64fn.1).

147. Copplestone and Myers 1970:39.
148. González 1951:217fn.222; O'Callaghan 1975:461.
149. Gil Torres 1953:58.
150. On Muslim town plans, see Torres Balbás 1971(1):86,
131, 423; Von Grunebaum 1955:147.
151. On municipal ordinances regarding craft locations in the
eighteenth century, see Ardemans 1760:107–8.
152. Torres Balbás 1945:177–96
153. Torres Balbás 1947:452, 466.
154. Ballesteros y Beretta 1913:35.
155. Carande 1925(2):306.
156. González 1951:316; Ladero Quesada 1970–71:279–84.
157. Ladero Quesada 1970–71:279–84; López Martínez
1935:13–5; Vicens Vives 1969:249.
158. Carande 1925:272; Ladero Quesada 1970–71:279–84.
159. González 1951:304, 462.
160. Ibid:464.
161. Gestoso y Pérez 1918:33.
162. Breisach 1973:41.
163. Ferguson 1962:12–3; González Jiménez 1980:97–304;
Payne 1973(1):74–7.
164. Gestoso y Pérez 1919:5; Glick 1979:223. Hillgarth
1976(1):180 indicates that pottery making continued uninterrupted by the reconquest, but provides no source for the information.
165. Ainaud de Lasarte 1952:80, 197.
166. Morgada 1887:421.
167. Ainaud de Lasarte 1952:197; Gestoso y Pérez 1919:3. A
similar gate name was known in Muslim Granada, but it usually
is interpreted as *Bab al-fajarim*.
168. López Martínez 1935:22.
169. Scanlon 1967:75.
170. Firth and Yamsey 1964:17.
171. It was in this village that the conqueror of the Aztecs,
Hernan Cortéz, died on December 2, 1547 (Gestoso y Pérez
1918:324).
172. Torres Balbás 1971(1):385.
173. González 1951:548. Torres Balbás 1971(1):351 describes
the pottery market as being on the street from the *plaza* where
bread was sold to that of the meat markets. It still appeared on a
city map of the early nineteenth century.
174. Persian cobalt, known as Mohammedan blue, also was
traded eastward to China in Mongol times to give rise to the blue
and white Ming porcelain that was destined to send shock
waves through the ceramics world for centuries (Charleston
1968:56). Chinese blue and whites did not reach the West, however, until the fourteenth century (Scanlon 1970:81–96).
175. Frothingham 1951:21.
176. Agricola 1950; Lewis, G.R. 1924:59–60.
177. Goitein 1973:86, 114, 127 thinks that until a century
earlier, Spanish tin had been plentiful enough to be exported to
the eastern Mediterranean. Matson 1941:62 has pointed out
that antimony, zinc, magnesium, or clay could also cause opacity
under certain conditions.
For unexplained reasons, cobalt pigment was slow in reaching
Spain; ceramic examples with blue decoration are known from

ninth century Mesopotamia on some of the earliest maiolica
created. For examples of the latter, see Charleston 1968:73, Figs.
200–1; Grube 1966:21, Fig. 7; Lane 1958:Figs. 8–9; Victoria and
Albert Museum 1969:Figs. 5–11.

Persian cobalt ore from mines near Kamsar, which had been
worked since antiquity, was pounded with potash and borax into
a fine powder, formed into a paste with grape syrup, and then
shaped into cakes. The cakes and ground quartz sand were
put into large earthenware pots to be heated for many hours.
When needed for painting, such cobalt was reground with
broken glass and borax, then calcined, and reground again. It
was applied to pottery, using a gum as the medium, this being
replaced by honey or syrup in modern practice. In the case of
cheap Sevillian pottery, the cakes of imported cobalt quite likely
were ground and thinned with water. Fortunately, cobalt is
such a strong colorant that very little is required for medium
hues. Its greyed appearance prior to the seventeenth century
results from the primitive processing (Frothingham 1951:21;
Wilkinson 1973:180).

178. An Almohad palace near Sevilla, occupied into Christian
times, yielded what must have been early examples of this
style. However, their exact temporal placement is uncertain (Collantes de Teran and Zozaya 1972:Fig. 12e). Frothingham 1951:73
comments on a combination of purple and blue decorations
on Nasrid pottery.

179. Llubiá 1967:115–6.

180. Pringle 1982:104–17; Whitehouse 1978:42–9.

181. Myers 1984:157–61, 166–8, Fig. 5–5; Redman 1977:5;
Redman and Boone 1979:32, Fig. 18B; Redman, Anzalone, and
Rubertone 1978:188, Fig. 1B.

182. Guerrero Lovello 1949; López Serrano 1974.

183. Fontaine 1978:Fig. 30; Torres Balbás 1957:Fig. 565. De
Montêquin 1976:52 says ablution fountains were of an inverted,
truncated pyramidal form.

184. Ainaud de Lasarte 1952:Figs. 563–8; Lane 1960:71.

185. Ladero Quesada 1976:26 notes devastating raids from
Morocco in 1275, 1277, 1278, 1282, and 1285.

186. Ruddock 1951:19–23.

187. Hurst 1977:77–9; Pérez Embid 1969a:43–96; 1969b:141–85;
Platt and Coleman-Smith 1975(2):171–2; Vince 1982:135–44.
Mannoni 1981:128 states that thirteenth-century Andalusian pot-
tery was imported into Genoa, but does not describe it.

188. Hurst 1977:96; 1979:1.

189. Oliveira Marques 1976:91–2.

190. To illustrate the remarkable stability of just one of the
Spanish utilitarian pottery forms, the *cantimplora*: for Roman
example, see Hispanic Society of America 1938:110; for caliphate
example, see Zozaya 1981b:40; for *taifa* example, see Llubiá
1967:Fig. 39; for thirteenth-century example, see Hurst 1977:Fig.
32, no. 52, and Platt and Coleman-Smith 1975(2):Fig. 204, no.
1289; for Nasrid example, see Llubiá 1967:Figs. 94, 96; for sixteenth-century example, see Goggin 1964:Fig. 29, Pl. 16; for
twentieth-century example, see Curtis 1962:Pl. 2f, and Pelauzy
1977:Fig. 148.

191. For example, see Posac Mon 1972.

192. Hurst 1977:Fig. 32, nos. 42–51; Vince 1982:138, Fig. 15.2
(20–21).

193. Llorens Artigas and Corredor Matheos 1970; Pelauzy
1977:77–118; Torres, P. 1982.

194. Hurst 1977:Fig. 34, no. 62; 1979:1 suggests their usual contents may have been dried fish. If that were so, the glaze would not have been necessary, but a matter of potter's choice. In actuality, no documentation supports its function as a shipping container.

195. Mannoni 1972:107–29; Wilkinson 1963:Fig. 17.

196. Blum et al 1970:37; González Jiménez 1980:184–5.

197. Grice-Hutchinson 1978:39 states that half of Castile's 200,000 Jews converted at this time.

198. Beinart 1979:161–7; González 1951:316; Ladero Quesada 1970–71:279–84.

199. Carande 1925:268–9; Jackson 1972:147.

200. Gestoso y Pérez 1903:76–80.

201. Berendsen 1967:24–7; Brett 1980:34; Burckhardt 1972:Figs. 42–4; Copplestone and Myers 1970:57; Jackson 1972:Fig. 75; Kuhnel 1966:133; Torres Balbás 1949:314–7, Fig. 357.

202. Ainaud de Lasarte 1952:Figs. 184–90; Charleston 1968:138, Fig. 389.

203. Lane 1939:10.

204. Torres Balbás 1945:183.

205. Ainard de Lasarte 1952:198; Lane 1939:69; Llubiá 1967:Figs. 198–9.

206. Ainaud de Lasarte 1952:198.

207. In Spain, local manufacture of lusterware was reported by Muslim travelers from eleventh-century Toledo in Castile and twelfth-century Calatayud in Aragón, but there never has been confirmation through artifacts (Lane 1946:246, 250; Talbot Rice 1965a:80; Torres Balbás 1949:62).

208. The earliest documented export from Málaga of *reflejo metálico* is cited by Hurst 1977:71 as 1249. Ibn Battuta is quoted in Johns 1973:670.

209. Brill 1970:376–7 provides an English translation from the German version of the 1300 Abū'l Qāsim luster recipe: "The preparation process for the glaze is as follows: One takes 1½ parts yellow and red arsenic, 1 part silver or gold marcasite, ½ part yellow vitriol from Tabas, and ¼ part burnt copper, which are pulverized and made into a paste. One-quarter of this is ground together with six dirham of pure burnt and pulverized silver, and pulverized 48 hours until the powder is extremely fine. This is then dissolved in grape juice or vinegar and painted on the vessels as you wish and is put again into a second oven made especially for this purpose, and then fired there for three days with little smoke so that they take on 'the color of two fires.' And when they are cooled one takes them out and rubs them with wet earth, so that the gold color becomes apparent. Other people add to the glaze certain things like red lead and verdigris, but instead of this, simple bloodstone with burnt silver does the same thing. The parts of this that are exposed to a constant fire will glow like red gold and shine like the sun."

210. Royal support for other industries is known for lead miners in Tunisia and textile workers in Egypt (Rodinson 1973:52).

211. Casamar 1961:185–90. Frick 1971:297 notes the finding of late fourteenth-century Nasrid lusterware in the debris of the destroyed Egyptian city of Fostat. Hurst 1977:68–105 and Vince 1982:135–7 discuss archaeological finds in England.

212. Ladero Quesada 1970–71:281–2.

213. Ettinghausen 1974:277.

214. Drey 1978:26. Benito del Cano and Roldán y Guerrero

1928:32 list six different forms used in Spain to contain drugs. These are *albarelos, cántaros, botellas, botijas, jarrones*, and *orzas*. Spanish Muslim writers on medicine, doctors, and pharmacists were famous from caliphate times. Avenzoar of Sevilla and Averroes of Córdoba were particularly well known, as was a medical school at Córdoba. For detailed discussion, see Frothingham 1941a.

215. The most famous of the lustered winged *tinajas* are fifteen extant whole or partially complete specimens now housed in museums across Europe and in the United States. They were found *in situ* as far away from Spain as Palermo and Cairo. One rested on a pilaster of the Carthusian monastery at Jérez de la Frontera and today is a prized exhibit at the Museo Nacional de Arqueología in Madrid (Ainaud de Lasarte 1952:Figs. 232–7; Charleston 1968:138, Fig. 390; Copplestone and Myers 1970:58, Fig. 87; Ettinghausen 1954:Figs. 21–5, 35–40; Frothingham 1951:Figs. 8, 11, 13, 15, 19; Gudiol 1964:Fig. 22; Kurz 1975:205–12; Torres Balbás 1936–39:Figs. 10–2; 1949:213, Fig. 232; Zozaya 1981b:48–9).

216. Museo Arqueológico Provincial de Granada.

217. Lane 1946:249.

218. Ibid:249.

219. Grabar 1976:Figs.12–3.

220. Hudson 1970:161.

221. Frothingham 1951:63–4; Torres Balbás 1936–39:421–2.

222. According to G. Ferguson 1959, fish represented Christ, griffin either the Saviour or those who oppressed the Christians, ships the church of Christ, and blue either heaven or heavenly love.

223. Torres Balbás 1935:434; 1949:210. Clay utilized typically fired red and contained schist temper (Vince 1982:135).

224. Torres Balbás 1934:388.

225. Ettinghausen 1954:154 suggests that this was a North African element taken to Egypt by the Fatimids and then rediffused back to southern Spain via the Moroccan Merinids.

226. Nonell 1973:60; Pelauzy 1977:113. Finds of the same kind of pottery at the sixteenth-century Portuguese installation at Mombasa on the Kenya coast and its continued occurrence as a modern Portuguese folk art underscores the widespread, longlasting nature of this style (Parvaux 1968:Pl. 1, nos. 33–4).

227. Frothingham 1951:2–3.

228. Sánchez Pacheco 1981a:62. Lane 1946:252 places an approximate date of 1414 on this development.

229. Domínguez Ortíz 1941:599.

230. Glick 1979:113.

231. Gestoso y Pérez 1903:118.

232. Ladero Quesada 1976:65.

233. Morgada 1887:421.

234. Until recently the group of buildings housed the Pickwick La Cartuja ceramic factory. Since the early nineteenth century this business has been producing English-style transfer ware. Its large bottle kilns are a prominent feature and are out of character with the ceramic past of Triana.

235. Domínguez Ortíz 1973:301.

236. Munzer 1924:201, 204fn.1.

237. Gestoso y Pérez 1903:374–5, 383–4, 390–1, 393, 401, 405, 407, 412.

238. Verlinden 1940:49.

239. Carande 1925:292–4; Ladero Quesada 1970–71:279–84; Vicens Vives 1969:275.

240. Ferguson, W.K. 1962:443; Wallerstein 1974(1):68.

241. For in-depth discussions of the decisive Isabelline period, see Davies 1937; Elliott 1963; Mariejol 1961; Payne 1973(1).

242. Pirenne 1937:131.

243. Payne 1973(1):178.

244. Beinart 1979:161–7.

245. Highfield 1972:265; Jackson 1972:147; Mariejol 1961:45–52; Morison 1942:109.

246. For a discussion of one of these modern industries, see Curtis 1962:486–503.

247. Maggetti, Westley, and Olin 1984:166.

248. Maniatis, Simopoulos, and Kostikas 1982:106; Mannoni 1982:91; Vince 1982:138.

249. Brownell 1976:212–3; Shepard 1956:21.

250. The first known instance in Spain of the use of a combination of complete vessels of different shapes and decorative modes and of random assortments of potsherds as construction fillers was observed in and about Barcelona and in Valencia (González Martí 1944[1]:Fig. 302; Llubiá 1967:123, 139, 153, Figs. 167, 169, 170, 180–3, 268). In Andalusia, the same use of jars in the haunches of vaulting was found to have occurred at several Visigothic churches near Granada and at the fifteenth-century Carthusian chapel at Jérez de la Frontera (Torres et al. 1940:447, 458). The latter structure is believed to have been erected by masons brought from Sevilla. The record of ceramic ballast at the Sevilla cathedral is thus far entirely documentary, with the exception of the seventeenth-century Sagrario. Its roof recently has been discovered to include two variations of large amphorae (Lister and Lister 1981:66–78).

251. Gestoso y Pérez 1903:370–5, 379–81, 383, 439.

252. Domínguez Ortíz and Aguilar Piñal 1976:18.

253. Ariño 1873:27–8.

254. The Cartujano breed forms the basic stock of the world famous Spanish Riding School in Vienna and Jérez. Beside its magnificent intelligent agility, the breed is unusual in the growth among some adults of incipient horns.

255. A sampling of comparable jars in the Museo Arqueológico Provincial de Sevilla, of unknown date but believed to be of the Christian period, found them varying from almost 90 cm to 60 cm in ht. and 1 m 26 cm in greatest diam.

256. Hurst 1977:96, 101, 103, Figs. 32 (no. 45, 49), 33 (no. 56); Pérez Embid 1969a:78; Redman 1978:22; Redman and Boone 1979:Fig. 18; Redman, Anzalone, and Rubertone 1978:188–95; Whitehouse 1972b:232–5.

257. Redman and Boone 1979:Fig. 18d.

258. A typical *atanor* at the Museo Arqueológico Provincial de Sevilla measured 38 cm in length, its ends measuring 17 cm and 12 cm in diam., respectively. A plumber's connection consisted of a bowl and right-angled lateral tube 29 cm in length.

To demonstrate the continuity from Roman practice, Pliny wrote: "The most convenient method of making a water course from the spring is by employing earthen pipes, two fingers in thickness, inserted in one another at the point of junction. The one that has the higher inclination fitting into the lower one and coated with quicklime macerated in oil" (quoted in Forbes 1964 [1]:154).

259. Piccolpasso 1980(2):29 illustrates a comparable technique being used by sixteenth-century Italian potters, who attached one of several sizes of round-bottomed, hemispherical, hollowed-out, wooden forms upside down to their wheel heads. This is not a convex wheel head, as sometimes described, but a jigger. Vessels for a number of purposes then were thrown over these devices, which could be removed from the wheels when other forms were desired. The bases of the jigger-produced forms were shaped before removal from the wheel by irons of different configurations. It is unknown whether the parallel Spanish jigger was wooden or a bisqued vessel. Moist clay could have been less likely to have adhered to a lubricated wooden form.

260. Kubler 1962:76 notes that increased markets and competition typically lead to simplified production methods and styles. Thus far, competition with the Sevillian potting industry from other sources for basic tableware cannot be demonstrated.

261. For *pilas*, see Gestoso y Pérez 1919:11–2, Fig. 27; for *tinajas*, see Sierra Fernández and Vega Porre 1982:459–70 for a suggested typology of specimens in the Museo Arqueológico Provincial de Sevilla; for *brocales*, see Llubiá 1967:Figs. 189–90, 195; for *jarras*, see Barber 1915:Fig. 27.

262. Lane 1939:11; Torres Balbás 1949:64.

263. *Cuerda seca* tiles are *in situ* in an altar room of the Casa de Pilatos, Sevilla (sixteenth century), and an altar frontal at Alanis (second half of fifteenth century) (Hernández Días et al 1939[1]:28).

264. González Martí 1954:Figs. 81–2; Llubiá 1967:82, Fig. 111; Martínez Caviró 1968:Figs. 125–9.

265. Martínez Caviró 1968:Figs. 90–124.

266. Ainaud de Lasarte 1952:Figs. 15–21; Caiger-Smith 1973:40; Charleston 1968:79, 83; Lane 1946:250; 1958:Figs. 22–3.

267. Compare with Torres Balbás 1957:779, Fig. 653, 780, Fig. 656.

268. Ainaud de Lasarte 1952:Figs. 624, 633; Gestoso y Pérez 1903:114, 120, Fig. 33; Martínez Caviró 1968:Figs. 88–9.

269. Gestoso y Pérez 1903:109.

270. The largest single collection was gathered early in this century by Don Guillermo J. de Osma, founder of a museum called Instituto Valencia de Don Juan in Madrid, where the collection is displayed.

271. Davillier 1949:409; Gestoso y Pérez 1919:6; Gómez Moreno 1924:70.

272. Mariejol 1961:218.

273. Llubiá 1967:121, Fig. 179.

274. Ainaud de Lasarte 1952:Fig. 579; Charleston 1968:Fig. 28; Gestoso y Pérez 1903:200.

275. Frothingham 1969:1; Gestoso y Pérez 1919:7.

276. López Martínez 1935:38.

277. Gestoso y Pérez 1903:149–52; 1919:5; Lister and Lister 1976a:59–60.

278. Domínguez Ortíz 1941:600; 1971:134; Pike 1967:1–3; Vicens Vives 1957(3):15.

279. Pike 1972:10–11.

280. On Sevillian sixteenth-century society, see Pike 1972.

281. Braudel 1974:16; Chaunu and Chaunu 1974:119.

282. Grice-Hutchinson 1978:45.

283. Braudel 1974:14; Domínguez Ortíz 1941:600; Pike 1966:12–3.

284. Morales Padron 1977:38.

285. Gestoso y Pérez 1899–1909.

286. Kubler 1962 points out that it is not uncommon for artistic florescence, such as that in late sixteenth- or early seventeenth-century Sevilla, to occur in times of staggering economic problems.

287. Wallerstein 1974(2):29. Braudel 1974:30 thinks twelve to fourteen million Mediterranean inhabitants were near starvation.

288. Domínguez Ortíz 1941:605; 1971:134; Domínguez Ortíz and Aguilar Piñal 1976:18.

289. Braudel 1967:400–1; 1979(3), calls the years between 1557 and 1627 the age of the Genoese.

290. Hamilton 1954:218.

291. Chaunu and Chaunu 1974:120.

292. For conditions in Sevilla during the seventeenth-century decline, see Domínguez Ortíz and Aguilar Piñal 1976.

293. Grice-Hutchinson 1978:45; Wallerstein 1974(2):130, 135, 148.

294. Goggin 1968:126–8; Lister and Lister 1982:Figs. 4.10, 4.11.

295. Goggin 1968:Pl. 5c–e; Lister and Lister 1982:Fig. 4.21.

296. Ainaud de Lasarte 1952:Figs. 624, 633; Gestoso y Pérez 1903:114, 120, Fig. 33; Goggin 1968:134–5; Lister and Lister 1982:Fig. 4.30; Martínez Caviró 1968:Figs. 88–9; Williams 1902(2):Fig. LXVIII.

297. Lister and Lister 1982:Fig. 5.2; Torres Balbás 1934:388; 1935:435.

298. Temboury Alvarez 1939:432–3.

299. Chaunu and Chaunu 1974:120.

300. Appendix 2.

301. The type was named Caparra Blue after an early Spanish site in Puerto Rico (Goggin 1968:134–5; Hostos 1938[1]).

302. Ruddock 1951:82.

303. Carrera Stampa 1949:2–24.

304. Lister and Lister 1976c:28–41; Pike 1966:177 fn.82. Pisa, captured in 1406, provided inland Florentines with a valuable port and trading fleet (Ferguson, W.K. 1962:427).

305. Mannoni 1981:129. For descriptions, see Comune di Sesto Fiorentino 1973; Vannini 1977.

306. Domínguez Ortíz 1956:103–4.

307. Morales Padrón 1977:147.

308. An intensive search of the Archives of the Indies confirms that the sixteenth-century cargoes from Sevilla to the Americas concentrated on grains, biscuits, wine, and olive oil (Chaunu and Chaunu 1974:120).

309. Appendix 2, 317, 314. The *cantimplora*, but not the *botija perulera*, was recovered at Qsar es-Seghir, Morocco, abandoned in 1550 (Redman, Anzalone, and Rubertone 1978:Fig. 2g–h). *Cantimplora* fragments were numerous in Nueva Cádiz, Venezuela, which was deserted by the 1540s (Willis, R. 1980b). Data compiled by Goggin suggested that the *cantimplora* form was disappearing in the Caribbean about 1580 (Goggin 1964:277).

310. James 1985:20, 29.

311. García Fuentes 1977:1–40, and 1980:244 puts usual *botija* capacity at 1.25 *arrobas* (approximately 3¼ gallons if using a 2.6 gallon per *arroba* ratio) and *botija perulera* capacity at 1.50 *arrobas* (approximately 3.9 gallons, using the same base for computations). This author cites a specific regulation in the law digest for the 1.25 *arroba* sizing.

312. Goggin 1964:266 gives average measurements of the

elongated version (his Middle A type) recovered in Florida as 52.87 cm ht., 26.36 cm greatest diam.; the round-bodied version (his Middle B type) from Panamá and a shipwreck off Florida as 26.40 cm ht., 21.32 cm greatest diam. A sample of specimens measured at the Museo Arqueológico Provincial de Sevilla yielded measurements for the elongated version of 50 cm ht., 26 cm greatest diam., and for the round-bodied version 29 cm ht., 25 cm greatest diam. James 1985:Tables 1, 3 measured a large series of complete specimens recovered from two eighteenth-century ships sunk off Hispaniola to obtain comparable results.

313. To the contrary, nearly three-fourths of the 600-piece collection of container jars recovered from two ships wrecked off Hispaniola in 1724 were of the spheroid form (James 1985:21).

314. García Fuentes 1980:244; see also, Appendix 2, 314–18.

315. Martin 1978:38–47; 1979:283–4.

316. Morales Padrón 1955:328.

317. World Health Organization 1977.

318. Carrera Stampa 1949:14; García Fuentes 1977:1–40; 1980:243. Usher 1932:209 computes a *pipa* of wine at about 1000 pounds dead weight.

319. Because of inconsistencies in the incomplete shipping records located during this study, it is impossible to present precise statistics and it is very easy to arrive at false conclusions. However, one interpretation of the records is that for ten different years in the sixteenth century when wine shipments were indicated, 15,047 *botijas peruleras* were dispatched empty to accompany *pipas* and 10,793 *botijas peruleras* were sent filled. The former practice dominated the first half of the century (1542–1550), the latter the second half (1551–1580). See Appendix 2, 314–18.

320. España. Sevilla. Archivo de Protocolos 1935:352, 389, 406–7.

321. Martin 1979:282.

322. Bonsor (1931:16) assumes a Roman relationship between makers of ceramic jars and wine producers. Later evidence comes from Vázquez de Espinosa, a Carmelite missionary from Jérez de la Frontera, who traveled widely in Mexico and Peru during the first several decades of the seventeenth century. Of Pisco, Peru, he wrote: "It has four potteries which produce plenty of jugs for all the vineyard owners, and their proprietors are the wealthiest and the persons most in demand. Each jug treated with pitch to hold wine, sells for 3 to 3½ reales, and even up to 4; and in addition to these, many vineyard owners have potteries and baking ovens on their ranches for the bottling of their wines." A similar statement about the Vitor Valley, also in Peru: "They get over 100,000 jugs of wine, because at this point the valley where the vineyards are planted is very wide. They have excellent establishments and storehouses to keep their wine (many vessels and) ovens where they bake the jars and jugs" (1942:484, 499).

323. Jiménez Barrientos 1982:394.

324. Morales Padrón 1955:328 reports that twenty-six of these jars went from Garachico, Canary Islands, to Puerto Rico in 1680. Carrera Stampa 1949:12–3 reports that the *botijuela* was used in New Spain for sale of honey, and the term also indicated ten kilos capacity.

325. Nasrid potters had made large decorated earthenware slabs to be used as grave markers and door jambs. These have not been identified in Sevilla as yet. Had they been produced, they could have been regarded as forerunners of the smaller polychrome tiles.

326. Frothingham 1969:5–8.

327. Ibid:18–20.

328. Vicens Vives 1969:336.

329. Barile 1975:23, 50–3, 211.

330. España. Sevilla. Archivo de Protocolos 1935:202.

331. Gestoso y Pérez 1903:242–5, 430. Citations provided by Italian maiolica expert Guido Farris (pers. comm. dated Nov. 22, 1974) are Alizeri, F., *Notizie dei Professori di Disegno dalle Origini al Secolo XVI*, Vol. 4, Genova, 1880; *Archivio di Stato di Genova, Atti Notaro Andrea Monaco*, Fogliazzo 1578–1579, and *Antiche Ceramche Liguri*, Scheiwiller, V., ed. Milano, 1965:36.

332. Domínguez Ortíz 1956:15; Frothingham 1969; Sancho Corbacho 1948; 1949:233–7.

333. Gestoso y Pérez 1919:12. Other renditions of Justa and Rufina are a pair of figurines modeled with a miniature Giralda tower between them, which is in the chapel dedicated to them in the Sevilla cathedral; a stained glass window dated 1686, showing the saints and some pieces of pottery, in the chapel of San Antonio in the cathedral; and a number of paintings by Strum, Goya, Murillo, and Zurbarán in the cathedral and various European galleries. The sisters predated by centuries the Giralda in both its Muslim and Christian forms; the pottery depicted was that of the artists' own time.

334. Gestoso y Pérez 1903:417.

335. Ainaud de Lasarte 1952:Figs. 592–5; Lister and Lister 1976c:Figs. 10–11; Martínez Caviró 1968:Figs. 146–53; Sánchez Pacheco 1981b:97.

336. Lister and Lister 1982:Fig. 4.28; Liverani 1960:Fig. 9a.

337. Farris 1972:323–30; Farris and Ferrarese 1969a:9–45; Lister and Lister 1982:62, Fig. 4.30; Mannoni 1969:75–96. Piccolpasso 1980(1):66, 68, 70 prepared composition drawings of three of those most typical on Ligurian Blue–on–Blue: arabesques, foliage, and porcelain motifs. He gives prices paid decorators, indicating they moved from shop to shop doing piece work. It is unknown whether the Italians working in Sevilla followed the same procedure.

338. Blake, H. 1981:114; Mannoni 1981:129. In Italy, the blue glaze was made in one of three ways: a combination of zafre and usual white tin glaze; a mixture of calcined wine lees, sand, lead, zafre, and salt; or another blend of massicot, tin, sand, and cobalt (Piccolpasso 1934:49; 1980(2):82, 84, 86). Spanish method is not known, but use of wine lees is unlikely.

339. Gestoso y Pérez 1903:307; Appendix 2, 318. Confirmation also comes from Schafer 1938:322–3, as quoted in Goggin 1968:212, who lists 260 dozen *loza de Pisa* and 260 dozen *loza de Sevilla de la Puerta de Goles que es como la de Pisa*. This refers to the Ligurian blue ware and the Sevillian copy of it.

340. Barile 1975:43.

341. Lister and Lister 1982:Fig. 4.24a.

342. Jan M. Baart, Amsterdam Historical Museum, pers. comm. 1983.

343. Home 1953:170, Fig. 10; Piccolpasso 1934; 1980.

344. Vossen et al 1975:67, 71, 197.

345. This practice is observed today at Puente del Arzobispo, which has preserved many traditional methods. In Triana, the ancient cylindrical kiln still functions for all production stages.

346. Farris and Ferrarese 1969b:99–110; Piccolpasso 1934:Fig. 22; 1980(2):40.

347. Piccolpasso 1934:68, Fig. 52; 1980(2):108. A modern variation is reported from Bailén, Andalusia. There, hollow cylin-

drical tubes with matching holes along their sides are set
between rimmed forms. Clay plugs are inserted horizontally in
the holes upon which the vessels to be fired rest (Curtis
1962:499).

348. Piccolpasso 1934:Fig. 52.

349. Home 1953:148, Fig. 8; Piccolpasso 1934:Fig. 15;
1980(2):29.

350. Frothingham 1969:21–2, 48; Martínez Caviró 1971:283–93.
Frans Andries became Francisco Andrea to the Spaniards. His
name appears in sixteenth-century archives in Sevilla in connection with a 1561 contract with potter Roque Hernández to teach
him the decorative methods of Pisa. In actuality, his family roots
were farther north in Italy (Gestoso y Pérez 1903:417).

351. Frothingham 1944b:20; 1969:48; Gestoso y Pérez
1903:249–52, 298–9; Vaca González and Ruíz de Luna Rojas
1943:21–37. It is of interest that Antonio Díaz appears to have
admired Talavera pottery while in residence in Sevilla and found
it a profitable commodity. In 1554 he received the comparatively
large sum of forty four *ducats* gold ($28.60) for a shipment of
eleven *cargas* of this ware (Gestoso y Pérez 1903:397).

352. Frothingham 1969:48; Vaca González and Ruíz de Luna
Rojas 1943:165.

353. Frothingham 1944b:23.

354. Donatone 1968:Figs. 1–2, 4–8, 28.

355. Frothingham 1944b:18–20; Gestoso y Pérez 1903:389–90,
412; Museo de Bellas Artes, Barcelona; Museo Ruíz de Luna,
Talavera; Museo de Artes y Costumbres Populares, Sevilla;
Museo Nacional de Arqueología, Madrid. Flemish-Italian potter
Frans Andries, working in Talavera, is recorded as having also
gone to shops in Sevilla (Gestoso y Pérez 1903:417).

356. Gestoso y Pérez 1899–1909(1):384–5; 1903:245. Frothingham illustrates a number of probable contemporary Sevillian
copies of Talaveran vessels (1944b:Figs. 142–52). It has been
habitual among Spanish students of ceramics to automatically
classify better pieces as from Talavera proper, poorer ones from
Sevilla. Such distinctions based upon quality may or may not
be valid, because in both industries there must have been superior and mediocre potters.

357. Gestoso y Pérez 1903:131.

358. Pescador del Hoyo 1965:256–8.

359. Lister and Lister 1982:48, 52, Fig. 4.8, where it is called
Columbia Gunmetal; Appendix 2, 317–18. Identification of this
type has been hampered by frequent black sulfide staining
caused by anerobic conditions of deposition following discard. A
test of a simple application of weak hydrogen peroxide will
bleach such accidental coloration, permitting accurate analysis
(Donald L. Hamilton, Institute of Nautical Archaeology, Texas A
& M University, pers. comm. 1983).

360. Appendix 1, 307–9. Frothingham 1944b:26 incorrectly
believed the vessels in the Zurbarán painting, *The Miracle of Saint
Hugh*, to be products of Talavera, or copies made in Sevilla.

361. Lister and Lister 1976c:Fig. 4a–c; 4d now is thought to be
Sevillian rather than Pisan; 1982:Fig. 4.46, 75–8.

362. Domínguez Ortíz 1956: 15. The authorities were objecting
to the large number of potters causing damage by extracting
clay from pits on the isle off the Cartuja land and along the east
banks in front of San Jerónimo.
*"En este lugar de Triana se hace mucha y buena loza de Málaga
blanca y amarilla, y de todas maneras y suertes. Hay casi cincuenta casas
donde se hace, y de donde se lleva por muchas partes; asi mismo se*

hace azulejo muy pulido de muchas diferentes labores y colores; y asi mismo muy hermosos bustos de hombres y de otras cosas. De este azulejo se labra mucha contidad que se lleva a muchas partes." Written by Pedro de Medina in commemoration of the 300th anniversary of the reconquest of Sevilla by Fernando III, published in 1548 (reproduced in España, Consejo Superior de Investigaciones Científicas 1944:76).

363. Gestoso y Pérez 1903:306–7.
364. Vicens Vives 1969:420.
365. Hurst 1977:96–8; 1979:2; Martin 1979:279–93; Platt and Coleman-Smith 1972(2):28–9, 171–9.
366. Hurst 1979:2; Martin 1979:300.
367. Similar imitations were noted by a priest writing in 1568 in Talavera (Riaño 1879:171).
368. Jean McClure Mudge, Museum of the American China Trade, pers. comm., Dec. 6, 1983.
369. Sánchez Pacheco 1981b:100–1 illustrates a cylindrical flower pot said to be Sevillian and decorated with a polychromatic bird-on-branch Chinese motif. It is thought to date to the seventeenth century, for reasons not stated. The identical pattern appears on a presumed eighteenth-century water jar, or *aguamanil*, executed in blue only. It also is regarded as of Sevillian manufacture. A few sherds noted at Sevilla and in Indies remains, where they were thought to be early seventeenth century in date and were called Ichtucknee Blue–on–White by Goggin 1968:148–51, possibly represent such a Sevillian imitation of Chinese blue–on–white porcelain.

Oriental porcelains had been known in the Muslim eastern Mediterranean since the thirteenth century, with porcelaneous types arriving earlier. Some fragments found in thirteenth-century Spain and attributed to eastern manufacture are questionable (Whitehouse 1972a:69–70). Perhaps these are what Glick had in mind when he said that Egyptian imitations of Chinese pottery were sold to Andalusian merchants (Glick 1979:132). Only beginning with Portuguese penetration of Far Eastern markets in the early sixteenth century did undoubted Chinese porcelains begin to appear in Spain. They seem never to have been as common there, even in royal collections, as elsewhere in western Europe. Certainly the amount of porcelain circulated in Spain never matched that in its overseas colonies in the Americas.

370. Benítez, J.R. 1929:120; Hamilton 1954:217.
371. Chaunu and Chaunu 1974:120.
372. Morales Padrón 1955:328.
373. García Fuentes 1980:249–50.
374. Goggin 1964:Fig. 37.

Notes to Diffusion Abroad of Andalusian Pottery

1. Phoenician amphorae have been found 600 miles south of Gibraltar at Mogador (Culiacan 1966:109).
2. Mercer 1976:70.
3. España. Ministerio del Ejército 1935(1):102.
4. Glick 1979:39.
5. Barbour 1966:17; Haquim 1955:67; Meakin 1901:238–87.
6. Le Tourneau 1961:83–113.
7. Bel 1918.
8. Ibid:104, Fig. 49.
9. Ibid:71, Fig. 20. For continuation of the pit wheel, see Beckett 1958:Fig. b; Lister and Lister 1975a:272–95.

10. Glick 1979:237; Myers 1983; Redman, Anzalone, and Rubertone 1978:Fig. 3E. According to Torres Balbás 1940:196, the first vertical water wheel in Fez was built in the second half of the thirteenth century by a refugee from Sevilla and was outfitted with many jars. It must have been preceded by many horizontal wheel lifts. The original vertical wheel, or a replacement, was still functioning in 1525, being mentioned in an account by Leon the African. Another Muslim writer, al Marrakushi, reported that at the beginning of the thirteenth century in Marrakesh 300 mills functioned through the use of water wheels (Smith, N. 1976:142).

11. Frothingham 1944b:282, fn. 5.

12. Redman and Myers (1981:295) agree that overt Spanish Muslim ceramic influence was not present at al Basra. The kiln and ceramics are more fully described in Redman 1983:359–67.

13. Ibid:370–2, 374.

14. Gil Torres 1953:47; España. Ministerio del Ejército 1935(1):199, 206–7, 245.

15. Gil Torres 1953:51.

16. Marcais 1913; 1916.

17. Glick 1979:131.

18. Krueger 1937:57–71; Verlinden 1953:206.

19. De Montêquin 1976; Hill 1976:145, 397; Le Tourneau 1961:10. Bernès and Jacob 1974:7 report eighteen pottery workshops in Fez in the Almohad period.

20. Myers 1983:Figs. 11, III; 1984:Figs. 5–2, 5–5, 5–6, 145–53; Myers and Blackman 1984:Fig. 2; Redman 1978:Fig. 3b; 1979a:Figs. 3A–F, 64—66; 1979b:251–63; 1985; Redman and Boone 1979:Figs. 18A–F, 19A–G.

21. Berendsen 1967:40. Hill 1976:146 writes that a contemporary Andalusian potter, Sidi Qāsim al Jalizi, introduced new pottery techniques to Tunisia. This may have included *alicatado*.

22. Puigaudeau n.d.:27–35.

23. Boone 1984:76–86; Myers 1983; Redman 1979a:Figs. 1H, I, L, 2A–C, 3M–S; 1982:233–4; Redman and Boone 1979:Fig. 2M–S; Redman, Anzalone, and Rubertone 1978:Figs. 1A, C, I, J, L, M, 2E, H, 3F, I; Sinopoli n.d.:1–9.

24. Lister and Lister 1975a:280–1, Fig. 28.

25. Bernès and Jacob 1974:7.

26. Hess 1978:178.

27. Mohamed 1967:627–39.

28. Arques 1966; España. Ministerio del Ejército 1941(2); Gil Torres 1953:65–6; Redman 1978:12–23.

29. Gil Torres 1953:107; Hess 1978:173.

30. Mercer 1980:21, Fig. 6.

31. Millares Torres 1974(9):155–6; Procacci 1968:52; Verlinden 1953:203–4.

32. Hale 1966:18.

33. Duncan 1972:9.

34. Ainaud de Lasarte 1952:Fig. 555; Gestoso y Pérez 1903:140–1 fn., Fig. 5.

35. Cespedes del Castillo 1957:505.

36. According to Jane 1960:204 fn.17, there was no such person as Rodrigo de Triana on the ships' lists. He suggests the seaman who sighted land first may have been one Juan Rodríguez Bermeo. Rodrigo de Triana also was omitted from a list provided by Martínez Hidalgo 1966.

37. Jane 1960:26, 36, 41, 116. For Spanish language versions, see Anghiera 1964(1):106; Casas 1957(1):145, 153, 191; Navarrete 1945(1):167, 176–7; Tío 1966:189.

38. Jane 1960:194, 196; Sanz 1961:9.

39. Dr. William Hodges, an American medical missionary who has spent his adult career in northern Haiti, believes Navidad is probably two miles from the sea at a locality where he has found bells and Spanish coins. A National Geographic Society expedition to the region failed to substantiate this belief (Scofield 1975:584–625). Presently, a University of Florida team is conducting a search in the same general area pinpointed by Hodges. An Arawak village that sheltered the hastily erected Spanish fortification may have been located. Analysis of results are pending (Deagan 1986).

40. Chanca 1907:452; Navarrete 1945(1):347; Thacher 1903 (2, pt.1):278; Tío 1966:64. Although pottery was not formally included by the Spaniards with trading goods, its popularity might have been sufficient to add it to later inventories. However, the Juan Pardo treks into North Carolina and Tennessee in 1566–68 make no mention of such items (DePratter and Smith 1980:67–78).

41. Palm 1955(1):48.

42. Colón (1959:109) wrote, "artisans of all kinds, laborers, and peasants to work the land." Irving (1868[1]:356–7) and Morison (1939:25) also mention the presence of artisans.

43. Fernández Armesto 1974:116, 136; Morison 1939; Palm 1945:299, 301; 1955(1):47–8; Sauer 1966:74–5; Tío 1966:186.

44. The vandalizing of Isabela begun by Las Casas and his contemporaries continued, so that by the mid-nineteenth century a local resident wrote to Washington Irving that only the pillars of the church, part of the royal storehouses, and some of Columbus's stone house remained, although he added that the ruins of a fort, a pillar, and flagstaff also could be seen (Palm 1945:299). By 1870 some stone walls had been reduced to a foot in height. The site was privately owned but could be purchased for $100 (Sauer 1966:75). Twenty years later, eight structures were mapped by the men and officers of an American steamship, the *Enterprise*. At that time only foundation outlines were visible (Thacher 1903[2, pt. 1]:285–7). In 1945, excavations found the foundations of a tower, arsenal, church, and fort. Remains of a well, quarries, and a forge likewise were located (Palm 1945:298–303). Unfortunately, by that time the Columbus house appeared to have crumbled from the cliff into the sea. At this date (1987), part of the site is covered by native huts, and there is not even a marker to inform a visitor of the historical significance of the spot.

45. Fernández de Oviedo 1959(2):191.

46. Ballesteros y Beretta 1945:373; Cruxent and Rolando 1961:19. Morison 1974:150 regards this *bacín* as one of brass rather than of earthenware. For a history of this form in Spanish ceramics, see Lister and Lister 1983:167–87.

47. Fuentes 1963:19.

48. Cruxent and Rouse 1958; Rouse and Cruxent 1963:134; Willis, R. 1980b:29.

49. Vigneras 1972:621–41.

50. *General Caribbean:* Fairbanks 1973:141–74; Goggin 1968:23–43; Lister and Lister 1974:19–23. *Cuba:* Domínguez González 1979a; 1979b; Morales Patiño and Pérez de Acevedo 1946:5–20. *Cubagua:* Cruxent and Rouse 1958; Rouse and Cruxent 1963:134; Willis, R. 1980b:27–40. *Darién:* American Geographical Society 1960:274–6; Cruxent 1956; Verlinden et al 1958:1–48. *Haiti:* Hodges 1979; 1980; Marrinan 1984; McEwan 1983, 1984; Willis, R. 1980a, 1984. *Jamaica:* for general background, see Goodwin

1946:55, who writes that a single sherd recovered at Don Christopher's Cove may have been left from the year-long stranding there in 1503–4 of the Admiral at the inglorious end of his fourth voyage; Morales Padrón 1952. *Panamá:* Baker 1969; Goggin 1968:163–8; Lister and Lister 1974:43–6; Long 1964; 1967; Manucy and Gagliano 1958; Rovira 1980. *Puerto Rico:* Hostos 1938; Smith, H.G. 1962:43–106. *Santo Domingo:* Caceres Mendoza 1980; Council 1975; Goggin 1964:253–98; 1968:23–43; Nieves Sicart 1980:89–97; Ortega and Cruxent 1974; Ortega and Fondeur 1978a; 1978b.

51. Gestoso y Pérez 1903:143.

52. Physical analyses of clay and glazes are confirming the Sevillian provenience previously based upon stylistic and historical evidence (Jornet 1984; Maggetti, Westley, and Olin 1984:151–91; Olin and Sayre 1975a, 1975b:57–61; Olin et al 1978:200–29; Vaz and Cruxent 1975:71–81; 1976:10–14).

53. Morison 1939:24; 1942:390. Numerous bisqued objects are noted by Ortega and Fondeur, 1978a.

54. Pike 1966:55.

55. Council 1975:46, Fig. 5A–D, F; Goggin 1968:144–6; Hostos 1938:Fig. 26; McEwan 1983:Table 5; Ortega and Fondeur 1978:Figs. 28E, 29C, 50A, 60A–B, 64B, 81A; Verlinden et al 1958:1–48; Willis, R. 1984:159.

56. The *flota* that brought Diego Columbus to his post as governor of Hispaniola in 1509 consisted of twenty galleons, or *naos*. With the exception of the flagship, *San Jorge*, all carried some pottery aboard, generally as containers for various food products of Andalusia. Other cargo varied from locks, nails, and scissors to velvets, thread, and shoes. A listing of the ships in this convoy and the pottery in the cargoes is given in Appendix 2. See also Otté 1964:475–503.

57. Haring 1964:131.

58. España, Archivo General de Indias, Contratación 1451. Francisco López to [consignee not named]: *1 canasta en que van 7 vasos de loza* (Gestoso y Pérez 1903:141).

59. Otté 1964:475–502; Hostos 1938(2):26–7, 54. According to Hostos, bricks were considered a bad load, and if they shifted during the voyage they may have been responsible for some of the shipwrecks. España, Archivo General de Indias, Contratación 4674, dated 1515, states *6000 ladrillos razonados en 12 tonelados los quales en su nao paso a las yndias para el monasterio de Santo Domingo en la isla Española*. A second archival entry (for which specific date and *contratación* number are lacking) states *16,500 ladrillos a 2 ducados el millar, destinado por el almirante y oficiales . . . que residen en la ysla Española . . .* 1508 and 1512 entries for 13,000 and 5,000 bricks, respectively, appear in the España. Sevilla. Archivos de Protocolos de Sevilla (1):58, 104, 203. A royal *cédula* dated 1512 from Burgos notes that King Fernando had received requests for tiles and bricks, as well as masons, carpenters, and cement men, and had ordered both supplies and artisans to be sent. He complained, however, that he could not understand why these requests were made, inasmuch as the islands had been reported to him as having substantial wood and clay resources and men calling themselves laborers had migrated there. Perhaps there is a royal explanation for the lack of records of shipments of bricks or roof tiles after about 1515, except for several to Tierra Firme and Puerto Caballos in the 1540s. The Spanish population in the latter regions still was very small, and pottery industries had not gotten underway.

60. Casas 1971:47, 96.

61. See Appendix 2, 311–13.

62. Goggin 1964:257, 291; Lister and Lister 1981:66–78; Ortega and Fondeur 1978a:Figs. 34B, 35a, 37b.

63. Ortega and Fondeur 1978a:Figs. 46c, 47a, 48a, 49a.

64. Gestoso y Pérez 1903:372; Goggin 1968:31. See Council 1975:Fig. 108 for so-called manioc griddle form.

65. Contrary to the suggestion made by Ortega and Fondeur (1978a:187, Fig. 47c), several cockspurs found at Sanate, some burned walls of a pit, and a shaped round stone that excavators felt might be the flywheel of a potter's wheel are inconclusive evidence for a sixteenth-century pottery industry.

66. Otté 1964:483.

67. For itemization, see Appendix 2, 313–14.

68. Gestoso y Pérez 1903:428.

69. Arnold 1978; Arnold and Weddle 1978:Fig. 45b–e. Specimens from ships sunk in a storm of 1554 formerly were housed at the Balcones Laboratory, University of Texas, Austin; they are now in the care of the Corpus Christi Museum. Other specimens from a 1715 sea disaster are at the Bureau of Historic Sites and Properties, Tallahassee, Florida. For popular accounts of the sea disasters involving Spanish shipping, see Marx 1971, and Peterson 1965, 1975.

70. Council 1975:44–6, 48, 55–112; Goggin 1964:253–98; 1968:32–4; Ortega and Fondeur 1978a. For reconstruction of colonial Santo Domingo, see Bearse 1979:33–9.

71. Cruxent and Rouse 1958; Goggin 1968:34–6; Domínguez González 1979a; McEwan 1983; 1984; Morales Padrón 1955:320–2, 324; Ortega and Fondeur 1978a; Willis, R. 1980a; 1980b:27–40; 1984:157–9, 162–4.

72. For archaeological examples in the New World, see Council 1975:Fig. 18A–B, 102; Deagan 1978:Figs. 9, 10; Fairbanks 1966:430–2; 1973:Fig. 9C–E; McEwan 1983:Table 5; Ortega and Fondeur 1978a:Fig. 44D, 63A; South 1982:Table 5; Willis, R. 1980b:Table 3; 1984:163. Redware inlaid with white feldspar chips also has remained as a folk art in central Mexico and Peru.

73. Caceres Mendoza 1980:110–1; McEwan 1983:Table 5; Ortega and Fondeur 1978b; Rouse and Cruxent 1963:138; Willis, R. 1980b:31. For suggested African ware, see Willis, R. 1984:165–71.

74. One extant record indicates one box of pottery from Genoa being exported in 1551 from Santa Cruz de la Palma, Canary Islands, to the Indies. Specific destination is not given (Morales Padrón 1955:324). See also, Cruxent and Vaz 1973; Lister and Lister 1976c:28–41; 1976d:311–20.

75. Barile 1975; Comune di Sesto Fiorintino 1973; Blake 1981:99–116; Farris 1972:323–30; Farris and Ferrarese 1969a:9–45; Goggin 1968:Pl. 1g, 7c–h; Lister and Lister 1974:22–3, Fig. 3b; Vannini 1977.

76. Blake 1981:114.

77. Haring 1964:107.

78. Lister and Lister 1976c:28–41; Pike 1966:3, 54–5, 101–2, 143. See Pike 1966:Table 6 for listing of Sevillian Genoese in America in the sixteenth century, most of whom resided in Santo Domingo. One Genoese, Francisco Pinelo, underwrote Columbus's first and second voyages and ultimately was appointed factor of the powerful *Casa de Contratación*, founded in Sevilla in 1503, as overseer of the transatlantic trade.

79. Appendix 2, 315. Colored glazed floor tiles were recovered in early fifteenth-century Islamic deposits at the Moroccan site of Qsar es-Seghir (Redman 1983:358). Such tiles very possibly also were used in Sevilla.

80. Appendix 2, 317–18. Fragments of candleholders discussed in Council 1975:55, 57, Fig. 8b,c might well be some of those listed in these bills of lading.

81. Council 1975:110, Appendix 2; Deagan 1978:36; Goggin 1968:38; McEwan 1983:Table 5; Smith 1962:71; South 1982:Tables 4–5; Willis, R. 1980b:Table 3.

82. Fairbanks 1973:54–5; Lister and Lister 1974:43–6; Long 1964:104–9; 1967; Rovira 1980. Remains of a rare kiln and excavations at Panamá Viejo, which was sacked by pirates and then abandoned in 1671, indicate a local maiolica industry operating prior to that date. It appears stylistically related to eastern rather than southern Spain. During what may have been a production period of no more than fifty to seventy-five years, Panamanian maiolica was dispersed down the west coast of South America to Ecuador and Peru. Later, a second industry appears to have been revived in Panamá Nueva, the present city, and that industry survived through the nineteenth century. Inasmuch as Panamá first was part of the Viceroyalty of Peru and later passed to the authority of the Viceroyalty of New Granada, its pottery-making activities are not considered here.

83. Council 1975:73–82.

84. Chaunu and Chaunu 1974:123; Council 1975:58–61; Ortega and Fondeur 1978a:Figs. 30F, 34D, 38A, 61A–B, 89A–B, 90C.

85. For Santa Elena, see South 1981; 1982; 1983; for St. Catherines Island, Georgia, see, Thomas, Jones, Durham, and Larsen 1978; for San Agustín, see Deagan 1978; 1983; for Puerto Real, see McEwan 1983 and Willis, R. 1984.

86. South 1972:96–122; 1982:85–92.

87. Cotter (1958:Pl. 82, lower) includes later Iberian ware that may have originated in Portugal; see also Jelks 1958:201–12. For distribution elsewhere on Atlantic Seaboard, see Goggin 1968:133, 139, 150.

88. Zavala and Castelo 1939–46(5):220–1 notes Indians under *repartimiento* arrangements making bricks and water ducts. Kubler 1948(2):169 states that bricks for floors were being made by Indian laborers by mid–century, with roof tiles common after the 1580s.

89. For repeated ordinances against littering, see Gómez de Cervantes 1944:102; Mexico City, Cabildo 1871–1919; Romero 1973(2, pt. 1):246–7; Rubió Mañe 1956:19–27; Simpson 1966:164.

90. Between 1650 and 1700 there are records for 939,370.5 *arrobas* (approximately 2,442,363 gallons at 2.6 gallons to one *arroba*) of wine having been sent from Sevilla to New Spain. It probably was shipped in *botijas peruleras* of 1.5 *arrobas* capacity. Shipments of olive oil amounted to 252,162.5 *arrobas*, of vinegar 11,658.75 *arrobas*. For these, ceramic jugs of several sizes were used. Also, 3695 *botijos* of olives, 896 *botijos* of capers, and 483 *botijos* of almonds were listed (García Fuentes 1977:1–40). See García Fuentes 1980:Table 3 for total shipments from Sevilla and the Canaries of wine, olive oil, and *aguardiente* during the half-century from 1650 to 1700. The destination listed in the Indies was, overwhelmingly, New Spain. Chaunu and Chaunu 1974:123 confirm a high point in the American trade between 1600–1620, with New Spain the primary market.

91. Two municipal projects beneath Mexico City have been responsible for the greatest amount of these sixteenth-century Spanish ceramics yet recovered in the Republic. One project was the installation of a subway system, one line of which travels directly under the north side of the *plaza*, or *zócalo*, and along the main colonial era roadway from the center of town to the west-

ern mainland village of Tacuba. The other was a restoration project at the cathedral, which faces the main *plaza*; the project involved subterranean reinforcement. Both these engineering works probed deep into the soil and muck under the city, where they encountered masses of debris resulting from Aztec and early Spanish occupation. Comparable finds have been made beneath numerous other edifices and streets of the former *traza*, but not in such volume. The complex of introduced Sevillian wares comprises a grouping in these studies designated as Morisco Ware to indicate its probable ethnic affiliation (Lister and Lister 1974:23–4; 1975b:31–2; 1978:3–8; 1982:1–9, 45–56; see also López Cervantes 1976a; 1976b; 1983). For Montelupo maiolicas, see Comune di Sesto Fiorintino 1973:Figs. 5, 11, 21, 29, 30, 49, 54; Lister and Lister 1976c:Fig. 2; 1982:71–2, Fig. 4.39; Liverani 1960:Figs. 80–2; Vannini 1977:Figs. 8, 19–23, 25, 32.

92. Physical tests now show the presence of volcanic inclusions in Mexican clay that were absent in Andalusian clay and are not visible to the naked eye. (Maggetti, Westley, and Olin 1984:159–64; Olin and Sayre 1975a; 1975b:57, 61; Olin et al. 1978:200–29).

93. Boyd-Bowman 1963:181; 1967:51; 1976:580–604. Neasham 1939:147–60 estimates the sixteenth-century emigration from Sevilla to the Americas in general at 50.6 percent of the total.

94. Kubler 1948(2):155; Lister and Lister 1982:98; Zorita 1909:299.

95. Charlton 1968:101.

96. Foster 1948:369–70; 1965:51; Kaplan 1976:244; Müller 1970–71:97–110; Müller and Hopkins 1974:50–6; Whitaker and Whitaker 1978. Winter and Payne (1976:37–40) report two aboriginal structures at the Oaxaca site of Monte Alban that they suggest had served as pottery kilns. Their features were amazingly comparable to those of the introduced *horno arabe*. Thus far, no similar constructions have been found elsewhere in pre-Columbian circumstances.

97. Mexico City, Cabildo 1871–1919(2):61, 135. In the 1509–1533 listing of passengers to the Indies prepared by the staff of the Archivo General de Indias there are eight persons named Francisco de Morales. One is identified as a bootmaker, but no occupations are given for the others. Six indicated they were from Sevilla (España, Archivo General de Indias 1930[1]). Another search of the Archivo General de Indias revealed that a Francisco de Morales from Jaén, Andalusia, went to New Spain in 1537, a date that corresponds exactly to the *merced* to a potter of the same name in Mexico City (Bermúdez Plata 1942[2]:217). Boyd-Bowman (1968[2]:113) notes a Francisco de Morales who came to Mexico in 1535, moved to Mexico City in 1538, and then went on to Puebla in 1547. He is described as *sin oficio*, without a trade, but he is another candidate for being the recipient of the *merced*. No information is available about the other potter indicated at Mexico City, one Francisco de la Reyna. No potters were on a list drawn up by the Archivo General de Indias of craftsmen emigrating to the Indies between 1492 and 1592 (Rubió y Moreno 1917[1]:49).

98. No specific locations for potteries of the sixteenth century are documented for Mexico City, such as that of the silversmiths on what is now Avenida Madero, the shoemakers on República de Argentina, the ropemakers on Cinco de Mayo, or a variety of other crafts along Calle Tacuba. See Romero 1973(2, pt. 1):254. However, later pottery and brick kilns are known to have been in the same part of town as was the parochial church of Santa

Veracruz, founded in 1526, where the seventeenth-century and eighteenth-century confraternity of the potters was reported to have met. At present, the church is opposite the Alameda Park, once a swampy area outside the *traza* on the edge of the mainland. A large volume of cockspurs may have been recovered in the vicinity by the trenches dug for construction of a metropolitan subway system, but exact provenience of these artifacts is uncertain. Nevertheless, all these factors can be signs of the existence in that sector of former potteries, now eradicated by urban development (Carrera Stampa 1954:90, 92, 197; Lister and Lister 1982:90; Marroqui 1900[3]:116; Santiago Cruz 1960:55; Toussaint 1967:265).

99. Physical tests conducted by the Smithsonian Institution confirm that the red clays used by early Mexican potters were similar, if not identical, to those used by aboriginal artisans at the sites of Tlatilco and Teotihuacán near Mexico City. That means that seemingly inexhaustible beds had provided this basic resource for two millennia. The Mexican clays were found to differ from Spanish clays in having volcanic inclusions (Olin and Sayre 1975a, 1975b:57–61; Olin et al. 1978:217).

100. Maggetti, Westley, and Olin 1984:151–91; Warren 1973. Spanish clays were found to contain twice the amounts of cerium, lanthanum, and thorium.

101. Bargalló 1955:26; Fuentes 1963:167; González Reyna 1956:165; Humboldt 1811(3):117; Prieto 1973:21.

102. In 1654 a master potter, Diego Salvador Carreto of Puebla, sold fifteen boxes of ceramics to a sargeant major in Peru for cash and nine hundred pounds of tin (Cervantes 1939(2):179).

103. In 1617 the administration prohibited the unauthorized cutting of *barrilla*, identified as *Batis maritima L.* (Uphof 1968:69), to conserve it for these industries (Mexico, Archivo Nacional de la Nación 1940:337; 1941:165; 1943:183). The Mexican Indians near Lake Texcoco used the substance to make soap to be sold to the Spaniards (Gibson 1964:339).

104. Cervantes 1939(1):11; Gibson 1964:339; González Reyna 1956:431; Humboldt 1811(3):16–7.

105. Cervantes 1939(1):17; Frothingham 1944b:21–2; Santiago Cruz 1960:90. Father Sahagún reported that some natives of central Mexico learned to make a glaze from a rocky material called *tetízatl* (Sahagún 1956(3):343).

106. Gibson 1964:397–402; Hakluyt 1907(6):287; Kubler 1948(1):155; Mayer 1961:30–1.

107. Dibble 1963:74, 103 notes entry by the Aubin drawing of 1576, "*Viernes 7 del mes de agosto se encaló detrás de la iglesia, donde se saca agua con noria.*" Instituto Indigenista Interamericano 1947 and Toussaint 1924:19 show two vertical water wheels lifting water to the site where the construction of the foundation for the Mexico City cathedral was under way. More probably the wheels were *norias de sangre*, with the horizontal gearing wheel being omitted from the drawing.

108. Gómez de Orozco 1941:65–70. In the eighteenth century three galleons sunk off the Florida Keys while returning to Spain were said to have carried *botijos* of resinous balsam, another clue to the usage of these jars by colonials (Peterson 1975:381). James (1985:42) also notes the possibility of cochineal dye being transported to Spain in ceramic jars.

109. This pottery has been designated as Valle Ware, with three types decorated in blue on a white ground and one type being plain white. These are Tlalpan Blue–on–White, Guadalupe Blue–on–White, Tlalpan Mottled, and Tlalpan White (Lister

and Lister 1982:30–3, Figs. 3.30–3.33, 3.42). For discussion of paste, see Maggetti, Westley, and Olin 1984:151–91.

110. Mexico City Ware, Fine Grade, is comprised of four decorated and one white stylistic types. These are San Juan Polychrome (also known as Fig Springs Polychrome), San Luis Blue–on–White, Tacuba Polychrome, La Traza Polychrome, and Mexico City White Variety One. Mexico City Ware, Common Grade, includes Mexico City Blue–on–Cream, Mexico City Polychrome, Mexico City Green–on–Cream, San Luis Polychrome, Santa María Polychrome, and Mexico City White Variety Two (Lister and Lister 1982:13–30, Figs. 3.1–3.6, 3.8–3.28, 3.40, 3.41).

111. Ibid:Fig. 3.7c; Frothingham 1969:145; Toussaint 1967:101, 174. Fray Hernando de Ojea in the late 1500s wrote that the Santo Domingo church in Mexico City had walls richly covered with tiles. According to Kubler (1948(2):528–9), these tiles would have dated between 1560 and 1607. By the latter date the massive building had sunk nine feet below street level, causing it to be rebuilt. The sixteenth-century tiles disappeared in the renovations, so it is now impossible to know whether they were imported from Sevilla or were made locally. Other tiles recovered *in situ* on facings of some tombs beneath the Mexico City cathedral are provincial, as proved by the quality of pigments and draftsmanship. They are late sixteenth or early seventeenth century in date. Peña Verchez, pers. comm., Mexico City, 1983; Valle Arizpe 1939:231). Some plain white impressed tiles in the Capilla del Rosario, Santo Domingo, Puebla, although treated in the *cuenca* manner, likely date from a late seventeenth-century Puebla revival of an earlier mode. The chapel was dedicated in 1690. See Cervantes 1939(2):87.

112. Gómez de Orozco 1949:189–212. According to Israel (1975:120), at the end of the sixteenth century the Italians resident in Mexico were primarily wealthy merchants from the areas of Genoa, the Piedmont, Venice, and Naples.

113. For the years 1590, 1592–3, see Appendix 2, 317–18. Torre Revello 1943:773–80 notes that some of the 2,805 ships coming to the Americas between 1504 and 1555 carried ceramics in their mixed cargoes. Such pottery is not identified as to kinds or amounts, nor are the ports of destination given. Friede (1952:467–96) places the figure at 2,550 registered ships to America, but the number of unregistered vessels is unknown. Benítez, J. R. (1929:120) gives number of convoys from 1565 to 1800, but the merchandise on board is not described. Chaunu and Chaunu (1974:119) report a 1500–1580 rise in annual tonnage from 3,000–4,000 tons to 30,000 tons, with a sharp drop after the loss of so many vessels in the 1588 defeat of the Spanish Armada. One important green lead-glazed specimen of this period, which must represent a Sevillian export, is a pedestal-based *pila bautismal* bearing molded Renaissance designs, an impressed Franciscan escutcheon, and the date 1599. It was found in the 1920s in the Franciscan monastery in the village of Tepepan at the south side of the Valley of Mexico. Local art historians have considered it a Mexican-made specimen, which seems unlikely (Cervantes 1939[1]:88–9; Toussaint 1967:Fig. 159).

114. Called Indígena Ware, the painted and etched style is Romita Sgraffito, the white Romita Plain (Lister and Lister 1982:34–40, 96–9). To compare Aztec design style with that appearing on this ware, see Franco 1945:163–86; 1949:162–208; Franco and Peterson 1957; Griffin and Espejo 1947(6, no. 2):137–47; (9, no. 1):118–69; Noguera 1965; 1967:7–11; Vega Sosa 1975.

115. Cruxent and Vaz 1980:71–85; Deagan 1978:Figs. 6–7; McEwan 1983:Appendix 3. Mexico City potters' guild ordinances of 1677 listed three kinds of pottery being made: white ware (maiolica), yellow ware (lead-glazed cook pots), and red ware (utility plainware). Those divisions in production likely existed from the beginning of pottery making in the Valley of Mexico (Barrio Lorenzot 1920:174; Toussaint 1967:265).

116. Goggin (1968:154, 156–7) assigns a beginning date of 1610 to the polychromatic palmette style (archaeologically known as Fig Springs Polychrome or San Juan Polychrome) and 1630–35 to the blue–on–white floral style (archaeologically known as San Luis Blue–on–White). Lister and Lister (1982:Table 2.1) place the beginnings of both in the second half of the sixteenth century as a consequence of finding them in deposits below a 1573 foundation capping at the Mexico City cathedral. These dates superceded those given in Lister and Lister 1976b:132. Caiger-Smith (1973:Fig. 152) illustrates a Puebla copy of Chinese styling that he claims was being made before 1630 and refers to Bernabé Cobo's report of that date that ware as fine as that of Talavera was being produced in Puebla. That would suggest that the two Mexico City styles were being replaced by the typical seventeenth-century Puebla styles at least by the third decade of the century. Terminal dates cannot be determined as yet, but probably they would fall at or before the middle of the seventeenth century. For other specific distributions, see DiPeso 1974(3):948–9; (8):195; Goggin 1968:153–4, 157; Ortega and Fondeur 1978a:233; Plowden 1958:Fig. 215–7; Snow 1965:Table 2. Scholes (1930:100–1), in a list of supplies sent north every three years from Mexico City to seventeenth-century Franciscan missions in New Mexico, indicates a number of items that normally might have been packed in earthenware containers. These were forty-five gallons of sacramental wine, twenty-six gallons of oil for illuminating the Holy Sacrament, eight gallons of oil for the friar's use, four gallons of vinegar, two jugs of Campeche honey, and other foods such as raisins, almonds, conserves, and spices. One box of *loza de Puebla* was dishes for altar or personal use. No tile has been recovered archaeologically from these missions.

117. Gerhard (1972:Table D) lists nine major epidemics between 1563 and 1634, several lasting more than a year and, as should be expected, most particularly devastating in areas of population concentration, such as Mexico City. Flooding was another recurring problem in the island city, with five major inundations from 1553 to 1629 forcing wholesale evacuation of the capital (Galindo y Villa 1925:161; Maza 1968:30). To quote Thomas Gage (1958:50), a seventeenth-century priest who traveled extensively in Spanish America, "In the year of 1634, when Mexico was like to be drowned with the inundation of the lake, thousands left it, and came with all their goods and families to Puebla . . ."

118. Maggetti, Westley, and Olin 1984:151–91.

119. Barrio Lorenzot 1920; Toussaint 1967:176.

120. Chevalier 1970:108. According to Kubler and Soria (1958:69), the gridiron city plan, although an admired Renaissance concept, was seldom used in Europe before 1600. The setting aside of craft neighborhoods is not discussed usually in connection with the city plans ordered for the Spanish Americas and may not be a factor recognized by historians. For example, see Borah 1972:35–54.

121. Ewald 1976:14.

122. Artes de Mexico 1966; Carrion 1896; López Rasado 1965.

123. Maggetti, Westley, and Olin 1984:151–91. The *tequesquite* came from Hacienda Ozumba, a holding of the Jesuit College of Espíritu Santo, on the east side of the peak of Malinche (Ewald 1976:10).

124. Cervantes 1939(1):1; Fernández de Echeverría y Veytia 1931(1):318. The latter originally wrote in 1779, at which time white-firing clay from San Baltasár is said to have been used. There is no mention of either two clays or the deposits of greyish clay (*negro*) from the hill of Loreto just east of colonial Puebla or whitish clay (*blanquizco*) from the village of Totimehuacán, the modern sources. The 1653 guild ordinances stipulate the proper sieving and cleaning of the raw clay, but do not give its origin (Barber 1908:20; Cervantes 1939(1):23). Cobalt used at Puebla came from Spain (Leicht 1934:124).

125. Cervantes (1939(2):197–8) lists a total of six potters, but implies the presence of three others who worked into the seventeenth century.

126. Ibid:15–8.

127. Peña Virchez, pers. comm. 1983; Lister and Lister 1982:Fig. 3.7c.

128. Cervantes 1939(2):185–96; Leicht 1934; Lister and Lister 1984:88–9, Fig. 1.

129. Lister and Lister 1984:89–91, Fig. 2.

130. Cervantes 1939(2):223; Fowst 1971:178.

131. Cervantes 1939(2):223; Fowst 1971:178.

132. An American counsul, A.M. Gottschalk (1907:15), in reporting to Washington, said: "In the early days of Puebla's history the Dominican friars, struck by the aptitude of their Aztec parishioners, at making crude native pottery, and desirous also of obtaining tiles for the monastery and church which they were building, sent word to the Dominican establishment at Talavera de la Reina, in the Province of Toledo, Spain, that they could make good use of five or six of the brotherhood who were acquainted with the Spanish processes of pottery making, if such could be sent out to them. Accordingly a number of Dominican friars, familiar with the clay-working processes in use at Talavera, were assigned to the Puebla house of their order, and under them were trained a generation of workmen, who for the first few succeeding years produced some excellent pieces." His source for such information is not given, but many writers thereafter repeated it as fact (for example, Barber 1911:5).

133. Cervantes 1939(2):209, 215, 227, 231–2, 236.

134. Toussaint 1939:603–8; 1946; 1967:125–8. As late as 1776 a *mestizo* Puebla potter married a young local girl identified as a *morisca*. She was the legitimate daughter of residents of the San Marcos parish (Cervantes 1939[2]:244). However, by that period in colonial Mexico the word *morisco* had come to mean a quadroon, a racial mixture of Spaniard and mulatto, rather than, as in Spain, a converted Muslim.

135. Blair and Robertson 1903–1909(3):214; (44):311; (45):40. A package (*balsa*) of porcelain was to be one *vara* high by two and a half *varas* in circumference. An official document states, "the citizens [of Manila] be allowed to send wax and porcelain at their pleasure, as these are commodities of little value, and needed by Nueva España." It is no surprise, therefore, that the large amount of Chinese porcelain found in excavations beneath Mexico City shows that it was very common in the colony, much more so than in Spain. Also inasmuch as it has been found at many of the humble frontier sites across the northern border-

lands, its cost could not have been prohibitive, although surely more than that of locally made wares. For discussion of the Manila Galleon trade, see Artes de Mexico 1971; 1977; Carrera Stampa 1959; Chaunu and Chaunu 1974:124; Schurz 1939. It cannot be demonstrated that Chinese influence on Mexican maiolica came through Spain, as has sometimes been suggested (Goggin 1968:11).

136. Chaunu and Chaunu 1974:124.

137. Barber 1908:21; Cervantes 1939(1):24.

138. Lister and Lister 1976a:58.

139. Toussaint 1967:167

140. For illustrations and/or descriptions of the three seventeenth-century Puebla maiolica styles (Puebla Polychrome, Abó Polychrome, and Puebla Blue–on–White) represented by complete specimens of museum caliber, see Angulo Íñiguez 1946; Banamex 1979; Barber 1908; 1911; 1915; Cervantes 1939; Hernández 1946; Peon Soler and Cortina Ortega 1973. For archaeological specimens, see Goggin 1968:169–82; Lister and Lister 1974:Figs. 5a, 6; Müller 1973: 97, 108–9; Toulouse 1949:Pl. 27–8. Goggin (1968:172, 180) suggests both Puebla Polychrome and Abó Polychrome began in the second half of the seventeenth century. Because they have been recovered in a number of sites in New Mexico dating as early as the first and second decades of the century, it is entirely likely they commenced some time in that period (Lister and Lister 1976b:132; Snow 1965:33). Cervantes (1939[1]:97–107) similarly places them in the first half of the century. Both may well have continued to be made through the rest of the seventeenth century, perhaps into the early eighteenth century.

141. May 1939:147, Fig. 158.

142. Lace-patterned maiolica believed to have originated in Lisbon was recovered in seventeenth-century Jamestown, Virginia (Cotter 1958:Pl. 82, lower left). Examples also are in the Museo de Bellas Artes, Lisbon.

143. Ainaud de Lasarte 1952:Figs. 741–3; Martínez Caviró 1968:Fig. 181; Seseña 1981:71.

144. Banamex 1979:Figs. 2–3; Cervantes 1939(1):104–7.

145. Cervantes 1939(2):315.

146. Banamex 1979:Fig. 1; Cervantes 1939(1):101, 103.

147. Cervantes 1939(1):28–9. (Abó Polychrome).

148. Banamex 1979:Fig. 5; Peon Soler and Cortina Ortega 1973:Fig. 7.

149. Goggin 1968:Pl. 14c; Peon Soler and Cortina Ortega 1973:Fig. 2.

150. Known to American archaeologists as Puebla Blue–on–White, the beginning date of this style should be pushed back into the mid seventeenth century. It has been recovered in a number of New Mexico sites and in the Casas Grandes convento, Chihuahua, which was abandoned by the 1680s (Barber 1908:27; DiPeso 1974(3):948; (8):194; Goggin 1968:194; Lister and Lister 1976b:134). Variations continued into the early nineteenth century, such continuity being another example of the extreme conservatism of this pottery-making complex. Puebla Blue–on–White was the style intended in the 1676 guild ordinance amendments, which translate: "Also in making the fine wares the coloring should be in imitation of the Chinese ware, very blue, finished in the same style and with relief work in blue . . ." (Barber 1908:27); for Spanish version, see Cervantes 1939(1):29.

151. Cervantes 1939(1):23.

152. Cervantes 1939(2):94–5.

153. Berendsen 1967:24; Cervantes 1939(2):21–5 for variations of brick and tile patterns. Toussaint believes the combination of plain and glazed terra cottas was a transfer of the *mudéjar olambrilla* pavement to the Puebla walls. Toussaint 1967:266.

154. Benítez, F. 1965:57; Vetancurt 1971:47.

155. Frothingham 1943:97–117.

156. Arcila Farias 1950:97; Barnes 1972:6–7; 1976:158–9; Deagan 1983:Table 5.2; DiPeso 1974(3):947–9; Goggin 1968:172, 179, 180, 194; Lister and Lister 1974:38–43; 1976b:113–40; Ortega and Fondeur 1978a:Figs. 31a, 33 c–f; Plowden 1958:212–19; Snow 1965:215–35.

157. Lister and Lister 1974:38–43.

Notes to The Potters: Their Work and Social Roles

1. Cervantes 1939(1):49–50.

2. Torres Balbás 1971(1):385. It is presumed that the Spanish Muslims likely had lived at their Sevilla workshops. Myers 1984:69 reports that this is not a typical arrangement in modern Morocco, but it did occur elsewhere in medieval Islam. For example, see Rye and Evans 1976:Fig. 2.

3. Excavation of an extensive pottery in Sirāf on the Persian gulf provides a model for former Muslim yards (Whitehouse 1971:1–18). Observation of modern shops in Morocco and Granada provides a continuum (Lister and Lister 1975a:290–2). For in-depth consideration of primitive pottery technology, see Rye 1981; for modern methods, see Bourry 1926; for present Spanish methods, see Giral 1981.

4. Collantes de Teran and Zozaya 1972:258; Morales Padrón 1977:33. An interesting petition of six potters to the city authorities of Sevilla in March, 1557, protested the taking of clay from pits at Castilleja de la Cuesta by some men without authority to do so. They stated that the local potters had used clay from this source for as long as anyone could remember, and they would fight to keep intruders out. Although the purpose of the memorial was to request the city to designate the clay reserves as a royal patrimony, no known action was taken. (Gestoso y Pérez 1903:61, 446).

5. Maggetti, Westley, and Olin 1984:151–91.

6. Cervantes (1939(1):1) says today a blackish clay comes from the Loreto hill on the east side of Puebla and a red clay is from a village near Tecali in the state of Puebla. Whether the same clay deposits were in use in the seventeenth century is not known.

7. Barrio Lorenzot 1920:174.

8. Cervantes 1939(1):5; Maggetti, Westley, and Olin 1984: 151–91.

9. West of what is now Calle 11 (Leicht 1934:200; Lister and Lister 1984:93).

10. Allan 1973:113. See Whitehouse 1971:Pl.VI for photograph of a calcination kiln.

11. For Spanish wares, Gestoso y Pérez 1903:101; Llubiá 1967:20. For finewares of Puebla, Mexico, guild ordinances called for l *arroba* (25 pounds) of lead to 6 pounds of tin, or a ratio of 4 to 1. For common grade wares, the proportions were 1 *arroba* to 2 pounds of tin, or a ratio of 12 to 1 (Cervantes 1939[1]:24). The Mexico City ordinances required 1 *arroba* lead to 4 pounds of tin for finewares, a ratio of 5 to 1, the common ware ratio being

the same as that at Puebla (Barrio Lorenzot 1920:174). The fine
glazes obviously were less opaque on Mexico City wares when
these ratios were carefully followed.

12. Allan 1973:113.

13. Singer et al 1954(2):354.

14. In 1621 an English trader described the processing of
barrilla (*Salsola webbi*) in the Valencia area, which likely was a procedure similar to that used in Andalusia. In both localities the
resulting soda ash was used in making soap, glass, and glazes.
"This Barrillia is a strange kind of vegetable, and it grows no
where upon the Surface of the Earth in That Perfection, as here;
It grows thus, It is a round thick earthy Shrub that bears Berries
like Barberries, betwixt blue and green; it lies close to the
Ground, and when it is ripe they dig it up by the Roots, and put
it together in Crocks, where they leave it to dry many Days
like Hay; then they make a Pit of a Fathom deep in the Earth,
and with an Instrument like one of our Prongs, they take the
Tuffs and put fire to them, and when the Flame comes to the
Berries, they melt and dissolve into an Azure Liquor, and fall
down into the Pit till it be full; then they dam it up, and some
Days after they open it and find this Barrillia Juice turned to a
blue Stone, so hard, that it is scarce malleable; and it is sold at
one hundred Crowns a Tun . . ." (Howell 1907(1):63–4; also
quoted in Frothingham 1963:12). The modern Pakistan production of *khār*, or sintered plant ash, is fully discussed in Rye
and Evans 1976:180–4. The process is essentially that of eighteenth-century Spain.

15. Scanlon 1965:7–30.

16. Frothingham 1941b:71–3. Glass slag is today the usual frit
in Triana potteries.

17. Glass factory was located on what is now Calle 5 Norte
400 (Leicht 1934:443).

18. In their analysis of Piccolpasso's work, Lightbown and
Caiger-Smith (1980(1):xv;[2]:68) suggest that Italian technique
reversed the more usual maiolica firing methods, with the highest temperatures being achieved during the bisque step. They
estimate the former to have been about 1000°C. and the latter
about 950°C. In their opinion, the structure of the updraft kilns
would not have withstood temperatures greater than 1100°C.
without collapse of the floor separating the two chambers.
Because Spanish Muslim technology did not include the additional weight of saggars, it is felt the higher temperature range
was possible, and, in some instances, likely.

19. An inventory made in 1556, at the time of the death of
Gaspar de Escobar, illustrates the sort of stockpiled materials and
equipment to be found in a typical sixteenth-century Sevillian
workshop. These included a jar with yellow pigment; a basin
with approximately 2 *arrobas* of blue; a basin of brown pigment of
about ½ *arroba* quantity; certain ground glass and a mill with
about 15 *arrobas* in it; a small amphora full of blue pigment; two
shovels of a type used in calcination kilns; a scale for weighing
galena; a large amphora with a certain amount of powder; a
marble mortar in which to grind glaze; three large earthenware
tubs; a certain quantity of fired and unfired roof tile; two cartons
of molds; three potter's wheels; 211 planks; one basin of the
size packed six to a carton and a smaller one of the size packed
ten to a carton; a certain quantity of clay; twelve loads of white
maiolica and green lead-glazed pottery; 155 pieces of green
[unfired] ware; 80 *arrobas* of white powder from the calcination of

white tin and green copper-colored lead glaze valued at 56 *reales;* and 18 pounds of tin (Gestoso y Pérez 1903:402).

20. Gestoso y Pérez 1899–1909(1):73–4, 76, 79, 81–3, 87, 383, 385; 1903:370–451.
21. Gestoso y Pérez 1903:448.
22. Ibid:437; 1919:6.
23. España, Sevilla, Archivo de Protocolos 1932(2):270; Gestoso y Pérez 1903:412.
24. Morales Padrón 1977:92–3.
25. Pike 1972:19, 161, 168.
26. Haring 1964:105; Mexico City, Cabildo 1871–1919(2):61, 135. Toussaint (1946:9, note 5) cites a half-dozen proper names with Arabic background, although none were those of potters. Avilez Moreno (1980:656) calls attention to a 1543 royal *cédula* prohibiting the further emigration to the Americas of *moriscos,* by inference substantiating their presence. He also notes that 200 *morisco* soldiers were in the army that aided the conquest of Peru.
27. Borah 1943:9; Liss 1975:57, 79, 101.
28. Santiago Cruz 1960:36.
29. The roles of Chinese, mulattoes, Negroes, and Mexican Indians are dealt with in Carrera Stampa 1954:227–8, and Cervantes 1939(2):206, 219, 228–30. Dubs and Smith (1942:387–9) note the beginnings of a Chinese colony in Mexico City as early as 1635. A 1676 ordinance prohibiting members of any of these racial groups from becoming an Inspector of Puebla guilds is to be found in Mexico, Archivo General de la Nación 1940–1:325.
30. Gestoso y Pérez 1899–1909(2):759; (3):265.
31. Barrio Lorenzot 1920:175; Cervantes 1939(1):23.
32. Hess 1978:173.
33. Glick 1979:151.
34. Goitein 1967(1):92.
35. Bennassar 1979:ix.
36. Pike 1972:130–1.
37. Among modern potters of Mexico, particularly those *mestizos* in village industries, there is a feeling that their occupation is a lowly, dirty one without status. They would prefer other occupations, even farming, which is similarly dirty (Foster 1965:46–7; Weigand and Weigand 1969:3). These attitudes must be traceable to those of the invading Spaniards, for the aboriginal potters exhibited no such negative outlook, so far as we know. It might be theorized that maiolists would place themselves in an intermediate position between makers of utility wares and of industrial ceramics. They are very aware of their historical linkage to Spanish culture, and their income exceeds that of the makers of plainwares.
38. Barsis 1973:99, 108, 137–8.
39. Ramazzini 1964:59.
40. Hillier 1968:19–20.
41. It has been suggested that the fall of the Roman Empire came about through endemic lead poisoning resulting from use of lead water pipes and lead-lined cook pots, even though the users were aware of the danger (Forbes 1956:665; Waldron and Stofen 1974:5). Vitruvius, a Roman architect at the beginning of the Christian Era, noted: "Lead is found to be harmful to the human system . . .: This we can exemplify from plumbers, since in them the natural color of the body is replaced by a deep pallor" (Briggs 1956:419). The Muslim potter Abū'l Qāsim recorded the method he and his co-workers used to deal with the lead problem in glazes (Allan 1973:113).

42. World Health Organization 1977.

43. Gestoso y Pérez 1903:377, 386, 387, 401, 445, 451 lists extant records for the first quarter of the sixteenth century of purchases of some supplies. These show 1700 pounds of iron costing 5000 *maravedíes* ($8.82) in 1503 and *chamiza* fuel of unknown quantity 4920 *maravedíes* ($8.68) in 1524. An unspecified amount of Viscayan lead amounted to 2703 *maravedíes* ($4.77) in 1505. Three hundred pounds of old tin, probably comprising discarded articles to be melted down, went for 4800 *maravedíes* ($8.47) in 1504. In 1527 an order of tin from a Genoese and an English merchant cost 17,969 *maravedíes* ($31.71). By contrast, two 1501 purchases from a Genoese trader of zafre, or refined cobalt, required the tidy sums of 30,000 *maravedíes* ($52.94) and 102,000 *maravedíes* ($180).

44. Ibid:413.

45. The itemized taxes collected for kiln firings in Sevilla all are in the 1570s. They ranged from 6 *reales* (36 cents) to 12,000 *maravedíes* ($21.18). The higher charge, plus another for 7 *ducats* ($4.63), was assessed against Tomás de Pésaro, the Ligurian craftsman who set up a *fábrica* in the old house formerly belonging to Columbus's son, and apparently was retroactive to include all previous firings (Ibid:430).

46. Wagner 1972:119–30.

47. Gestoso y Perez 1903:385.

48. Pike 1972:141. Taking information from a 1559 parish survey made by a priest in Málaga, which reported that 70 percent of his parishioners fell into a category termed *pequeños* (little ones), Braudel (1974:33) estimates their annual income at from 7500 to 15,000 *maravedíes*. Artisans likely comprised the bulk of this group.

49. Gestoso y Pérez 1903:391.

50. Pike (1967:345) reports that in 1567 there were 6,327 slaves in the Sevillian population of 85,538, or one slave for every fourteen persons.

51. Bennassar (1979:108, 112–3) says that in 1620 slaves represented five percent of Sevilla's population and were owned by all classes, from churchmen and administrators to artisans. See also, fn.48.

52. Gestoso y Pérez 1903:242.

53. Pike 1972:149.

54. Sailing time for the fleet bound for New Spain was May; that for the Tierra Firme fleet was August.

55. Bennassar (1979:145, 169) considered the average work day to have been no more than six hours. With obvious disapproval, he wrote, "Such was the seductive power of festival and diversions that they pressed a continual offensive against the time assigned to labor; the whole object seemed to be to rescue as many days as possible from labor, and to limit the length of the workday so that time was left for recreation."

56. Carrera Stampa 1954:167.

57. Hamilton 1976:872.

58. Gestoso y Pérez 1903:307–8.

59. Domínguez Ortíz 1956:15.

60. Díez Borque (1975:112) quotes a seventeenth-century traveler to Spain, Countess D'Aulnoy, who wrote of Spanish artisans, "It is not possible to see a carpenter, harness maker, or any other shopkeeper who does not go dressed in velvet and satin, like a king, having a sword, dagger, and a guitar hanging in his shop."

61. Delfourneaux 1971:43.

62. Lévi-Provencal 1957:179. Myers (1984:188–91) argues that even with some self-regulation, craft organizations in North Africa were under tighter state control than in Europe.

63. Von Grunebaum 1955:151.

64. Gestoso y Pérez 1903:164.

65. Domínguez Ortíz (1956:103–4) and Gestoso y Pérez (1899–1909[1]:xxvii) assume a guild but could not locate documents that pertained to it. Montoto de Sedas (1938:165) categorically states that potters and tilers were not organized.

66. Gestoso y Pérez 1903:102; Montoto de Sedas 1938:165.

67. Gestoso y Pérez 1903:443.

68. For an exhaustive study of Spanish craft guilds and their effects upon the national economy and the attitudes of workers, see Colmeiro 1965(1 and 2); Klein 1967:164–88; Rumeu de Armas 1942; Vicens Vives 1972:248–75.

69. According to Borah and Cook (1958:47), in 1555 a skilled carpenter in Mexico made 36 *maravedíes* daily; in 1569 an unskilled worker earned 12 *maravedíes* daily. Guthrie (1939:131) places unskilled laborer wages at about one-fourth a *peso* daily, but notes that a person could exist well in the city for a half *peso* per day.

70. Cervantes 1939(1):21–2; (2):203; Leicht 1934:32; Lister and Lister 1984:90.

71. Cervantes (1939(2):216) gives a 1687 rental inventory for the Carreto shop to include: 16 dozen good and bad saggars; 50 boxes used as molds; 7 dozen saggar lids; 3 dozen saggars for small plates for nuns; one large and one small mill; a template; two wooden potter's wheels; a 25-*vara* long wooden scaffold; one large and one small kiln; a calcination kiln; three pits for sieving ingredients; a large block on which to crush *tequesquite* and a wooden sledge; and a grinding stone (*piedra mexicana*) to prepare pigments. Ibid:222 gives a similar 1697 rental inventory for Talavera, in addition to the kilns: a mill in which to grind glaze materials, which would have been animal driven; two other mills for preparing and applying glaze; a grinding stone on which to pulverize mineral pigments; 126 loads of plates, half of which were in poor condition; and 8 dozen broken and 2½ dozen complete saggar lids.

72. Ibid:211.

73. Ibid:198–238.

74. One well documented family passing its workshop down through successive generations was that founded by Nicolás de Zayas, who was married in 1674. His business went to José in 1724, to Nicolás in 1740, to Sebastián in 1744, to Antonio in 1783. The colonial street that carried the Zayas name is modern Avenida 10 Poniente 700. The present factory of most importance still occupies a house established by a potter ancestor in 1868. (Leicht 1934:9–10, 385–6, 469–70; Lister and Lister 1984:90–1).

75. Cervantes 1939(2):114–5; Leicht 1934.

76. México, Archivo General de la Nación 1941 (12, #2):325.

77. Santiago Cruz (1960:12) states that Charles V ordered the disbandment of Spanish confraternities in 1552, but they continued as popular, rather than semi-religious or trade, organizations.

78. Cue Canovas 1963:87–8. According to Santiago Cruz (1960:13), ironworkers formed a guild in 1524, but this is unverified in other sources.

79. Carrera Stampa (1954:92) and Cervantes (1939(1):22–5) reaffirm that a potters' guild in Puebla was organized in June, 1659; another in Mexico City appeared in October, 1681 (Barrio

Lorenzot 1920:173–5). The content of their ordinances was nearly identical. In a 1675 listing of craft organizations, that for potters ranked thirty-fifth (J.R. Benítez 1929:180–1).

80. See Weckmann 1951:130–41 for other medieval attributes in the Spanish New World. See also Konetzke 1949:483–524.

81. How completely cockspurs replaced saggars is shown in an eighteenth-century inventory of the equipment of a workshop that listed 7,000 such items (Barber 1908:18–23; Cervantes 1939[1]:23–5, 49–50; [2]:310).

82. Cervantes 1939(1):52–3.

83. The clothes were specifically itemized as a vest, breeches, cloak, two shirts, stockings, shoes, and hat (Ibid:55–6).

84. Cervantes 1939(1):55–6; Santiago Cruz 1960:28–9.

85. Gestoso y Pérez 1903:376.

86. Cervantes 1939(2):197–238.

87. For a perceptive discussion of how modern Puebla utility grade potters learn their craft and contribute to a continuity of style from generation to generation, see Kaplan 1976:243–8.

Glossary

aceite olive oil

aceituna olive

adarve secluded district within city

aging process in which moistened clay is stored to permit water to become more uniformly dispersed, thus improving plasticity

aguador water peddler

aguamanil water jar; usually large, high-shouldered, narrow-based, with a spigot near bottom

alaria fettling tool

albarelo cylindrical vessel, often with indrawn walls at midsection, used to contain drugs; form was said to have been suggested by section of bamboo; in early periods was sealed with piece of parchment or linen spread over wide mouth, in eighteenth century with ceramic lid

albornía cup-shaped vessel or larger ovoid jar often used in pharmacies to dispense medicines

alcaicería shopping center, or bazaar, with small stalls that could be closed and locked; usually sold luxury goods, but one in Sevilla sold common pottery

alcalde guild officer elected annually by guild members to deal with authorities

alcaparra caper

alcarraza unglazed jar for cooling water

alcázar castle-fortification

alcohol galena (lead sulphide) used as flux in most common earthenware glaze

alcuza earthenware pot attached to water wheel; jar for storing water; also called *arcaduz* or *cangilón*

alfar or *alfarero* potter

alicatado mosaic tile panels composed of number of fragments covered with opaque glaze of diverse colors; technique persists in modern Morocco

alicer individual glazed tile fragment used in mosaic panels

alisios trade winds

almajena earthenware pot for glaze solutions

almajo saltwort burned to obtain soda ash for tin glaze

almalluquero peddler of rejected or damaged pottery

almártaga litharge (a fused lead monoxide)

almendra almond

almijarra long-handled tool used to remove melted minerals from calcination kiln

almojarifazgo import-export duty

almotácen Muslim overseer of market

alpañata chamois used to smooth and compact soft rims

alpetije wooden trimming tool

alquitrán pitch, tar

amin   Muslim official whose task was to arbitrate between municipal authorities and artisans

anafe   earthenware brazier consisting of cylindrical base with opening for insertion of charcoal and open bowl-shaped upper portion with pierced base in which to place cook pot

ánfora   amphora; generally large jar with pointed base, high shoulders, short neck, and two stout handles at each upper side

appliqué   raised elements attached with slurry to a leather hard vessel surface

aprendiz   apprentice

arcaduz   earthenware jar attached in series to rim of water wheel; also called *cangilón*

arista   tile with arrises, or impressed raised salient angles, to form pattern, the ridges preventing flow of molten glaze

arroba   liquid measure varying from 2.6 to 3.6 (in more extreme cases to 4.26) gallons, or 16.13 liters; dry measure of 25 pounds

arroz   rice

artesanado   body of artisans

atanor   cylindrical earthenware tubes open at both ends, used as water drains

ataurique   Islamic design element of heavy scroll with lobed borders

atífle   cockspur

azafrán   saffron

azulejero   maker of tile

azulejo   smooth–surfaced tile, usually decorated in several or many colors

azumbre   liquid measurement of 4 pints or 4 *cuartillas*; 8 *azumbres* equaled 1 *arroba*; also name of a Muslim vessel form of unknown contours

bacín   cylindrical chamber pot with straight sides, flat base, and broad horizontal brim; usually, but not always, with a pair of handles on the upper walls to aid in pouring; often confused by English speakers with basin

back   shallow vat for holding water

barbotine   Roman decorative mode using raised slip pattern over a base provided by smooth vessel wall

barreño   deep, flat-bottomed earthenware basin or tub with straight sides

barrilla   saltwort, *Salsola soda*, used in soap, glass, glaze manufacture

barrio   district

barro   clay

bat   wooden or plaster of paris disk temporarily attached to potter's wheel head; could be removed without disturbing freshly thrown object on top of it

berenjena   eggplant

birlo   fired ceramic rod used by Muslim potters as support within a kiln

bisque   biscuit; pottery fired one time; can be used in this state or may be covered with glaze and refired; *biscocho* in Spain, *juaguete* in Mexico

bodegón   painting still life

borujo   residue of skins and pits from olive pressing; in Andalusia and Morocco, used as fuel for kilns

bote   squat, round-bodied, neckless jar used in pharmacies for medicines or conserves *botella*   bottle form with tall narrow neck, round body, and flat base

boticario   pharmacist

botija   measurement for wine, alcohol, and other liquids, varying from 5 to 8 liters; 115 gallons in another context; also a vessel form

botija perulera   round-bodied, round-based jug with brief neck; lacked the spouts and upper arched handle of *botijo*; probably principal variation of form commonly known by American archaeologists as olive jar; was the standard container for Andalusian products shipped to the Americas; *vacía*, empty; *llenada*, filled.

botijería   industry for making earthenware containers

botijo   enclosed, bulbous, flat-based jar with tapered small-mouthed pouring spout, a large vertical filling spout, and an arched handle over the top

botijuela   measure of 10 kilos for honey; also jar of that capacity

brocal   massive ceramic well mouth; usually approximately 3 feet in diameter, moldmade of circular or quadrangular form, with heavy walls, thick rim, and frequently with relief decoration on exterior walls; comparable undecorated cylindrical sections formed well casing

caballito   Mexican term for cockspur; literally, small horse

cabildo   town council

cacharrería   cheap earthenware crockery; *cacharrero*, dealer in such crockery

caja   box; saggar

cajón   large box

caldera   caldron

canasta   basket

candelero   candleholder; recovered forms of sixteenth and seventeenth century are of tubular form, seated in a saucer, topped by a wide disk to catch dripping wax, with a socket for candle above it

candil de piquera   oil lamp consisting of tiny, flat-based jar with a long horizontal trough to accommodate a wick

canela   cinnamon

cántara   large pitcher of approximately 32 pints capacity; also defined as oil jar; also liquid measurement of 4.26 liters of oil or 3.32 liters of other liquids

cántaro   earthenware jar with prominent neck, high shoulders, bulging mid-section tapering to narrow flat base, generally with a pair of handles from upper neck to shoulders, occasionally small spout; used for liquid storage; spouted variant for medicines; one more-or-less standardized size held 12.56 liters

cántiga   song

cantimplora   round-bodied canteen or pilgrim bottle; pair of small handles from brief neck to upper shoulders

carrera de indias   Spanish sea-lanes to the Americas; also the transatlantic trade

carta de examen   guild papers indicating successful passing of craft examination

casa de ollería   combination living and working quarters where pottery was manufactured

cascajo   broken or discarded piece of pottery

cavetto   concave area between obverse center and rim of open vessel form

cazuela   casserole; round-bodied, relatively broad, low-walled cook pot

ceramista potter of high caliber ware

chamiza brushwood utilized for kiln fuel

cintillo narrow border tile

clavo small, triangular-shaped, earthenware headpin inserted through saggar walls to provide support during glaze firing for horizontal rims of plates suspended from them; literally, nail

clay earthy mineral substance that becomes plastic when wet, rocklike when fired

clepsydra earthenware jar with small hole in base used to measure time by the gradual flow of water through the opening; water clock

cobija saggar

cockspur tripod-shaped piece of fired clay used to separate vessels during glaze firing

cofradía lay brotherhood

colador settling tank used to soak raw clay for preliminary processing

collación precinct

colorant mineral oxide used to produce color in glaze solution or decorative pigment; in oxidizing atmosphere typical of Spanish production, iron gave golden to dark brown, copper gave green, manganese gave purple to brown, cobalt gave blue, tin gave white

compadrazgo relationship between parents and godparents of child

comunidad community; chapter house

conserva conserve, preserve

contrahecho counterfeit, imitation

converso Jewish convert to Catholicism

coperta In Italian methods, thin layer of clear lead glaze applied over maiolica surfaces prior to firing; served to protect patterns, itensify decorative colors and luster of glaze, and hide imperfections

corral Sevillian term for house compound, consisting of living and working rooms and galleries around a central courtyard

cortijo farm or country home in Andalusia

crackling intentional crazing

crazing unintentional network of tiny fissures in glaze coat due to improper fit of glaze to body

criollo American Spaniard born of European parents, as opposed to *gachupín*, a peninsular Spaniard living in Latin America

cuartilla liquid measurement of 4.03 liters; *cuartillo*, of one-half liter; both frequently used for olive oil

cuenca tile bearing impressed patterns, the ridges of which confined glazes of different colors during firing

cuenco bowl form typical of Spanish Muslim repertory, with widely flaring walls tapering down to a very narrow base; used today as ceremonial form for serving couscous, the national dish of Morocco

cuerda seca Islamic decorative technique common in Spain, wherein sections of glaze were separated during firing by a greasy medium to which glaze would not adhere; wax resist

Cufic Early Arabic script notable for angular characters; design element on Spanish Muslim ceramics

dehydration first stage in baking cycle of greenware when clay is deprived of chemically combined water, clay permanently loses plasticity

de lo blanco   maker of white maiolica

docena   dozen

dorado   golden, in reference to lusterware

ducat   gold coin of variable worth, usually 375 *maravedíes*

earthenware   low-fired (800°C.–1050°C.) pottery that when unglazed generally is relatively porous; most commonly of fusible iron-bearing clay; worldwide distribution

engobe   wet coating of fine-grained clay, sometimes colored with mineral oxides, applied prior to firing; served to cover imperfections and provide smooth, uniform ground over which patterns could be applied or through which they could be etched; generally known to archaeologists as slip

entrefino   middle grade of fineware

epigrafiada   inscribed

escudilla   small earthenware bowl, often with horizontal-lobed lug handles; used as porringer

esmalte   glaze

esparto   native Spanish grass, either *Slipu tenacissima* or *Lygeum spartum*, used for weaving cordage or baskets or as packing material

espiga de maiz   decorative motif adopted in Spain; based on corn tassel

estrella de pluma   Spanish decorative motif of plumed star; most characteristic of late sixteenth century

fábrica   factory, workshop

faience   earthenware with tin-opacified glaze coat; also known as maiolica

fanega   1.6 bushels

fettling   removal of excess clay left at edges of vessel during shaping

fino   top grade ware

fire rods   solid, fired earthenware rods; see *birlo*

flatware   vessels with predominately horizontal contour, such as platters or plates

flota   convoy; system of Spanish shipping to and from the Americas to prevent pirate attacks

flux   glaze component, such as lead, which combines readily with silica to promote melting and vitrification

foot   ring base on vessel for added support and more refined contours

franquesa   exemption from taxes

frit   glaze ingredients that are melted, ground, and then added to glaze solution to reduce toxic effects of lead and promote smoother surfaces; ground glass serves same purpose

frontera   frontier; in Andalusia the no-man's-land between Muslim and Christian occupation

fruta   fruit

fuente   deep bowl

furze   spiny evergreen shrub commonly used in Europe for fuel or fodder

galena   lead sulphide; used as flux for earthenware glazes

glaze   aesthetic and functional glassy coat fused to ceramic surface at high temperature; glaze with lead fluxant characteristic of Spanish ceramic tradition

glost   glaze, generally used in reference to a firing

greenware   unfired pottery

gremio   guild

grog   nonplastics added to clay to open its composition so that steam can escape during firing; also called temper

harina flour

headpin see *clavo*

higo fig

hispanidad Spanishness

hollow ware vessels more perpendicular than horizontal, i.e.,
pitchers, bowls, basins, cups; also means pottery in general

horma earthenware sugar mold consisting of large, wide-
mouthed, conical jar, with basal drip hole

horno kiln; *horno árabe*: Muslim updraft kiln of two vertical
chambers in rough beehive elevation; *horno quadrado*: two-
chambered updraft style with squared elevation typical of
Spain after mid sixteenth century

imágen image, figurine

impronta impressed pattern

incising cutting a design into a leather hard surface

jabuja large earthenware jar of twenty *arrobas* dry capacity; used
in Spanish Muslim period as a measuring device

jarra jar; also liquid measurement of 2.17 gallons

jarrón large jar

jícara small cup, usually without handles, used for drinking
chocolate; also called *pocillo*

jigger metal template attached to wheel frame; trims excess clay
on vessel exterior as wheel revolves

jolly plaster mold on wheel head over which soft clay is placed
to form vessel interior as wheel revolves

kiln furnace used for firing pottery; in Andalusia and dependencies it was composed of two units, a lower one for fuel and
an upper one for pottery; combustion gases pass upward
from firebox, through the stacked objects directly above, and
out one or more roof ports (hence the kiln is termed updraft)

kiln furniture fire rods, cockspurs, and saggars used to aid
in stacking a kiln for firing

lacería pattern of interlaced elements; characteristic of Muslim
art

ladrillo brick

leather hard condition of unfired vessel when most of moisture
has evaporated from clay but walls are still soft enough to
be worked

lebrillo broad earthenware basin having vertical walls and flat
base; basin

limeta squat, long-necked bottle; may be of glass or earthenware

locero in Mexico, a maker of glazed pottery; *locero oficial*, journeyman; *locero maestro*, master potter

loza ceramics, generally tableware; *loza amarilla*, unglazed utility
pottery; *loza basta* or *loza común*, lowest grade of domestic
utensils, generally lead-glazed; *loza fina*, top quality ceramics,
generally tin-glazed; *loza de Génova*, Genoese ceramics,
assumed to be blue–on–blue maiolica

lute to join pieces of leather hard clay with slurry

madrasa Muslim educational house

maestro master craftsman

maiolica earthenware with tin-opacified lead glaze

malvasía variety of grape that produces wine of same name;
wine also known as malmsey

manteca lard

maravedí Spanish copper coin with value of approximately one-
sixth of a cent; basic monetary unit; preferred plural, *maravedíes*, but also *maravedís*, *maravedises* (Real Academia Española,
Diccionario de la Lengua Española 1970: 845).

massicot   mixture of one part sand to five parts of carbonate of
   soda, calcined, ground, and added to glaze to gain high
   coefficiency of expansion
matte   dull surface, not glossy
maturing temperature   firing temperature at which ceramic
   body has developed required degree of vitrification
melado   honey-colored lead glaze achieved by adding iron oxide
   as colorant
merced   grant of land or water
mestizo   mixed blood; In Mexico, Indian and Spaniard
mirador   watchtower
mold   plaster of paris form containing hollow negative shape
   into which moist clay can be pressed or poured
montepío   widows' and orphans' relief fund maintained by craft
   confraternity
morería   district of Sevilla in which Muslim population was
   confined following the reconquest
morisco   converted Muslim
moro   unconverted Muslim, a Moor
mortero   mortar; could be either earthenware or brass; most
   commonly used to crush crude salt
mozarab   Christian residing in Spain under Muslim political
   control
mudéjar   Muslim living under Christian political rule; art style of
   Spanish Muslims
mudejarismo   influence of *mudéjar* thought and art
muffle   control that protects wares from direction of kiln gases
naranjada   orange cordial
Nashki   cursive Arabic script; used as pottery decoration
niello   process of decorating metal objects with incised, filled
   designs
noria   water-lifting wheel composed of several hundred wooden
   parts, onto the outer circumference of which were fastened
   wide-mouthed ceramic jars to contain water as the mechanism
   revolved to a dumping position
noria de sangre   combination of vertical wheel and geared horizontal wheel turned by animal power to raise well water;
   smaller than *noria de vuelo*; also called *saquiyah*
noria de vuelo   large vertical water wheel turned by water current
oficial   journeyman
oficios mecánicos   mechanical arts
ollería   unit of pottery; *olla*, wide-mouthed earthenware jar;
   ollero, generic term in fifteenth and sixteenth centuries for a
   potter
opacifier   chemical, such as tin, whose particles remain in
   suspension in a glaze solution and so prevent light from pene-
   trating the glaze; makes glaze opaque
orza   high-shouldered, bulbous jar lacking handles; used as drug
   or sweets receptacle
oxidation   kiln atmosphere achieved when supply of oxygen is
   ample to allow fires to burn freely and without smoking
padilla   calcination kiln
par   pair
parrilla   pierced floor separating fire chamber from baking chamber in kilns; literally, grill
pasa   raisin
paste   clay body
pez   fish
pico   sharp-edged cutting tool used in *alicatado*, or mosaic tile,
   process

piedra mexicana   grinding stone

pila bautismal   baptismal font consisting of very large, wide-mouthed bowl set on a tall, narrow stem support

pila de agua bendita   holy water stoup

pilgrim bottle   earthenware canteen, named for use by persons traveling to holy shrines

pilón   large pounding mortar

pimienta   pepper

pinholing   tiny holes in glaze finish caused by air pockets, too rapid firing, or too rapid cooling

pipa   wooden cask, with capacity variously given as 120.5 gallons, 27½ *arrobas*, or 456 liters

pisano   term specifically applied to flat-surfaced polychrome tiles introduced to Sevilla by an Italian craftsman; anything Italian

plasticity   property of clay that allows stretching and shaping of vessels without collapse; malleability

plato   plate

poblano   of Puebla

pocillo   small cup made by Puebla potters in imitation of Chinese tea cup

polvo azul   cobalt; literally, blue powder

porcelain   high-fired (1250°C–1450°C.) ceramic made of white kaolin clay and feldspathic rock covered with feldspar glaze; notable for translucence

potsherd   fragment of fired pottery

potter's wheel   device to supply centrifugal force to a clay ball on its center surface (wheel head), which a potter's hand pressure can cause to rise into a hollow circular form

pottery   articles of prepared clay that have undergone chemical changes produced by heat of 600°C. or more

pounce   dark powder pushed through perforated stencil to indicate faint outline of pattern for decorators to follow; burns out in firing

punteada   term identified a late sixteenth-century ceramic style suggested by Faenza models of an earlier date; dotted

qadus   Arabic term for well jar; see *arcaduz*

quesera   wide-mouthed jar for storing cheese

quintal   unit of weight equaling 46 kilograms or 100 pounds

qulla   earthenware jar of 6 gallons liquid capacity; used in Spanish Muslim period as measuring device

ramón   branches and leaves of olive trees, used in Andalusia for kiln fuel

real   coin worth approximately 6 cents, 34 *maravedíes* in Spain, 44 *maravedíes* in Mexico, depending on period

reduction   kiln atmosphere characterized by low oxygen, so that carbon dioxide is produced; smoky

reflejo metálico   lusterware, or maiolica that underwent a third, brief, specialized firing to set overglaze decorations of copper or silver oxides

regla   law

remate   roofline finial, often of glazed earthenware, popular in medieval Sevillian architecture

rib   shaped hand tool used in contouring a vessel

roulette   repeated pattern achieved by moving an incised roller over moist clay

sábalo   shad

saggar   fired earthenware box in which glazed vessels were placed during firing to reduce chances of mishaps

salero   salt cellar; often in small bowl shape; sometimes molded square or rectangular receptacles

salvadera   small vessel to hold the sand or pouncing material
    sprinkled upon ink in order to hasten its drying on unsized
    paper
sera   basket
sgraffito   method of decorating ceramics by cutting through or
    scratching through an engobe layer to reveal body color
shrinkage   contraction of clay during drying and firing
slurry   fine clay in liquid suspension; used for attaching appen-
    dages or appliqué decorations to leather hard objects
stanniferous   glaze containing tin
tabla   flat tablet on which pills were counted or dispensed
tahona   grinding mill
taifa   small principality
tapadera   lid
tasación   regulation
taza   small bowl with vertical upper walls slanting sharply down
    below mid section to a base that was either unfooted or
    ring-footed; used as drinking vessel
teja   curved terra cotta roof tile
terra cotta   coarse, low-fired clayware, usually of structural
    nature and brick red in color
terra sigillata   moldmade Roman red gloss pottery characterized
    by thin-walled, sharply defined contours borrowed from
    metal prototypes, often with delicate raised decorations based
    on mythological themes
tequesquite   Mexican term for raw sodium used in glaze prepara-
    tion
throwing   forming pottery on revolving potter's wheel; throw-
    ing rings are concentric ridges left by finger pressure
thumn   small earthenware jar of 4 pints liquid capacity or one-
    eighth *arroba* dry capacity; used during Spanish Muslim
    period as measuring device; also called *azumbre*
tibor   Mexican term for large, high-shouldered, narrow-based jar
    with short vertical neck; inspired by Chinese form commonly
    called a ginger jar
tinaja   large earthenware jar of cylindrical shape, usually with
    tapered base, brief neck, and two opposed handles; tapered
    base often abandoned by sixteenth century in favor of flat base
tinajero   maker of *tinajas*; also loosely used as term for potter
tonelada   unit of measure equaling volume occupied by three
    pipas of 27½ *arrobas* each, 10 sacks of tableware, or 5 *botijas* of
    wine; used as basis for calculating assessments
torno   potter's wheel
torno lento   pivoted turntable or disk of wood revolved by hand
traza   district of Mexico City reserved for Spanish residence
turn   to trim walls and foot of pot while leather hard; also
    throwing
vasija   pottery vessels in general
vaso   carton or container used for shipping standardized lots of
    pottery; also a glass
veedor   guild officer elected annually by guild members to police
    the craft
vicole   cockspur
vidrio   glass; *vidriado*, glazed
vinagre   vinegar
vino   wine
volatilization   turning of some glaze elements to gaseous state
    under high temperature
waster   vessel, or fragments from it, damaged in manufacturing
    process and then discarded

wax resist   decorative mode utilizing wax emulsion over certain
    vessel parts so that glaze will not adhere
wedging   process of kneading clay to eliminate trapped air
    bubbles and increase workability
zacate   brush used as fuel or fodder in Mexico

Bibliography

Agricola, Georgius
  1950 *De re Metallica*. Trans. by H.C. Hoover and L.H. Hoover from first Latin edition of 1556. Dover, New York.

Ainaud de Lasarte, Juan
  1952 Cerámica y Vidrio. *Ars Hispaniae*, Vol. 10. Editorial Plus Ultra, Madrid.

Allan, J.W.
  1971 *Medieval Middle Eastern Pottery*. Ashmolean Museum, Oxford.

  1973 Abū'l Qāsim's Treatise on Ceramics. *Iran*, Vol. 11, 111–20.

Almagro Basch, Martín
  1946 Arte Prehistórico. *Ars Hispaniae*, Vol. 1. Editorial Plus Ultra, Madrid.

American Geographical Society
  1960 Santa María la Antigua del Darién. *Geographical Review*, Vol. 50, 274–6.

Amiran, Ruth
  1965 The Beginnings of Pottery-Making in the Near East. In Ceramics and Man, Frederick R. Matson, ed. *Viking Fund Publications in Anthropology*, No. 41, 240–7.

Anderson, William J.
  1927 *The Architecture of Ancient Rome*. Charles Scribner's Sons, New York.

Anghiera, Pietre Martire D'
  1964 *Décadas del Nuevo Mundo*. Vol. 1. Porrúa, México.

Angulo Íñiguez, Diego
  1946 La Cerámica de Puebla (Méjico). *Publicaciones de la Escuela de Artes y Oficios Artísticos de Madrid*, No. 24.

Arcila Farias, Eduardo
  1950 *Comercio Entre Venezuela y México en los Siglos XVI y XVII*. Colegio de México, México.

Ardemans, Teodoro
  1760 *Ordenanzas de Madrid, y Otros Diferentes, que se Practican en los Ciudades de Toledo, y Sevilla con Algunas Advertencias a los Alarifes, y Particulares y Otros Capítulos Añadidos a la Perfecta Inteligencia de la Materia, que Todo se Cifra en el Gobierno Político de las Fábricas*. Antonio Pérez de Soto, Madrid.

Ariño, Francisco
  1873 *Sucesos de Sevilla de 1592 a 1604*. Sociedad de Bibliofilos Andaluces, Sevilla.

Arnold, J. Barto III
  1978 The Flota Disaster of 1554. Paper presented to Ninth Conference on Underwater Archeology, San Antonio.

Arnold, J. Barto III and Robert Weddle
    1978   *The Nautical Archeology of Padre Island: The Spanish*
            Shipwrecks of 1554. Academic Press, New York.
Arques, Enrique
    1966   *Las Adelantadas de España. Las Plazas Españolas del Litoral*
            Africano del Mediterraneo. Consejo Superior de
            Investigaciones Científicas, Madrid.
Arribas, Antonio
    1964   *The Iberians.* Praeger, New York.
Arslan, Ermanno
    1967   El Significato Spaziale delle Volte Sottili Romane e
            Paleocristiane. *Mesopotamia,* Vol. 2, 185–93.
Artes de México
    1966   Puebla. *Artes de México,* Vol. 13, No. 81–2.
    1971   El Galeon de Manila. *Artes de México,* Vol. 18, No. 143.
    1977   El Arte en el Comercio con Asia. *Artes de México,* Vol.
            22, No. 190.
Avilez Moreno, Guadalupe
    1980   El Arte Mudéjar en Nueva España en el siglo XVI.
            Anuario de Estudios Americanos, Vol. 37, 649–63.
Baker, Henry Alexander
    1969   Archaeological Excavations at Panama la Vieja, 1968.
            M.A. thesis, University of Florida, Gainesville.
Ballesteros y Beretta, Antonio
    1913   *Sevilla en el Siglo XIII.* Tipografía de Juan Pérez Torres,
            Madrid.
    1945   *Cristóbal Colón y el Descubrimiento de América.* Colección
            de Documentos Inéditos para la Historia de Hispano-
            América, Vol. 5. Salvat, Barcelona.
Banamex
    1979   *Talavera Poblana.* Fomento Cultural Banamex, México.
Barber, Edwin Atlee
    1908   *The Maiolica of Mexico.* Pennsylvania Museum,
            Philadelphia.
    1911   *Catalogue of Mexican Maiolica Belonging to Mrs. Robert W.*
            de Forest. Hispanic Society of America, New York.
    1915   *Hispano-Moresque Pottery in the Collection of the Hispanic*
            Society of America. Hispanic Society of America, New
            York.
Barbour, Neville
    1966   *Morocco.* Walker, New York.
Bargalló, Modesto
    1955   *La Minería y la Metalurgía en la América Colonial.* Fondo
            de Cultura Económica, México.
Barile, Costantino
    1975   *Antiche Ceramichie Liguri. Maioliche di Genova e Savona.*
            Cassa di Risparmio, Savona.
Barnes, Mark R.
    1972   Majolica of the Santa Cruz Valley, Arizona. Pacific
            Coast Archaeology Society, *Occasional Papers,* No. 2, 1–
            24.
    1976   Non-Indian Material in Mission Guevavi: Excavations
            in the Convento. *Kiva,* Vol. 42, No. 2, 156–70.
Barraclough, Geoffrey
    1976   *The Crucible of Europe, the Ninth and Tenth Centuries in*
            European History. University of California Press,
            Berkeley.
Barrio Lorenzot, Francisco del
    1920   *Ordenanzas de Gremios de la Nueva España.* 173–5.
            Talleres Gráficos, México.

Barsis, Max
  1973   *The Common Man Through the Centuries, a Book of
          Costume Drawings*. Frederick Ungar, New York.
Bearse, Grace M.
  1979   History is Alive and Well and Living in Santo
          Domingo. *Americas*, Vol. 31, No. 9, 33–9.
Beckett, T.H.
  1958   Two Pottery Techniques in Morocco. *Man*, Vol. 58,
          185–8.
Beinart, Haim
  1979   The Jews in Spain. In *The Jewish World. History and
          Culture of the Jewish People* (161–67). Elie Kedourie, ed.
          Abrams, New York.
Bel, Alfred
  1918   *Las Industries de la Ceramique a Fez*. A. Lebroux, Paris.
Beltrán Lloris, Miguel
  1978   *Cerámica Romana: Tipología y Clasificación*. Vol. 1. Libros
          Pórtico, Zaragoza.
Benítez, Fernando
  1965   *The Century After Cortes*. University of Chicago Press,
          Chicago.
Benítez, José R.
  1929   *Historia Gráfica de la Nueva España*. Cámara Oficial
          Española de Comercio en los Estados Unidos
          Mexicanos, México.
Benito Del Cano, Ciro and Rafael Roldán y Guerrero
  1928   *Cerámica Farmaceutica*. Jesus López, Madrid.
Bennassar, Bartolomé
  1979   *The Spanish Character. Attitudes and Mentalities from the
          Sixteenth to the Nineteenth Century*. Benjamin Keen,
          trans. University of California Press, Berkeley.
Berendsen, Anne
  1967   *Tiles, a General History*. Viking, New York.
Bermúdez Plata, Cristóbal
  1942   *Catálogo de Pasajeros a Indias Durante los Siglos XVI,
          XVII, y XVIII*. Vol. 2. Sevilla.
Bernès, J.P. and Alain Jacob
  1974   *Arts et Objets du Maroc. Céramique, Bijoux, Armes*. Paris.
Blair, Emma H. and James A. Robertson, eds.
  1903–09 *The Philippine Islands, 1493–1898* (in 55 vols.).
          Arthur H. Clark, Cleveland.
Blake, Hugo
  1981   Pottery Exported from Northwest Italy Between 1450
          and 1830; Savona, Albisola, Genoa, Pisa, and
          Montelupo. In *Archaeology and Italian Society* (99–124).
          Graeme Barker and Richard Hodges, eds. BAR
          International Series 102, London.
Blake, Marion Elizabeth
  1973   Roman Construction in Italy from Nerva Through the
          Antonines. American Philosophical Society, *Memoirs*
          96.
Blanco Freijeiro, Antonio
  1979   *La Ciudad Antigua: De la Prehistoria a los Visigodos*.
          Universidad de Sevilla, Sevilla.
Blum, Jerome, Rondo Cameron, and Thomas G. Barnes
  1970   *The European World, a History*. Little Brown, Boston.
Bonsor, George Edward
  1931   *The Archaeological Expedition Along the Guadalquivir,
          1889–1901*. Hispanic Society of America, New York.

Boone, James L. III
1984 Majolica Escudillas of the 15th and 16th Centuries: a Typological Analysis of 55 Examples from Qsar es-Seghir. *Historical Archaeology*, Vol. 18, No. 1, 76–86.

Borah, Woodrow
1943 Silk Raising in Colonial Mexico. *Ibero-Americana* 20.
1954 Early Colonial Trade and Navigation Between Mexico and Peru. *Ibero-Americana* 38.
1972 European Cultural Influence in the Formation of the First Plan for Urban Centers That has Lasted to Our time. In *Urbanización y Proceso Social en América* (35–54). Proceedings of the International Congress of Americanists, Lima, 1970.

Borah, Woodrow and Sherborne F. Cook
1958 Price Trends of Some Basic Commodities in Central Mexico, 1531–1570. *Ibero-Americana* 40.

Bosch Gimpera, Pedro et al
1935 España Romana (218 a. de J.C.–414 de J.C.) *Historia de España*, Vol. 2. R. Menéndez Pidal, ed. Espasa-Calpe, Madrid.

Bourry, Emile
1926 *A Treatise on Ceramic Industries*. Scott, Greenwood, London.

Boyd, E.
1963 Houghton Sawyer Collection of Puebla Majolica. Manuscript, International Folk Art Foundation, Santa Fe.

Boyd-Bowman, Peter
1963 La Emigración Peninsular a América: 1520–1539. *Historia Mexicana*, Vol. 13, 165–92.
1964 *Indice Geobiográfico de Cuarenta Mil Pobladores Españoles de América en el Siglo XVI*, Vol. 1. Instituto Caro y Cuervo, Bogotá.
1967 La Procedencía de los Españoles de América: 1540–1559. *Historia Mexicana*, Vol. 17, 37–71.
1968 *Indice Geobiográfico de Cuarenta Mil Pobladores Españoles de América en el Siglo XVI*, Vol. 2. Editorial Jus, México.
1976 Patterns of Spanish Emigration to the Indies Until 1600. *Hispanic American Historical Review*, Vol. 56, No. 4, 580–604.

Braudel, Fernand
1967 *Capitalism and Material Life, 1400–1800*. Harper and Row, New York.
1974 The Mediterranean Economy in the 16th Century. In *Essays in European Economic History, 1500–1800* (1–44). Peter Earle, ed. Clarendon, Oxford.
1979 *Civilization and Capitalism, 15th–18th Centuries*. Harper and Row, New York.

Breisach, Ernst
1973 *Renaissance Europe, 1300–1517*. Macmillan, New York.

Brett, Michael
1980 *The Moors, Islam in the West*. Orbis, London.

Briggs, Martin S.
1956 Building Construction. In *A History of Technology* (397–448), Vol. 2, Charles Singer et al, eds. Clarendon, Oxford.

Brill, R.H.
1970 Chemical Studies of Islamic Luster Glass. In *Scientific Methods in Medieval Archaeology* (351–77). Rainer Berger, ed. University of California Press, Berkeley.

Brownell, W.E.
1976 *Structural Clay Products*. Springer-Verlag, New York.
Burckhardt, Titus
1972 *Moorish Culture in Spain*. Allen and Unwin, London.
Caceres Mendoza, Lourdes
1980 Cerámica de las Ruinas de la Vega Vieja. *Casas Reales*, Vol. 5, No. 11, 101–13.
Caiger-Smith, Alan
1973 *Tin-Glaze Pottery, in Europe and the Islamic World. The Tradition of 1000 Years in Maiolica, Faience, and Delftware*. Faber and Faber, London.
Callender, M.H.
1965 *Roman Amphorae, with Index of Stamps*. Oxford University Press, London.
Carande, Ramón
1925 Sevilla, Fortaleza y Mercado. *Anuario de Historia del Derecho Español* 2, 233–391.
Carrera Stampa, Manuel
1949 The Evolution of Weights and Measures in New Spain. *Hispanic American Historical Review*, Vol. 29, 2–24.
1954 *Los Gremios Mexicanos*. Ibero Americana de Publicaciones, México.
1959 La Nao de la China. *Historia Mexicana*, Vol. 9, 97–118.
Carrion, Antonio
1896 *Historia de la Ciudad de Puebla de los Angeles*. Dávalos, Puebla.
Casamar, Manuel
1961 Fragmentos de Jarrones Malagueños en los Museos de El Cairo. *Al Andalus*, Vol. 26, No. 1, 185–90.
Casas, Bartolomé de las
1957 *Obras Escogidas. Historia de las Indias* (in 2 vols.). Edited by Juan Pérez de Tudela and Emilio López Oto. Atlas, Madrid.
1971 *History of the Indies*. Andres Collard, trans. Harper and Row, New York.
Cervantes, Enrique A.
1933 *Nomina de Loceros Poblanos Durante el Período Virreinal*. México.
1939 *Loza Blanca y Azulejo de Puebla* (in 2 vols.). México.
Cespedes del Castillo, G.
1957 Las Indias en el Reinado de los Reyes Católicos. In *Historia Social y Económica de España y América* (493–547), Vol. 2. Jaime Vicens Vives, ed. Teide, Barcelona.
Chanca, Diego Alvarez
1907 The letter of Dr. Diego Alvarez Chanca, Dated 1494, Relating to the Second Voyage of Columbus to America. A.M. Fernández de Ybarra, trans. *Smithsonian Miscellaneous Collections*, No. 48.
Charleston, Robert J.
1968 *World Ceramics*. Paul Hamlyn, London.
Charlton, Thomas H.
1968 Post-Conquest Aztec Ceramics: Implications for Archaeological Interpretations. *The Florida Anthropologist*, Vol. 21, No. 4, 96–101.
Chatterton, E. Keble
1913 *Ships and Ways of Other Days*. Lippincott, Philadelphia.
Chaunu, Pierre and Huguette Chaunu
1974 The Atlantic Economy and the World Economy. In

Essays in European Economic History (113–26). Peter
Earle, ed. Clarendon, Oxford.

Chejne, Anwar
1974   *Muslim Spain, its History and Culture*. University of
Minnesota Press, Minneapolis.
1980   The Role of Al-Andalus in the Movement of Ideas
Between Islam and the West. In *Islam and the Medieval
West* (110–33). Khalil L. Semaan, ed. State University
of New York Press, Albany.

Chevalier, Francois
1970   *Land and Society in Colonial Mexico*. University of
California Press, Berkeley.

Collantes de Teran, F. and J. Zozaya
1972   Excavations en el Palacio Almohade de la Buhayra
(Sevilla). *Noticiario Arqueológico Hispánico*, Vol. 1,
221–59.

Colmeiro, Manuel
1965   *Historia de la Economía Política en España* (in 2 vols).
Taurus, Madrid.

Colón, Fernando
1959   *The Life of the Admiral Christopher Columbus by His Son
Ferdinand*. Trans. and annotated by Benjamin Keen.
Rutgers University Press, New Brunswick.

Comune di Sesto Fiorentino
1973   *Ceramiche Antiche di Montelupo*. Comune di Sesto
Fiorentino, Montelupo.

Copplestone, Trewin and Bernard S. Myers, eds.
1970   *Art Treasures in Spain*. Paul Hamlyn, London.

Cotter, John L.
1958   Excavations at Jamestown, Virginia. *National Park
Service Archeological Research Series*, No. 14.

Council, Robert Bruce
1975   Archaeology of the Convento de San Francisco. M.A.
thesis, University of Florida, Gainesville.

Cruxent, José M.
1956   Informe Sobre un Reconocimiento Arqueológico en el
Darién (Panamá). Museo de Ciencias Naturales, *Boletín*
No. 9.

Cruxent, José M. and Irving Rouse
1958   *An Archaeological Chronology of Venezuela*. Social Science
Monograph No. 6, in 2 vols. Pan American Union,
Washington.

Cruxent, José M. and Maruja Rolando
1961   Tipología Morfológica de Tres Piezas de Cerámica.
Instituto Venezolano de Investigaciones Científicas,
Boletín Informativo No. 2, 7–19.

Cruxent, José M. and J.E. Vaz
1973   Provenience Studies on Majolica Pottery: Type
Ichtucknee Blue on Blue. Manuscript, Instituto
Venezolano de Investigaciones Científicas, Caracas.
1980   Hidroceramos Mexicanos en la República Dominicana.
Casas Reales, Vol. 5, No. 11, 71–85.

Cue Canovas, Agustín
1963   *Historia Social y Económica de México (1521–1854)*. F.
Trillas, México.

Culiacan, William
1966   *The First Merchant Venturers in History and Commerce,
and Ancient Levant*. Thomas and Hudson, London.

Curtis, Freddie
  1962 The Utility Pottery Industry of Bailén, Southern Spain. *American Anthropologist*, Vol. 64, No. 3, Pt. 1, 486–503.
Daumas, Maurice
  1969 *A History of Technology and Invention, Vol. 1: The Origins of Technological Civilization*. Eileen B. Hennessy, trans. Crown, New York.
Davies, R. Trevor
  1937 *The Golden Age of Spain*. Macmillan, London.
Davillier, Charles
  1949 *Viaje por España*. Castilla, Madrid.
Dayton, J.E.
  1971 The Problem of Tin in the Ancient World. *World Archaeology*, Vol. 3, No. 1, 49–70.
Deagan, Kathleen
  1978 The Material Assemblage of 16th Century Spanish Florida. *Historical Archaeology*, Vol. 12, 25 50.
  1983 *Spanish St. Augustine: The Archaeology of a Colonial Creole Community*. Academic Press, New York.
  1986 The Search for "La Navidad" in North Haiti. Paper presented at annual meeting, Society for Historical Archaeology, Sacramento.
Defourneaux, Marcelin
  1971 *Daily Life in Spain in the Golden Age*. Praeger, New York.
Delaney, John L. and James Edward Tobin
  1961 *Dictionary of Catholic Biography*. Doubleday, Garden City.
De Montêquin, Francoise
  1976 *Compendium of Hispano-Islamic Art and Architecture*. Hamline University, St. Paul.
De Pratter, Chester B. and Marvin T. Smith
  1980 Sixteenth Century European Trade in the Southeastern United States: Evidence from the Juan Pardo Expeditions (1566–1568). *Spanish Borderlands Research*, No. 1, 67–78.
Deutsch, Karl W.
  1967 Medieval Unity and the Economic Conditions for an International Civilization. In *Early Medieval Society* (247–60). Sylvia L. Thrupp, ed. Appleton-Century Crofts, New York.
Dibble, Charles E.
  1963 *Historia de la Nación Mexicana Reproducción a Todo Color del Codice de 1576. Codice Aubin*. Porrúa, Madrid.
Díez Borque, José María
  1975 *La Sociedad Española y los Viajeros del Siglo XVII*. Sociedad General Española de Librería, Madrid.
Di Peso, Charles C.
  1974 *Casas Grandes, a Fallen Trading Center of the Gran Chichimeca*. Vols. 3, 8. Northland Press, Flagstaff.
Domínguez González, Lourdes S.
  1979a Mayolica Colonial en Sitios Arqueológicos Cubanos del Siglo XVI y XVII: Consideraciones Generales. Manuscript, Museo Nacional de Arqueología, Havana.
  1979b Carta Informativa. Manuscript, Museo Nacional de Arqueología, Havana.
Domínguez Ortíz, Antonio
  1941 La Población de Sevilla en la Baja Media y en los

Tiempos Modernos. Sociedad Geográfica Nacional, *Boletín*, No. 67, 595–608.

1956   *Orto y Ocaso de Sevilla*. Imprenta de la Diputación Provincial, Sevilla.

1971   *The Golden Age of Spain, 1516–1659*. Basic Books, New York.

1973   *Las Clases Privilegiadas en la España del Antigua Regimen*. ISTMO, Madrid.

1980   La Sociedad Bajo Andaluza. In *Historia de Andalucia* (293–316), Vol. 4. Cuspa, Madrid.

Domínguez Ortíz, Antonio and Francisco Aguilar Piñal

1976   *El Barroco y la Ilustración. Historia de Sevilla*, 4. Universidad de Sevilla, Sevilla.

Donatone, Guido

1968   *La Ceramica di Cerreto Sannita*. Museo del Sannio, Sannio.

Dozy, Reinhart

1978   *Spanish Islam*. F.G. Stokes, trans. Karimsons, Karachi.

Drey, Rudolf E.A.

1978   *Apothecary Jars. Pharmaceutical Pottery and Porcelain in Europe and the East, 1150–1850*. Faber and Faber, London.

Dubs, Homer H. and Robert S. Smith

1942   Chinese in Mexico City in 1635. *Far Eastern Quarterly*, Vol. 1, No. 4, 387–9.

Duda, Dorothea

1972   Die Frühe Spanisch-Islamische Keramik von Almería. *Madrider Mitteilungen*, Vol. 13, 345–432.

Duncan, T. Bentley

1972   *Atlantic Islands, Madeira, the Azores, and the Cape Verdes in Seventeenth-Century Commerce and Navigation*. University of Chicago Press, Chicago.

Elliott, J.H.

1963   *Imperial Spain, 1469–1716*. St. Martins, New York.

España. Archivo General de Indias

1930   *Catálogo de Pasajeros a Indias Durante los Siglos XVI, XVII, y XVIII. Vol. 1 (1505–1533)*. Espasa-Calpe, Madrid.

n.d.   Contratación records 1079, 1080, 1089, 1090, 1091, 1099, 1100, 1451, 4674.

España. Consejo Superior de Investigaciones Científicas

1944   *Libro de Grandezas y Casas Memorables de España*. Madrid.

España. Ministerio del Ejército, Servicio Histórico Militar

1935   *Acción de España en Africa. Vol. 1, Iberos y Bereberes*. Talleres del Ministerio de la Guerra, Madrid.

1941   *Acción de España en Africa. Vol. 2, Cristianos y Musulmanes de Occidente*. Servicio Geográfico y Cartográfico, Madrid.

España. Museos Arqueológicos Provinciales

1945   *Memorias*, Vol. 7.

España. Sevilla. Archivo de Protocolos

1932   *Catálogo de los Fondos Americanos* (in 3 vols.). Instituto Hispano-Cubano de Historia de América, Sevilla.

1935   *Documentos Americanos del Siglo XVI de Protocolos de Sevilla*. Instituto Hispano-Cubano de Historia de América, Madrid.

Etayo, Carlos

1971   *Naos y Carabelas de los Descubrimientos y Las Navas de Colón*. Pamplona.

Ettinghausen, Richard
    1954   Notes on the Lusterware of Spain. *Ars Orientalis*, Vol.
           1, 133–56.
    1974   The Decorative Arts and Painting: Their Character and
           Scope. In *The Legacy of Islam* (274–92). Joseph Schacht
           and C.E. Bosworth, eds. Clarendon, Oxford.
Ewald, Ursula
    1976   *Estudios Sobre la Hacienda Colonial de México*. Franz
           Steiner, Wiesbaden.
Fairbanks, Charles H.
    1966   A Feldspar-Inlaid Ceramic Type from Spanish Colonial
           Sites. *American Antiquity*, Vol. 31, No. 3, 430–2.
    1973   The Cultural Significance of Spanish Ceramics. In
           Ceramics in America (141–74). University of Virginia
           Press, Charlottesville.
Farris, Guido
    1972   Note Stilistiche su un Nuovo Genere Decorativo della
           Maiolica Ligure del XVI Secolo. Convegno
           Internacionale della Ceramica, *Atti*, Vol. 5, 323–30.
Farris, Guido and V.A. Ferrarese
    1969a Contributo alla Conoscensa della Tipologia e della
           Stilistica della Maiolica Ligure del XVI Secolo.
           Convegno Internacionale della Ceramica, *Atti*, Vol. 9,
           No. 2, 9–45.
    1969b Metodi di Produzione della Ceramica en Liguria nel
           XVI Secolo. Convegno Internacionale della Ceramica,
           Atti, Vol. 9, No. 2, 99–110.
Ferguson, George
    1959   *Signs and Symbols in Christian Art*. Oxford University
           Press, New York.
Ferguson, Wallace K.
    1962   *Europe in Transition, 1300–1520*. Houghton Mifflin,
           Boston.
Fernández Armesto, Felipe
    1974   *Columbus and the Conquest of the Impossible*. Weidenfeld
           and Nicolson, London.
Fernández de Echeverría y Veytia, Mariano
    1931   *Historia de la Fundación de la Ciudad de la Puebla de los
           Angeles en Nueva España (c. 1749–79)* (in 2 vols.).
           México.
Fernández de Oviedo, Gonzalo
    1959   *Historia General y Natural de las Indias* (in 2 vols.).
           Gráficas Orbe, Madrid.
Firth, Raymond and B.S. Yamsey
    1964   *Capitol, Saving, and Credit in Peasant Societies*. Aldine,
           New York.
Fletcher, Banister
    1961   *A History of Architecture*. Charles Scribner's Sons, New
           York.
Folch y Torres, Joaquin
    1929   *La Cerámica*. David, Barcelona.
Fontaine, Jacques
    1978   *El Prerrománico*. Ediciones Encuentro, Madrid.
Forbes, R.J.
    1956   Hydraulic Engineering and Sanitation. In *A History of
           Technology* (663–94), Vol. 2. Charles Singer et al, eds.
           Clarendon, Oxford.
    1964   Water. In *Studies in Ancient Technology* (153–4), Vol. 1.
           Brill, Leiden.

1965a   Irrigation and Drainage. In *Studies in Ancient Technology* (1–79), Vol. 2. Brill, Leiden.

1965b   Kiln. In *Studies in Ancient Technology* (70–2), Vol. 6. Brill, Leiden.

1965c   Tin. In *Studies in Ancient Technology* (128), Vol. 9. Brill, Leiden.

Foster, George M.

1948   Some Implications of Modern Mexican Mold-Made Pottery. *Southwestern Journal of Anthropology*, Vol. 4, No. 4, 356–70.

1954   Aspectos Antropológicos de la Conquista Española de América. *Estudios Americanos*, Vol. 8, No. 35–6, 115–71.

1959a   The Coyotepec Molde and Some Associated Problems of the Potter's Wheel. *Southwestern Journal of Anthropology*, Vol. 15, No. 1, 53–63.

1959b   The Potter's Wheel: An Analysis of Idea and Artifact in Invention. *Southwestern Journal of Anthropology*, Vol. 15, No. 2, 99–119.

1960   Culture and Conquest: America's Spanish Heritage. *Viking Fund Publications in Anthropology*, No. 27.

1965   The Sociology of Pottery: Questions and Hypotheses Arising from Contemporary Mexican Work. In Ceramics and Man. Frederick R. Matson, ed. *Viking Fund Publications in Anthropology* (43–61), No. 41.

Fowst, G.

1971   Ceramisti Liguri in Messico Nei Secoli XVI e XVII. Convegno Internazionale della Ceramica. *Atti*, Vol. 9, No. 4, 177–9.

Franco, José Luis C.

1945   Comentarios Sobre Tipología y Filogenía de la Decoración Negra Sobre Color Natural del Barro en la Cerámica Azteca II. *Revista Mexicana de Estudios Antropológicos*, Vol. 7, Nos. 1–3, 163–86.

1949   Algunos Problemas Relativos a la Cerámica Azteca. *El México Antiguo*, Vol. 7, 162–208.

Franco, José Luis C. and Frederick A. Peterson

1957   Motivos Decorativos en la Cerámica Azteca. *Serie Científica*, No. 5. Museo Nacional de Antropología, México.

Frick, Fay Arrieh

1971   *A Typology of Fustat Ceramics.* University Microfilms, Ann Arbor.

Friede, Juan

1952   Algunas Observaciones Sobre la Realidad de la Emigración Española a América en la Primera Mitad del Siglo XVI. *Revista de Indias*, Vol. 12, No. 49, 467–96.

Frierman, J.D.

1970   Physical and Chemical Properties of Some Medieval Near Eastern Glazed Ceramics. In *Scientific Methods in Medieval Archaeology* (379–88). Rainer Berger, ed. University of California Press, Berkeley.

Frothingham, Alice Wilson

1941a   Apothecaries' Shops in Spain. *Notes Hispanic*, 100–23. Hispanic Society of America, New York.

1941b   *Hispanic Glass.* Hispanic Society of America, New York.

1943 Talavera Pottery Decorations Based on Designs by Stradanus. *Notes Hispanic*, 97–117. Hispanic Society of America, New York.

1944a Aragonese Lustreware from Muel. *Notes Hispanic*, 78–91. Hispanic Society of America, New York.

1944b *Talavera Pottery, with a Catalogue of the Collection of the Hispanic Society of America*. Hispanic Society of America, New York.

1951 *Lustreware of Spain*. Hispanic Society of America, New York.

1963 *Spanish Glass*. Faber and Faber, London.

1969 *Tile Panels of Spain, 1500–1650*. Hispanic Society of America, New York.

1974 Spanish Pottery and its Exportation to the New World. In *Europe in Colonial America*, Antiques Forum, 5–7. Williamsburg.

1975 The Pottery of Spain. *American Ceramic Circle, Bulletin*, No. 1, 129–38, 170–1.

Fuentes, Patricia de
1963 *The Conquistadores. First-Person Accounts of the Conquest of Mexico*. Orion, New York.

Gage, Thomas
1958 *Thomas Gage's Travels in the New World*. J. Eric Thompson, ed. University of Oklahoma Press, Norman.

Galindo y Villa, Jesús
1925 *Historia Sumaria de la Ciudad de México*. Cultura, México.

García Fuentes, Lutgardo
1977 Exportación y Exportadores Sevillanos a Indias, 1650–1700. *Archivo Hispalense*, No. 184, 1–40.

1980 *El Comercio Español con América, 1650–1700*. Publicaciones de la Escuela de Estudios Hispano-Americanos de Sevilla, No. CLLXV, Sevilla.

García Rodríguez, Carmen
1966 *El Culto de los Santos en la España Romana y Visigoda*. Consejo Superior de Investigaciones Científicas, Madrid.

García y Bellido, Antonio
1946a Colonizaciones Púnica y Griega. *Ars Hispaniae*, Vol. 1, 137–98. Editorial Plus Ultra, Madrid.

1946b El Arte Ibérico. *Ars Hispaniae*, Vol. 1, 199–300. Editorial Plus Ultra, Madrid.

Gerhard, Peter
1972 *A Guide to the Historical Geography of New Spain*. Cambridge University Press, Cambridge.

Gestoso y Pérez, José
1899–1909 *Ensayo de un Diccionario de los Artífices que Florecieron en Sevilla Desde el Siglo XIII al XVIII Inclusivo* (in 3 vols.). Sevilla.

1903 *Historia de los Barros Vidriados Sevillanos Desde Sus Origenes Hasta Nuestros Días*. Tipografía la Andalucía Moderna, Sevilla.

1910 *Curiosidades Antiguas Sevillanos*. Editorial Correo de Andalucía, Sevilla.

1918 *Guia Artistica de Sevilla*. Zarzuela, Sevilla.

1919 Cerámica Sevillana. Sociedad Española de Excursiones, *Boletín*, Vol. 27, 2–19.

Gibson, Charles
    1964   *The Aztecs Under Spanish Rule, 1519–1810.* Stanford
           University Press, Palo Alto.
Gil Torres, Rodolfo
    1953   *Andalucismo Africano.* Instituto de Estudios Africanos,
           Madrid.
Giral, María Dolors
    1981   Técnica Cerámica. In *Cerámica Esmaltada Española* (15–
           34). Labor, Barcelona.
Glick, Thomas F.
    1977   Noria Pots in Spain. *Technology and Culture,* Vol. 18,
           No. 4, 644–50.
    1979   *Islamic and Christian Spain in the Early Middle Ages.*
           Princeton University Press, Princeton.
Goggin, John M.
    1964   The Spanish Olive Jar. In *Indian and Spanish Selected
           Writings* (253–98). University of Miami Press, Coral
           Gables.
    1968   Spanish Majolica in the New World, Types of the
           Sixteenth to Eighteenth Centuries. *Yale University
           Publications in Anthropology,* No. 72.
Goitein, S.D.
    1966   *Studies in Islamic History and Institutions.* Brill, Leiden.
    1967   *A Mediterranean Society. The Jewish Communities of the
           Arab World. Vol. 1: Economic Foundations.* University of
           California Press, Berkeley.
    1973   *Letters of Medieval Jewish Traders.* Princeton University
           Press, Princeton.
Gómez de Cervantes, Gonzalo
    1944   *La Vida Económica y Social de la Nueva España al Finalizar
           del Siglo XVI.* Carreno, México.
Gómez de Orozco, Federico
    1941   Las Primeras Comunicaciones Entre México y Peru.
           Universidad Nacional Autonomo de México, Instituto
           de Investigaciones Estéticas, *Anales,* Vol. 7, 65–70.
    1949   Italianos Conquistadores, Exploradores y Pobladores
           de México en el Siglo XVI. Academia Mexicana de la
           Historia, *Memorias,* Vol. 8, No. 3, 189–212.
Gómez Moreno, Manuel
    1924   *Cerámica Medieval Española.* Universidad de Barcelona,
           Barcelona.
    1951a El Arte Árabe Español Hasta los Almohades. *Ars
           Hispaniae,* Vol. 3, 11–354. Editorial Plus Ultra,
           Madrid.
    1951b Arte Mozarabe. *Ars Hispaniae,* Vol. 3, 355–410.
González, Julio
    1951   *Repartimiento de Sevilla.* Madrid.
González Jiménez, Manuel
    1980   Origines de la Andaluciá Cristina. In *Historia de
           Andaluciá* (97–304), Vol. 2. Cuspa, Madrid.
González Martí, Manuel
    1944   *Cerámica del Levante Español, Siglos Medievales* (in 3
           vols.). Labor, Barcelona.
    1954   *Cerámica Española.* Labor, Barcelona.
González Reyna, Jenaro
    1956   *Riqueza Minera y Yacimientos Minerales de México.* 20th
           Congreso Geológico Internacional, México.
Goodwin, William B.
    1946   *Spanish and English Ruins in Jamaica.* Meador, Boston.

Gottschalk, A.M.
  1907 Mexican Pottery, Heraldic Patterns, Medieval in
        Design. Department of Commerce and Labor, Bureau
        of Manufacture, *Daily Consular and Trade Reports* No.
        2975, Sept. 18, 15.
Grabar, Oleg
  1976 Islamic Art and Byzantium. In *Studies in Medieval
        Islamic Art* (69–88). Variorum Reprints, London.
Grace, Virginia R.
  1956 The Canaanite Jar. In *The Aegean and the Near East* (80–
        109). Saul S. Weinberg, ed. Augustin, New York.
Grice-Hutchinson, Marjorie
  1978 *Early Economic Thought in Spain, 1177–1740.* Allen and
        Unwin, London.
Griffin, James B. and Antonieta Espejo
  1947 La Alfarería Correspondiente al Último Período de
        Ocupación Nahua del Valle de México. Academia
        Mexicana de la Historia, *Memorias*, Vol. 6, No. 2, 137–
        47; Vol. 9, No. 1 (1950), 118–69.
Grube, Ernst J.
  1965 The Art of Islamic Pottery. Metropolitan Museum of
        Art, *Bulletin*, Vol. 23, No. 6, 209–28.
  1966 *The World of Islam.* McGraw Hill, New York.
  1976 *Islamic Pottery of the Eighth to the Fifteenth Century in the
        Keir Collection.* Faber and Faber, London.
Guasch, Ricardo Pascual
  1963 Las Ánforas de la Plaza del Rey. *Ampurias*, Vol. 25,
        224–34.
Gudiol, José
  1964 *The Arts of Spain.* Doubleday, New York.
Guerrero, Manuel Esteve
  1960 Nuovo Hallazgo de Cerámica Árabe en Mesas de Aste
        (Jérez), *Al Andalus*, Vol. 25, No. 1, 200–03.
Guerrero Lovello, José
  1949 *Las Cántigas. Estudio Arqueológico de sus Miniaturas.*
        Consejo Superior de Investigaciones Científicas,
        Madrid.
Guthrie, Chester L.
  1939 Colonial Economy, Trade, Industry, and Labor in 17th
        Century Mexico City. *Revista de Historia de América*,
        No. 7, 103–34.
Hakluyt, Richard
  1907 *The Principal Navigations, Voyages, Traffiques, and
        Discoveries of the English Nation, Made by Sea or Overland
        to the Remote and Farthest Distant Quarters of the Earth at
        Any Time Within the Compasse of These 1600 Yeres*, Vol.
        6. Dent, London.
Hale, John R.
  1966 *Age of Exploration.* Time-Life Books, New York.
Hamer, Frank
  1975 *The Potter's Dictionary of Materials and Techniques.*
        Pitman, London.
Hamilton, Earl J.
  1954 The Decline of Spain. In *Essays in Economic History*
        (215–26). E.M. Carus-Wilson, ed. Arnold, London.
  1976 What the New World Gave the Economy of the Old.
        In *First Images of America* (853–84), Vol. 2. Fredi
        Chiappelli, ed. University of California Press,
        Berkeley.

Haquim, Mohammad Ibn Azzuz
    1955   *Historia de Marreucos Hasta la Dominación Almoravide.*
        Consejo Superior de Investigaciones Científicas,
        Madrid.

Haring, Clarence Henry
    1964   *Trade and Navigation Between Spain and the Indies in the
        Time of the Hapsburgs.* Peter Smith, Gloucester.

Heer, Friedrich
    1961   *The Medieval World, Europe 1100–1350.* World Pub.,
        Cleveland.

Hernández, Francisco Javier
    1946   Mayolicas Poblanas. *Arte y Plata*, Vol. 2, No. 20, 6–12.

Hernández Días, José, Antonio Sancho Corbacho, and Francisco
Collantes de Teran
    1939   *Catálogo Arqueológico y Artístico de la Provincia de Sevilla*
        (in 3 vols.). Servicio de Defensa del Patrimonio
        Artístico Nacional, Sevilla.

Hess, Andrew G.
    1978   *The Forgotten Frontier. A History of the Sixteenth-Century
        Ibero-African Frontier.* University of Chicago Press,
        Chicago.

Highfield, John Roger, comp.
    1972   *Spain in the Fifteenth Century, 1369–1516.* Macmillan,
        New York.

Hill, Derek
    1976   *Islamic Architecture in North Africa.* Archon, Hamden.

Hillgarth, J.N.
    1976   *The Spanish Kingdoms, 1250–1516* (in 2 vols.).
        Clarendon, Oxford.

Hillier, Bevis
    1968   *The Social History of the Decorative Arts, Pottery and
        Porcelain, 1700–1914. England, Europe, and North
        America.* Meredith, New York.

Hispanic Society of America
    1938   *Handbook.* Hispanic Society of America, New York.

Hodges, Henry
    1970   *Technology in the Ancient World.* Knopf, New York.

Hodges, William H.
    1979   Puerto Real and Limbé, an Analysis. Manuscript,
        Limbé, Haiti.
    1980   Puerto Real Sources. Manuscript, Limbé, Haiti.

Hoffmann, Eleanor
    1965   *Realm of the Evening Star, a History of Morocco and the
        Lands of the Moors.* Chilton, Philadelphia.

Home, Ruth M.
    1953   *Ceramics for the Potter.* Bennett, Peoria.

Hostos, Adolfo de
    1938   *Investigaciones Históricas: Vol. 1, Las Excavaciones de
        Caparra; Vol. 2, El Fondeadero de Colón en Puerto Rico.*
        San Juan.

Howard, Hilary and Elaine L. Morris, eds.
    1981   *Production and Distribution: A Ceramic Viewpoint.* BAR
        International Series 120, Oxford.

Howell, James
    1907   *Epistolae Ho-Elianae. The Familiar Letters of James Howell,*
        Vol. 1. Houghton Mifflin, Boston.

Hudson, G.F.
    1970   The Medieval Trade of China. In *Islam and the Trade of
        Asia* (159–68). D.S. Richards, ed. Bruno Cassirer,
        Oxford.

Humboldt, Alexander von
1811 *Political Essays on the Kingdom of New Spain* (in 4 vols.).
John Black, trans. Longman, Hurit, Rees, Orme, and
Brown, London.
Hurst, John G., ed.
1969 Red-Painted and Glazed Pottery in Western Europe,
from the Eighth to the Twelfth Century. *Medieval
Archaeology*, Vol. 13, 93–147.
Hurst, John G.
1977 Spanish Pottery Imported into Medieval Britain.
Medieval Archaeology, Vol. 21, 68–105.
1979 Portuguese Tour, June, 1979. Manuscript in possession
of authors.
Imamuddin, S.M.
1965 *Some Aspects of the Socio-Economic and Cultural History of
Muslim Spain*. Brill, Leiden.
Irving, Washington
1868 *The Life and Voyages of Christopher Columbus*, Vol. 1.
G.P. Putnam's Sons, New York.
Israel, J.I.
1975 *Race, Class, and Politics in Colonial Mexico, 1610–1670*.
Oxford University Press, London.
Jackson, Gabriel
1972 *The Making of Medieval Spain*. Harcourt Brace
Jovanovich, New York.
James, Stephen Robert
1985 The Analysis of the Conde de Tolosa and the Nuestra
Senora de Guadalupe Olive Jar Assemblage. M.A.
thesis, Texas A & M University, College Station.
Jane, Cecil
1960 *The Journal of Christopher Columbus*. Clarkson N. Potter,
New York.
Jelks, Edward B.
1958 Ceramics from Jamestown. In Archeological
Excavations at Jamestown (201–12). *National Park
Service Archeological Research Series*, No. 1.
Jenkins, Marilyn
1968 The Palmette Tree: A Study of the Iconography of
Egyptian Lustre Painted Pottery, *American Research
Center in Egypt Journal*, Vol. 7, 119–26.
Jiménez Barrientos, Juan Carlos
1982 Un Grupo de 17 Anforitas en el Museo Arqueológico
Provincial de Sevilla. In *En Homenaje a Conchita
Fernández Chicarro* (393–8). Dirección del Museo
Arqueológico de Sevilla, Sevilla.
Johns, Jeremy
1973 Excavations at Tuscania, 1973: Report on the Finds
from Six Selected Pits. The Medieval and Renaissance
Pottery. *Papers of the British School at Rome*, Vol. 41, 49–
111, 670.
Jornet, Albert
1984 Elemental Analysis of Spanish Colonial Majolica to
Determine Provenance. Paper presented to annual
meeting of Society for Historical Archaeology,
Williamsburg.
Kaplan, Flora S.
1976 Learning and the Transmission of Style Among Folk-
Urban Potters in Puebla, Mexico. Congreso
Internacional de Americanistas, *Actas*, Vol. 3, 243–8.

Kingery, W.D.
1980 Social Needs and Ceramic Technology. American Ceramics Society, *Bulletin*, Vol. 59, No. 6, 598–600.
1982 Plausible Inferences from Ceramic Artifacts. In *Archaeological Ceramics* (37–45), Jacqueline S. Olin and Alan D. Franklin, eds. Smithsonian Institution Press, Washington.

Klein, Julius
1967 Medieval Spanish Gilds. In *Facts and Factors in Economic History* (164–88). Edwin Francis Gay, ed. Augustus M. Kelley, New York.

Konetzke, Richard
1949 Las Ordenances de Gremios Como Documentos Para la Historia Social de Hispano-América Durante la Época Colonial. *Estudios de Historia Social de España*, 483–524.

Kramers, J.H.
1970 Islamic Geography and Commerce. In *The Islamic World and the West, A.D. 622–1492* (66–78). Archibald L. Lewis, ed. Wiley, New York.

Kremers, Edward and George Urdang
1976 *History of Pharmacy*. Revised by Glenn A. Sonnedecker. Lippincott, Philadelphia.

Krueger, Hilmar G.
1933 Genoese Trade with Northwest Africa in the Twelfth Century. *Speculum*, Vol. 8, 377–95.
1937 The Wares of Exchange in the Genoese-African Traffic of the Twelfth Century. *Speculum*, Vol. 12, 57–71.

Kubiak, Wladyslaw B.
1970 Medieval Ceramic Oil Lamps from Fustat. *Ars Orientalis*, Vol. 8, 1–18.

Kubler, George
1948 *Mexican Architecture of the Sixteenth Century*. (in 2 vols.). Greenwood, Westport.
1962 *The Shape of Time*. Yale University Press, New Haven.

Kubler, George and Martin Soria
1959 *Art and Architecture in Spain and Portugal and Their Dominions, 1500 to 1800*. Penguin, Baltimore.

Kuhnel, Ernst
1966 *Islamic Art and Architecture*. Bell, London.

Kurz, Otto
1975 The Strange History of an Alhambra Vase. *Al Andalus*, Vol. 40, No. 1, 205–12.

Ladero Quesada, Miguel Angel
1970–71 Algunas Consideraciones Sobre Granada en el Siglo XIV. *Anuario de Estudios Medievales*, Vol. 7, 279–84.
1976 *La Ciudad Medieval (1248–1492)*. Universidad de Sevilla, Sevilla.

Lane, Arthur
1937 Medieval Finds at Al Mina in North Syria. *Archaeologia*, Vol. 87, 19–78.
1939 *A Guide to the Collection of Tiles*. Victoria and Albert Museum, London.
1946 Early Hispano-Moresque Pottery: A Reconsideration. *Burlington Magazine for Connoisseurs*, Vol. 88, 246–52.
1947 Early Islamic Pottery in the Collection of Sir Ernest Debenham. *Connoisseur*, Vol. 119, 21–6, 59.
1958 *Early Islamic Pottery*. Faber and Faber, London.

1960 *A Guide to the Collection of Tiles.* 2nd ed. Victoria and Albert Museum, London.

Leicht, Hugo
1934 *Las Calles de Puebla. Estudio Histórico.* Mijares, Puebla.

Lemoine, C., S. Walker, and M. Picon
1982 Archaeological, Geochemical, and Statistical Methods in Ceramic Provenance Studies. In *Archaeological Ceramics* (57–64), Jacqueline S. Olin and Alan D. Franklin, eds. Smithsonian Institution Press, Washington.

Lerner, Martin
1978 *Blue and White Early Japanese Export Ware.* Metropolitan Museum of Art, New York.

Le Tourneau, Roger
1961 *Fez in the Age of the Marinides.* University of Oklahoma Press, Norman.

Lévi-Provencal, E.
1957 España Musulmana Hasta la Caída del Califato de Córdoba (711–1031 de J.C.). Instituciones y Vida Social e Intelectual. In *Historia de España* (3–300), Vol. 5. R. Menéndez Pidal, ed. Calpe, Madrid.

Lévi-Provencal, E. and Emilio García Gómez
1948 *Sevilla a Comienzos del Siglo XII. El Tratado de Ibn' Abdun.* Madrid.

Lewis, Archibald
1978 Mediterranean Maritime Commerce, A.D. 300–1100: Shipping and Trade. In *The Sea and Medieval Civilizations* (1–21). Variorum Reprints, London.

Lewis, George Randall
1924 *The Stannaries, a Study of the English Tin Miner.* Harvard University Press, Cambridge.

Liss, Peggy K.
1975 *Mexico Under Spain, 1521–1556.* University of Chicago Press, Chicago.

Lister, Florence C. and Robert H. Lister
1969 Majolica, Ceramic Link Between Old World and New. *El Palacio*, Vol. 76, No. 2, 1–15.
1974 Maiolica in Colonial Spanish America. *Historical Archaeology*, Vol. 8, 17–52.
1975a An Overview of Moroccan Maiolica. *Papers of the Archaeological Society of New Mexico*, Vol. 2, 272–95.
1975b Non-Indian Ceramics from the Mexico City Subway. *El Palacio*, Vol. 81, No. 2, 25–48.
1976a *A Descriptive Dictionary for 500 Years of Spanish-Tradition Ceramics, 13th Through 18th Centuries.* Special Publication Series 1, Society for Historical Archaeology, Columbia.
1976b Distribution of Mexican Maiolica Along the Northern Borderlands. *Papers of the Archaeological Society of New Mexico*, Vol.3, 113–40.
1976c Italian Presence in Tin Glazed Ceramics in Spanish America. *Historical Archaeology*, Vol. 10, 28–41.
1976d Ligurian Maiolica in Spanish America. Convegno Internazionale della Ceramica, *Atti*, Vol. 9, 311–20.
1978 The First Mexican Maiolicas: Imported and Locally Produced. *Historical Archaeology*, Vol. 12, 1–24.
1981 The Recycled Pots and Potsherds of Spain. *Historical Archaeology*, Vol. 15, 66–78.

1982 Sixteenth Century Maiolica Pottery in the Valley of Mexico. *Anthropological Papers of the University of Arizona*, No. 39.

1983 One Pot's Pedigree. *Papers of the Archaeological Society of New Mexico*, Vol. 8, 167–87.

1984 The Potters' Quarter in Colonial Puebla, Mexico. *Historical Archaeology*, Vol. 18, 87–102.

Liverani, Giuseppe
1960 *Five Centuries of Italian Majolica*. McGraw Hill, New York.

Llorens Artigas, José and José Corredor Matheos
1970 *Cerámica Popular Española Actual*. Blume, Barcelona.

Llubiá, Luis M.
1967 *Cerámica Medieval Española*. Labor, Barcelona.

Llubiá Munné, Luis María and Miguel López Guzman
1951 *La Cerámica Murciana Decorada*. Cámara Oficial de Comercio, Industria y Navegación de Murcia, Murcia.

Long, George A.
1964 Excavations at Panama Vieja. *Florida Anthropologist*, Vol. 17, No. 2, 104–09.

1967 Archeological Investigations at Panama Vieja. M.A. thesis, University of Florida, Gainesville.

López, Robert S. and Irving W. Raymond
1970 Moslem Trade in the Mediterranean and the West. In *The Islamic World and the West, A.D. 622–1492* (30–8). Archibald Lewis, ed. Wiley, New York.

López Cervantes, Gonzalo
1976a Cerámica Colonial de la Ciudad de México. Instituto Nacional de Antropología e Historia, *Colección Científica, Arqueología*, No. 38.

1976b Cerámica Española en la Ciudad de México. Instituto Nacional de Antropología e Historia, *Boletín*, Vol. 18, 33–8.

1983 *Cerámica Mexicana*. Editorial Everest Mexicana, México.

López de Coca Castañer, José Enrique
1980 Los Reinos de Taifas y las Dinastias Bereberes. In *Historia de Andaluciá* (97–304), Vol. 2. Cuspa, Madrid.

López Martínez, Celestino
1935 *Mudéjares y Moriscos Sevillanos*. Tipografía Rodríguez, Giménez y Cia., Sevilla.

López Rosado, Diego
1965 *Historia Económica de México*. Pormaca, México.

López Serrano, Matilde
1974 *Cántigas de Santa María de Alfonso X el Sabio, Rey de Castilla*. Editorial Patrimonio Nacional, Madrid.

Maggetti, Marino, Harold Westley, and Jacqueline S. Olin
1984 Provenance and Technical Studies of Mexican Majolica Using Elemental and Phase Analysis. *Advances in Chemistry* Series, No. 205, 151–91.

Malaquer de Motes, J. Antonio García y Bellido, Blas Taracena, and Julio Caro Baroja
1957 Pintura Cerámica. *Historia de España* (599–765), Vol. 2. R. Menéndez Pidal, ed. Calpe, Madrid.

Maniatis, Y., A. Simopoulos, and A. Kostikas
1982 The Investigation of Ancient Ceramic Technologies. In *Archaeological Ceramics* (97–108), Jacqueline S. Olin and Alan D. Franklin, eds. Smithsonian Institution Press, Washington.

Mannoni, Tiziano
  1969   Gli Scarti di Fornace e la Cava del XVI Secolo en Via S.
         Vincenzo a Genova. Convegno Internazionale della
         Ceramica, *Atti*, Vol. 9, No. 2, 75–96.
  1972   Nuove Analisi Techniche e Mineralogiche della
         Ceramiche Medievali di Importazioni Renvenute in
         Liguria. Convegno Internacionale della Ceramica, *Atti*,
         Vol. 12, 107–29.
  1981   The Archaeological Evidence for Commerce: A
         Ligurian Case Study. In *Archaeology and Italian Society*
         (125–32). Graeme Barker and Richard Hodges, eds.
         BAR International Series 102, London.
  1982   Present Day Knowledge of Mediterranean Pottery
         After Ten Years of Thin-Sectioning at the University of
         Genoa. British Museum, *Occasional Paper*, No. 32,
         89–91.
Manucy, Albert and Joseph A. Galiano
  1958   *Spanish Colonial Sites in the Panama Canal Zone*. National
         Survey of Historic Sites and Buildings, National Park
         Service, Washington.
Marcais, Georges
  1913   *Les Poteries y Faiences de la Qal'a des Beni Hammad (XIe
         Siecle)*. Braham, Constantine.
  1916   *Les Poteries y Faiences de Bougie*. Braham, Constantine.
Mariejol, Jean Hippolyte
  1961   *The Spain of Ferdinand and Isabella*. Rutgers University
         Press, New Brunswick.
Marrinan, Rochelle A.
  1984   Puerto Real, Haiti: Test Excavation in an Early 16th-
         Century Spanish Town. Paper presented at annual
         meeting of Society for Historical Archaeology,
         Williamsburg.
Marroqui, José María
  1900   *La Ciudad de México*. (in 3 vols.). México.
Martin, Colin
  1978   La Trinidad Valencera, a Spanish Armada Wreck.
         Archaeology, Vol. 31, No. 1, 38–47.
  1979   Spanish Armada Pottery. *International Journal of
         Nautical Archaeology*, Vol. 8, No. 4, 279–302.
Martínez Caviró, Balbina
  1968   *Catálogo de Cerámica Española*. Instituto Valencia de Don
         Juan, Madrid.
  1969   *Cerámica de Talavera*. Instituto Diego Velázquez del
         Consejo Superior de Investigaciones Científicas,
         Madrid.
  1971   Azulejos Talaveranos del Siglo XVI. *Archivo Español de
         Arte*, Vol. XLIV, Nos. 173–6, 283–93.
Martínez Hidalgo, José María
  1966   *Columbus' Ships*. Barre Publishers, Barre, Mass.
Marx, Robert F.
  1971   *Shipwrecks of the Western Hemisphere, 1492–1825*. World,
         New York.
Mata Carriazo, Juan de
  1973   *Tartesos y el Carambolo* (417–650). Patronato Nacional de
         Museos, Madrid.
Matson, Frederick R.
  1941   A Review of "The Ceramic Art in Islamic Times. C.
         Techniques." *Ars Islamica*, Vol. 8, 59–63.
  1951   Ceramic Technology as an Aid to Culture

Interpretation. Techniques and Problems. *Museum Anthropological Papers*, No. 8, 102–16. University of Michigan, Ann Arbor.

1955   Ceramic Archaeology. American Ceramic Society, *Bulletin*, Vol. 34, No. 2, 33–44.

1965   Ceramics and Man. *Viking Fund for Publications in Anthropology*, No. 41.

May, Florence Lewis
1939   *Hispanic Lace and Lace Making*. Hispanic Society of America, New York.

Mayer, William
1961   *Early Travellers in Mexico, 1534 to 1816*. Mexico.

Maza, Francisco de la
1968   *La Ciudad de México en el Siglo XVII*. Fondo de Cultura Económica, Mexico.

McEwan, Bonnie G.
1983   *Spanish Colonial Adaptation on Hispaniola: The Archaeology of Area 35, Puerto Real, Haiti*. M.A. thesis, University of Florida, Gainesville.

1984   Domestic Adaptation at Puerto Real. Paper presented at annual meeting of Society for Historical Archaeology, Williamsburg.

Meakin, Budgett
1901   *The Land of the Moors*. Swan Sonnenschein, London.

Medina, Pedro de
1944   *Libro de Grandezas y Cosas Memorables de España*. Consejo Superior de Investigaciones Científicas, Madrid.

Menéndez Pidal, Ramón
1957   *Historia de España*. Vol. 1: *España Prerromana*, Vol. 2: *España Romana, 218 a. de J.C. - 414 de J.C.)*; Vol. 3, *España Visigoda, 414–711 de J.C.*; Vol. 5, *España Musulmana, 711–1031 de J.C.* Calpe, Madrid.

Mercer, John
1976   *Spanish Sahara*. Allen and Unwin, London.
1980   *The Canary Islanders, Their Prehistory, Conquest, and Survival*. Rex Collings, London.

México. Archivo General de la Nación
1940   Indice del Ramo de Ordenanzas, *Boletín*, Vol. 11, No. 2, 303–44.

1941   Indice del Ramo de Ordenanzas, *Boletín*, Vol. 12, No. 1, 141–75; Vol. 12, No. 2, 297–375.

1943a   Indice del Ramo de Ordenanzas. *Boletín*, Vol. 13, No. 1, 161–92.

1943b   Cartas de Examen y Algunas Ordenanzas de Gremios. *Boletín*, Vol. 13, 429.

México. Instituto Indigenista Interamericano
1947   *Codice Osuna. Reproducción Facsimilar de la Obra del Mismo Título. Editada en Madrid, 1878*.

Mexico City. Cabildo
1871–1919   *Actas de Cabildo de la Ciudad de México*. Paleography by Ignacio Bejarano.

Millares Torres, Agustín
1974   *Historia General de las Islas Canarias*. Inventarios Provisionales Editores, Las Palmas.

Mohamed, Ataallah
1967   La Ceramique Museulmane a Paroi Fine Incisee au Peint e de Lixus. *Bulletin d'Archeologie Marocaine*, Vol. 7, 627–39.

Montoto de Sedas, Santiago
  1938 *Sevilla en el Imperio, Siglo XVI.* Nueva Libreriá, Sevilla.
Morales Padrón, Francisco
  1952 *Jamaica Española.* Sevilla.
  1955 El Comercio Canario-Americano, Siglos XVI, XVII, y
        XVIII. *Publicaciones de la Escuela de Estudios Hispano-
        Americanos de Sevilla*, No. 91.
  1977 *La Ciudad de Quinientos.* Universidad de Sevilla, Sevilla.
Morales Patiño, Oswaldo and Roberto Pérez de Acevedo
  1946 El Período de Transculturación Indohispánico. *Revista
        de Arqueología e Etnología*, Vol. 1, No. 1, 5–20.
Morgada, Olonso de
  1887 *Historia de Sevilla.* Ariza, Sevilla.
Morison, Samuel E.
  1939 *The Second Voyage of Christopher Columbus, From Cádiz to
        Hispaniola and the Discovery of the Lesser Antilles.*
        Clarendon, Oxford.
  1942 *Admiral of the Ocean Sea. A Life of Christopher Columbus.*
        Little Brown, Boston.
  1974 *The European Discovery of America. The Southern Voyages,
        A.D. 1492–1616.* Oxford University Press, New York.
Müller, Florencia
  1970 Efectos de la Conquista Española Sobre la Cerámica
  –71   Prehispánica de Cholula. Instituto Nacional de
        Antropología e Historia, *Anales*, Época 7a, Vol. 3, 97–
        110.
  1979 Estudio de la Cerámica Hispánica y Moderna en la
        Región Tlaxcala-Puebla. Comunicaciones 16. 2nd
        Symposium. *Proceedings.* Proyecto Puebla-Tlaxcala.
Müller, Florencia and Barbara Hopkins
  1974 *A Guide to Mexican Ceramics.* Minutiae Mexicana,
        México.
Munzer, Gerónimo
  1924 Viaje por España y Portugal en los Años 1494 y 1495.
        Julio Puyol, trans. *Boletín de la Real Academia de la
        Historia*, Vol. LXXXIV, 32–119, 197–279.
Myers, Joseph Emlen
  1983 Pottery Production and Distribution in a Medieval
        Economy. Paper presented at 83rd Annual Meeting,
        American Anthropological Association, Chicago.
  1984 The Political Economy of Ceramic Production: A Study
        of the Islamic Commonware Pottery of Medieval Qsar
        es-Seghir. Ph.D. dissertation, State University of New
        York at Binghamton.
Myers, Joseph Emlen and M. James Blackman
  In Press Conical Plates of the Hispano-Moresque Tradition
            from Islamic Qsar es-Seghir. Paper submitted for
            publication in Proceedings of the Third
            International Congress on Medieval Ceramics in
            the Western Hemisphere, Siena.
Navarrete, Martín Fernández de
  1945 *Colección de los Viajes y Descubrimientos que Hicieron por
        Mar los Españoles Desde Fines del Siglo XV: Vol. 1, Viajes
        de Colón, Almirantazgo de Castilla.* Guarania, Buenos
        Aires.
Neasham, V. Aubrey
  1939 Spain's Emigrants to the New World, 1492–1592.
        Hispanic American Historical Review, Vol. 19, 147–60.

Needham, Joseph
    1949   Central Asia and the History of Science and
            Technology. Royal Central Asian Society, *Journal*, Vol.
            36, 135–45.
Nicklin, Keith
    1971   Stability and Innovation in Pottery Manufacture. *World
            Archaeology*, Vol. 3, No. 1, 13–48.
Nicocini, Gerard
    1974   *The Ancient Spaniards.* Jean Stewart, trans. Heath,
            Hants.
Nieves Sicart, María
    1980   Piezas Cerámicas Conservadas en los Depósitos del
            Departamento de Ceramología Histórica del Museo de
            las Casas Reales. *Casas Reales*, Vol. 5, No. 11, 89–97.
Noguera, Eduardo
    1965   *La Cerámica Arqueológica de Mesoamerica.* Universidad
            Nacional Autonoma de México, México.
    1967   Motivos Naturalistas de la Cerámica Azteca IV.
            Ministerio de Hacienda y Crédito Público, *Boletín
            Bibliográfico*, Vol. 13, No. 377, 7–11.
Nonell, Carmen
    1973   *Cerámica y Alfarería Populares de España.* Everest,
            Madrid.
O'Callaghan, Joseph F.
    1975   *A History of Medieval Spain.* Cornell University Press,
            Ithaca.
Olin, Jacqueline S. and Edward V. Sayre
    1975a Identification of the Provenience of Maiolica From
            Sites in the Caribbean Using Neutron Activation
            Analysis. Paper presented at University of California
            Conference on Analytical Studies in Ceramics, March,
            1975.
    1975b Neutron Activation Analysis of Majolica From
            Spanish Colonial Sites in Meso-America. *Bulletin of
            the American Institute for Conservation of Historic and
            Artistic Works*, Vol. 15, No. 2, 57–61.
Olin, Jacqueline S., Garman Harbottle, and Edward V. Sayre
    1978   Elemental Compositions of Spanish and Spanish-
            Colonial Majolica Ceramics in the Identification of
            Provenience. In *Advances in Chemistry Series*, No. 171,
            200–29.
Olin, Jacqueline S. and Alan D. Franklin, eds.
    1982   *Archaeological Ceramics.* Smithsonian Institution Press,
            Washington.
Olivar Daydí, Marcal
    1952   *La Cerámica Trecentista en los Países de la Corona de
            Aragón.* Seix Barral, Barcelona.
Oliveira Marques, A.H. de
    1976   *History of Portugal.* Columbia University Press, New
            York.
Ortega, Elpidio and José M. Cruxent
    1974   Informe Preliminar Sobre las Excavaciones en las
            Ruinas del Convento de San Francisco, Santo
            Domingo, República Dominicana. Paper presented to
            Congreso Internacional de Americanistas, Mexico City.
Ortega, Elpidio and Carmen Fondeur
    1978a *Arqueología de los Monumentos Históricos de Santo
            Domingo.* Universidad Central de Este, San Pedro de
            Macorís.

1978b Estudio de la Cerámica del Período Indo-Hispano de la Antigua Concepción de la Vega. Fundación Ortega Alvarez, *Serie Científica* No. 1.

Ortíz Muñoz, Luis
1973 *Sevilla Eterna.* Seix Barral, Barcelona.

Otté, Enrique
1964 La Flota de Diego Colón, Españoles y Genoveses en el Comercio Tras-Atlántico de 1509. *Revista de Indias,* Vol. 24, Nos. 97–8, 475–503.

Palm, Erwin Walter
1945 Excavations of La Isabela, White Man's First Town in the Americas. *Acta Americana,* Vol. 3, 298–303.
1955 *Los Monumentos Arquitectónicos de la Española, con una Introducción a América* (in 2 vols.). Universidad de Santo Domingo, Ciudad Trujillo.

Parvaux, Solange
1968 *La Ceramique Populaire du Haut-Alentejo.* Presses Universitaires de France, Paris.

Pavón Maldonado, Basilio
1966 *Memoria de la Excavación de la Mesquita de Medinat al-Zahra.* Ministerio de Educación Nacional, Madrid.
1967 Notas Sobre la Cerámica Hispano-Musulmana. *Al Andalus,* Vol. 32, 415–37, 457–8.
1968 Influjos Occidentales en el Arte del Califato de Córdoba. *Al Andalus,* Vol. 33, No. 1, 206–19.
1972 La Loza Doméstica de Medinat al-Zahra. *Al Andalus,* Vol. 37, No. 1, 191–227.

Payne, Stanley G.
1973 *A History of Spain and Portugal,* Vol. 1. University of Wisconsin Press, Madison.

Peacock, D.P.S.
1974 Amphorae and the Baetican Fish Industry. *Antiquaries Journal,* Vol. 54, 232–44.
1977 *Pottery and Early Commerce.* Academic Press, New York.

Pelauzy, María Antonia
1977 *Artesanía Popular Española.* Blume, Barcelona.

Peñafiel, Antonio
1910 *Cerámica Mexicana y Loza de Talavera de Puebla.* Secretariá de Fomento, México.

Peon Soler, Alejandra and Leonor Cortina Ortega
1973 *Talavera de Puebla.* Comermex, México.

Pérez Embid, Florentino
1969a Navegación y Comercio en el Puerto de Sevilla en la Baja Edad Media. In *Les Routes de l'Atlantique* (43–96). Noveno Coloquio Internacional de Historia Marítima, Sevilla.
1969b La Marina Real Castellana en el Siglo XIII. *Anuario de Estudios Medievales,* 141–85.

Pescador del Hoyo, María del Carmen
1965 La Loza de Talavera y Sus Imitaciones del Siglo XVII. *Archivo Español de Arte,* Vol. 38, Nos. 151–2, 245–60.

Pesce, Giovanni
1969 I Vase da Farmacia del Secolo XVI nei Reperti di Scavo di Genova e Savona. Convegno Internazionale della Ceramica, *Atti,* Vol. 9, No. 2, 49–53.

Peterson, Mendel
1965 *History Under the Sea.* Smithsonian Institution, Washington.
1975 *The Funnel of Gold.* Little Brown, Boston.

Philon, Helen
    1980   *Early Islamic Ceramics, Ninth to Late Twelfth Centuries.* Islamic Art Publications, London.

Piccolpasso, Cipriano Cavaliere
    1934   *The Three Books of the Potter's Art.* Intro. and trans. by Bernard Rackham and Albert Van de Put. Victoria and Albert Museum, London.
    1980   *I Tre Libri Dell'Arte del Vasaio* (in 2 vols.) Trans. and ed. by Ronald Lightbown and Alan Caiger-Smith. Scholar Press, Ilkley.

Pike, Ruth
    1966   *Enterprise and Adventure, the Genoese in Sevilla and the Opening of the New World.* Cornell University Press, Ithaca.
    1967   Seville in the Sixteenth Century: Slaves and Freemen. *Hispanic American Historical Review*, Vol. 41, No. 1, 1–30.
    1972   *Aristocrats and Traders, Sevillian Society in the Sixteenth Century.* Cornell University Press, Ithaca.

Pirenne, Henri
    1937   *Economic and Social History of Medieval Europe.* Harcourt, Brace, New York.

Platt, Colin and Richard Coleman-Smith
    1975   *Excavations in Medieval Southampton, 1953–1969: Vol. 2, The Finds.* Leicester University Press, Leicester.

Plowden, William W.
    1958   Spanish and Mexican Majolica Found in New Mexico. *El Palacio*, Vol. 65, No. 6, 212–19.

Plumer, James Marshall
    1968   Certain Celadon Potsherds from Samarra Traced to Their Source. *Ars Islamica*, Vol. 4, 195–200.

Pope, Arthur Upham
    1964   *A Survey of Persian Art: Vol. 4, The Ceramic Arts;* Vol. 10, *Plates, Pottery, and Faience.* Oxford University Press, Oxford.

Pope, E.M.
    1956   Ceramics: Medieval. In *A History of Technology*, Vol. 2, 284–310. Charles Singer et al, eds. Clarendon, Oxford.

Pope, John Alexander
    1956   *Chinese Porcelains from the Arbedil Shrine.* Smithsonian Institution, Washington.

Posac Mon, Carlos
    1972   La Villa Romana de Marbella. *Noticiario Arqueológico Hispánico*. Vol. I: *Arqueología*. Comisaría General de Excavaciones Arqueológicas, Madrid.
    1981   Candiles de la Ceuta Islamica. Jornadas de Cultura Árabe e Islamica, *Actas*, 287–92.

Prieto, Carlos
    1973   *Mining in the New World.* McGraw Hill, New York.

Pringle, Denys
    1982   Some More Proto-Maiolica from 'Athlit (Pilgrims' Castle) and a Discussion of its Distribution in the Levant. *Levant*, Vol. 14, 104–17.

Proccaci, Guilano
    1968   *History of the Italian People.* Harper and Row, New York.

Puig i Cadafalch, J.
    1927–31   Les Anfores per a la Construccio de Voltes a Tarragona. *Seccio Histórico Arqueológico*, Vol. 8, 114. Institut d'Estudis Catalana, Barcelona.

Puigaudeau, Odette du
n.d.   Safi Potters. *Morocco Tourism*, No. 48, 27–35.
Ramazzini, Bernardino
1964   *De Morbis Artificum: Diseases of Workers*. Trans. from
        1713 Latin text by William Cave Wright. Hafner, New
        York.
Redman, Charles L.
1977   Late Medieval Ceramics from Qsar es-Seghir.
        Manuscript, State University of New York,
        Binghamton.
1978   Qsar es-Seghir, an Islamic Port and Portuguese
        Fortress. *Archaeology*, Vol. 31, No. 5, 12–23.
1979a   Description and Inference with Late Medieval Pottery
        from Qsar es-Seghir, Morocco. *Medieval Ceramics*, Vol.
        3, 63–79.
1979b   La Céramique Médiévale en Mediterranée
        Occidentale. X^e–XVe Siecles. *Colloques Internationaux
        du Centre National de la Recherche Scientifique*, No. 584,
        251–63.
1982   The Role of Italian Tradeware in an Early 16th Century
        North African Colony. *Archeologia Medievale*, Vol. 9,
        227–36.
1983   Comparative Urbanism in the Islamic Far West. *World
        Archaeology*, Vol. 14, No. 3, 355–77.
1985   *Qsar es-Seghir, An Archaeological View of Medieval Life*.
        Academic Press, New York.
Redman, Charles L. and James L. Boone
1979   Qsar es-Seghir (Alcacer Ceguer): a 15th and 16th
        Century Portuguese Colony in North Africa. *Studia*,
        No. 41–2.
Redman, Charles L. and J. Emlen Myers
1981   Interpretation, Classification, and Ceramic Production:
        a Medieval North African Case Study. In *Production
        and Distribution: A Ceramic Viewpoint* (285–307). Hilary
        Howard and Elaine L. Morris, eds. BAR International
        Series 120.
Redman, Charles L. and Patricia E. Rubertone
1976   Preliminary Report on the Qsar es-Seghir Ceramic
        Analysis, 15th and 16th Century Ceramics from a
        North African Portuguese Colony. Manuscript, State
        University of New York, Binghamton.
Redman, Charles L., Ronald D. Anzalone, and Patricia E.
Rubertone
1978   Qsar es-Seghir, Three Seasons of Excavation. *Bulletin
        d'Archeologie Marocaine*, Vol. 11, 151–95.
Riaño, Juan R.
1879   *The Industrial Arts in Spain*. Chapman and Hall,
        London.
Richter, Gisela M.A.
1956   Ceramics, from 700 B.C. to the Fall of the Roman
        Empire. In *A History of Technology* (259–83), Vol. 2.
        Charles Singer et al, eds. Clarendon, Oxford.
Rodinson, Maxime
1973   *Islam and Capitalism*. Pantheon, New York.
Romero, Hector Manuel
1973   *Anatomía de la Ciudad de México*, Vol. 2, Pt. 1. México.
Romero de Terreros y Vinent, Manuel
1923   *Las Artes Industriales en la Nueva España*. Robredo,
        México.

Ronsheim, Marian G. Riebe
    1977   Folk Pottery in Israel. *Ceramics Monthly*, Vol. 25, No. 1,
            31–4.
Rosselló Bordoy, Guillermo
    1964   Hallazgos Cerámicos en el Colegio de Montesión
            (Palma de Mallorca). *Al Andalus*, Vol. 29, No. 2,
            329–36.
    1981   Elementos Decorativos en la Cerámica Árabe de los
            Siglos X y XI. Jornadas de Cultura Árabe e Islamica,
            Actas, 271–6.
Rothschild-Boros, Monica C.
    1981   The Determination of Amphora Contents. In
            Archaeology and Italian Society (79–89). Graeme Barker
            and Richard Hodges, eds. BAR International Series
            102, London.
Rouse, Irving and José M. Cruxent
    1963   *Venezuelan Archaeology*. Yale University Press, New
            Haven.
Rovira, Beatriz E.
    1980   La Cerámica Histórica en la Ciudad de Panamá: Tres
            Contextos Estratigráficos. Paper presented to
            International Congress of Americanists, Manchester.
Rubió Mañe, J. Ignacio
    1956   Ordenanzas para la Limpieza de la Ciudad de México.
            Archivo General de la Nación, *Boletín*, Vol. 27, No. 1,
            19–27.
Rubió y Moreno, Luis
    1917   Pasajeros a Indias. Catálogo Metodológico de las
            Informaciones y Licencias de los Allí Pasaron,
            Existentes en el Archivo General de Indias. Siglo
            Primero de la Colonización de América, 1492–1592.
            *Colección de Documentos Inéditos para la Historia de
            Hispano-América*, Vol. 8. Ibero-Americana de
            Publicaciones, Madrid.
Ruddock, Alwyn A.
    1951   *Italian Merchants and Shipping in Southampton, 1270–
            1600*. University College, Southampton.
Rumeu de Armas, Antonio
    1942   *Historia de la Previsión Social en España. Cofradías,
            Gremios, Hermandades, Montepíos*. Editoria Revista de
            Derecho Privado, Madrid.
Rye, Owen A.
    1981   *Pottery Technology; Principles and Reconstruction*.
            Taraxacum, Washington.
Rye, Owen S. and Clifford Evans
    1976   Traditional Pottery Techniques of Pakistan. *Smithsonian
            Contribution to Anthropology*, No. 21.
Sahagún, Bernardino de
    1956   *Historia General de las Cosas de Nueva España*, Vol. 3.
            Porrúa, México.
Said, Hakim Mohammed
    1980   *Pharmacy and Medicine Through the Ages*. Hamdard
            Foundation, Karachi.
Sánchez Pacheco, Trinidad
    1981a   Paterna y Manises. In *Cerámica Esmaltada Española*
            (53–72). Labor, Barcelona.
    1981b   Sevilla. In *Cerámica Esmaltada Española* (93–108).
            Labor, Barcelona.

Sancho Corbacho, Antonio
  1948 *La Cerámica Andaluza*. Universidad de Sevilla, Sevilla.
  1949 Los Azulejos de Madre de Dios de Sevilla. *Archivo Español de Arte*, Vol. 22, 233–7.
Santiago Cruz, Francisco
  1960 *Las Artes y los Gremios de la Nueva España*. Jus, México.
Santos, Samuel de los
  1952 Botella de Cerámica Hispano-Musulmana con Representaciones Humanas. *Al Andalus*, Vol. 17, 401–03.
Sanz, Carlos
  1961 *La Carta de Colón Anunciado el Descubrimiento del Nuevo Mundo, 15 Febrero–14 Marzo, 1493*. Gráficas Yagues, Madrid.
Sauer, Carl Ortwin
  1966 *The Early Spanish Main*. University of California Press, Berkeley.
Sayas Abengochea, Juan José
  1957 La Vida Privada. In *Historia de España*, Vol. 4, 707–11. R. Menéndez Pidal, ed. Calpe, Madrid.
Scanlon, George T.
  1965 Preliminary Report: Excavations at Fustat, 1964. *American Research Center in Egypt Journal*, Vol. 4, 7–30.
  1967 Fustat Expedition: Preliminary Report 1965, Part II. *American Research Center in Egypt Journal*, Vol. 6, 65–86.
  1970 Egypt and China: Trade and Imitation. In *Islam and the Trade of Asia* (81–96). D.S. Richards, ed. Bruno Cassirer, Oxford.
Scavizzi, Giuseppe
  1966 *Maioliche dell' Islam e del Medioevo Occidentale*. Fretelli Fabbri, Milano.
Scheufler, Vladimir
  1968 Classification System of Pottery Making. VIIIth Congress of Anthropological and Ethnological Sciences, *Proceedings*, Vol. 3, Section B-10, 1–3.
Schlindler, A.D.
  1896 *Eastern Persian Irak*. Royal Geographical Society, London.
Scholes, France V.
  1930 The Supply Service of the New Mexico Missions in the 17th Century. *New Mexico Historical Review*, Vol. 5, No. 1, 93–115.
Schurz, William Lytle
  1939 *The Manila Galleon*. Dutton, New York.
Scofield, John
  1975 Christopher Columbus and the New World He Found. *National Geographic Magazine*, Vol. 148, No. 5, 584–625.
Scott, Lindsay
  1954 Pottery. In *A History of Technology* (376–412), Vol. 1. Charles Singer et al, eds. Clarendon, Oxford.
Seseña, Natacha
  1968 The Pottery of Talavera de la Reina. *Oro Verde*, Vol. 8, No. 58, 53–62.
  1975 *La Cerámica Popular en Castilla la Nueva*. Nacional, Madrid.
  1981 Talavera and Puente del Arzobispo. In *Cerámica Esmaltada Española* (73–92). Labor, Barcelona.

Shepard, Anna O.
  1956 *Ceramics for the Archaeologist*. Carnegie Institution (Pub.
         No. 609), Washington.
Sierra Fernández, Juan Alonso de la, and María de Gracia Lasso
de la Vega Porre
  1982 Tinajas Mudéjares de Museo Arqueológico de Sevilla,
         Tipología e Decoración. In *En Homenaje a Conchita
         Fernández Chicarro* (459–70). Dirección del Museo
         Arqueológico, Sevilla.
Simpson, Wesley Bird
  1953 Mexico's Forgotten Century. *Pacific Historical Review*,
         Vol. 22, No. 2, 113–21.
  1966 *Many Mexicos*. University of California Press, Berkeley.
Singer, Charles, E.J. Holmyard, A.R. Hill, and Trevor I.
Williams
  1954 *A History of Technology*: Vol. 1, *From Early Times to the
         Fall of Ancient Empires*; Vol. 2, *The Mediterranean
         Civilizations and the Middle Ages, c. 700 B.C. to c. A.D.
         1500*; *Epilogue: East and West in Retrospect*. Clarendon,
         Oxford.
Sinopoli, Carla M.
  In Press The Blue-on-White Majolica of Qsar es-Seghir. In
            Qsar es-Seghir, Vol. 2: The Portuguese Period (1–9).
            C.L. Redman, ed. Villes et Sites Archeologique
            Morocaine, Rabat.
Smith, Hale G.
  1962 Archaeological Excavation at El Morro, San Juan,
         Puerto Rico. *Florida State University Notes in
         Anthropology*, Vol. 6.
Smith, Norman
  1976 *Man and Water, a History of Hydro-Technology*. Peter
         Davies, London.
Smith, Rhea Marsh
  1965 *Spain, a Modern History*. University of Michigan Press,
         Ann Arbor.
Snow, David H.
  1965 The Chronological Position of Mexican Maiolica in the
         Southwest. *El Palacio*, Vol. 72, No. 1, 25–35.
Sotomayor, Manuel
  1972 Andújar (Jaén), Centro de Producción y Exportación
         de Sigillata a Mauritania. *Noticiario Arqueológico
         Hispánico*, Vol. 1, 263–89.
Sotomayor, Manuel, A. Pérez Casas, and M. Roca Coumens
  1976 Los Alfares Romanos de Andújar (Jaén). *Noticiario
         Arqueológico Hispánico*, Vol. 4, 113–42.
South, Stanley
  1972 The Horizon Concept Revealed in the Application of
         the Mean Ceramic Formula to Spanish Majolica in the
         New World. *Site Archaeology Papers*, Vol. 7, 96–122.
  1981 Summary of the Archeological Discoveries at the
         Sixteenth Century Spanish Colonial City of Santa
         Elena on Parris Island, South Carolina. Manuscript
         proposal to Explorers Club, New York.
  1982 Exploring Santa Elena 1981. Institute of Archeology
         and Anthropology, University of South Carolina,
         Research Manuscript Series 184.
  1983 Revealing Santa Elena 1982. Institute of Archeology
         and Anthropology, University of South Carolina,
         Research Manuscript Series 188.

Stevenson, Robert B.K.
  1954   Medieval Lead Glazed Pottery: Links Between East
         and West. *Cahiers Archeologiques*, Vol. 7, 89–94.
Sutherland, C.H.V.
  1939   *Romans in Spain*. Methuen, London.
Tablada, José Juan
  1927   *Historia del Arte de México*. Nacional Editora Aguilas,
         México.
Talbot Rice, David
  1965a *Islamic Art*. Praeger, New York.
  1965b The Pottery of Byzantium and the Islamic World. In
         *Studies in Islamic Art and Architecture in Honour of Prof.
         K.A.C. Creswell* (194–236). Center for Arabic Studies,
         Cairo.
Taracena, Blas
  1946   Arte Romano. *Ars Hispaniae*, Vol. 2, 11–182. Editorial
         Plus Ultra, Madrid.
Taylor, F. Sherwood and Charles Singer
  1956   Pre-Scientific Industrial Chemistry. In *A History of
         Technology* (347–74), Vol. 2. Charles Singer et al, eds.
         Clarendon, Oxford.
Temboury Alvarez, Juan
  1939   La Cerámica Vidriada de Málaga Después de la
         Reconquista de la Ciudad. *Al Andalus*, Vol. 4, 432–3.
Thacher, John Boyd
  1903   *Christopher Columbus: His Life, His Work, and His
         Remains*, Vol. 2, Pt. 1. G.P. Putnam's Sons, New York.
Thomas, David Hurst, Grand D. Jones, Roger S. Durham, and
Clark Spencer Larsen
  1978   The Anthropology of St. Catherines Island, I: Natural
         and Cultural History. *Anthropological Papers of the
         American Museum of Natural History*, Vol. 55, Pt. 2.
Thompson, E.A.
  1969   *The Goths in Spain*. Clarendon, London.
Thursdon, Herbert and Donald Attwater
  1963   *Butler's Lives of the Saints*. P.J. Kenedy and Sons, New
         York.
Tío, Aurelia
  1966   *Dr. Diego Alvarez Chanca*. Universidad Interamericana
         de Puerto Rico, San Juan.
Torre Revello, José
  1943   Merchandize Brought to America by the Spaniards
         (1534–1586). *Hispanic American Historical Review*, Vol.
         23, No. 4, 773–80.
Torres, Manuel et al
  1940   España Visigoda, 414–711 de J.C. In *Historia de España*,
         Vol. 3. R. Menéndez Pidal, ed. Calpe, Madrid.
Torres, Pablo
  1982   *Cántaros Españoles*, Vol. 1. Artemos, Madrid.
Torres Balbás, Leopoldo
  1934   Cerámica Doméstica de la Alhambra *Al Andalus*, Vol.
         2, 387–8.
  1935   Tenería en el Secano de la Alhambra de Granada. *Al
         Andalus*, Vol. 3, 434–7.
  1936–1939 De Cerámica Hispano-Musulmana. *Al Andalus*,
         Vol. 4, 412–31.
  1940   Las Norias Fluviales en España. *Al Andalus*, Vol. 5,
         195–208.
  1945   Notas Sobre Sevilla en el Época Musulmana. *Al
         Andalus*, Vol. 10, No. 1, 177–96.

1947 Plazas, Zocos, y Tiendas de la Ciudades Hispanomusulmanas, *Al Andalus*, Vol. 12, No. 2, 437–76.

1949 Arte Almohade, Arte Nazarí, Arte Mudéjar. *Ars Hispaniae*, Vol. 4. Editorial Plus Ultra, Madrid.

1957 Arte Hispanomusulman Hasta la Caída del Califato de Córdoba. In *Historia de Espana* (333–788), Vol. 5. R. Menéndez Pidal, ed. Calpe, Madrid.

1959 Letrinas y Bacines. *Al Andalus*, Vol. 14, No. 1, 221–34.

1971 *Ciudades Hispanomusulmanas* (in 2 vols.). With collaboration of Henri Terrasse. Instituto Hispano-Árabe de Cultura, Madrid.

Toulouse, J.H.

1949 *The Mission of San Gregorio de Abó*. School of American Research (Monograph No. 13), Santa Fe.

Toussaint, Manuel

1924 *Iglesias de México, Vol. 12: La Catedral de México.* Cultura, México.

1939 Arte Mudéjar en América. Congreso Internacional de Americanistas, *Actas*, Vol. 2, 603–08.

1946 *Arte Mudéjar en América*. Porrúa, México.

1967 *Colonial Art in Mexico*. University of Texas Press, Austin.

Uphof, J.C. Th.

1968 *Dictionary of Economic Plants*. J. Cramer, Lehre.

Usher, Abbott Payson

1932 Spanish Ships and Shipping in the Sixteenth and Seventeenth Centuries. In *Facts and Factors in Economic History* (189–213). Russell and Russell, New York.

Vaca González, Diodoro and Juan Ruíz de Luna Rojas

1943 *Historia de la Cerámica de Talavera de la Reina y Algunos Datos Sobre de la Puente del Arzobispo*. Nacional, Madrid.

Valle Arizpe, Artemio de

1939 *Historia de la Ciudad de México, Según los Relatos de Sus Cronistas*. Robredo, México.

Vannini, Guido

1977 *La Maiolica di Montelupo. Scavo di Uno Scarico di Fornace*. Montelupo.

Vaz, J. Eduardo and José M. Cruxent

1975 Determination of the Provenience of Majolica Pottery Found in the Caribbean Area Using Its Gamma-Ray Induced Thermoluminescence. *American Antiquity*, Vol. 40, No. 1, 71–81.

1976 The Gamma-ray Induced Thermoluminescence of 15th and 16th Century Azulejos as an Indicator of Their Provenience. Congreso Internacional de Americanistas, *Actas*, Vol 2, 10–14.

Vázquez de Espinosa, Antonio

1942 Compendium and Description of the West Indies. *Smithsonian Miscellaneous Collections*, Vol. 102.

Vega Sosa, Constanza

1975 Forma y Decoración en las Vasijas de Tradición Azteca. Instituto Nacional de Antropología e Historia, *Colección Científica* No. 23.

Velázquez Bosco, Ricardo

1912 *Medina Azzahra y Alamiriya*. José Blas, Madrid.

Verlinden, Charles

1940 The Rise of Spanish Trade in the Middle Ages. *Economic History Review*, Vol. 10, 44–59.

1953   Italian Influence in Iberian Colonization. *Hispanic American Historical Review*, Vol. 33, No. 2, 199–211.

Verlinden, C., J. Mertens, and G. Reichel-Dolmatof
1958   Santa María la Antigua del Darién, Premiere "Ville" Coloniale de la Terre Ferme Americaine. *Revista de Historia de América*, No. 45, 1–48.

Vetancurt, Agustín de
1971   *Teatro Mexicano. Descripción Breve de los sucesos Exemplares de la Nueva España en el Nuevo Mundo Occidental de las Indias*. Porrúa, México.

Vicens Vives, Jaime
1957   *Historia Social y Económica de España y América*, Vol. 3. Teide, Barcelona.
1969   *An Economic History of Spain*. Princeton University Press, Princeton.
1972   The Economy of Ferdinand and Isabella's Reign. In *Spain in the Fifteenth Century, 1369–1516* (248–75). Roger Highfield, ed. Macmillan, New York.

Victoria and Albert Museum
1957   *Hispano Moresque Pottery*. Victoria and Albert Museum, London.
1969   *Islamic Pottery, 800–1400 A.D. An Exhibition Arranged by the Islamic Art Circle and Held at the Victoria and Albert Museum, 1 Oct to 30 Nov 1969*. Hillington, London.

Vigneras, Louis Andre
1972   The Three Brothers Guerra of Triana and Their Five Voyages to the New World, 1498–1504. *Hispanic American Historical Review*, Vol. 52, No. 4, 621–41.

Vince, Alan
1982   Medieval and Post-Medieval Spanish Pottery from the City of London. British Museum, *Occasional Paper*, No. 32, 135–44.

Von Grunebaum, G.E.
1955   Islam, Essays in the Nature and Growth of a Cultural Tradition. American Anthropological Association *Memoirs*, No. 81.

Vossen, Rudiger, Natacha Seseña, and Wulf Kopke
1975   *Guía de los Alfares de España, 1971–73*. Nacional, Madrid.

Wagner, Klaus
1972   Apuntes para el Coste de Vide en Sevilla. Agosto 1544–February 1545. *Archivo Hispalense*, No. 170, 119–30.

Waldron, H.A. and D. Stofen
1974   *Sub-Clinical Lead Poisoning*. Academic Press, New York.

Wallerstein, Immanuel
1974   *The Modern World-System* (in 2 vols.). Academic Press, New York.

Warren, A.H.
1973   Majolica—New World or Old? Petrographic Notes on the Aplastic Inclusions of Majolica Sherds from Middle America and Spain. Paper presented at Gran Quivira Conference, Rio Rico, Arizona, 1973.

Watt, W. Montgomery
1963   *A History of Islamic Spain*. Edinburgh University Press, Edinburgh.

Weckmann, Luis
1951   The Middle Ages in the Conquest of America. *Speculum*, Vol. 26, 130–41.

Weigand, Phil C. and Celia García de Weigand
    1969   The Lozeros of San Marcos, Jalisco, Mexico. Specialia
           3, *Interamericana* 2.
Whitaker, Irwin and Emily Whitaker
    1978   *A Potter's Mexico.* University of New Mexico Press,
           Albuquerque.
Whitehouse, David
    1966   Medieval Painted Pottery in South and Central Italy.
           Medieval Archaeology, Vol. 10, 30–44.
    1971   Excavations at Sīrāh: Fourth Interim Report, *Iran,* Vol.
           9, 1–18.
    1972a Chinese Porcelain in Medieval Europe. *Medieval
           Archaeology,* Vol. 16, 63–78.
    1972b Excavation and Survey at Tuscania, 1972: A
           Preliminary Report. *Papers of the British School at Rome,*
           Vol. 40, 232–5.
    1978   The Origins of Italian Maiolica. *Archaeology,* Vol. 31,
           No. 2, 42–9.
Wilber, Donald N.
    1968   The Development of Mosaic Faience in Islamic
           Architecture in Iran. *Ars Islamica,* Vol. 6, 16–47.
Wilkinson, Charles K.
    1963   *Iranian Ceramics.* Asia House, New York.
    1973   *Nishapur: Pottery of the Early Islamic Period.* Metropolitan
           Museum of Art, New York.
Williams, Leonard
    1908   *The Arts and Crafts of Older Spain,* Vol. 2. McClurg,
           Chicago.
Willis, Michael D.
    1977   Folk Pottery in Saudi Arabia. *Ceramics Monthly,* Vol.
           25, No. 1, 35–8.
Willis, Raymond
    1980a Excavations at Puerto Real, Haiti. Paper presented at
           Annual Meeting of Society for Historical
           Archaeology, Albuquerque.
    1980b Nueva Cádiz. *Spanish Borderland Research,* No. 1.
           27–40.
    1984   Empire and Architecture at 16th Century Puerto Real,
           Hispaniola: An Archeological Perspective. Ph.D.
           dissertation, University of Florida, Gainesville.
Winter, Marcus C. and William O. Payne
    1976   Hornos Para Cerámica Hallados en Monte Alban.
           Instituto Nacional de Antropología e Historia, *Boletín,*
           Vol. 16, 37–40.
Wiseman, F.J.
    1956   *Roman Spain.* Bell, London.
World Health Organization
    1977   Ceramic Foodware Safety; Sampling, Analysis, and
           Limits for Lead and Cadmium Release; Report of a
           WHO Meeting, Geneva, Switzerland. WHO/FOOD
           ADD/77.44. Extracted in *Ceramics Monthly,* Vol. 25, No.
           10, 69–75.
Wulff, Hans E.
    1966   *The Traditional Crafts of Persia.* MIT Press, Cambridge.
Zavala, Silvio and María Castelo
    1939–1946 *Fuentes Para la Historia del Trabajo en Nueva
               España.* Fondo de Cultura Económica, México.
Zbiss, Slimane Mostfa
    1956   Mahdia et Sabra-Mansouriya. *Journal Asiatique,* Vol.
           244, 79–93.

Zorita, Alonso de
  1909 *Historia de la Nueva España*, Vol. 1. Fortanet, Madrid.
  1963 *Life and Labor in Ancient Mexico*. Benjamin Keen, trans.
        Rutgers University Press, New Brunswick.
Zozaya, Juan
  1969a Red-Painted and Glazed Pottery in Western Europe
        from the 8th to 12th Centuries, Spain. *Medieval
        Archaeology*, Vol. 8, 133–6.
  1969b El Comercio de Al Andalus con el Oriente: Nuevos
        Datos. *Boletín de la Asociación Española de Orientalistas*,
        Vol. 5, 191–200.
  1981a Aproximación a la Cronología de Algunas Formas
        Cerámicas de Época Taifas. Jornadas de Cultura
        Árabe e Islamica, *Actas*, 277–86.
  1981b Cerámica Andalusí. In *Cerámica Esmaltada Española*
        (35–50). Labor, Barcelona.
  1983 Excavaciones en la Fortaleja de Qal'at'abd-al-Salam
        (Alcalá de Henares, Madrid). *Noticiario Arqueológico
        Hispánico*, No. 17.
Zozaya, Juan, M. Fernández Miranda, and A. Moure
  1972 El Yacimiento Medieval de Almallut (Escores,
        Baleares), *Noticiario Arqueológico Hispánico*, No. 1,
        199–220.

Index

336n.10; jars for, 12, 22–23, 27–
28, 70, 91, 100, 107, 140, 177,
181, 224, 321n.50, 321n.51,
336n.10; in Mexico, 224,
342n.107; in Morocco, 177,
336n.10. *See also arcaduz;*
cangilón; irrigation; *noria de*
sangre; noria de vuelo
Wattasid Dynasty, 175
wedging, 258, 279
wellhead, 46, 61–63, 114, 126;
casing for, 61–62. *See also brocal*
well jar, 12
wine, 8–11, 16, 20, 25, 60, 70, 73,
81–82, 102; Muslims and,
321n.48; shipment of, 124, 128,
131–36, 165, 191–92, 205, 207,
217, 224, 278, 282, 311–12, 314
17, 331n.308, 332n.318, 340n.90,
344n.116; lees, 263, 333n.338

wineries: ban against, 131
Windward Islands, 194
workshop, 8, 11–12, 16, 25, 27,
29, 33, 35, 46, 50, 53–54, 73–74,
80, 84, 94, 104, 106, 113, 119,
127, 135, 137–38, 140–41, 145–
46, 151, 160–61, 164, 167–68,
176–77, 185, 196, 201, 205, 212,
216–17, 221–23, 232, 241, 243–
44, 248, 254–55, 257, 259–61,
266, 268–70, 273, 276, 279, 282,
285, 292, 294, 298, 300, 304,
336n.19, 347n.2, 347n.3,
350n.45, 352n.81; inventory of,
348n.19; plan of, 256. *See also*
pottery

Yemenites, 56
Yucatan, 198, 211
Yueh ware, 323n.103

zacate, 221. *See also* fuel: kiln
Zacatecas, 217
zafre, 157, 333n.338, 350n.43. *See*
also cobalt
Zaida, 271
Zaragoza, 86
Zayas, Antonio de, 351n.74
Zayas, Diego de, 312
Zayas, José de, 351n.74
Zayas, Nicolás de (no. 1), 351n.74
Zayas, Nicolás de (no. 2), 351n.74
Zayas, Sebastián de, 351n.74
zinc, 225, 325n.177
zócalo, 340n.91
Zuffo, Giovanni, 141
Zumárraga, Bishop, 273
Zurbarán, Francisco de, 147, 160–
61, 163, 308, 333n.333, 334n.360

FLORENCE C. LISTER and ROBERT H. LISTER devoted nearly
20 years of archaeological, documentary, and empirical
research to the creation of *Andalusian Ceramics in Spain and
New Spain*. Robert Lister, who earned the M A. and Ph.D
in anthropology from Harvard University, taught for
many years at the University of Colorado and for seven
years served as chief of the Chaco Center, operated by the
National Park Service and the University of New Mexico.
Florence Lister holds a B.A. in anthropology from the
University of New Mexico and pursued graduate studies
in art history at the University of New Mexico and the
University of Colorado. Together they have written a
number of scholarly and popular books, including *Those
Who Came Before: Southwestern Archaeology in the National
Park System* (University of Arizona Press, 1983), *Anasazi
Pottery*, and *In Search of Maya Glyphs*. They also have pub-
lished many technical articles on Spanish and New World
ceramics.